THE SIGN OF THE CANNIBAL

New Americanists

A Series Edited by Donald E. Pease

THE SIGN OF THE CANNIBAL

Melville and the Making of a Postcolonial Reader

Geoffrey Sanborn

Duke University Press   *Durham and London, 1998*

© 1998 Duke University Press
All rights reserved
Printed in the United States of America on acid-free paper
Typeset in Sabon by Tseng Information Systems, Inc.

Library of Congress Cataloging-in-Publication Data
Sanborn, Geoffrey.
The sign of the cannibal : Melville and the making
of a postcolonial reader / by Geoffrey Sanborn.
Includes bibliographical references and index.
ISBN 0-8223-2102-5 (acid-free paper).
— ISBN 0-8223-2118-1 (pbk. acid-free paper)
1. Melville, Herman, 1819–1891—Political and social views.
2. Imperialism in literature.   3. Literature and
anthropology—United States—History—19th century.
4. Authors and readers—United States—History—19th
century.   5. Books and reading—United States—History—
19th century.   6. Decolonization in literature.
7. Cannibalism in literature.   8. Reader-response criticism.
9. Colonies in literature.   I. Title.
PS2388.I45S26   1998   813'.3—dc21   97-44323   CIP

TO SOFIE, WHOEVER SHE MAY BE

CONTENTS

Abbreviations   ix

Preface   xi

Introduction   3

1   In the Wake of the *Resolution:*
The Post-Enlightenment Discourse on Cannibalism   21

2   The Terror of Their Name: Reflections on *Typee*   75

3   The Aftersight: *Moby-Dick* and the Spectacle
of Savagery   119

4   Walking Shadows: "Benito Cereno" and the
Colonial Stage   171

Afterword   201

Notes   209

Works Cited   239

Index   251

BB   *Billy Budd, Sailor.* Ed. Harrison Hayford and Merton M. Sealts Jr. Chicago: University of Chicago Press, 1962.

BC   "Benito Cereno." In *The Piazza Tales and Other Prose Pieces.* Ed. Harrison Hayford, Alma A. MacDougall, and G. Thomas Tanselle. Evanston, IL: Northwestern University Press/Newberry Library, 1987.

C   *Correspondence.* Ed. Harrison Hayford, Hershel Parker, and G. Thomas Tanselle. Evanston, IL: Northwestern University Press/Newberry Library, 1993.

CM   *The Confidence-Man: His Masquerade.* Ed. Harrison Hayford, Hershel Parker, and G. Thomas Tanselle. Evanston, IL: Northwestern University Press/Newberry Library, 1984.

CP   *Collected Poems of Herman Melville.* Ed. Howard P. Vincent. Chicago: Hendricks House, 1947.

IP   *Israel Potter: His Fifty Years of Exile.* Ed. Harrison Hayford, Hershel Parker, and G. Thomas Tanselle. Evanston, IL: Northwestern University Press/Newberry Library, 1982.

J   *Journals.* Ed. Harrison Hayford, Hershel Parker, and G. Thomas Tanselle. Evanston, IL: Northwestern University Press/Newberry Library, 1989.

M   *Mardi; and a Voyage Thither.* Ed. Harrison Hayford, Hershel Parker, and G. Thomas Tanselle. Evanston, IL: Northwestern University Press/Newberry Library, 1970.

MD   *Moby-Dick; or, The Whale.* Ed. Harrison Hayford, Hershel Parker, and G. Thomas Tanselle. Evanston, IL: Northwestern University Press/Newberry Library, 1988.

O   *Omoo: A Narrative of Adventures in the South Seas*. Ed. Harrison Hayford, Hershel Parker, and G. Thomas Tanselle. Evanston, IL: Northwestern University Press/Newberry Library, 1968.

P   *Pierre; or, The Ambiguities*. Ed. Harrison Hayford, Hershel Parker, and G. Thomas Tanselle. Evanston, IL: Northwestern University Press/Newberry Library, 1971.

PT   *The Piazza Tales and Other Prose Pieces*. Ed. Harrison Hayford, Alma A. MacDougall, and G. Thomas Tanselle. Evanston, IL: Northwestern University Press/Newberry Library, 1987.

R   *Redburn: His First Voyage*. Ed. Harrison Hayford, Hershel Parker, and G. Thomas Tanselle. Evanston, IL: Northwestern University Press/Newberry Library, 1969.

T   *Typee: A Peep at Polynesian Life*. Ed. Harrison Hayford, Hershel Parker, and G. Thomas Tanselle. Evanston, IL: Northwestern University Press/Newberry Library, 1968.

WJ   *White-Jacket; or, The World in a Man-of-War*. Ed. Harrison Hayford, Hershel Parker, and G. Thomas Tanselle. Evanston, IL: Northwestern University Press/Newberry Library, 1970.

T he process of putting this book together began about eight years ago, when I read Melville's "Benito Cereno" in a graduate seminar on race and American literature. Like so many other readers of that story, particularly first-time readers, I was troubled by the climactic unveiling of the slave owner's bones. What was Melville suggesting here? That the blacks on board the *San Dominick* had cannibalized their former master? That the ambiguities of identity in the early sections of the story were not in fact mysteries but mystifications, ultimately dispelled by this revelation of the blacks' bedrock savagery? I was temporarily convinced otherwise by some of the other participants in the seminar, who argued that Melville intended us to balance the image of the skeleton against subsequent images of white-on-black violence, and to conclude, accordingly, that the stirrings of savagery were not limited to any one race. But I was still troubled. It had taken substantial effort on the part of a group of late-twentieth-century academics sympathetic to Melville and slave rebellions to defuse that explosive image. Could Melville have counted on a similar effort from the average reader of the story at the time of its initial publication? Could we conclude anything about the story's racial politics without knowing more about the meanings that were conventionally attached to the image of cannibalism in the mid-nineteenth century?

With these questions in mind, I began researching the history of the discourse on cannibalism between 1770, when the first Cook expedition discovered signs of cannibalism in New Zealand, and 1855, when Melville published "Benito Cereno." I was guided in this research by an assumption that I had not yet come to recognize as an assumption: that whatever cannibalism might have *seemed* to be to post-Enlightenment writers, it was *really* a phenomenon that could only be decoded through reference to the idea of culture. Every step of the way, I divided the writers on cannibalism into two categories: bad witnesses who saw only what they were enabled to see by the discourse on savagery, and good witnesses who glimpsed the culturalist truth. Largely on the strength of *Typee,* Melville became, for me, the greatest of these good witnesses. In the dissertation that this project became, I started off by arguing that *Typee* embodied Melville's imperfectly formulated recognition that culture structures everything, even the seemingly unstructured act of cannibalism. In his attention to superstition among the Typee, particularly the superstition of the taboo, I thought that Melville was attempting to replace the assumption that cannibals were creatures of the primitive night with the recognition that their thoughts and acts were just as structured, just as meaningful on their own terms, as those of humans who did not eat human flesh.

But as I wrote my way through Melville's career, toward the concluding chapter on "Benito Cereno," I became less sure of this argument. By the time I completed the dissertation, I was very worried about it. Six months later, I was sure it was wrong. Though I still believed that Melville had opposed himself to essentializations of savagery, I no longer believed that this act of opposition had propelled him onto the terrain of the anthropological idea of culture. Instead, I realized, it had propelled him first onto the terrain of the masculinist romance of vengefulness, and from there, into the shadowy border territory of the phenomenon that Lacan refers to as "the missed encounter": the "appointment to which we are always called with a real that eludes us." [1] Because I had thought of the assertion of the truth of culture as the most valuable act of opposition that Melville could perform, I had minimized all of the indications that vengefulness was, in fact, the explanation of cannibalism that Melville most favored. And although I had argued, especially in my chapter on "Benito Cereno," that Melville ultimately hollows out the conventional image of savagery, I had strained far too hard to hear in that echo chamber the voice of Clifford Geertz. In my chapter on *Typee,* for instance, I had overread references to superstition—which generally signified, in the nineteenth century, nothing more than the contraction and petrifaction of the sphere of reason—as intimations of culture. And in my chapter on "Benito Cereno," I had been unnecessarily apologetic about the fact that Melville does not replace the conventional image of savagery with a culturalist image of human difference. Now that the culturalist hypothesis was out of the way, I was finally able to see that there was no need to apologize for Melville's habit of suggesting that cannibalism represented a masculinity without limits, and that the dreamed-of encounter with this figure of masculinity was always missed. In both its content and its form, it was a distinctly postcolonial vision, oriented toward the renovation of a complexly colonized world.

To some, this argument may appear to be an inappropriate application of postcolonial theory—either because it does not square with Melville (an objection that can only be answered by the book as a whole) or because Melville, as a white American writing in the early nineteenth century, does not square with it. In my introduction, I have attempted to respond to the latter objection by theorizing the position of white or "first-world" writers within postcolonial critiques. What I am ascribing to Melville is a very specific postcolonial *function*: the articulation of the dynamics of anxiety and menace in the colonial encounter. That function, which we now associate with the work of Homi Bhabha, is a logically necessary element of any postcolonial critique that aims to question the ontology of the colonial subject. Though the primary source of such critiques is the indigenous resistance to the territorial and discursive advances of Westerners, the signal of this resistance cannot be broadcast to the metropoles without the aid of translators—white or nonwhite, colonial or metropolitan—like Melville. As Gareth Griffiths has said, in the course of a similar argument, "this is not to deny the vital importance for the various indigenous communities of recovering their own tongues and cultures as vital recuperative strategies. It is rather to indicate that unless this is accompanied by a wider strategy of disruption within the field of the dominant discourse . . . the possibilities for winning the larger discursive battle may be lost even as local 'tactical' victories are won."[2] In the secondary but vital act of discursive disruption, writers like Melville are capable of making a distinctly postcolonial difference.

Such disruptions are rare, of course, and they are radically dependent on what Ernesto Laclau defines as "conditions of possibility."[3] In chapter 1, I attempt to show that those conditions were in fact present to an unusual degree within the post-Enlightenment discourse on cannibalism. The crucial historical event, in this case, was the rejection of medieval and early Renaissance accounts of cannibalism, on the grounds that travelers' tales of "Anthropophagi" were no more reliable than their tales of "men whose heads/Do grow beneath their shoulders."[4] From the mid-eighteenth century through the mid-nineteenth century, compilers of travel narratives, reviewers of travel narratives, and travelers themselves raised two fundamental questions about those tales: Do they allow us to conclude that cannibals actually exist? And if so, do they allow us to provide an explanation of their motives? The most common response to these questions was that cannibals do indeed exist, and that they eat human flesh simply because they like its taste. The argument at the opposite end of the spectrum, that cannibals do not exist, enjoyed a brief period of respectability in the mid-eighteenth century, but was discredited shortly thereafter by a series of reasonably credible accounts of cannibalism. In the early-nineteenth century, a more common way of challenging the use of cannibalism as an image of bestial lust was to suggest another motive to the act: either famine, vengeance, superstition, or a desire to terrorize. As a result of this longstanding controversy over the existence and extent of cannibalism, it was unusually evident to the early-nineteenth-century participants in this discourse that the cannibal had not yet been captured. On the basis of this recognition, it was entirely possible for any one of these participants to go one step further, and to argue that the textual image of the cannibal was, as Slavoj Žižek has said of the anti-Semitic image of the Jew, "a scenario filling out the empty space of a fundamental impossibility, a screen masking a void."[5]

In chapter 2, I show that this is in fact the argument that Melville makes in *Typee*. In that book, a fictionalized account of his captivity among the supposedly cannibalistic inhabitants of a Marquesan island, he begins from the belief that cannibalism is motivated by lust, takes his readers through the suggestion that it does not exist, and then turns to the idea that it is motivated by vengeance. The appeal of this third idea is that it makes cannibalism out to be a romantically unfettered expression of the masculine spirit and enables us to think of the Typeean chiefs and warriors as especially manly incarnations of the Noble Savage. But Melville doesn't stop here; in the last chapters of the book, he encourages us to see that the Typees are not actually as spontaneous and sincere as they initially appeared to be. At the climax of the narrative, when the narrator discovers the disarticulated bones of a rival warrior, we are asked to consider the possibility that the Typeean nobility are using the *appearance* of cannibalism to terrorize enemies, subordinates, and overly curious strangers into submission. Melville is not asking us to see the Typees as the members of a "culture"—he explicitly rejects the explanation of cannibalism that ascribes it to the influence of custom— and he is certainly not asking us to see them as the symbols of a savagery that lurks within all people or within all men. Instead, he is asking us to experience the tension between two competing perceptions of the Typees: first, that they are the exemplars of an authentically masculine spirit, and second, that they are the spectral objects of the humane gaze.

In chapter 3, I argue that Melville extends the implications of this discovery in *Moby-Dick*. The critical depiction of *Typee* as nothing more than a work of "popular reading" had taught him that he could not get his readers to reflect on the spectrality of their Other without first leading them away from the idea that savages were nothing better than curiosities. To encourage the readers of *Moby-Dick* to see Queequeg outside the dehumanizing frame of the spectacle, he satirizes the contemporary practice of presenting cannibals, or parts of them, in museum shows. That accomplished, he allows Queequeg to wane away, thereby suggesting that we should not uncritically identify with that romantically masculine figure, and that we should instead turn toward the more general "truth" embodied in the equally elusive whale. It is a remarkably sophisticated piece of pedagogy, one that bears a striking resemblance to Kaja Silverman's description of the ideal post-humanist textual intervention. The first step in that intervention, Silverman says, is to " 'light up' dark corners of the cultural screen, and thereby make it possible for us to identify both consciously and unconsciously with bodies which we would otherwise reject with horror and contempt." The second step is to "inhibit our attempt to assimilate those coordinates to our own in order to 'become' the ideal image." The third and final step is to "bring us to a conscious knowledge of both the purely provisional nature of the illuminated image, and our own capacity to turn the light on or off." [6] In all of these ways, Melville attempts to transform the spectral cannibal of *Typee* into the basis of a reformulated vision of humanity and its Other.

In chapter 4, I demonstrate that in "Benito Cereno," Melville returns one last time to the tension at the heart of the discourse on cannibalism. With the unveiling of the bones of Don Alexandro Aranda on the prow of the *San Dominick,* he again transports us from the dream of unforced expression to the waking world of gestures and asks us to recognize that savagery is *produced,* both by the acts of the "savage" and the expectations of the "humane." It is Melville's most expert evocation of the unilluminated territories behind the mask of the savage, but it is also his most chilly. Rather than idealizing the de-idealized savage and then hollowing out that ideal, he simply denies us the possibility of any kind of romantic identification with Babo, the leader of the slave revolt. And rather than using a likable persona to model the reader's successive responses to the spectacle of savagery, he forces us to walk the decks in the company of Amasa Delano, an especially dull-witted racist. This is not to say that he has given up on the possibility of making meaningful contact with his readers; throughout the story, but particularly in

Cereno's final speech, he tries to get us to see around the limitations of Delano's vision. The difference is that he now refuses to present us with anything even temporarily substantial beyond the horizon of the naïve white consciousness. The only way out of that prison of the imagination is through the vacant eyes of the master and the slave, and the theatrical babble of the deck and the courtroom. It is harder that way, but it is the way that Melville did it, and he thinks that it is at least possible for some of his readers to use that exit too.

I have many thanks to give, for all kinds of reasons. To my family, first of all, every last one of you. To my friends: Todd Arms, Sam Smiley, Dave Rosenthal, Bill Clark, Dave Fruman, John Paul Roberts, Andy Schultz, Jill Gilbert, Karin MacDonald, Suzy Brundage, Jim Harris, Michael Connell, Roxanne Eberle, Jason Rosenberg, Libby Gruner, Mark Gruner, Cassandra Cleghorn, Shawn Rosenheim, and Karen Shepard. To my professors at Stanford and UCLA, especially John L'Heureux, Michelle Carter, Ehud Havazalet, Martha Banta, and Eric Sundquist. Special thanks to the readers and editors at Duke University Press; to the New York Public Library, for permission to quote from their Melville manuscripts; to *Arizona Quarterly*, for permission to reprint portions of "Where's the Rest of Me? The Melancholy Death of Benito Cereno" (an early version of chapter 4 that appeared in the spring 1996 issue); to Jim Shepard and the late Michael Bell, for their thoughtful and helpful readings of the manuscript; and to Beth Boquet, for her equally helpful readings, but especially for her patience, good taste, and taste for wasting time.

My deepest thanks go out to my dissertation director, Michael Colacurcio, and to my wife, Kristy Carter-Sanborn. From you, Michael, even more than from Melville, I learned that ideas have shapes, that those shapes unfold in time, and that time is all we have. You, Kristy, are my reflection, intimate, set apart, and when I put my lips to the glass—lo, they are yours, and not mine. I feel that the Godhead is broken up like the bread at the Supper, and that we are the pieces. Hence this infinite fraternity of feeling.

THE SIGN OF THE CANNIBAL

1. Lt. James Burney with the hand of Thomas Hill.
Journal of the Resolution's *Voyage*. 1775.
Reprint, New York: Da Capo Press, 1967.

INTRODUCTION

It is the cause, it is the cause, my soul;
Let me not name it to you, you chaste stars,
It is the cause.
—*Othello*

Eight white men are gathered together on a beach; their ship is anchored in the harbor behind them (figure 1). The leader of the group, taller and better dressed than the others, is holding up a human hand that he has apparently just taken from a basket held by the man beside him. The hand is oddly oversized, sharply defined against a background of sky, and its palm, inscribed with the letters *TH,* faces the viewer. The eyes of the leader and the man directly across from him in the foreground of the picture are riveted on this object, but the men surrounding them have turned their faces away; several of them appear to be staring into space. In the middle distance, we see three shadowy figures on the shore, one of whom is running from a canoe with his arm outstretched. In the lower left corner, a dog has found some shapeless object and has it in his teeth.

The source of the picture is the *Journal of the* Resolution*'s Voyage,* published anonymously in 1775. The text that accompanies the picture tells of a search party from the *Resolution*'s sister ship, the *Adventure,* discovering in a New Zealand cove the dismembered bodies of some sailors who had gone among the Maoris the day before. The party, led by Lt. James Burney, found in a Maori canoe "a pair of shoes tied up together. On advancing farther up the beach, they found several of their peoples baskets, and saw one of their dogs eating a piece of broiled flesh, which upon examining they suspected to be human, and having found in one of the baskets a hand, which they knew to be the left hand of Thomas Hill, by the letters T. H. being marked on it, they were no longer in suspence about the event."[1]

In his representation of the event, the artist obviously means to capture that moment of perfect conviction, when the members of the search party can no longer doubt that the Maoris are cannibals and that they have eaten British sailors. Confronted by the sign of the most outrageous act of savagery imaginable, these eight white men on the edge of a strange land have been rendered speechless and immobile: their jaws are slack, their gazes are frozen or averted, and their guns are balanced loosely on their shoulders. In their shared sensation of horror, they express a shared "humanity," a moral sentiment that is defined by its abhorrence of all forms of "savagery." But even as the picture invites its European viewers to join in this involuntary expression of an innate morality, it suggests, in the urgency of its invitation, that the humanity of these viewers is peculiarly dependent on the spectacle it abhors. It suggests this in its hyperbolic representation of the hand, not just enlarged but also drawn to our attention by the fixed gazes of the two figures in the foreground and the pointing finger of another man. It suggests it, as well, in its depiction of the meat-tugging dog, which indicates that even the enormous hand requires corroborating evidence. Though these images are intended to point us in the direction of the absent cannibals, they also point us in the direction of the "humane" observers, so anxious to dispel their suspense and so strangely in need of the signs of the cannibal.

Another example may help to make this point more clear. In his *Narrative of a Residence in New Zealand* (1832), the British artist Augustus Earle reports that during his brief stay on the north island, he got wind of a rumor that the corpse of a female slave was about to be eaten in a nearby village. Because "much [had] been written to prove the nonexistence of so hideous a propensity," he and his companion, Captain Duke, immediately "resolved to witness this dreadful scene."[2] As they neared the village, they caught sight of a Maori oven, a hole filled with stones that had been heated in a nearby fire.

> We ran towards the fire, and there stood a man occupied in a way few would wish to see. He was preparing the four quarters of a human body for a feast; the large bones, having been taken out, were thrown aside, and the flesh being compressed, he was in the act of forcing it into the oven. While we stood transfixed by this terrible sight, a large dog, which lay before the fire, rose up, seized the bloody head, and walked off with it into the bushes; no doubt to hide it there for another meal! The man completed his task with

the most perfect composure, telling us, at the same time, that the repast would not be ready for some hours!

Here stood Captain Duke and myself, both witnesses of a scene which many travellers have related, and their relations have invariably been treated with contempt; indeed, the veracity of those who had the temerity to relate such incredible events has been every where questioned. In this instance it was no warrior's flesh to be eaten; there was no enemy's blood to drink, in order to infuriate them. They had no revenge to gratify; no plea they could make of their passions having been roused by battle, nor the excuse that they eat their enemies to perfect their triumph. This was an action of unjustifiable cannibalism. Atoi, the chief, who had given orders for this cruel feast, had only the night before sold us four pigs for a few pounds of powder; so he had not even the excuse of want of food. After Captain Duke and myself had consulted with each other, we walked into the village, determined to charge Atoi with his brutality. (113)

Like the picture of the *Adventure*'s search party, Earle's description magnifies the signs of cannibalism in order to legitimate the tableau of humanity frozen in horror by the spectacle of savagery. Even more obviously than in the picture, moreover, Earle's intense desire for these signs overtakes and undermines the nominal subject. Unlike the search party, he has gone looking for these signs for their own sake; it is abundantly clear that he *wants* to see a Maori "occupied in a way few would wish to see." Once he finds the scene he is looking for, he repeatedly reminds us that he and his companion are indeed witnessing it—"Here stood Captain Duke and myself"—and that they are united in horror: "we stood transfixed by this terrible sight." Finally, by dwelling at length on the conclusions he draws while standing there, he indicates both that he understands his own spontaneous reflections on the event to be the preeminent object of interest and that he finds it hard to drag himself away. After being rebuffed by the chief, in fact, he and Captain Duke return to "the spot where this disgusting mess was cooking" (114). They sit "gazing on this melancholy place; it was a lowering gusty day, and the moaning of the wind through the bushes, as it swept round the hill on which we were, seemed in unison with our feelings." In consonance with nature, they too give "full vent to the most passionate exclamations of disgust" and proceed to dig up "the shocking spectacle" of the half-roasted body and rebury it, as the gathered members of two Maori villages look on (115). It is a purely gratuitous act, as he later admits, for when he goes back the next day the grave is empty. But it is, for that reason, a signal event: a consummate proof of the Englishmen's involuntary humanity and the Maoris' unquestionable savagery.

Earle is not entirely unaware of the fact that his revisitings of this site, both at the time and in the act of writing about it, might look a little peculiar to his readers. In the midst of an ensuing account of the origin of cannibalism in New Zealand, he suddenly declares, "I will no longer dwell on this humiliating subject. Most white men who have visited the island have been sceptical on this point; I myself was, before I had 'ocular proof.' Consequently, I availed myself of the first opportunity to convince myself of the fact" (116–17). But neither is he able to keep it from looking peculiar; in protesting that he does not actually take any pleasure in seeing or dwelling on the signs of cannibalism, Earle only calls more attention to the fact that he has been dwelling on the subject for a very long time. And in his allusion to "ocular proof"—a phrase that shows up again and again in early-nineteenth-century accounts of cannibalism—he undermines his position still further; whether he intends it or not, he is situating his intense desire for evidence within one of the most damning contexts imaginable.³ The source of the allusion is the scene in *Othello* in which Othello, his jealousy aroused, says to Iago, "Villain, be sure thou prove my love a whore;/Be sure of it. Give me the ocular proof." The point of the rest of that play, of course, is that if the jealous desire for evidence of infidelity is strong enough, the quality of the evidence is irrelevant; as Emilia says, jealous souls "are not ever jealous for the cause,/But jealous for they're jealous."⁴ The object that ultimately satisfies Othello's desire for ocular proof is nothing more than a planted handkerchief, not a "cause" to which his jealousy can be objectively referred, but an indifferent object that Iago's machinations and Othello's mounting jealousy have invested with the aura of a cause. In comparing his visual evidence of cannibalism to Othello's ocular proof, Earle invites a similar critique of his own efforts to discover a "cause" for humane horror in the spectacle of savagery. As Sir John Barrow, a well-known writer and reviewer of travel narratives, would observe a few years later, "though we are not at all disposed to impeach Mr. Earle's veracity, we should much like to have some clear evidence that he was not *hoaxed—in terrorem*."⁵ Like the hand, Earle's ocular proof may be said to signify the excessiveness of his desire for it; like the handkerchief, it may also be said to indicate that he does not *discover* his "cause," but that the illusion of that cause was awaiting his arrival.

In my reading of these scenes, I am operating on the basis of assumptions that are quite different from the ones that most Westerners have applied, and continue to apply, to their interpretations of the colonial encounter. In Tzvetan Todorov's *The Conquest of America,* to take a particularly prominent recent example, we are told that the Spanish subjugation of the Aztecs was made possible by their advanced " 'technology' of symbolism." [6] Because the Spaniards were able to write, Todorov says, they were able to improvise; alienated from their representations of themselves, they were able to project those representations into any conceivable context. Because the Aztecs were not able to write, they were not able to improvise; "the necessary memorization of laws and traditions" led to "the predominance of ritual over improvisation," which is to say the "predominance of presence over absence, of the immediate over the mediatized" (156, 157). One of the most telling signs of this weakness, for Todorov, is the Aztecs' practice of cannibalism. Together with human sacrifice and adornment with the skins of flayed enemies, cannibalism indicates "a certain inadequacy in the Aztecs' conception of the other" (157). Unlike the Spanish, who can strategically symbolize otherness, the Aztecs always "act as if they were confusing the representative with what he represents: what begins as a representation ends as a participation and identification; the distance necessary to the symbolic functioning seems to be lacking" (158). Rather than conceiving of bodies as figurations of an absent but real spirit, human or divine, the Aztecs address them in the most brutally literal of ways, as things to be torn, burned, chewed, or worn.

The assumptions that Todorov applies to his reading of the Spanish-Aztec encounter—Westerners are ironic and adaptable, non-Westerners are literal and tradition-bound—are so widely agreed upon in the West that they are virtually unrecognizable *as* assumptions.[7] But assumptions they are, and questionable ones, as the two scenes I began with should suggest.[8] In each of those scenes, it is the *explorers,* not the natives, who value ritual over improvisation, presence over absence, the immediate over the mediated. This is not as strange as it might seem; as Stephen Greenblatt has pointed out, there is good reason to believe that such behavior is less the exception than the rule, the entirely predictable consequence of the dream of discovery and possession. Everything in that imperial dream "rests on witnessing, a witnessing understood as a form of significant and representative seeing." But "[t]he discoverer sees only a fragment and then imagines the rest in the act of appropriation"; he must therefore force "the bit that has actually been seen" to become "by metonymy a representation of the whole."[9] The hand expands, and points beyond itself; the ocular proof materializes, repeatedly, before the discoverer's covertly hungry eyes. Through their absorption in their fetish-objects, the viewers in these scenes reveal, in Todorov's words, "a certain inadequacy in [their] conception of the other." To keep from consciousness the recognition of how much they have not seen, they inflate what they *have* seen to outlandish proportions. But by insisting on the adequacy of the signs themselves, they inadvertently emphasize the material presence of those signs. To return to Todorov's words, "the distance necessary to the symbolic functioning seems to be lacking"; as a result of the desire for a purely immaterial signified, the material presence of the sign becomes all in all.[10]

Even more important, perhaps, the scene in Earle's narrative links the fetishism of the Western "discoverers" to a complementary *anti*fetishism in the "discovered." As I have argued above, it is entirely possible to read that scene as a terrorist hoax, both capitalizing and commenting on Earle's credulity. Read in this way, the dismemberment of the corpse is not a sign of the Maoris' destructive literalism, as the Todorovian model might suggest. It is, instead, a strategic appeal to *Earle's* destructive literalism, his fetishistic tendency to carve out parts and mistake them for wholes. Far from being incapable of improvisatory play, the Maori are, in this reading, highly competent producers of the spectacle of savagery. In addition to suggesting this reading in his reference to "ocular proof," Earle explicitly offers it as an explanatory option in his subsequent account of a meeting between the Maori and some visiting Tikopians. When the Tikopians openly express their dread of the Maoris, "whose character for cannibalism had reached even their remote island," the Maoris, "with characteristic cunning, perceiving the horror they had created, tormented them still more cruelly, by making grotesque signs, as if they were about to commence devouring them" (159). The essence of the Maoris' "characteristic cunning" is their ability to use the sign of the cannibal as, in Lacanian terms, a screen. "In the case of display," Lacan says, "the being gives of himself, or receives from the other, something that is like a mask, a double, an envelope, a thrown-off skin, thrown off in order to cover the frame of a shield." Through the consciously instrumental use of these "grotesque signs," the so-called cannibal "isolates the function of the screen and plays with it."[11] In doing so, he takes on that form of subjectivity that Todorov values most: one that depends on supplementarity and *knows* it.

Readers of the postcolonial theorist Homi Bhabha will have already recognized the style of interpretation I am practicing here. For a decade and a half now, Bhabha has been chipping away at the conventional reading of the colonial encounter by drawing attention to the question of "how newness enters the world"—a phrase, borrowed from Salman Rushdie, that he uses as the title of one of his essays. By "newness," Bhabha means the mode of identity that emerges from "the momentous, if momentary, extinction of the recognizable object of culture in the disturbed artifice of its signification, at the edge of experience." [12] The instruments of that extinction—the means by which newness enters the world—are, for him, the fetishism of the colonialist and the mimicry of the native. Observing that the colonial stereotype is "an arrested, fixated form of representation" (75), he suggests that it has, as a result, a peculiarly "phantasmatic quality—the *same old* stories of the Negro's animality, the Coolie's inscrutability or the stupidity of the Irish *must* be told (compulsively) again and afresh, and are differently gratifying and terrifying each time" (77). And if the colonialists' repetition of the stereotype can make their authority ghostly, so can the *natives'* repetition of that stereotype make their visibility uncertain. Through a "mode of negation that seeks not to unveil the fullness of Man but to manipulate his representation" (62), Bhabha's native "terrorizes authority with the *ruse* of recognition, its mimicry, its mockery" (115). Opposing himself to those "purists of difference" (111) who argue that the colonialists' authority is seamless and total, or that the natives' identity is recognizable and whole, Bhabha contends that the essence of the colonial encounter is its *hybridity:* in every such encounter, the colonialist must come into being by way of a postulated native, and the native must come into being by way of a postulated colonialist. This way of reading colonial discourse "does not merely recall the past as social cause or aesthetic precedent; it renews the past, refiguring it as a contingent 'in-between' space, that innovates and interrupts the performance of the present" (7).

There are, however, a couple of crucial differences between my work and Bhabha's. His métier is the essay, a form that enables him to be, in Emerson's words, an "endless seeker," an "experimenter" who does not pretend "to settle any thing as true or false." [13] I would not ask him, or Emerson, to be anything else. Other critics have begun to find fault with this habit of mind and style, however, arguing that it leads Bhabha to overgeneralize his account of colonial subjectivity and underemphasize the material conditions of colonial experience. Although there are indeed grounds for such complaints, these critics have tended to use them as a warrant either to dismiss his suggestions, or to grant those suggestions some small region of relevance and then go on with business as usual.[14] What this means, I think, is that we have reached a point in the development of colonial discourse analysis at which it may be useful to establish Bhabha's assertions on a broader base of data and to flesh out his account of the means by which "newness" achieves its anticolonial effects. To keep "newness" new, we need to do something more than illustrate it with isolated anecdotes; we need to enact it, and thereby complicate it, in the course of more extended historical and literary analyses.

With that in mind, I have tried here to add weight to Bhabha's description of "newness," and to adjust, in the process, our understanding of the ways in which it "enters the world." My central argument is that within at least one field and period of colonial discourse, newness became so visible that it was possible for a popular American author to articulate it for a mass audience. For this kind of argument, it is clearly not sufficient to allude to a couple of examples, such as those I began with, and then move on to the author in question. It is necessary to show, instead, a *pattern* of newness within the more general pattern of the discourse as a whole. Toward that end, I have gathered and analyzed over four hundred discussions of cannibalism produced between 1770 and 1855, in venues including travel narratives, novels, plays, poems, periodical essays, newspaper articles, pamphlets, and unpublished journals. In reading these documents, together with a great many others produced just before and after that period, I have tried to do more than identify the existence of newness; I have tried to identify the *degree of its emergence* with respect to the other elements of the discourse. As I show in chapter 1, and in the sections of later chapters devoted to the related discourses on peddled heads and discovered bones, newness tended to emerge from the shadows cast by other interpretive positions within the discourse on cannibalism. It emerged, nevertheless, with surprising regularity, and very often in explicit terms. Though it was by no means the dominant element—no element that threatens the ontological basis of its discourse ever could be—it did indeed constitute a recognizable interpretive position. As such, it offers us a small but strong confirmation of Bhabha's claim that postcoloniality, understood as the interrogative aftermath of colonial truth-claims, was capable of being *experienced as such* in the colonial era.[15]

But this is not the same thing as showing that newness has entered the world. Though it was a recognizable interpretive position in the post-Enlightenment discourse on cannibalism, its challenge to the stability of that discourse, and of colonial discourse more generally, did not inevitably follow from its recognition. As Bhabha himself obliquely suggests, newness cannot be converted from an available opinion into a world-altering challenge without a translator, someone capable of bringing the discursive dynamics of anxiety and menace to the consciousness of colonialists and natives alike. This, I take it, is the import of such passages as the following:

> *Read as a masque of mimicry,* Anund Messeh's tale emerges as a question of colonial authority, an agonistic space. (121; my emphasis)

> In general terms, there is a colonial contramodernity at work in the eighteenth- and nineteenth-century matrices of Western modernity that, *if acknowledged,* would question the historicism that analogically links, in a linear narrative, late capitalism and the fragmentary, simulacral, pastiche symptoms of postmodernity. (173; my emphasis)

> Through the natives' strange questions, it is possible to see, *with historical hindsight,* what they resisted in questioning the presence of the English. (118; my emphasis)

All of these passages call attention, in a subdued, partial way, to the possibility that the forces of "colonial contramodernity" are not present in colonial discourse unless we say they are. To be fully present, Bhabha suggests, they must be acknowledged, and to be acknowledged, they must be read in a way that sometimes seems to be available only in "historical hindsight." If that last suggestion is correct, if it was indeed impossible to interpret the implications of colonial contramodernity *at the time,* then critics like Abdul Jan-Mohammed are right to say that Bhabha has "represse[d] the political history of colonialism" by imputing to it, "at this late date, and through the back door," an ambivalence that only he is capable of sensing.[16]

As Houston Baker has argued, however, we can in fact find examples of that style of interpretation in the historical record. In Frederick Douglass's 1845 autobiography, for instance, we are asked to *"hear between the lines"* of the songs that Douglass remembers singing with his fellow slaves. For those readers who respond to that request, Baker writes, "[t]he visual and *voiceless* slave is finally set spiritually, meaningfully, and resistantly singing. And what is overheard by effective readers is a lyrical repudiation of the master's exclusive right to meaningful being in the world." One of the more important lessons of this section of Douglass's narrative is that the slave songs "have to be *written* before they can become fully agential as interpretive protests or negations."[17] Though the primary source of resistance may be found in the souls of black folk, the ultimate effectiveness of that resistance depends on the secondary work of "[e]xegesis, hermeneutics, the offices of *interpretation* and fitting analysis vis-à-vis Afro-America."[18] The name that Baker gives to the office of interpretation is "renaissancism" (*Modernism,* 106), a word that succinctly indicates the answer he would give to the question of how newness enters the world. The birth of an effective cultural and political organization is always a *re*birth, for Baker, an interpretive recovery of intimations of newness that have not yet been given a voice. That interpretive recovery is not always taken up in turn by "effective readers"; "it seems obvious," he says, "that the implications of Douglass's literate metasonics were not seriously heard or heeded by the United States of his era" ("Scene," 41). It is, nevertheless, a recognizably postcolonial act: a sustained effort to alter the material conditions of encounters between "whites" and "blacks" by altering the conventional representation of those terms.

For an even better example of "renaissancism," one that I will be building on throughout this book, I want to turn now to a somewhat lengthy passage from W. E. B. DuBois's *The Souls of Black Folk.* In it, we are not asked to hear an obscure but real note of resistance; instead, we are asked to hear in the voices of humanists, racists, and insurgents alike an obscure but real wavering:

> From the shimmering swirl of waters where many, many thoughts ago the slave-ship first saw the square tower of Jamestown, have flowed down to our day three streams of thinking; one swollen from the larger world here and over-seas, saying, the multiplying of human wants in culture-lands calls for the world-wide cooperation of men in satisfying them. Hence arises a new human unity, pulling the ends of earth nearer, and all men, black, yellow, and white. The larger humanity strives to feel in this contact of living Nations and sleeping hordes a thrill of new life in the world, crying, "If the contact of Life and Sleep be Death, shame on such Life." To be sure, behind this thought lurks the afterthought of force and dominion,—the making of brown men to delve when the temptation of beads and red calico cloys.
>
> The second thought streaming from the death-ship and the curv-

ing river is the thought of the older South,—the sincere and passionate belief that somewhere between men and cattle, God created a *tertium quid,* and called it a Negro,—a clownish, simple creature, at times even lovable within its limitations, but straitly foreordained to walk within the Veil. To be sure, behind the thought lurks the afterthought,—some of them with favoring chance might become men, but in sheer self-defence we dare not let them, and we build about them walls so high, and hang between them and the light a veil so thick, that they shall not even think of breaking through.

And last of all there trickles down that third and darker thought, —the thought of the things themselves, the confused, half-conscious mutter of men who are black and whitened, crying "Liberty, Freedom, Opportunity—vouchsafe to us, O boastful World, the chance of living men!" To be sure, behind the thought lurks the afterthought,—suppose, after all, the World is right and we are less than men? Suppose this mad impulse within is all wrong, some mock mirage from the untrue?

So here we stand among thoughts of human unity, even through conquest and slavery; the inferiority of black men, even if forced by fraud; a shriek in the night for the freedom of men who themselves are not yet sure of their right to demand it. This is the tangle of thought and afterthought wherein we are called to solve the problem of training men for life.[19]

I can think of no other passage from a colonial-era text that so evidently embodies the mode of critical consciousness that we now associate with Bhabha. Like Bhabha, DuBois asks his readers to conceive of ideological positions as performative utterances, haunted by the silence they temporarily break. In doing so, he enables them to conceive of that silence as a space in which it is possible for thought to double back on itself, in which it is possible to begin hearing something other than what is given to be heard. That he does all this without the aid of "theory" is remarkable; that he does it at the grimmest moment in the history of American race relations is truly extraordinary. Even at the turn of the twentieth century, when the attention to the delicate ambiguities of colonial subjectivity was most likely to appear frivolous, DuBois was willing to declare that the revelation of the intrinsic anxiety of colonial discourse could make a material difference. As in the case of Douglass, the actual number of contemporary minds and lives he changed is less important than the fact that he *thought* he could change them. In his expression of that faith, he indicates not only that it was possible to conceive of colonial subjectivity as a "tangle of thought and afterthought," but also that it was possible to imagine, on the basis of that conception, some form of collective renewal.

The search for early articulators of a postcolonial sensibility is neither fruitless nor pointless, in other words; they are out there, and they matter. My treatment of Melville has been guided by those beliefs, and by the corollary belief that although we are more likely to find these articulators among writers of color, we should not be overly surprised to find them among white writers. The work of translation requires no racial or cultural visas, after all, and the direct and ongoing experience of oppression is not the only factor contributing to the desire to do that work. If we pursue the project of identifying those writers who have actively assisted in the birth of newness, we should be prepared to recognize figures like Melville among them, and to give an evenhanded account of the difference they represent. Although Melville does not share all the motives and tactics of writers like Douglass and DuBois, he does address with a similar acuity the limits of the consciousness nurtured within an ideology of "whiteness." Especially in his representations of the encounters between white men and cannibals, he calls his readers back, again and again, to the "afterthought" that haunts all efforts to ascertain and explain the existence of savagery. Positioned, like Douglass and DuBois, between murmured sounds and inattentive ears, he attempts to transpose his readers into the space in which those sounds are clearest and loudest, and then, in Douglass's words, "let [them], in silence, analyze the sounds that shall pass through the chambers of [their] soul[s]." [20]

The most representative example of that mode of articulation is a chapter in *Moby-Dick* called "The Cabin-Table." At first glance, the chapter seems to be premised on a relatively ordinary distinction between the ways in which the "civilized" and the "savage" occupy the same space: when the white officers eat at the cabin table, they are constrained by "nameless invisible domineerings"; when the nonwhite harpooners eat at the cabin table, they express themselves with an "entire care-free license and ease." But the chapter does not in fact offer us an authoritative demonstration of the difference between civility and savagery; instead, it filters the *perception* of that difference through the mind of the steward, Dough-Boy, "a very nervous, shuddering sort of little fellow" (*MD*, 152). When Dough-Boy is not quick enough in bringing out the harpooners' food, he finds Tashtego "singing out for him to produce himself, that his bones might be picked," or Daggoo "snatching him up bodily, and thrusting his head into a great empty wooden trencher" (153, 152). As for Queequeg, "he had a mortal, barbaric smack of the lip in eating—an ugly sound enough—so much so, that the trembling Dough-Boy almost looked to see whether any marks of teeth lurked in his own lean arms. . . . How could he forget that in his Island days, Queequeg, for one, must certainly have been guilty of some murderous, convivial indiscretions. Alas! Dough-Boy! hard fares the white waiter who waits upon cannibals. Not a napkin should he carry on his arm, but a buckler" (153). By showing us that the harpooners express their supposedly cannibalistic tendencies "ostentatiously," to weigh on the steward's "credulous, fable-mongering" mind, Melville breaks down the opposition that the chapter nominally constructs. Just as the harpooners' "intrepid exclamations" when rowing toward a whale are not spontaneous, but calculated "to set an example of superhuman activity to the rest" (287), so do their performances before Dough-Boy refer not to an internal condition, but to the effect that they expect their performances to have on that trembling, soft-headed, redundantly white man.

What makes this chapter especially representative is that it is so evidently an "overhearing" of a prior moment in the history of colonial discourse. Besides being influenced in a general way by the structure of the discourse on cannibalism, it is rooted in a very specific description of a causelessly panicked steward in Capt. Edmund Fanning's *Voyages Round the World* (1833). In 1798, Fanning writes, he and a few of his men landed on the Marquesan island of Nukuheva and were led in a ceremonial procession to the quarters of the king. When the procession came to a stream, the islanders walking behind the sailors "formed a sort of seat, by clinching their hands together, then by striking the inner or hinder part of the knee." Having been informed by a local missionary that this might happen, Fanning was on his guard. But "not so the steward, poor fellow":

> he was most sadly frightened at being thus unceremoniously treated, and as a small return for the favor, gave them a most tremendous scream: from his station, which was a little behind us, he had a fair view of the human hair which topped the rods of those chiefs at our side, and in all probability was thinking of the barbarous custom, which some of the South Sea islanders had, of murdering and eating their foes, when he was thus unwittingly seated, and perhaps he now conceived that his own hair was to decorate some other rod; but be this as it may, the effect of the scream was to make

himself the laughing stock of all the natives, for all eyes had been instantly turned upon him, and raised as he was in the world, his countenance still made it very evident that he was much alarmed. This complete success of their manoeuvre, pleased the natives prodigiously, and was the source of a great deal of laughter at the poor steward's expense, till some one good naturedly told him not to be frightened, but to join in the laugh, if he wished them to cease.[21]

Fanning is not entirely aware of the implications of this scene; shortly thereafter, he himself recoils from an equivocal sign of cannibalism without reflecting on the possibility that he, like the steward, has been the victim of a Nukuhevan "manoeuvre."[22] Like so many other authors of colonial-era travel narratives, Fanning hears only the sounds of shrieks and laughter, and not the critique of "white" consciousness that they are capable of founding. Before that critique can "enter the world," those inarticulate sounds must be transformed, through the strategic dramatization of their anxiety and menace, into a powerfully broadcast signal. That signal does not emanate from Melville alone—it is radically dependent on the Nukuhevan maneuverers, on Fanning, and on the conditions of the discourse on cannibalism—but it would not exist, in any meaningful sense, without him.

Within the context of postcolonial theory, then, the major claims of the book are these: Bhabha's "newness" existed as a *pattern* of interpretation within at least one colonial discourse, and this pattern was translated as a *challenge* to the structure of colonialism by at least one contemporary author. But postcolonial theory is not the only relevant context of my argument; I am also positioning myself within the fields of cannibal studies[23] and Melville studies, to such a degree that my ordering of contexts could easily be rearranged: the book could also be said to be a revisionary interpretation of cannibalism that has implications for Melville studies and postcolonial theory, or a revisionary interpretation of Melville that has implications for postcolonial theory and cannibal studies. I have begun with a discussion of the postcolonial context because it is the most general of the three. By way of conclusion, I now want to describe, very briefly, where I have positioned myself within the other two fields.

My treatment of cannibalism is closest in spirit to the one we find in the work of the postcolonial critics Peter Hulme and Gananath Obeyesekere. Like Hulme, I am arguing that the representations of cannibalism in Western texts should not be expected to reveal, upon closer analysis, the authentically "cultural" meaning of the act.[24] Like Obeyesekere, I am arguing that we can nonetheless speak of a native presence in these texts, a presence whose origin and point of reference is not the dim, distant home of "culture," but the eerily lit terminals of the encounter.[25] Where I depart from these critics is in my response to a question that arises for everyone who investigates the textual image of the cannibal: *Why* were Western travelers to the Americas, Asia, the Pacific, and Africa so obsessed with the thought of cannibalism, even before their hosts provided them with a reason to think it? For both Hulme and Obeyesekere, the answer lies in the realm of the drives; hungry for land and labor, colonial-era travelers unconsciously projected their "cannibalistic" desires onto the people they encountered, thereby concealing and justifying their own unacknowledged avarice.[26] For me, however, the crucial element in these accounts of cannibalism is their anxiety. Anxiety, as Joan Copjec says, is "that which nothing precedes," that which signals the "overproximity" of nothingness.[27] By stressing the manifest anxiety of figures like Earle, rather than searching for signs of their latent aggression, I will be suggesting that the image of the cannibal is not the projection of a secret lust, as so many critics have argued, but the trace of a secret lack.

By characterizing Melville as an archaeologist of that lack, moreover, I will be offering an alternative to the three most influential ways of reading his representations of savagery. The first is that he universalizes the savagery conventionally ascribed to dark-skinned peoples; the second is that he evokes the numinous meaningfulness of apparently savage behavior; the third is that he does neither of these things as well as he should, that he is neither as humanist nor as culturalist as he ought to be.[28] My position is closest to the third style of interpretation, with the important difference that I do not see the resituation of "savagery" within the holistic space of "humanity" or "culture" as his aim, or even as his responsibility.[29] Although Melville was indeed inclined to search for hidden points of origin and reference, he retained, throughout his career, a profound distrust of universal organizing principles. With respect to the doctrine of original sin, for example, his strongest statement of belief is this radically hesitant passage from "Hawthorne and His Mosses": "[Hawthorne's] great power of blackness . . . derives its force from its appeals to that Calvinistic sense of Innate Depravity and Original Sin, from whose visitations, *in some shape or other,* no *deeply thinking* mind is *always and wholly* free. For, *in certain moods,* no man can weigh this world, without throwing in *something, somehow like* Original Sin, to strike the uneven balance" (*PT,* 243; my emphasis).[30] Like the wind in "The Conflict of Convictions" that "spins *against* the way it drives" (*CP, 6*), his prose tends to move forward on the strength of, and in spite of, such odd inward circlings. If we neglect or minimize that quality of style, we may come away from his work with a sense of him as, if not an anthropologist (which he certainly was not), at least a tragic liberal humanist, for better or for worse. But if we read his sentences, paragraphs, chapters, and books with an attention to the process of their unfolding, we are far more likely to come away from his work with the sense that his thought orbits away from, and spirals toward, an emptiness no humanist principle could contain.

In the place of the humanist/culturalist Melville, then, I am offering a Lacanian/postcolonial Melville, a writer who explores, in Toni Morrison's phrase, "the cul de sac, the estrangement, the non-sequitur that is entailed in racial difference."[31] In making that claim, I hope to avoid, as much as possible, the implication that Melville "walked in and out at will of the categories that controlled most thinking in his time."[32] As I have already suggested, what makes Melville special is his ability to articulate the undervoiced, to receive and retransmit the indistinct sounds of newness. That is why I begin the book with my discussion of the post-Enlightenment discourse on cannibalism: not to contrast its foolishness to Melville's wisdom, but to identify the categories *within which* Melville generates his critique. The time-bound nature of Melville's critique of whiteness — and, as we will see, of his intimately related critique of masculinity — is perhaps the most interesting thing about it. Beginning in the late nineteenth century, the collection and arrangement of "other knowledges" would become a major concern of novelists and social scientists. Before that time, however, white male writers were far more likely to stress the impossibility of attaining such knowledge — to dwell, with Hawthorne, on "that mute mystery which so hopelessly perplexes us, whenever we attempt to gain an intellectual or sympathetic knowledge of the lower orders of creation."[33] When Melville evacuates the categories of whiteness and masculinity without referring, by way of contrast, to the "other knowledges" of nonwhites and women, he bears witness to the fact that he is not, in Roy Harvey Pearce's phrase, "our contemporary."[34] Although he sees something that Lacanian and postcolonial theorists would eventually see, he does so by other means, in another time, under different conditions of visibility.

Reconfigured in this way, as a writer who means "to place incendiary devices within the dominant structures of representation and not to confront these with another knowledge," Melville may not be to everyone's liking.[35] If we accept the argument that the encounter with "savagery" is the point of origin and reference for the concept of "humanity," that concept instantly becomes *unheimlich,* unhomelike, unsafe for occupation. If the façade of "savagery" does not subsequently fall away, revealing the prefabricated space of "another knowledge," we are left waiting, with gradually diminishing expectations, in the open air. But this is not necessarily a bad thing. By refusing to resettle us in a new home, Melville makes it possible for us to see "humanity" as "a project of political construction, not something that has always been there, waiting to be recognized."[36] Left without "another knowledge," we are not left without hope; it is not so terrible, in the end, to be expelled from the humanist Eden. If we learn how to share his determination to do without a "cause," we may find ourselves, as he did, in a world ringed round with a new horizon—a world that is, within those mobile yet constant limits, "all before us."[37]

1 🖐 IN THE WAKE OF THE *RESOLUTION:*

THE POST-ENLIGHTENMENT DISCOURSE

ON CANNIBALISM

On the afternoon of November 23, 1773, the British officer Richard Pickersgill brought a recently severed human head on board the *Resolution,* then anchored in Queen Charlotte's Sound on the north island of New Zealand. "[S]ome Indians of a different party were on board," Pickersgill would later write in his log of the expedition, "and were very desirous of a piece of it." At first he refused to give up any part of the head, which he had just bought for the price of two nails at a Maori encampment, but after Lt. Charles Clerke got one of the Maoris on board to affirm that "he'd eat a peice there directly" if given one, Pickersgill agreed, "for curiosity's sake," to give up a slice of the cheek. Clerke "then cut a peice of[f] carry'd [it] to the fire by his desire and gave it a little broil upon the Grid Iron then deliver'd it to [the Maori]—he not only eat it but devour'd it most ravenously, and suck'd his fingers 1/2 a dozen times over in raptures."[1] The naturalist George Forster confirmed the officers' accounts of this transaction in his published journal of the voyage, emphasizing how thoroughly *witnessed* it was; after the piece of flesh was broiled "in presence of all the ship's company," he says, it was "devoured . . . before our eyes with the greatest avidity."[2]

The *Resolution*'s captain, James Cook, returned to the ship shortly thereafter to find "the quarter-deck crowded with the natives, and the mangled head, or rather part of it (for the under jaw and lip were wanting) lying on the tafferal. The scull had been broken on the left side, just above the temples; and the remains of the face had all the appearances of a youth under twenty." Initially, he says, the scene, together with the officers' reports as to what had taken place, "struck me with horror, and filled my mind with indignation against these cannibals." But he was intensely "desirous of becoming an eye-witness of a fact which many doubted," and soon "ordered a piece of the flesh to be broiled and brought to the quarter-deck, where one of these cannibals eat it with surprising avidity. This had such an effect on some of our people as to make them sick."[3] The astronomer William Wales, apparently not one of the sick, recorded the results of this second experiment in more detail, with an undisguised thrill: "another Steake was cut off from the lower part of the head, behind, which *I saw* carried forward, broiled, and eaten by one of them with an avidity which amazed me, licking his lips and fingers after it as if affraid to lose the least part, either grease or gravy, of so delicious a morsel" (Beaglehole, *Journals,* 2:818).

Wales's conclusions regarding this episode are worth citing at length:

> 1st) They do not, as I supposed might be the Case, eat them only on the spot whilst under the Impulse of that wild Frenzy into which they have shewn us they can & do work themselves in their Engagements; but in cool Blood: For it was now many Days since the Battle could have happened.
>
> 2d) That it is not their Enemies only whom they may chance to kill in War; but even any whom they meet with who are not known Friends: since those who eat the part of the head on board, could not know whether it belonged to a friend or Enemy.
>
> 3d) It cannot be through want of Annimal food; because they every day caught as much Fish as served both themselves and us: they have moreover plenty of fine Dogs which they were at the same time selling us for mere trifles; nor is there any want of various sorts of fowl, which they can readily kill if they please.
>
> 4th) It seems therefore to follow of course, that their practice of this horrid Action is from Choice, and the liking which they have for this kind of Food; and this was but too visibly shewn in their eagerness for, and the satisfaction which they testified in eating, those inconsiderable scrapts, of the worst part on board the Ship. (2:819)

For Wales, the afternoon's experiments had definitively resolved two major points of philosophical contention. Cannibals do indeed exist; he begins his journal entry by saying, "I have this day been convinced beyond the possibility of a doubt that the New-Zealanders are Cannibals; but as it is possible others may be as unbelieving, as I have been in this matter, I will, to give all the satisfaction I possibly can, relate the whole affair just as it happened" (2:818). And cannibals do indeed eat human flesh because they like its taste, not because they are maddened by vengefulness or pressed by famine. Not only in Wales's journal, but in several of the other accounts of this episode, the dominant tone is, fittingly, *resolution*. "That the New Zealanders are cannibals, can no longer be doubted," Cook declares, adding that whatever the original impetus to this custom may have been, at present "it was but too evident, that they have a great liking for this kind of food" (*South Pole*, 1:245, 246).[4] The reason the journalists on the *Resolution* were so concerned with setting down the fact that they saw the Maoris avidly eating human flesh is that the uncertainty over the existence and extent of cannibalism had revealed a fissure running along the surface of their knowledge. By means of these extraordinary experiments, that fissure was closed.

But it didn't stay closed. In 1790, Joseph Banks told a naturalist about to accompany Vancouver to the Pacific that "if you find the abominable custom of eating human flesh, which they are said to practice, to be really in use among them, you are, if you can do it with safety and propriety, to be present at some of their horrid repasts in order to bear witness to the existence of a practice all but incredible to the inhabitants of civilised countries, and discover, if you can, the original motives of a custom for which it seems impossible to suggest any probable cause." And in 1821, a British commissioner asked an officer recently stationed in New Zealand the same two questions: first, whether "cannibalism still prevails amongst them," and second, "whether the practice arises from some superstition, or from the gratification of revenge on their enemies, or a fondness for eating human flesh?"[5] No matter where late-eighteenth- and early-nineteenth-century travelers came from—England, America, France, Russia, or Germany—they brought those two questions with them.[6] And no matter where they went—New Zealand, Hawaii, the Marquesas, the Fijis, Melanesia, Sumatra, the northwest coast of America, the Amazon basin, or central Africa—they drew on the same small set of available answers.[7] These answers were, very briefly, lust, denial, famine, vengeance, superstition, and the desire to terrorize (which I will abbreviate, in my references to it, as "terror").[8] With some background on these answers, and on the questions that prompted and interrupted them, we will know better how to interpret the exchange on the subject of cannibalism between Melville and his contemporary readers.

Lust

The most powerful answer was the one that the members of the *Resolution* expedition generally agreed upon: cannibalism does exist, and it proceeds from what Cook calls, following Wales, "a great liking for this kind of food."⁹ It was an old answer, as many late-eighteenth- and early-nineteenth-century travelers knew. In Greek and Roman histories, in early modern accounts of the Orient and Africa, and in the narratives of the Americas, the margins of the known world were very often represented as the homes of humans who feast on human flesh.¹⁰ The "discovery" of Pacific island cannibals in the late eighteenth century was widely hailed as a confirmation of those earlier accounts, shoring up their authority against an erosion that had begun a few decades earlier. After citing Cook's proofs that the Maoris were indeed "addicted to the custom of devouring one another," the American historian Jared Sparks declared that "[t]he stories related by Herodotus, Strabo, Pliny, and other ancients, about anthropophagi, which have been regarded as fables in modern times, are more than realized at this day in many islands of the southern ocean."¹¹ This reclamation of the ancient image of cannibalism was part of a more general shift from the Enlightenment conception of humanity as "everywhere the same" to the racist conception of humanity as a moral substance inherent in white bodies. Because accounts of lustful cannibalism tended to weld together the moral, physical, and social connotations of "savagery," they were an especially important component of that shift. As the "crime more calculated than all others to excite the horror and detestation of the civilized world," it provided an especially potent "cause" for that form of humanity that could only know itself in the act of shrinking from the spectacle of savagery.¹²

For this reason, accounts of lustful cannibalism were generally accompanied by images of humane horror.¹³ In the case of the cannibal experiments on the *Resolution*, the representative of humanity was a Tahitian named Oedidee, who was, in Cook's words, "so affected with the sight as to become perfectly motionless, and seemed as if metamorphosed into the statue of Horror." After being roused from this trance, Oedidee "burst into tears; continued to weep and scold by turns; told them they were vile men; and that he neither was, nor would be any longer their friend. He even would not suffer them to touch him; he used the same language to one of the gentlemen who cut off the flesh; and refused to accept, or even touch, the knife with which it was done. Such was Oedidee's indignation against this vile custom; and worthy of imitation by every rational being" (*South Pole*, 1:244).

We are asked to imitate two things here: Oedidee's initial motionlessness and his subsequent rejection of everyone and everything associated with the experiment—including, we must imagine, the captain who ordered it. Being "humane," Cook suggests, means experiencing an involuntary physical revulsion when confronted with the spectacle of savagery and disavowing any participation in the production of that spectacle. In asking us to imitate Oedidee's reaction, he is asking us to conceive of humanity as a sensibility that exists entirely outside the realm of representation, insofar as it resides *in the body* and is in no way a cause of the spectacle that occasions its expression. If we conceive of humanity in this way, and ascribe it not only to Oedidee but also to his admirer, it is possible that we might be seduced into forgetting that Cook has contributed to the staging of the experiment, and that he has, in that sense, *produced* his humanity in the space of representation, rather than experiencing it in the space of the body.

When the humane body did not freeze into a "statue of Horror," a prop in an allegorical tableau, its most common response was to shudder. Before describing the feast that supposedly followed the Maoris' 1809 massacre of the crew of the *Boyd*, John Liddiard Nicholas writes that it is a scene "at which humanity will shudder, as well as the person who records it."[14] For Jared Sparks, the episodes of cannibalism that accompanied the intensification of tribal warfare in New Zealand in the early 1820s constitute "a scene, which words have not power to express, and which humanity shudders to contemplate."[15] The American captain David Porter writes that at the moment when he believed he was about to see human flesh being eaten, his "blood recoiled with horror"; for James Oliver, simply thinking about "cannibal orgies" in the midst of an 1829 visit to New Zealand is enough to bring on "an involuntary shuddering."[16] By characterizing cannibalism as a practice "from which the first instincts of our nature so strongly recoil,"[17] these authors characterize humanity as a moral substance, a thing that lies, as a reviewer of *Typee* insisted, beyond the horizon of knowledge. The only sensible way of responding to Melville's willful defense of cannibalism, the reviewer says, is to allude to "certain feelings, which we have no intention of analyzing, and which are implanted in us by nature."[18]

The most elaborate and influential articulation of this way of thinking about humanity may be found in Henry Bolingbroke's *Voyage to Demerary* (1807), where we learn that "it is a principle of our nature, to be averse to devouring what has been an object of love":

> Man is the object of our strongest affection—the tenderest emotions of the heart are excited by individuals of the human race and these emotions are extended by association in some degree to all mankind. The form, the countenance, the lineaments of man, excite

in our minds faint traces of the love which we had felt for individuals of this kind. It is not surprising, therefore, that we should have the most invincible antipathy to eating human flesh; that we should shudder at devouring that which is so peculiarly associated with our strongest affections. . . . Cannibalism is the practice only of the most savage and ferocious nations, of those who have little sensibility of heart to render them capable of loving, and who are devoid of the amiable qualities of the mind, which are the objects of love.[19]

For Bolingbroke, the definition of humanity is, in part, *people who love people who love people;* he understands the "amiable qualities of the mind" to be both the agents and the objects of humane love. But if we cannot detach ourselves from this tautology long enough to establish it as an object of reflection, our humanity will be something we *are,* unknowingly, rather than something we have and use. Accordingly, humanity must be additionally defined as *people who do not love people who eat people.* When our bodies shudder at the very idea of cannibalism, we discover the limit of humanity—"I cannot love a cannibal"—and thereby become capable of recognizing ourselves as humane subjects. Cannibalism is in this sense *constitutive* of humanity. Without the presence of some such image of inhumanity, humanity could never be anything more than a notion, an endlessly extensive and purely contentless set.

Though the body that shuddered at the sight or thought of cannibals did not have to be white, many late-eighteenth-century writers and most early-nineteenth-century writers assumed that it was. Because whites dominated the writing and reading of travel narratives, their references to "the first instincts of our nature" tended to imply, unless modified, "white nature." Exceptions like Oedidee did little to change that rule; because these noble savages were almost always light-skinned, they were all too easily interpreted as proofs of the racist axiom that one's character approaches humanity as one's color approaches whiteness. Such exceptions were extremely rare, moreover, in comparison to the number of dark-skinned people who were thought to harbor an instinctive love of human flesh. Among Africans, Hegel writes in *The Philosophy of History,* "cannibalism is looked upon as quite customary and proper. Among us instinct deters from it, if we can speak of instinct at all as appertaining to man. But with the Negro this is not the case, and the devouring of human flesh is altogether consonant with the general principles of the African race; to the sensual Negro, human flesh is but an object of sense—mere flesh."[20] In the Reverend Michael Russell's *Polynesia* (1843), we learn that the Fijians properly "belong to the black tribes" of Melanesia and New Guinea, for "[w]ith strong indications of negro ferocity, they combine some of the worst habits which disgrace the whole population of the Southern Pacific, especially the horrible practice of eating their enemies, now abhorred by all the fairer-skinned families of the windward clusters." [21] And in the Reverend Josiah Priest's *Slavery* (1844), we are informed that "[t]he horrid and heart-appalling practice of *cannibalism* has, in *all* ages, attached more to the African race than to any other people of the earth." For the past three thousand years, Priest says, the black-skinned people of Africa and the western Pacific "have been, irrespective of civilization, actually more or less in the practice of the dreadful crime of eating human flesh, as an article of food; not from necessity, nor on account of the requirements of their religion, but wholly from the common desire of that kind of food, the same as dogs or any other carnivorous animal." [22]

These odd and deadly ideas were reinforced, throughout the early nineteenth century, by the belief that human flesh is an addictive substance. One of the most influential sources of that belief was Defoe's *Robinson Crusoe* (1719), in which Crusoe finds that Friday, his redeemed cannibal, "had still a hankering stomach after some of the flesh, and was still a cannibal in his nature." For Defoe, this hankering is difficult but not impossible to overcome; Crusoe ultimately succeeds in weaning his servant away from "the relish of a cannibal's stomach" by letting him taste goat's flesh, which he quickly learns to prefer. [23] By the early decades of the nineteenth century, however, the habit of cannibalism had begun to be represented as a much more formidable barrier to the reformation of savages. Samuel Patterson, an American whaleman shipwrecked on the Fijis in 1808, reports that "[t]he greediness of these people, and all cannibals, for human flesh is astonishingly great; and perhaps there is no evil habit so hard to be eradicated as this inhuman one: it has been known, that even after the practice has been renounced, and the persons christianized, still a lurking hankering appetite has remained a long time." [24] In his narrative of a visit to the Marquesan islands in 1804, George von Langsdorff makes the more sweeping claim that many cannibals, worldwide, "feed upon human flesh merely on account of its delicacy, and as the height of *gourmandise*." It is such an amazingly delicious food—especially "the inside of the hand and the sole of the foot" and the "flesh of young girls and women, particularly of new-born children"—that it is almost impossible for a cannibal to become anything other than a cannibal: "human flesh is found so grateful, that those who have once eaten it can with difficulty abstain from it." [25]

By the mid-nineteenth century, thanks in part to the widespread acceptance of the idea "that a depraved and unnatural appetite, when once formed, has a tendency, not only to continue, but to increase," it had become a virtual dictum that "when cannibalism is found common among races of men, sensual love of human flesh invariably influenced the continuance of the custom."[26] Given the addictiveness of human flesh, several writers argued, there was really no point in speculating on the primary cause of cannibalism, since that cause, whatever it was, bore no meaningful relationship to present conditions. In *The New Zealanders* (1830), George Craik declares that though "superstitious notions" may have influenced the development of cannibalism among the Maori, it "has now become an enjoyment in which they not unfrequently indulge without any reference to the considerations which originally tempted them to partake of it."[27] Joel Polack similarly contends, in *New Zealand* (1838), "that the *present practice* of cannibalism, has little or no reference to the original causes of its institution; that continual indulgence from earliest infancy, has wholly obliterated any disgust that might have anciently accompanied the horrid rites; but it is a vice indulged in from a depraved taste that scarcely the powerful feelings of shame can subdue."[28] And in his *Narrative of the United States Exploring Expedition* (1845), after noting that the "existence of cannibalism, independent of superstitious notions, has been doubted by many," Charles Wilkes asserts that there can be "no question that, although it may have originated as a sacred rite, it is continued in the Feejee Group for the mere pleasure of eating human flesh as a food."[29] Through its association with race, the fixed desire for human flesh had been made visible; through its association with addictiveness, the visible sign of cannibalism—dark skin—was fixed.

Scholars who have examined these kinds of discursive links among race, lust, and cannibalism have tended to explain their existence in one of two ways. The first has been to link them to the economic interests of colonialists. The historian Francis Barker, for example, argues that ancient accounts of cannibalism in Africa began to be "embellished" once "the slave trade introduced new motives for emphasis on native cruelty."[30] There is some truth to this claim; in the case of Columbus, which I will discuss in chapter 4, it seems fairly clear that the navigator's failure to find gold encouraged him to find people who could be made slaves in Christ's name. But in the late eighteenth and early nineteenth centuries, the image of lustful cannibals was more likely to obstruct colonial projects than to clear a way for them. In the case of New Zealand, for instance, the Maoris' reputation as "a race of atrocious

cannibals, wholly unfit to be admitted within the pale of civilization,"
operated as a serious deterrent to colonial settlement from the 1770s
through the 1820s.[31] As Edward Jerningham Wakefield observed in 1845,
"[i]n the Parliamentary debates which led to the establishment of New
South Wales in 1788, New Zealand was mentioned as very suitable for
an experiment of penal colonization, and narrowly escaped through a
terror of its savage inhabitants and their cannibalism."[32] That terror was
exacerbated by the *Boyd* massacre of 1809, in which Maoris at the Bay
of Islands killed and apparently ate nearly everyone on board in retaliation for a prior insult. The effect of the massacre, William Fox wrote in
1842, "was to stamp the character of the natives as one of irreclaimable
ferocity, and to deter all navigators from approaching these inhospitable coasts, where they could only expect to be plundered and killed,
and could hope for no other grave than the ovens of their murderers."[33]
Not until the 1830s, after the more favorable reports of missionaries like
Samuel Marsden had removed "the impressions of fear which had been
made by the savage character of the natives," would the project of colonizing New Zealand gain any real momentum in England.[34]

The other way of explaining the image of the lustful cannibal has been
to suggest that it is an unconscious projection of the colonialist's own
aggression. As I indicated in the introduction, however, this explanation
simply repeats, from another angle, the thoroughly conventional association of cannibalism with the instinctual drives. As a result, it does
nothing to disrupt the structure of the relationship between cannibalism and humanity; the only difference is that "humane" beings are now
encouraged to shudder at a latent or metaphorical "cannibalism" in the
souls of bad white folk. More importantly, perhaps, it does not make
sense of the ways in which the image of lustful cannibalism was actually deployed in the late eighteenth and early nineteenth centuries. The
reason so many white writers found this image appealing is that it promised a moral and social fixity: black people love eating people, white
people hate people-eaters, and these two states of being are both natural
and permanent. But as everyone who used the image knew, this instrument of fixity was itself unfixed. When these writers declared, again and
again, and at high volume, that cannibals *do* exist, and that they *do* like
the taste of human flesh, they were attempting to fill a gap in knowledge with an assertion that had only recently been delegitimated. For
that reason, the efforts to establish the fixity of lustful cannibalism are
better understood as displacements of *anxiety* than as displacements of
aggression. At least in the period we are studying, the image of the lust-

ful cannibal was neither a rationalization of seizure nor a projection of hidden greed. It was, instead, an insecure instrument of security, a key that had to be forced to fit in a door that would not quite close.

Denial

The element of the discourse on cannibalism that would do the most to disrupt the authority of the lust explanation made its most prominent early appearance in John Atkins's *Voyage to Guinea, Brasil, and the West Indies* (1735). In his preface, Atkins announces that one of the principal features of the narrative will be "[t]he Denial of *Canibals,* against the Authority of *grave* Authors." [35] He goes on to confess, very candidly, what has motivated this denial; it "has proceeded from a Persuasion, that the Charge carries the highest Reproach on Humanity, and the Creator of it" (xxii). As he says later on, his faith in the essential unity and orderliness of "Humanity" has led him to be so "prejudiced indeed against the Opinion of Cannibals," that he doubts "whether there be any such men on the face of the Earth" (123). He is willing to admit that in extreme situations, human beings might have been driven to the act, either "when provoked by Famine, as has unfortunately happened in Voyages: Or possibly with Savages, single Instances may have been, as their way to express an intense Malice against a particular Enemy, and *in terrorem,* or to cement with a Bond of Secrecy some very wicked Societies of Men" (123–24). What he resists is the notion that cannibalism could ever have been *habitual* with any human being. In those cases in which it has been represented as a habit, he says, "the Accusation every where has probably proceeded from *Fear* in some, to magnify the Miracle of escaping an inhospitable and strange Country, and from *Design* in others, to justify Dispossession, and arm Colonies with Union and Courage against the *supposed Enemies of Mankind*" (xxii–xxiii). Nearly two hundred and fifty years before the anthropologist William Arens radicalized the academic study of cannibalism with the publication of *The Man-Eating Myth,* that is, Atkins was openly suggesting the existence of "a universal taboo on cannibalism." [36]

In the three decades following the publication of Atkins's narrative, his argument was taken up by several compilers of travel narratives, who decried the continuing tendency to represent newly discovered peoples "as the most savage and barbarous, and particularly being fond of devouring all the white men whom they can get into their power." The editors of one such collection declare that "the people of many countries who, when little known, were described as anthropophagi, or man-eaters, have been found to be friendly, benevolent and enemies to cruelty."[37] By the time Cook first sailed for the Pacific, the denial of cannibalism had become popularly associated with the figure of the editor, whose assertion of authority over texts gleaned from other sources was increasingly perceived as "a proprietary, interpretive, appropriative, and often imperial act."[38] In his *Essay on the Natural History of Guiana* (1769), the American doctor Edward Bancroft bemoans the fact "that the very existence of Cannibals has been lately denied by several modern Compilers of History, notwithstanding the repeated attestations of Travellers to the contrary." He is particularly offended by the a priori nature of this denial, declaring that "[f]or persons . . . who have never quitted their native country, to determine concerning the manners of distant unknown nations, and, on the strength of plausible appearances, to impeach the veracity of Travellers, and positively deny those things which, at most, they are but permitted to doubt, is a culpable temerity, which well deserves reprehension."[39] Though the denial of cannibalism was first popularized by the report of a traveler, by the late 1760s it had begun to be linked to men who were liable to be dismissed, in George Forster's words, as "[p]hilosophers, who have only contemplated mankind in their closets" (*Voyage*, 1:514).

In the context of this debate, the significance of "ocular proof" should be clear. Without it, those who believed in the existence of cannibals were vulnerable to the accusation that they were old-fashioned dogmatists; with it, they were free to characterize their accusers as new-fangled dogmatists. Nowhere is the centrality of the Cook discoveries in the history of this debate more evident than in William Marsden's *History of Sumatra* (1781), in which Marsden uses the ocular proof of cannibalism among the Maori as the basis of his argument that the Battas of Sumatra are cannibals too. Marsden begins that argument with the acknowledgment that "[m]any of the old travellers had furnished the world with accounts of *anthropophagi* or man-eaters, whom they met with in all parts of the old and new world, and their relations, true or false, were in those days, when people were addicted to the marvellous, universally credited."[40] In the early years of the Enlightenment, "when a more sceptical and scrutinizing spirit prevailed, several of these asserted facts were found upon examination to be false; and men, from a bias inherent in our nature, ran into the opposite extreme. It then became established as a philosophical truth, capable almost of demonstration, that no such race of people ever did or could exist." But now, he says, the era of this "philosophical truth" is over, since "[t]he voyages of our late famous circumnavigators, the veracity of whose assertions is unimpeachable, have already proved to the world that human flesh is eaten by the savages of *New Zealand*" (390). In the aftermath of these discoveries, the critics who continue to harass travelers for "eye-witness" evidence of cannibalism can only be motivated by a credulous belief in the universality of the humane instinct. Although it is true that his own proofs of cannibalism come "through a second, or perhaps a third hand," critics who refuse to "assent to fair, circumstantial evidence, because it clashes with a systematic opinion" are simply doing willful harm "to the cause of truth" (392).

Though Marsden's characterization of the eighteenth-century denial of cannibalism as a "systematic opinion" is obviously strategic, it also seems to have been reasonably accurate. Atkins openly declares that he is "prejudiced" against the idea that cannibals exist because he wishes to maintain his belief in the existence of a humanity that is uniformly stamped with the mark of divinity. A similar sentiment animates the naturalist Joseph Banks, who accompanied Cook on his first expedition. Only the most unequivocal of proofs, he declares in his journal, could lead him to accept the existence of "a custom which human nature holds in too great abhorrence to give easy credit to." [41] Though he briefly succumbs to the idea after discovering gnawed human bones among the Maori in January 1770, he soon resumes his resistance on slightly modified grounds; two months later, he writes in his journal that "[a]s for the flesh of men, although they certainly do eat it I cannot in my own opinion Debase human nature so much as to imagine that they relish [it] as a dainty or even look upon it as a part of common food" (19). Like Atkins, he grudgingly accepts that cannibalism might occur in single instances, when frenzied by the "Thirst of Revenge" or "when the stings of hunger have overcome the precepts of nature" (19–20), but he holds firm against the idea that it is possible for human beings to prey on one another in the same way that fish and insects do. If he were to admit "that any human beings could have among them so brutal a custom" (443), he would have to surrender his belief that humanity was a universal and imperishable moral substance, and that was something that he remained unwilling to do.

This may help to explain why the late-eighteenth-century deniers of cannibalism had difficulty responding to their opponents' charges. Although their position was nominally skeptical, it seems to have been, in practice, a statement of principle. As such, it was extremely vulnerable to the commonsensical observation that "the varieties, inconsistencies, and contradictions of human manners, are so numerous and glaring, that it is scarcely possible to fix any general principle that will apply to all the incongruous races of mankind, or even to conceive an irregularity to which some or other of them have not been accustomed" (Marsden, *History*, 390). On the authority of John Locke, who had cited the existence of cannibals as a proof of his proposition that there is no "practical Truth, that is universally received without doubt or question, as it must be if innate," the defenders of the existence of cannibalism were able to dismiss the deniers as philosophically incorrect.[42] Immediately after witnessing a cannibal feast in New Zealand, the protagonist of the fictional *Travels of Hildebrand Bowman* (1778) observes that although the citizens of "all civilized nations" tend to believe that the detestation of cannibalism is "an innate principle in our natures," his recent experience has taught him otherwise. And if the detestation of cannibalism is not an innate principle, then "there was no such thing; but education and habit was all in all; and had I been born in that part of New Zealand, I most certainly should have been a cannibal."[43] For the most part, the defenders of the existence of cannibalism did not push their argument this far. What most of them wanted, as we have seen, was to replace the conception of humanity as a *universally* innate substance with the conception of humanity as a *racially* innate substance, and for that, all that was really needed was a rhetorical flourish that tagged the deniers as implicitly French and feminine "theorists" and the defenders as implicitly British and masculine "empiricists." With the aid of this mode of rhetoric, which David Simpson has convincingly identified as a common feature of British and Anglo-American "resistance to theory," the defenders were able to create a popular consensus that the deniers were men of a bygone era, soft-hearted French types who refused to face up to the ferocious lusts of their supposedly noble savages.[44]

Under these circumstances, it is astonishing that the denial of cannibalism persisted in any form. But persist it did, thanks in large part to the efforts of Sir John Barrow, second Lord of the Admiralty and prolific contributor to the *Quarterly Review*. Between 1810 and 1836, Barrow published seven essays in the *Quarterly Review* in which he produced variations on his central thesis that "the world has long been abused with regard to cannibals or eaters of human flesh, and perhaps no such people exist."[45] In the early stages of this campaign, Barrow sounds like a nineteenth-century incarnation of John Atkins; he actually repeats some of Atkins's formulations in the first of these essays, in which he declares that "we yet doubt exceedingly if there exists upon the face of the earth, a race of beings who delight in devouring human flesh; and we are persuaded that, if the practice exists at all, it must either arise from a mere ceremonial of tasting the flesh and blood of some powerful and detested enemy, or from being driven to it, as the last resource, by famine." [46] But over time, as he becomes more aware of the criticism that he will receive if he is thought to be arguing that cannibalism is a human impossibility, he is increasingly careful to present himself not as a Gallic theorist, but as a red-blooded Englishman who is capable of out-empiricizing the empiricists. One by one, he takes apart the accusations of cannibalism that we find in the narratives of D'Entrecasteaux, Krusenstern, Langsdorff, Cruise, Anderson, Raffles, and Earle, exposing the epistemological gaps that each of these travelers has attempted to paper over. Rather than committing himself to the idea that "no such people exist," he learns to limit himself to the still-controversial claim that although cannibalism may be motivated by famine, vengefulness, superstitiousness, and a love of display, there is no support for the idea that it is motivated by lust. Though his mode of criticism did not survive very long after the conclusion of his campaign, it had an unusually profound effect on the discourse and practice of travelers who encountered signs of cannibalism in the early nineteenth century.

The best example of Barrow's method of attack is his review of Capt. Richard Cruise's *Journal of a Ten Months' Residence in New Zealand* (1824). He begins by adverting to the fact that "[t]he New Zealanders have been pretty generally stigmatized with the odious practice of cannibalism—a vice which we have always maintained to be much less common among the worst of savages than is so often and so vaguely asserted." [47] When writers circulate "theories and conjectures" on this topic, he says, they are chargeable with "a culpable acquiescence in the odious prejudice against [the Maori]," a prejudice that has contributed to the Western visitor's habit of "looking on all improvement as hopeless, and, by an unrestrained and vicious intercourse, rendering them even worse than they now are" (58, 59). He finds it surprising, then, that in a book otherwise respectful of the Maori, Cruise includes "a piece of information which, if true, would at once throw all their good qualities into the shade; it is 'that anthropophagy exists among them, and is practised, not only as a superstition, but as a *sensual animal gratification*.'" The only possible explanation, he says, is that Cruise "had heard, and read, and believed long before he landed among them, that the New Zealanders were cannibals, and could not, as it would seem, during his stay, eradicate this impression from his mind, though no one fact came to his knowledge which could justify even a suspicion of such a practice" (60). To avoid the stigma of the Enlightenment theorist, Barrow immediately adds a note of clarification: "Let it not be supposed that we are seeking to exculpate the New Zealanders altogether from the disgusting and horrible practice of eating human flesh. We have little doubt that savages of their violent disposition, whose passions are easily and strongly excited, occasionally indulge a spirit of revenge by mangling and gnawing the bodies of their enemies. . . . To this extent, but no further, we are willing to admit that the New Zealanders, as well as certain other savage tribes, are in the habit of eating human flesh" (61).

The two basic moves that Barrow makes in this essay show up in most of his treatments of this subject. The first is to lament the absence of scientific procedure among the travelers who "report such hearsay stories of anthropophagi, on such slight grounds."[48] With such low standards of evidence, he says, it has become all too easy to include, "in almost every modern voyage which has been published, vague accounts of cannibalism, that are as discreditable to the relaters of them as they are calumnious and injurious to the character of the people of whom they are related" ("Porter's *Cruize*," 367). In two separate essays, he elaborates on this point by referring to the testimony of Alexander Dalrymple, the late hydrographer of the Admiralty, who "used to say, that he had seen most parts of the world himself, and believed that he had read every account of voyages and travels that had ever been published; but that he had never met one tittle of evidence on the question of man-eating, that would be received in a court of justice" (*"Expeditions*," 18). In the absence of "such direct and positive evidence" ("Porter's *Cruize*," 367), the only responsible thing to do is to conclude that the case is unproven. The second move is to insist that he is questioning not the existence of cannibalism but its extent, that he is emphatically not under the sway of eighteenth-century theories about the perfection of man in the state of nature. "Of the existence of cannibals we can no longer entertain any doubt," he writes in 1811, "but we confess ourselves rather skeptical as to the usually assigned motive for their becoming so, namely, the love of human flesh. We can conceive that famine, revenge, and even superstition, may drive these wretched men to this horrible expedient; but that they should make war for the sole purpose of eating one another, is too monstrous to be believed."[49] In reducing his opposition to a quarrel with the "usually assigned motive" for cannibalism, he attempts to dissociate himself from the likes of Atkins while continuing to undermine what he considers to be the most dangerous aspect of the discourse on cannibalism.

But in implying that the primary reason he is skeptical of lustful cannibalism is that it is "too monstrous to be believed," he leaves himself open to the same kind of criticism that the earlier deniers of cannibalism had encountered. His skepticism is "amiable," says a later writer in the *Quarterly Review,* but even if cannibalism is "less common than is supposed," its existence "appears to us to rest on incontestable evidence." [50] The force of Barrow's criticism was repeatedly blunted by this tendency to reduce it to a laudable but misguided attempt to think the best that could be thought about human nature. After noting that "[t]he cannibalism of the inhabitants of New-Zealand, and other islands of the Pacific, has been doubted by some, and denied by others," the missionary William Ellis expresses some sympathy with this tradition: "every mind influenced by the common sympathies of humanity must naturally resist the conviction of his species ever sinking to a degradation so abject, and a barbarity so horrible, until it be substantiated by the clearest evidence of indisputable facts." Unfortunately, he says, sympathy must here give way to science, for "the circumstantial accounts of the missionaries and other who have resided among them no longer admit any doubt to be entertained of the revolting and humiliating fact." [51] Defined as a blinkered humanism, Barrow's skepticism was stripped of much of its power to disturb the certainties of the discourse on savagery. As in the cases of Arens, Atkins, and Banks, this way of defining his position is not entirely inaccurate. Facts that did not fit into his idea of the natural order of things did seem to make him unusually uncomfortable; confronted by the story of a whale ramming and sinking the *Essex,* he declares that "we must decline giving the smallest credit to an anecdote so contrary to all experience of the habits of any class of whales—in short the story is worthy of Sinbad the Sailor." [52] His model of truth was essentially syllogistic, in that the only experiences he allowed to be true were those that could be made to coexist with prior beliefs. In an empiricist age, this was a difficult position to defend, and it is surely one of the major reasons he had no long-term successor in that role.

But even after the thickening file of reports of cannibalism had begun to be accepted as a sufficient rebuttal to his argument, Barrow's habit of inquiring into the means by which these reports were obtained continued to present an obstacle to the explanatory ambitions of travelers. In the late 1830s, toward the end of his tenure with the *Quarterly Review,* he and an acquaintance who reviewed for the newly prestigious London *Athenaeum* brought their collective weight to bear on Joel Polack, a one-time merchant in New Zealand whose stories about the Maori laid unusual emphasis on the horrors of their cannibalism. Barrow remarks in an 1836 essay that in one of their conversations, Polack had been "very indignant at our doubting the veracity of one of the chiefs—who had amused him with an account of the delicious repasts which he frequently indulged in, afforded by the flesh of a young girl—and boasted that he had recently caught the wife of a hostile chief while bathing, whose carcase, *after being steamed with potatoes,* made a glorious feast" (*"Expeditions,"* 18). Perhaps provoked by Barrow's doubts, Polack went on to highlight these kinds of tales of cannibal lust in his 1838 book on New Zealand, characterizing them as evidences of the fact that "[f]ew persons can conceive by theory alone, the disposition of man in a state of barbarism."[53] As the *Athenaeum* reviewer noted, however, Polack "never once witnessed an act of cannibalism." The reviewer instantly inserts the standard disclaimer, pointing out that "[w]e do not, indeed, mean to deny that the New Zealanders are cannibals; the concurrent testimony against them, though far from explicit, is yet too strong to be easily thrown aside." But cannibalism is "a theme on which vulgar minds have always delighted to amplify," and Polack's mind is unusually vulgar: "he absolutely revels in the thoughts of man-eating; he delights to fancy himself quivering in the jaws of some tattooed ogre; he is unable to satiate himself with 'supping full of horrors.' " "We cannot but think," the reviewer says, "that Mr. Polack's six years' experience of New Zealand, would have led him to entertain some doubts of the frequency of cannibalism among its inhabitants, if he had not begun with assuming the fact."[54]

Polack returned fire in *Manners and Customs of the New Zealanders* (1840), in which he notes, after relating an account of cannibalism, that "[i]t has become a fashion, among a certain portion of readers, to decry narratives of a similar nature to the above anecdote; to such readers, who would solely oppose personal prejudices to assured facts, the writer does not address himself."[55] But he can't help himself; the accounts of Maori cannibalism recorded by Anglican and Wesleyan missionaries are so indisputable, he says later on, that "even Sir John Barrow himself must become a convert" (1:288). Barrow did not deign to reply, but the *Athenaeum* reviewer did. Once again, he says, "we confess our inability to discover a single fact in Mr. Polack's volume calculated to change our opinion, which is, that cannibalism, though often the result of famine, or of that phrenzy to which barbarians in the hour of triumph, and actuated by feelings of revenge, can work themselves up, is not, never was, and cannot be familiar and usual, even among the most savage of the human race." The reviewer goes on to say that he was present when Barrow "pressed Mr. Polack to state distinctly whether he had ever had ocular testimony of the fact of cannibalism," and that Polack was "compelled to acknowledge, that he never saw a human being killed and eaten; that he could say nothing as to the existence of cannibal rites from his own knowledge; and that his belief rested altogether on hearsay evidence and presumptions."[56] As late as 1840, then, the skepticism of cannibalism was being publicly promoted by, in Polack's words, "those intelligent and highly intellectual gentlemen" who are "attached to the leading literary and public journals."[57] It was still powerful enough to serve as a warning to travelers inclined to pass along stories about cannibalism: before you set up camp, check the solidity of your epistemological ground. And it continued to play a major role in the elaboration of alternative explanations of cannibalism, particularly, as we will see, the notion that acts of cannibalism are motivated by a desire to imbue an audience with terror.

Famine

For a brief time in the mid-eighteenth century, one of the more popular arguments against the existence of lustful cannibalism was the claim that the act was motivated not by desire but by need. In Voltaire's *Candide* (1759), Cacambo justifies the cannibalism of the Oreillons by telling them that "you haven't the same resources we have," and that those who "have other means of making a good meal" should not criticize this sensible use of dead enemies.[58] Voltaire generalizes this argument in his *Philosophical Dictionary* (1764), suggesting that cannibalism has always and everywhere derived from the exigencies of small hunting clans: "The habit of nourishing themselves on what they killed easily led them to treat their enemies like their stags and their boars. It was superstition that caused human victims to be immolated; it was necessity that caused them to be eaten."[59] His argument was immediately picked up by Corneille de Pauw, who noted, "It is a subject of controversy among writers, whether the repast preceded or followed the sacrifice," but "[a]s the practice must have had its origin among savages, most of whom have but vague ideas of worship, and many of them no ideas at all, it is probable that hunger and revenge first impelled them to devour prisoners of war."[60] And in 1773, it received its most notorious expression in a comment that John Hawkesworth inserted into his edition of Cook's journal of his first voyage. After passing along Cook's initial report of the signs of cannibalism in New Zealand—mostly gnawed bones in baskets— Hawkesworth suggests that the constant threat of famine in that country "will enable us to account . . . for the horrid practice of eating those who are killed in battle; for the hunger of him who is pressed by famine to fight, will absorb every feeling, and every sentiment which would restrain him from allaying it with the body of his adversary."[61]

These arguments are quite clearly on the minds of the *Resolution* journalists; as I have noted, one of Wales's conclusions is that cannibalism cannot be explained "through want of Annimal food." Cook notes at one point that he has "heard people argue, that no nation could be cannibals, if they had other flesh to eat, or did not want food; thus deriving the custom from necessity" (*South Pole*, 2:60), and George Forster explicitly blames "the very learned canon *Pauw*," whose "sentiments are copied by Dr. Hawkesworth," for promoting the incorrect notion "that men were first tempted to devour each other from real want of food and cruel necessity" (*Voyage*, 1:514). In the wake of the Cook expeditions, the famine explanation very quickly fell from favor. By the early nineteenth century, it had virtually disappeared, partly because the evidence from the Pacific was not providing much support for it, and partly because the environmentalist theory of human behavior that it was based on had been superseded by theories emphasizing the deep, dark forces of irrationality and race. As a grand unifying theory, it would not return until the late 1970s, when the work of Michael Harner and Marvin Harris would again provide this interpretation of cannibalism with a brief vogue.[62] But this is not to say that it simply and suddenly vanished from post-Enlightenment narratives of travel. Within the discourse on "savage" cannibalism, it served as a foil for the lust explanation; within the distinct but related discourse on white cannibalism, it offered a way of enacting, in a new location, the conflicts among the conventional understandings of the relationship between humanity and savagery.

In accounts of "savage" life, writers tended to invoke the famine explanation only to discredit it, a strategy that allowed them to characterize the lust explanation not as a credulous first impression, but as a rational second thought. In his *Journal of Researches into the Geology and Natural History of the Various Countries* (1846), for instance, Charles Darwin reports that a young native of Tierra del Fuego told an Englishman "that when pressed in winter by hunger, they kill and devour their old women before they kill their dogs: the boy, being asked by Mr. Low why they did this, answered, 'Doggies catch otters, old women no.' "[63] Rather than representing the act as an exercise of practical reason, as someone like Voltaire certainly would have, Darwin launches into a reverie on the horrors of savagery:

> This boy described the manner in which they are killed by being held over smoke and thus choked; he imitated their screams as a

joke, and described the parts of their bodies which are considered best to eat. Horrid as such a death by the hands of their friends and relatives must be, the fears of the old women, when hunger begins to press, are more painful to think of; we were told that they then often run away into the mountains, but that they are pursued by the men and brought back to the slaughter-house at their own fire-sides! (214)

Told in this way, the boy's story authorizes and extends Darwin's initial representation of the "abject and miserable" Fuegians: "Viewing such men, one can hardly make oneself believe that they are fellow creatures, and inhabitants of the same world" (213). For Darwin, famine cannibalism is by no means the sign of a common human nature pressed by a common necessity. It is, instead, an occasion for the expression of a racially specific lust, a lust that transports the Fuegians into a world apart from Darwin's, and thereby transforms them into an occasion for the experience of a racially specific "humanity."

But dark-skinned people were not the only ones who were driven by hunger to eat one another. As A. W. Brian Simpson has shown, it was a "socially accepted practice" during the age of sail for shipwrecked white sailors to feed on the bodies of their shipmates.[64] This "custom of the sea" was not the sailor's dirty little secret, either; throughout the early nineteenth century, narratives of maritime suffering enjoyed a wide popularity, and the stories of white men and women driven to the "last extremity" of feeding on human flesh were one of their staples. According to Keith Huntress, close to fifty compilations of shipwreck narratives were published in English between 1800 and 1849, along with nearly twice as many narratives of individual shipwrecks. Some compilations ran to as long as six volumes, and the most popular of them went through multiple editions. Of the compilations that Huntress was able to examine, almost every one contains accounts of famine cannibalism. In part, this is because the compilers endlessly rehashed the same old narratives of shipwrecks and, in doing so, inevitably repeated the most famous tales of cannibalism, such as the stories of the *Nottingham Galley*, the *Luxborough*, the *Tyrell*, the *Dolphin*, the *Anne and Mary*, the *Peggy*, the *Thomas*, the *Medusa*, the *Nautilus*, the *Essex*, the *Frances Mary*, and the *Francis Spaight*. But it also has something to do with the appeal that these narratives of the "last extremity" had for their readers—not just for the impoverished sailors and curious children who were so often addressed in the prefaces, but also for poets and novelists such as Byron, Poe, Thackeray, Dickens, Whittier, Twain, and Melville, all of whom made use of them in their work.[65] Despite the fact that these narratives seemed to threaten the ordinary way of dividing up the moral substances of humanity and savagery—or perhaps *because* of that threat, and its attendant frisson—they were highly visible elements of early-nineteenth-century Anglo-American literature.

To resolve some of the tension that these narratives created, most writers chose to distinguish between the reprehensible desire of dark-skinned beings and the piteous need of whites. Rather than signifying the presence of an inhuman lust, cannibalism among whites was made to signify humanity at its limits, at the point where it experiences most fully its subjection to the forces of God and Nature. Understood in this way, it was not really cannibalism at all, insofar as that word implied both an animal interior and a racially marked exterior. In the index to the influential *Shipwrecks and Disasters at Sea* (1812), Sir J. G. Dalyell does not include an entry on cannibalism, but he does include one entitled "Human flesh ate," with six separate page references. There is only one place in the entire three volumes where a variant of the word cannibalism is used to describe white men eating human flesh; in every other instance, it is softened by circumlocutions like "the last extremity" or "the cruel and barbarous resolution of devouring our own species."[66] Throughout Dalyell's collection, eating human flesh when pressed by famine is generally presented as an unlovely but understandable act, capable of being justified by a plea of extenuating circumstances. The survivors of the 1807 wreck of the *Nautilus*, for instance, "were not ignorant of the means whereby other unfortunate mariners in the like situation had protracted life, yet they viewed them with disgust. Still, when they had no alternative, they considered their urgent necessities and found them affording some excuse" (*Shipwrecks*, 3:452). The utilitarian decision making that had been rejected as a justification for cannibalism among dark-skinned peoples survived well into the nineteenth century as a justification for cannibalism among whites. Whereas cannibalism among hungry savages tended to be depicted as an inexcusable first impulse, cannibalism among hungry white sailors tended to be represented as a horrible but ultimately comprehensible last resort.

Narrated in this way, stories of shipwreck cannibalism offered their readers an image of humanity shrunken to its smallest possible scope. The sailors in these stories are agonizingly stripped of the range of choices necessary to a human identity understood in terms of the freedom of the will, until they are left with only one, purely negative mode of identification: to choose against death. In the dominant tradition of shipwreck narratives, this choice is still understood as an act of will that identifies the subject as human, but the humanity it represents is that of the subject reduced to its fragmentary essence, to the most objectlike thing it can become while still remaining itself. *Reduced* is, in fact, one of the words most frequently used to describe the white man who prefers cannibalism to death.[67] As Archibald Duncan suggests in his preface to *The Mariner's Chronicle* (1806), shipwreck cannibalism represented in this way was intended to force a moment of recognition in its white, Christian readership. When attending to "the recital of the cruel necessity to which many of them were reduced," he says, the readers of his anthology should recognize in the image of the famine-stricken sailors a diminished image of themselves, and respond not with outright horror, but "with mingled horror and compassion" (1:7). The children's author Peter Parley makes the same appeal, beginning his retelling of the *Francis Spaight* story with an apology for mentioning "such a proof of the dreadful excesses into which extreme sufferings have forced seamen," but explaining that "[o]ne of my objects in mentioning this terrible fact is, that you may not be altogether ignorant of the weakness of human nature, unassisted by Almighty power, to endure extreme trial without committing crime."[68] Like the narratives of famine cannibalism in Leviticus and Deuteronomy, these accounts were made to signify "the consequences of disobedience," the necessary diminishment of human beings who are "unassisted by Almighty power."[69] Although they did not deny them their anticipated shudder of horror, the writers and compilers of these accounts asked their readers both to understand white cannibalism, in utilitarian terms, and to sympathize with it, as the last possible choice of ordinary sinners like themselves, crushed in the hand of an angry God.

To a certain degree, then, the mid-eighteenth-century image of cannibals as rational, humane beings without any other rations may be said to have become, in the late eighteenth and early nineteenth centuries, an element of discourse marked "For Whites Only." But only to a certain degree; as I have already indicated, not every writer thought of shipwreck cannibalism as the unfortunate but necessary sustenance of a humanity that never entirely disappears. For at least some of these writers, humanity does indeed flicker out at the moment when human flesh is consumed—in some cases, at the moment when the *thought* of eating human flesh first crosses the white person's mind. Even among white people, in other words, eating human flesh could be said to entail the deformation or annihilation of the eater's moral nature. One potential interpretation of that flickering out, as I will suggest in the afterword, is that the idea of a God-given humanity is nothing more than a beautiful notion. We get hints of this interpretation in several compilations of shipwreck narratives, despite the fact that the compilers offered those narratives as affirmations of humanity's real presence. Ann Saunders, who was driven by hunger to eat the body of her fiancé, explains the entire experience of drifting for twenty-two days after a shipwreck as something that "the Almighty, for his own wise and good purposes, saw fit" to cause. She notes, however, that other survivors "appeared almost disposed impiously to accuse the Supreme Being, with being unjustly the author of their wretchedness."[70] When it turned out to be untrue "that God, who made man, always found him something to eat" (Dalyell, *Shipwrecks*, 3:370)—when it became horrifyingly evident that they would have to *take* something unlawful in order to live—sufferers like these understandably began to feel like creatures without a Creator. If God was indeed absent, or malevolent, then "humanity" could only be a spurious growth, a phosphorescent glow on the surface of a character, rather than a beating heart of light.

For most writers and readers, this was a very unpleasant idea. Accordingly, the more common way of upsetting the conventional understanding of white cannibalism was to suggest that at the moment when humanity flickers out, a deeply embedded savagery flames up. In his narrative of the 1710 wreck of the *Nottingham Galley,* for instance, Capt. John Dean reports that he only permitted his men to feed on the body of a dead comrade "[a]fter mature reflection and consultation on the lawfulness or sinfulness of the act on the one hand, and absolute necessity on the other" (Dalyell, *Shipwrecks*, 2:16). But once his men submitted to that necessity, their powers of reason and sympathy died away; within a few days, he says, "[t]heir eyes were wild and staring, their countenances fierce and barbarous, and, instead of obeying my commands, as they had universally and readily done before, I found that all I could say, and even prayers and entreaties, were vain and fruitless" (2:17-18). In *The Shipwreck and Adventures of M. Pierre Viaud* (1771), the narrator undergoes an even more striking transformation. Wandering through the jungles of Florida with his slave, Viaud begins to remember stories of previous voyagers casting lots to determine who should die to preserve the lives of the rest. "While the situation of these voyagers was running in my head," he says, "my roving eyes happened to fall upon the negro, though without design or direction; but they fastened themselves upon him, for some moments, with a greediness that I could not conquer or resist."[71] The greediness of those eyes steadily grows, and he strikes the slave once before being immobilized by protests that seem to come from other parts of his body: "My uplifted arm, now trembling, refused to repeat the stroke; my heart shook within me, as if loosened from my body, whilst struggling humanity unnerved every sinew that was necessary to complete the murder" (168–69). But in the end, the eyes have it, successfully stifling "the voice of pity" sounding from within his body. "I became a wolf again, a crocodile, an hyaena!" he tells us, and "distracted beyond the power of reason," he finishes the job of killing his slave for the sake of his flesh, "roaring out, at the same time, to increase my frenzy, and smother his cries" (169–70).

Although such narratives did blur the line between the humanity of whites and the inhumanity of nonwhites, they did not go so far as to question the idea that humanity is a real moral substance. In Viaud's narrative, for instance, the onset of savagery actually enables him to feel, more intensely than ever before, the "struggling humanity" of his heart. All that has happened here is that the conventional opposition between humanity and savagery in the encounter between Christians and cannibals has been reproduced in Viaud's body, where the only evidence necessary to guarantee the truth of that opposition is the evidence of his own private feelings. It is, in this sense, an even more powerful way of establishing these two moral states as natural facts. That is not to say that the suspension of the distinction between white and nonwhite cannibalism is entirely conservative, or that it offers us no glimpse of a radical critique; under certain circumstances, as the example of Charles Dickens indicates, it was capable of provoking some remarkably anxious denunciations.[72] For the most part, however, the literary critics who have addressed these kinds of texts have assumed that the mere blurring of the distinction between "humanity" and "savagery" is in itself a radical act.[73] Just as I suggested in my discussion of Oedidee that there is nothing intrinsically radical about the rhetorical isolation and elevation of individual "savages," I want to suggest here that there is nothing intrinsically radical about the rhetorical isolation and degradation of individual "humans." As Fredric Jameson has pointed out, because all such transgressions "presuppos[e] the laws or norms or taboos against which they function," they "end up precisely reconfirming such laws."[74] Whenever we dramatize a transgression, we both reify the prior existence of a border and establish the conditions under which that border may be redrawn, with an even heavier hand.

In the late eighteenth and early nineteenth centuries, the fundamental effect of scenes like Viaud's was to enable, and very often to enact, the redrawing of that border. The usual mode of reinscription was punishment: readers were given to understand that white people who ate human flesh would either go mad and die or develop a lifelong addiction to the substance. In the frequently reprinted narrative of a 1765 famine on board the *Peggy*, we hear of a sailor named James Campbell who "was so ravenously impatient" after the execution of a slave who was part of the ship's cargo "that, tearing the negro's liver from the body, he devoured it raw." Three days later, he "died raving mad." His madness and death were "imputed by the crew to his voracity," and, "dreading the consequence of subsisting on Campbell's body, they threw it overboard, though not without reluctance" (Dalyell, *Shipwrecks*, 2:452). The same thing happens in the story of cannibalism among the twelve white survivors of a 1797 insurrection on board the British slave ship *Thomas;* lots are drawn, and the surgeon who bleeds the victim to death immediately "drank the blood as it flowed, while the rest anxiously watched the victim's departing breath, that they might satisfy the hunger which preyed upon them." But this act is followed by consequences that assume all the force of a providential judgment: "[t]hose who glutted themselves with human flesh and gore, and whose stomachs retained the unnatural food, soon perished with raging insanity," and "[t]hose who remained attributed the preservation of their lives to their having refused to follow the example of their fellow sufferers" (Duncan, *Chronicle,* 1:109). Although these kinds of narratives do indicate that the border between humanity and savagery is not impassable, they also represent that border as a very real thing, a tremulous line that becomes dark and broad as soon as it is crossed.

More often, writers made that point by raising the specter of addiction. After citing some cases of famine cannibalism in India in which those who ate human flesh "acquired such an irresistible desire for this food, that they would even way-lay the living to kill and eat them," George von Langsdorff declares that "a strong conclusion may be drawn against the morality of even eating a corpse in times of the greatest scarcity, or pressed by the most gnawing hunger" (*Voyages*, 142, 143). W. Cooke Taylor similarly cautions against eating human flesh by referring to the case of a man "who, under pressure of famine at sea, had eaten a part of one of his companions. He declared, that the feeling of disgust disappeared at the second or third meal, and did not return during the five days that the crew were reduced to this horrid fare." Now, even "after the lapse of many years, he never thought upon the subject without finding desire strangely mixed with loathing."[75] Rather than being a purely exterior occasion, famine cannibalism is, in arguments like these, a circumstance that initiates the growth of a preexistent interior essence. To suggest that a single indulgence will transform us into addicts for life is to suggest that there is something in us but beyond us that is inclined to love the taste of human flesh, even before the occasion presents itself.

It was not at all uncommon for that "something" to assume a racial coloration. Beginning in the 1810s, writers became increasingly willing to bypass the earlier euphemisms and simply attach the race-linked term *cannibal* to white eaters of human flesh. In James Fenimore Cooper's *The Red Rover* (1827), for instance, the white sailor Dick Fid tells the governess Mrs. Wyllys that he once decided not to eat the body of a young boy when drifting in an open boat because, as he told his black companion, Guinea, at the time, " 'If we eat the boy, we shall be no better than the people in your own country, who, you know, my lady, are cannibals."[76] As that convention of representation changed, it became more acceptable for writers to associate the "something" that peered out of the eyes of famished white people with an explicitly racialized savagery. In a later version of the *Thomas* incident, we hear that "[t]hose who indulged their cannibal appetite to excess, speedily perished in raging madness" (Dalyell, *Shipwrecks,* 3:357), and in a section of Byron's *Don Juan* heavily indebted to that story, we are told that after a week in an open boat, the sufferers "glared upon each other . . . and you might see / The longings of the cannibal arise / (Although they spoke not) in their wolfish eyes."[77] As I have already argued, such passages do not necessarily embody a radical critique of "humanity," however much they may seem to compromise the integrity and purity of the humane subject. Once it was possible to declare of hungry castaways that "[t]he cannibal was, already, in their looks," it was less necessary to secure the truth of humanity by seeking a cannibal outside of oneself.[78] The signs of *this* cannibal were both secure from doubt and immediately available, and when they emerged, in oneself or in others, they called down an instant supernatural judgment. For all its apparent radicalness, then, the discourse on famine cannibalism among whites was, on the whole, a remarkably useful accessory to the discourse on lustful cannibalism. Only in those texts that exhibit, without roars or prayers, the sustenance of the unsustained, does the idea of "humanity" receive the scrutiny it deserves.

Although the famine explanation was an available means of palliating the cannibalism of nonwhite people in the late eighteenth century, it was not the one that most concerned those who believed that the fundamental motive for that behavior was lust. In Wales's list of the conclusions that could be drawn from the *Resolution* experiments, the first two—that cannibals do not eat human flesh "only on the spot whilst under the Impulse of that wild Frenzy into which they have shewn us they can & do work themselves in their Engagements" and that "it is not their Enemies only . . . since those who eat the part of the head on board, could not know whether it belonged to a friend or Enemy"—are attempts to respond to the argument that cannibalism is the natural outcome of the desire for revenge. This was an argument that was particularly popular among Enlightenment philosophers of human evolution, including Wales's companions John and George Forster. In their published narratives of the expedition, the Forsters acknowledge that the *Resolution* experiments indicated that at least some cannibals might take pleasure in the taste of human flesh, but, as George observes, "it would be absurd to suppose from such circumstances, that killing men for the sake of feasting upon them, has ever been the spirit of a whole nation; because it is utterly incompatible with the existence of society." It would be more logical, he thinks, to assume that vengeance is the master "spirit" of this cannibal nation: "Revenge has always been a strong passion among barbarians, who are less subject to the sway of reason than civilized people, and has stimulated them to a degree of madness which is capable of all kinds of excess" (*Voyage*, 1:516). Those accused of cannibalism should be at least partially excused, he suggests, because they are not really responsible for their actions. Especially in the late eighteenth century, and to a lesser degree in the early nineteenth century, the vengeance explanation offered an effective means of mediating between the extremes of the discourse on cannibalism. It did not deny the existence of cannibalism, but neither did it accept the general applicability of the lust explanation; it simply shifted the site of cannibal desire from the body to the spirit, from the physical to the mental passions.

In doing so, it drew on one of the more common assumptions about the nature of savages: that they were permanently occupied by a spirit of vengeance that periodically took possession of their imperfectly regulated minds. In his *History of America* (1777), the Scottish historian William Robertson declares, "As it is impossible to appease the fell spirit of revenge which rages in the heart of a savage, this frequently prompts the Americans to devour those unhappy persons, who have been the victims of their cruelty."[79] Because there is no limit to the expansiveness of that spirit, there is nothing to prevent it from finding its satisfaction in the grandest of human enormities; there is, accordingly, nothing particularly surprising about the existence of cannibalism in savage communities. In his edition of William Mariner's *Account of the Natives of the Tonga Islands* (1820), John Martin goes so far as to suggest that "in those uncultivated nations, where a spirit of national hatred and thirst of revenge, on some extraordinary occasions, run very high, it appears to be an instinct of uncultivated nature, to crown the catastrophe by a feast at which civilized humanity revolts."[80] Although it continued to situate cannibalism within the realm of the instinctual passions, the vengeance explanation made it possible to characterize cannibalism as a temporary and extraordinary event that originates in an uncontrollable spiritual faculty. In *An Account of New Zealand* (1835), the missionary William Yate argues that although the Maori "are to be ranked among the Anthropophagi," he "cannot, however, think that it is from any desire that the generality of them have to satisfy or to gratify their appetite for human flesh; but from the diabolical spirit of revenge with which they are actuated, which appears in all their movements, and which is never satisfied till exercised to the utmost upon its object." Once this virtually autonomous "spirit" is roused, he warns, "it is impossible to say to what lengths of reckless and desperate revenge he will go, or where his fury will end."[81]

Defined in this way as a species of madness, vengeance is clearly capable of serving as a palliation of cannibalism. What is not quite so immediately obvious is that it is also capable of transforming cannibalism into a strangely appealing act. Vengeance has historically been cast in the role of justice's evil twin, the horror that emerges when individuals do not merely take the law into their own hands, but explicitly reject the notion that their actions ought to be fitted to the prescriptions of the law. When we recoil from acts of vengeance, it is because they reject the idea that the self ever could or should justify its actions through reference to the conventions of its society, and because they seem to contain within themselves the seeds of a terrible determinism, a cycle of retributions without end. But even when we refuse the delusive promise of a perfect liberation, that promise retains its power to haunt and beckon. In Foucault's discussion of classical attitudes toward madness, for example, the condition of being free from "the sway of reason" and "capable of all kinds of excess" emerges as something like a positive good, an escape from the prison of disciplinary subjectivity into "the threatening space of an absolute freedom."[82] "We have now got into the habit," Foucault says,

> of perceiving in madness a fall into a determinism where all forms of liberty are gradually suppressed . . . [so that] madness threatens modern man only with that return to the bleak world of beasts and things, to their fettered freedom. It is not on this horizon of *nature* that the seventeenth and eighteenth centuries recognized madness, but against a background of *Unreason;* madness did not disclose a mechanism, but revealed a liberty raging in the monstrous forms of animality. . . . [T]he madman, tracing the course of human degradation to the frenzied nadir of animality, disclosed that underlying realm of unreason which threatens man and envelops—at a tremendous distance—all the forms of his natural existence. It was not a question of tending toward a determinism, but of being swallowed up by a darkness. (*Madness,* 83–84)

Within the terms of the fantasy of Unreason that Foucault describes here, it is possible for cannibalism to be represented not as a condition of fetteredness, but as the consummate expression of a purely independent agency.

Consider, for instance, the following sentence from John Forster's 1778 discussion of the origins of the cannibal spirit among the Maori:

> The men train up the boys in a kind of liberty, which at last degenerates into licentiousness: they suffer not the mothers to strike their petulant, unruly, and wicked sons, for fear of breaking that spirit of independency, which they seem to value above all things, and as the most necessary qualification for their societies; this naturally brings on an irascibility, which, in the men, cannot brook any controul, action or word, that can be construed according to their manners and principles, into an affront, or injury; inflamed by passion, they are impatient to wreak their vengeance: wild fancy paints the injury so atrocious, that it must be washed in blood; they know not where to stop, and being more and more incensed by the power of imagination, they go to battle with a loud and barbarous song; each feature is distorted, each limb is set in a cadenced motion; they brandish their destructive weapons, and stamp upon the ground with their feet, while the whole band join in an awful, tremendous groan; the

song begins anew, and at last the whole troop is lost in frenzy and rage; they fall to, and every one fights as if animated by furies; and destruction and carnage await the routed party: whoever falls, is murdered without mercy, and the corses of the slain immediately serve to glut the inhuman appetites of the conquerors.[83]

The sentence itself partakes of the masculine excess that it describes; it seems to "know not where to stop," except in the cannibalistic climax of the Maoris' system of education. By catching up the reader in the accelerating cadence of the Maori boy's development of a "spirit of independency" that knows no limit, Forster encourages a sympathy with this spirit. At its heart, the sentence is a romance of masculine freedom, an envious depiction of the spiritually naked by the spiritually clothed, in which cannibalism is not the sign of a miserable reduction to the condition of beasts but the sign of an absolute triumph over all insults to the honor of the immaculate self.

Forster goes on, in fact, to enshrine this spirit of excess within his theory of the means by which savages rise to civilization. From the homeostatic condition of an absolute savagery, in which the savage "has no other impulse for action, than want" and accordingly exists in "stupid indolence," the only avenue of escape is the one opened up by the visitation of the spirit of vengeance. The combustive force of this spirit awakens the savage's dormant "powers and faculties," which then develop exponentially as that spirit feeds on itself, carrying him "from the first excentric action to a second, from one enormity to another" (*Observations*, 330). Though that evolutionary process may seem dangerous, its dangers are only apparent, because the process contains within itself a regulatory mechanism that will forestall a cannibal apocalypse and encourage the formation of a new social order. At some point, the cannibals' development of new faculties will enable them to think in terms of the social welfare; they will then decide to engage in fewer battles, in order to avoid the decimation of their people, and to enslave captured enemies, in order to profit from their labor. "To us," Forster says, "who are used to live in better regulated societies, where for many years backwards, anthropophagy has been in disuse, it is always a horrid idea, that men should eat men. But I cannot help observing, that this barbarism is one of the steps, by which debased humanity, is gradually prepared for a better state of happiness" (330).[84]

Within the terms of Forster's argument, cannibalism is not the act that establishes the breadth and depth of the gulf between civilized and savage man, but the act that promises to bridge it. It identifies the savage as a man in the process of becoming civilized, and it enables the civilized man to see in the savage an image of his own limitless energies at a stage in which they are absolutely liberated from any restraining feminine influence. In Forster's masculinist fantasy, vengeful cannibalism represents a declaration of independence from the feminized social sphere, a declaration the civilized white man may at least nostalgically admire, if not emulate. The same dream of liberation animates the discussion of vengeful cannibalism in John Crawfurd's *History of the Indian Archipelago* (1820), in which we are told that "[i]n a state of society where there is no regular administration of justice, but where the security of every man's honour, life, and property, depends in no small degree upon his own arm, we may almost hesitate whether to pronounce the passion of revenge a virtue or a vice. Without it, at all events, society could not exist." Though this state of society may be permanently insecure, it has definite advantages over more settled states of existence; in Indonesia, the societies under the "regular administration of justice" are those "whose government is most despotic, and whose character is necessarily most servile and tame." [85] Believing that "there is something in [cannibalism] designating a fierce, warlike, and manly spirit" (J. Martin, *Account*, 137), writers like Forster and Crawfurd could not reject it as an unequivocal horror without thereby aligning themselves with a feminized principle of justice, a principle that they obviously longed to escape.

As we might expect, given the somewhat childish masculinism of this position, the image of vengeful cannibalism was not nearly as liberatory as it was made out to be. For one thing, it was used throughout the 1830s as a justification for transforming the Maori into colonial subjects. In *The New Zealanders*, a book written with an eye toward that island's "strong claim upon our attention as a commercial people" (17), George Craik freely admits that the Maoris have an unusual passion for warfare and that "they carry on that excitement in the most terrific way that the fierceness of man has ever devised;—they devour their slaughtered enemies" (15). But Craik takes this to be one of the many signs of "[t]he masculine independence they at once manifested in their first encounters with us," which "served to stimulate the feelings of curiosity with which we are now accustomed to regard them" (14). As the sign not only of masculine independence, but also of "an intellectual vigour, which is the root of ultimate civilization" (15), cannibalism indicates to Craik that the Maori are not, after all, "in the lowest stages of savage life" (13). The British resident James Busby echoes Craik's argument two years later, declaring that though the Maoris are indeed "stained with the habitual practice of cannibalism, a crime more calculated than all others to excite the horror and detestation of the civilized world," they "will not, on that account, be debarred from the efforts of the philanthropist." Clearly referring only to the men, he argues that "[t]he New Zealander's point of honour is revenge, and this he will pursue in spite of danger and difficulty. For this he will encounter every fatigue, and submit to every privation. No distance of time or space will conquer his resolution. His whole soul is engaged in the pursuit." Such "noble qualities . . . cannot fail to excite the sympathy, and to encourage the endeavours of those who may interest themselves in his improvement." [86] Strangely enough, the spirit of vengeance that deterred an earlier generation of Englishmen from colonizing the island is for these later writers a sign that the Maori are worthy of their paternalistic attention.

Even when we limit ourselves to the consideration of its use as a fantasy object for Westerners, the image of vengeful cannibalism is still a deeply conflicted image of freedom. There are a couple of reasons for this. First, its foundation in the instincts made it easily assimilable to the lust explanation; John Forster himself allows that one of the reasons vengeful cannibalism eventually becomes habitual is that humans are "reputed to be one of the most palatable dishes" (*Observations*, 329). Though vengeance was carefully distinguished from lust, as a "moral" rather than "physical" passion, the fact that both of these passions were imagined to exist outside language made them uncomfortably close neighbors. Second, it was only possible to maintain this vision in all its purity if one was able to conceive of savagery as a condition in which all forms of signification were radically tenuous; any sign that the act might be mediated by the conventions of religion, law, or social communication was a sign that the cannibal was not in fact lost in frenzy, not in fact "swallowed up by a darkness." This meant that the vision of vengeful cannibalism as an absolute freedom was troubled at its edges by all of the experiential evidence that indicated that the actions of savages were indeed mediated by various forms of signification. More specifically, this vision was troubled by the presence of the two explanations of cannibalism that I will turn to now: superstition and terror. Each of these explanations suggested, in very different ways, that cannibalism was not as liberated from the realm of language as some people wanted to believe.

In the late eighteenth century, very few travelers and commentators drew on the superstition explanation; it is absent not only from Wales's careful account of the possible motives for the act of cannibalism on board the *Resolution,* but from every other account of that expedition. It shows up briefly in Cook's narrative of his third voyage, in which he claims that in the Maori "system of belief, the soul of the man whose flesh is devoured by the enemy, is doomed to a perpetual fire, while the soul of the man whose body has been rescued from those who killed him, as well as the souls of all who die a natural death, ascend to the habitations of the Gods." [87] And in a noticeably different form, it also appears in La Perouse's journal of his Pacific expedition, first published in English in 1799. At Monterey Bay in 1786, La Perouse was told that when the natives "have vanquished and killed the chiefs, or bravest men, on the field of battle, they devour some small portions, less in token of hatred and vengeance, than as a homage due to their valour, and from the persuasion that this food is calculated to increase their courage." [88] But neither of these ways of explaining the existence of cannibalism—as a consequence of the superstitious belief that it assures the damnation of an enemy or of the superstitious belief that it assures the incorporation of his prowess—left much of a mark on the late-eighteenth-century discourse on cannibalism. When writers of that time attempted to explain how an act defined as "savage" could logically coexist with other acts defined as "humane," they tended to invoke the spirit of vengeance, as we have seen, rather than what Cook called "the power of superstition to counteract the first principles of humanity" (Cook and King, *Pacific,* 2:41).

Beginning around 1820, however, "the power of superstition" became one of the principal forces that writers alluded to in their explanations of cannibalism. One of its earliest articulations was in John Liddiard Nicholas's *Narrative of a Voyage to New Zealand* (1817), where it is very carefully situated in relation to the earlier theories on the subject. After briefly disposing of Hawkesworth's attribution of cannibalism to famine, Nicholas cites in full the passage from John Forster that I have quoted above, both "to oppose that part which ascribes to the New Zealanders a particular liking for human flesh" (2:67), and, more important, to amend the part that ascribes the origins of cannibalism to vengefulness. In attributing the Maoris' cannibalism to their education, Nicholas says, Forster is only partially correct. For Nicholas, the crucial factor in that education is not what men teach their sons in the absence of women, but what superstition teaches them all: "My opinion on the subject is, that a kind of superstitious revenge is the grand actuating principle that incites them to this horrible practice. Born in the grossest ignorance, and nurtured amidst wild dissensions, they give loose to all the violence of their ungovernable passions; while superstition teaches them to believe that their revenge can reach beyond the grave, and that the future existence of their wretched victims must be totally annihilated, by this unnatural destruction of their mortal remains" (2:68). He goes on to argue that this is true not only of the Maori, but of other Pacific islanders as well. Those Fijians who recently "massacred and devoured fourteen of the people belonging to two vessels that had sailed from Port Jackson" (2:69) were "actuated, I doubt not, by the same principle with the New Zealand cannibals; they were led on to the massacre by the terrible impulse of uncontrouled frenzy, and to the devouring of their victims by the implacable rage of a vengeful superstition" (2:70).

This theory is clearly based more on Cook than on personal experience; Nicholas never actually witnessed any signs of this superstition himself. And it is also pretty clearly motivated by Nicholas's desire to reconcile two competing principles of savagery: its unconstrained vengefulness and its superstitious constraints. In several passages, he echoes Forster in arguing that the savage's "favorite passion is revenge" (1:147) and that if this revenge is, in the case of cannibalism, "so disproportioned to the offence, it is because the barbarian draws no comparisons in these cases, and has never learned to employ an exact scale of retribution" (1:152). Cannibalism functions in passages like these as the preeminent sign of that tendency toward disproportion that the proportionality of the law exists to contain, a tendency so deeply ingrained in the masculine character that it can never quite be eradicated: "Man, whether in a rude or civilized state, is never disposed to passive quiescence under the goading hand of oppression" (1:152). But Nicholas also envisions the savage as a being who "stands enveloped in the dark clouds of ignorance" and consequently can only view "the works of his Creator through the medium of a blind superstition" (1:86–87). "Superstition is natural to man," he declares, so much so that "[c]ivilized nations are not exempt from its influence, nor is it to be expected that they will be, as long as some men are born with weaker minds than others" (2:308). The disproportionately strong will of the savage is naturally accompanied, Nicholas thinks, by a disproportionately weak reason. By arguing that both of these characteristics are expressed in the act of cannibalism,

Nicholas simultaneously denies vengeance its aura of absolute liberation and transforms superstition into a thing of unaccustomed horror.

That same movement through and past the vengeance explanation takes place on a serial basis in the journals of Nicholas's companion on this voyage, the Anglican minister Samuel Marsden. Marsden, the patriarch of the New Zealand mission, wrote in the *Church Missionary Register* for 1816 that he "was unable to ascertain whether they ever ate human flesh as a meal, or from choice, or in cool blood" but that he was inclined to believe that it was "only from mental gratification and in retaliation for some great injury."[89] In subsequent reports from the struggling mission, he began to modify that position. In 1819, he repeated the earlier argument that "[t]hey eat the slain, not so much as an object of food but as a mental gratification and to display publicly to the enemy their bitter revenge" (174), but added a new piece of information: "From all that I have been able to learn, relative to the New Zealanders eating human flesh, this custom appears to have its origin in religious superstition" (169). Unlike Cook and Nicholas, he argues that this superstition is oriented toward the incorporation of the enemy's spirit, rather than the damnation of his soul. The Maoris "believe that, by eating the flesh and drinking the blood of the departed chief, his system becomes incorporated into their system, and by that means they are secured from all danger from the departed ghost of the dead chief, and his spirit will then take up its residence in their bodies as being part of its former habitation" (220). This leads Marsden to a speculation that would get him in trouble with at least one other clergyman. "[O]ne would be led to think that [this belief] had been derived from Divine revelation," he suggests, since it calls up memories of what "[o]ur Saviour told the Jews: 'He that eateth my flesh and drinketh my blood dwelleth in me and I in him'" (220). It is this argument that the Australian minister John Dunmore Lang has in mind when he writes, in 1834, that he is "somewhat sceptical" of the claim that cannibalism is "a religious observance—bearing a sort of symbolical resemblance, forsooth, to the doctrine of the atonement—as certain *wise men of the east* have supposed."[90]

Marsden was not, however, putting the religious observances of Maoris and Christians on any kind of common footing. In an 1823 journal, he remarks that "[h]owever horrid and revolting this custom is to the Christian's mind—and nothing can be more so—yet the New Zealander feels himself as much bound by his superstition to kill and eat human sacrifices as the Christian does to offer up his sacrifices of prayer and praises to the true God" (Elder, *Letters and Journals,* 373). The "revolting" custom of cannibalism bears only a very distant resemblance to the rites of "the true God," and Marsden mentions the resemblance only as way of supporting the diffusionist theory of the origins of human differences. Like most early-nineteenth-century evangelicals, he believed that savages were not the products of a separate creation, but the children of a common Father who had long ago wandered from the light of reason and revelation into what are called, in Psalms, "the dark places of the earth . . . full of the habitations of cruelty." By characterizing cannibalism as a twisted version of Christian ritual, Marsden suggests both that the Maoris are capable of redemption, because they remain children of the light, and that they are badly in need of this redemption, because they are presently the inhabitants of the dark places of the earth. He goes out of his way to stress this last point in his 1823 journal, repeatedly characterizing the life of a cannibal as a condition of spiritual bondage. "Satan has got fast hold of the consciences of these poor heathen and leads them captive at his will" (372), he says; the "bloody rites" of cannibalism "will never be laid aside by the natives until the fetters of their superstition are broken by the sword of the Spirit" (373). In his new emphasis on the Maoris' enslavement to their superstitions, he makes a decisive turn away from the vengeance explanation. By the 1820s, cannibalism had become, for Marsden, anything but a sign of freedom.

The image of cannibalism as an enslavement to superstition quickly picked up adherents. The American captain Benjamin Morrell declared in his *Narrative of Four Voyages* (1832) that Maori cannibalism does not proceed from "a physical appetite or relish for human flesh, as many suppose," but from "a moral appetite, far more voracious than that of hunger." The source of this "moral appetite" is "an insatiable malice that would pursue its victim beyond the confines of the grave; for it is an article of their religious creed that the soul of a man thus devoured is doomed to eternal fire." [91] George Craik also drew on this theory, attributing it to Cook, but went on to say, citing Marsden, that "more recent authorities, concur in shewing that the person who eats any part of the body of another whom he has slain in battle, fancies he secures to himself thereby a portion of the valour or good fortune which had hitherto belonged to his dead enemy" (*New Zealanders*, 106). Because Marsden's explanation carried a greater weight of experiential authority than Nicholas's, it tended to be the one that mid-nineteenth-century writers turned to most. William Breton somewhat tentatively suggests in 1834 that the Maoris believe "that if the body of an enemy be devoured, his soul will pass into everlasting fire," but then says with more assurance that "[e]ven granting this not to be the fact, those persons who have been most among them, and who had opportunities of studying their character, assert most positively, that in eating an enemy whom they have slain, they are persuaded they will become possessed of the valour and abilities of the defunct."[92] W. Cooke Taylor similarly remarks in 1840 that "[t]hose who have had opportunities for close examination, inform us that the revolting practice appears to have originated in the superstitious belief, that those who partook of the banquet would imbibe some portion of the heroism for which the deceased was distinguished."[93]

The sudden popularity of the superstition explanation is a startling development, and it demands some explanation of its own. One possible explanation—perhaps the one that will come first to many people's minds—is that it is true. Thanks to the widespread diffusion of the anthropological concept of culture in the mid- to late twentieth century, we now tend to believe that the most scientifically accurate way of addressing behavior that strikes us as "savage" is to describe it as meaningful on its own terms. Accordingly, the theory that cannibalism is motivated by superstition is more likely to seem true to us than the other explanations I am presenting in this chapter, because it is easily articulated both with general conceptions of cultural practice and with specific interpretations of cannibalism by professional anthropologists. In *Divine Hunger* (1986), for instance, the anthropologist Peggy Reeves Sanday defines the foundations of the practice in a way that resonates with nineteenth-century explanations of cannibalism as an act that either exorcises or incorporates the spirit of the other. Worldwide and throughout time, she says, cannibalism is predicated by "the notion that the bodily substances of the corpse consumed in the cannibal meal are endowed with a significance that derives from its status in life as the social other, either as enemy or revered compatriot. . . . Thus, parts of the body may be consumed to imbibe the characteristics or the fertile force of the other; or, consumption may break down and destroy characteristics of the other in the self. In either case a self is made—either by synthesizing the other as part of the self or by negating the other in the self."[94] These resonances could easily be taken as signs that the reason the superstition explanation showed up so often in early-nineteenth-century texts is because it was empirically true—because a more intimate contact with native peoples had allowed observers to finally get it right.

There are, however, some important differences between the nineteenth-century understanding of superstition and the twentieth-century understanding of culture. In its most common anthropological formulation, culture is, as Sanday says, the medium within which "a self is made," the locally established sign system within which the self comes into meaningful being. Superstition, on the other hand, does not evoke what Clifford Geertz calls "local knowledge," but what the philosophers of the Enlightenment called "error."[95] It was generally thought to originate in the faulty reasoning of beings who had been degraded by their subordination to arbitrary rule—either of nature or of a tribal elite—and to perpetuate that degradation, insofar as the erroneous conclusions of limited minds were passed down to subsequent generations as unquestioned truths. It signified a condition of powerlessness, ignorance, and fear, an immobility of mind that was frequently dramatized in evangelical rhetoric as the source and consequence of the natives' abject obedience to stone or wooden idols.[96] When early-nineteenth-century writers refer to the "system" of "superstition," then, they are not anticipating the twentieth-century development of the culture-concept, as Christopher Herbert has recently argued.[97] Rather, they are evoking the horror of a humanity slowly stifled by the constrictions of error, a horror that enables them to enjoy, by contrast, a sense of their own imaginative freedom.

With this gap between superstition and culture in mind, I want to turn from the question of what these cannibalistic practices *really mean* to the question that I have been asking of every other element of the discourse on cannibalism: not Is it true? but What interests are at stake in the efforts to establish its truth? Whatever the truth of cannibalism may have been, there were factors other than factuality involved in the rise of the superstition explanation in the early nineteenth century. For one thing, as I have suggested above, it offered another way of enacting the constitutive opposition between savagery and humanity. When Marsden mourns over the Maoris' cannibalism as a sign that "Satan has them in sore bondage" (Elder, *Letters and Journals,* 408), he is establishing, through his horror and pity, his own liberty and humanity in Christ. For another, because it attributed the differences between savagery and humanity to the cumulative effects of restrictive as opposed to expandable conditions of existence, it played an important role in the rhetoric of the missionary project. It enabled missionaries to argue that they both should and could eradicate native practices and to measure their progress in terms of what Satanic practices had been eradicated, rather than in terms of how many natives had experienced a genuine conversion. In his 1848 reflections on the state of the New Zealand mission, for example, James Oliver says that "[t]he missionaries have succeeded tolerably well in civilizing the natives, and especially in checking the horrible practice of cannibalism, which is now of less frequent occurrence than formerly. We are not to judge of the first success of missionaries in any part of the world so much from the actual progress made by those, to whom they are sent, in civilization and religion, as from the thoroughness with which their old prejudices and superstitious notions are eradicated."[98] As an *Athenaeum* reviewer noted in 1841, this piecemeal process of destruction, undertaken in the name of humanity, allowed missionaries "to be always doing (which is perhaps their object), and never done."[99]

For the same kinds of reasons, the superstition explanation matched up nicely with the interests of Pacific colonialists. In an 1839 letter of instruction to Capt. William Hobson, Lord Normandy informs him that one of his primary duties after he secures the annexation of New Zealand will be to put an immediate end to "the savage practices of human sacrifice and cannibalism," for "such atrocities, under whatever plea of religion they may take place, are not to be tolerated in any part of the dominions of the British Crown" (McNab, *Records,* 1:735). Hobson asked, quite sensibly, for "more explicit instruction on this important subject"; in particular, he wanted to know if he was "authorized, after the failure of every other means, to repress these diabolical acts by force" (752). Normandy's reply is an especially telling example of how easily humanist rhetoric could be articulated with the colonial project. Though force is indeed authorized, he says, he is "convinced that habits so repulsive to our common nature as cannibalism and human sacrifice may be checked with little difficulty, because the opposition to them will be seconded by feelings which are too deeply rooted in the minds of all men, the most ignorant or barbarous not excepted, to be eradicated by customs, however inveterate, or by any errors of opinion, however widely diffused" (755). The superstition explanation allows him to represent cannibalism as a savage atrocity that is obscuring a humane capacity for sentiment; it operates as a sign that intervention is both necessary and possible. And unlike the vengeance explanation, which locates the humanity of cannibals in the masculine boundlessness of the act itself, the superstition explanation invokes the existence of a subterranean and universal humanity that is defined by its radical opposition to the heartlessness of cannibal rites. The superstition explanation is, in this sense, the element of the discourse on cannibalism that is most suited to the rhetoric of those who wanted both to enact their own humanity — through their horror at the savage's acts mingled with their pity for the presumably humane intentions trapped within his soul—and to use the energy created by that friction between "humanity" and "savagery" as a resource for colonial development.

Even with these seals of scientific and colonial approval, however, the superstition explanation remained as precarious as any of the others we have discussed so far. To promote it as a sufficient explanation of why cannibals do what they do, writers had to assume that the promptings of instinct could be distinguished from the promptings of education— that "nature" and "habit" could be cleanly separated from one another. Some did in fact attempt to make that distinction; in *New Zealand* (1842), a promotional tract intended to ease the minds of potential emigrants, Charles Terry argues that a "dispassionate inquiry and reflection on their customs" will demonstrate that although the Maoris do have a history of cannibalism, we should not assume "that they are, naturally, ferocious and cruel. . . . Much as the custom is to be deplored and deprecated, it must be remembered, that it was their education and religion. Their true natural character and disposition, therefore, should rather be considered and appreciated by their conduct, since they have been informed of the cruelty and wickedness of such practices."[100] But this distinction was repeatedly blurred, as I have already shown, by those who believed that customs in general, and this one in particular, were liable to be addictive. In the face of that belief, those who insisted, with William Breton, "that there is no proof of any nation being *naturally* cannibals," usually ended up conceding that the force of habit may have caused some nations "not only [to] have overcome the repugnance usually felt by mankind to eat human flesh, but even to have contracted a liking for it."[101] Because it was so difficult, under these circumstances, to distinguish between nature and habit, the superstition explanation was incapable of being perceived as orthodox, in Pierre Bourdieu's sense of the term: a "straight, or rather *straightened,* opinion." It was simply one of several "*competing possibles,*" each of which was employed, vainly, as a prospective means of resolving the "objective crisis" that had brought it into being.[102]

In offering this observation, I may seem to be suggesting that what kept the post-Enlightenment discourse on cannibalism from achieving resolution was a surplus of signification, an experiential plurality that could not easily be boiled down to a discursive singularity. As Judith Butler and Joan Copjec have shown, this is the vision of discourse that Foucault most consistently promotes.[103] Power is fragile, Foucault argues, because the discourse that transmits it is as infinitely mobile as the humans that use it. Its crucial features, for him, are its logically limit-less dispersal and proliferation: it is "a *series* of discontinuous segments whose tactical function is neither uniform nor stable," "a *multiplicity* of discursive elements that can come into play in various strategies."[104] If Foucault is right, then the explanation I turn to now could not be understood as anything other than another one of these discontinuous segments. What I want to argue, however, is that although this expla-nation was indeed capable of being read and used in that way, it was also capable of performing a function that separates it from every one of the explanations we have seen so far. In every symbolic structure, Slavoj Žižek says, there is "an element which embodies its 'stain,' its own point of impossibility around which it is articulated."[105] Within the post-Enlightenment discourse on cannibalism, the following expla-nation is the place where it is possible to touch, obliquely, that "point of impossibility."

Terror

The idea that cannibalism was an act with an audience in mind, intended to induce terror, was not new to the eighteenth century. A thirteenth-century Dominican friar declared that the Mongols devoured human flesh "sometimes out of necessity, sometimes out of pleasure, and some-times in order to strike fear and terror in the people who will hear of it."[106] The sixteenth-century traveler Jean de Lery suggested the same thing of the Tupi of South America: "their chief intention is that by pursuing the dead and gnawing them right down to the bone, they will strike fear and terror into the hearts of the living."[107] When writers began to question the standard representations of cannibalism in the early decades of the Enlightenment, this tradition was available to them as a means of resistance to the idea that cannibalism is an unmediated expression of savage "nature." As we saw earlier, one of the few excep-tions to John Atkins's rule against the existence of cannibalism is that human flesh is sometimes eaten "to express an intense Malice against a particular Enemy, and *in terrorem.*" More suggestively, Jonathan Carver observes in 1778 that when the Iroquois "assert that they will eat the flesh and drink the blood of their enemies, the threat is only to be consid-ered as a figurative expression. Notwithstanding they sometimes devour the hearts of those they slay, and drink their blood, by way of bravado, or to gratify in a more complete manner their revenge, yet they are not naturally anthropophagi, nor ever feed on the flesh of men."[108] In arguing that both in speech and in act, Iroquois behavior in the encounter with the enemy is "figurative," Carver makes it clear that the "bravado" conventionally attributed to savages has some profoundly unsettling implications. For one thing, if we allow that the signs of savagery must be considered in the light of their intended and actual effect, it becomes difficult to refer those signs back to noncontingent causes such as "race" and "nature." For another, if we understand the relationship between savages to be performative, it is a very short step to the suggestion that the relationship between savages and their civilized interlocutors is equally theatrical. As Sir John Barrow says in a passage that I quoted in the introduction, even the eyewitness account of the roasting of a human body is not proof of cannibalism, since it is possible that the viewer was "*hoaxed — in terrorem.*"

For the most part, the terror explanation emerged in discussions of cannibalism at the moment when the light of the vengeance explanation began to fail. In *Some Account of New Zealand* (1807), for instance, John Savage declares that although "[t]he natives of this island have hitherto been considered cannibals of the worst description,"

> I apprehend their character, in this respect, is not so horrible as represented; for although they acknowledge that they have been driven to the dire necessity of eating human flesh, in times of great scarcity of food, yet it does not appear that they have any predilection for the practice: the motive which impels them to this inhuman deed, as customary at present, is vengeance, but even this passion is not pursued without limitation. Thus, after a conquest, the victors do not devour the whole of their prisoners, but are content with shewing their power to do so, by dividing the chief of the vanquished tribe among them: he is eaten, it is true, but I do not believe that food is the inducement.[109]

Savage begins by arguing that lust does not motivate the customary practice of cannibalism in New Zealand; the Maoris have no "predilection for the practice," and so they should not be ranked as "cannibals of the worst description." They may have been driven to it on occasion by famine, but as Savage rightly observes, that tells us nothing about their character. This seems to leave the way open for the identification of vengeance as "the motive which impels them to this inhuman deed." But vengeful cannibalism conventionally signified the obliteration of the sense of proper limits, and Savage insists that among the Maori "this passion is not pursued without limitation." That limitation is emphatically not superstitiousness, with its connotations of ignorance, fear, and enslavement to tradition. Rather, it is the understanding and use of cannibalism as a sign, an act intended to produce an effect on an audience. Maori cannibalism is not situated in the realm of vengeful frenzy or of superstitious degradation, but in the realm of rhetoric, where identity is a function of display, dependent on a "shewing" of power.

Savage's reading of Maori cannibalism was reinforced by the subsequent observations of missionaries, and by the middle of the century, it was a relatively well-established explanation; in *The Story of New Zealand* (1859), Arthur Thomson would declare, as an uncontroversial matter of fact, that "[t]o strike terror was one of the motives of cannibalism" (146). But although the Maori were associated with the terrorist use of cannibalism throughout most of the early nineteenth century, the people who embodied this practice, in the Western imagination, were the Battas, a tribe occupying the interior regions of the Indonesian island of Sumatra. The principal authority on the Battas was William Marsden, who asserted that they "do not eat human flesh as the means of satisfying the cravings of nature," nor "as a gluttonous delicacy," but "as a species of ceremony; as a mode of shewing their detestation of certain crimes by an ignominious punishment; and as a savage display of revenge and insult to their unfortunate enemies" (*History*, 391). Like Savage, Marsden clears away famine and lust as possible explanations, and then argues for an alternative that is something other than vengeance or superstition. Their cannibalism is not the product of a desire for vengeance that "knows not where to stop," as Forster would have it, but a desire to "display" vengefulness to enemies and "shew" detestation of certain crimes. And if it is "a species of ceremony," it is far more judicial than superstitious, invoking no otherworldly powers and producing no fear and trembling among the participants. Marsden reports that the criminals and captured enemies are given a trial and, after sentencing, "delivered into the hands of the injured party." All of those who were in some way injured subsequently tie the offender to a stake, kill him with spears, and then "run up to him, as if in a transport of passion, cut pieces from the body with their knives, dip them in the dish of salt, lemon-juice, and red pepper, slightly broil them over a fire prepared for the purpose, and swallow the morsels with a degree of savage enthusiasm" (391). The most noticeable feature of this event, in the context of the late-eighteenth-century discourse on cannibalism, is its theatricality; the Battas aren't particularly fond of the taste of human flesh, as Marsden has told us, but they eat it anyway, "with a degree of savage enthusiasm." The executioners are only behaving "as if in a transport of passion," simulating a spontaneous rage for the sake of its effect on those who see it or hear about it.

The next major authority on the Battas, Sir Stamford Raffles, places an even greater emphasis on this aspect of their cannibalism. In an 1820 letter to Marsden, he tells the older traveler that his inquiries into cannibalism have confirmed that this practice is "the result of much deliberation among the parties, and seldom, except in the case of prisoners in war, the effect of immediate and private revenge." In most cases, the criminal or prisoner is "eaten quietly, and in cold blood, with as much ceremony, and perhaps more, than attends the execution of a capital sentence in Europe." Their devotion to the law is even deeper than Marsden had represented it, he says, and so is their cruelty, as they frequently cut flesh off criminals before they are dead.[110] The unexpected mingling of conventionally civilized and savage traits in this practice quickly made it notorious as, in William Breton's words, "[t]he most strange instance of cannibalism known to exist" (*Excursions*, 151). It was staggering, George Craik wrote, that a people who had advanced far enough in civilization to "have a regular government, and deliberative assemblies" could be "cannibals upon principle and system." Raffles's letter had made it clear that cannibalism among the Battas was not confined "to the accustomed cases of prisoners taken in war and to other gratifications of revenge," but that some unaccustomed principle was at work. That principle seemed to be something like the superstition that Craik had attributed to the Maoris, but not identical to it; superstition implied ignorance, and every visitor to the interior of Sumatra had concurred that the Battas were a highly intelligent people. As a kind of knowing superstition, a custom practiced for a reason other than a belief in its magical efficacy, it constituted "the most extraordinary instance of cannibalism which is known to exist in the world" (*New Zealanders*, 108).

What made it so extraordinary, again, was its characterization as a deliberate "shewing," as a systematic display of the abstract qualities associated with the cannibal. Motivated, as Jeremiah Reynolds writes in 1835, by a desire "to manifest the utter detestation in which they hold their enemies; or their abhorrence of the crimes for which their malefactors may have suffered death," Batta cannibalism is a form of political theater, enacting a collective attitude by means of a spectacle of punishment.[111] In this sense, it closely resembles the model of social organization that Foucault constructs in the first part of *Discipline and Punish*, in which the exercise of power on the body of the condemned appears to be "an extreme expression of lawless rage" but is in fact "a technique."

Once it is recognized as the main act in a "theater of terror," cannibalism, the dark heart of "savagery," is uncannily transposed to the surface of the savage character, where it has the same status as an ornament or a tattoo.[112] And, borrowing language now from Lacan, once the savage is seen as having projected the appearance of cannibalism onto the surface of social existence, his self "breaks up, in an extraordinary way, between its being and its semblance, between itself and that paper tiger it shows to the other" (*Concepts*, 107). The location of cannibalism in the realm of semblance, rather than being, and the definition of this semblance as a paper tiger consciously scissored and pasted by the savage himself, present an obvious threat to the stability of every other element of the discourse on cannibalism. This is why the terror explanation shows up less often than the other explanations, and why it sometimes appears as a hesitant suggestion. But if its presence within the discourse is often ghostlike, it is nonetheless real. Like the skull that appears in the corner of Holbein's *The Ambassadors* just as we turn away from the picture, the terror explanation functions as a mirror "of our nothingness" (*Concepts*, 92), waiting for the moment when it will be possible to trap our gaze.

An even better example of this dynamic may be found in the two pictures of Marquesan warriors reproduced in Langsdorff's *Voyages and Travels* (figures 2 and 3). Though both engravings are intended "to illustrate the observations in the text upon the subject of tattooing" (Langsdorff, *Voyages*, xiv), they present the viewer with very different images of the Marquesan character. In the first, the body is frontally exposed, the benign facial features are fully visible, and the arms are held away from the sides, as if in welcome. The man expresses both a frankness and a willingness to be observed; though the tuft of hair on the top of his club signifies that he is an experienced warrior, and hence, for Langsdorff, a cannibal, he is still represented as being appealingly openhearted. The same cannot be said of the man in the second engraving, which comes two pages later in the original edition. He is turned away from the viewer, his eyes, nose, and mouth barely visible. He bristles all over with sharp points: the spear, the earrings, the oddly clawlike finger, the hog's tusks decorating the skull that dangles from his left hand. Because the designs on the surface of his body do not run together, as they do in the previous engraving, they appear more as discontinuous, unfinished gestures than as a luxurious manifestation of spirit. And if we go looking for signs of an interior offered to us by the picture, all we find are the empty sockets of that inverted skull, staring straight back at us.

By means of that depthless gaze—repeated by the circles and ovals

2. "An Inhabitant of the Island of Nukahiwa." George von Langsdorff,
Voyages and Travels in Various Parts of the World. 1813.
Reprint, New York: Da Capo Press, 1968.

on the man's calves, thighs, buttocks, back, and shoulders—we are reminded of the terrorist tendencies of "savages," the other side of the
spontaneity attributed to them in the first engraving. Nominally, the
people who are intended to be terrified by this sign are the members of
rival tribes; the skull signifies that the owner has not just killed the victim, but also "swallow[ed] the blood and brains upon the spot," and it
is displayed "at future opportunities as a token of valour" (Langsdorff,

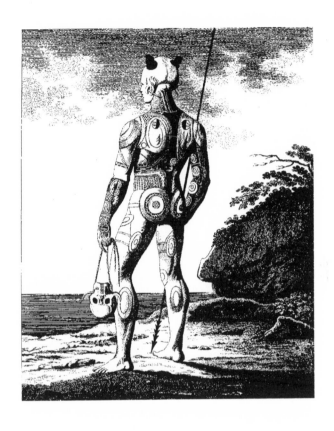

3. "A Young Nukahiwan Not Completely Tattooed." George von Langsdorff, *Voyages and Travels in Various Parts of the World*. 1813. Reprint, New York: Da Capo Press, 1968.

Voyages, 150). But the eyes of the skull look out at the implicitly white viewer, and, as Melville observes in his reference to this engraving, the warrior stands "upon the beach, with his back turned upon his green home, to hold at bay the intruding European" (*T,* 205). The terror of the skull teeters between two potential objects, in other words: enemy tribes and Western invaders. In either case, the Westerner's knowledge of the truth of the cannibal is threatened; in the latter case, however, the collectors of that knowledge are "literally called into the picture, and represented here as caught" (Lacan, *Concepts*, 92). By denying the desire for interiority, and thereby exposing the intrusiveness of the act of viewing, the picture suggests just how far in the direction of a critique of "humanity" the image of the terrorist cannibal might take us.

It is not at all clear that these effects were intended by Langsdorff or the engraver. The image is still useful, however, as a representation of a form of terrorism that did indeed enter into the relationship between suspected cannibals and their Western interrogators in the late eighteenth and early nineteenth centuries. That terrorism was made possible, and even encouraged, by three historically contingent factors. First, and most obviously, the suspects had something to gain from terrorizing their interrogators: a more exclusive possession of their territory. Second, most of the interrogators dreaded cannibalism, so much so that they "felt a greater horror of being devoured than of dying." [113] Once that dread was exposed, in obsessive questions or panicked withdrawals, the suspects were quite capable of turning it to their advantage. After the death of Cook in 1779, a party of Hawaiians delivered a piece of flesh to the Englishmen still in their harbor, telling them that it was a part of Cook's thigh. "[W]hen we enquired what had become of the remaining part of him," John Ledyard says, one of the islanders "gnashed his teeth and said it was to be eaten that night." [114] In 1772, a French lieutenant similarly observed in his journal that after asking a group of Maoris whether or not they were cannibals, "one of the chiefs, who well understood what I asked him, told me that after they had killed their enemies, they put them in a fire, and having cooked the corpses, ate them. Seeing that I was greatly disgusted with what he told me, my informant burst into laughter, and proceeded to reaffirm what he had just told me" (McNab, *Records*, 2:401–2). The chief's laughter is not merely the laughter of the practical joker; as elsewhere, it expresses the pleasurable discovery that the threat of cannibalism may be used as an instrument of power in the encounter with the Western invader. [115]

The third factor, which has already been suggested by the above scenes, is that the communication between the suspects and their interrogators was carried on almost entirely by means of signs. Many of these signs centered on the arm, probably because it was the most easily displayed fleshy part of the body. Upon being asked, repeatedly, if he was a cannibal, a Maori interviewed by the first Cook expedition "took hold of the flesh of his own arm with his teeth and made shew of eating" (Beaglehole, *Journals*, 1:236). While dining with a Maori chieftain, the Russian captain Faddey Bellingshausen says, "I indicated my arm, and asked him if he ate human flesh. He declared that he ate it willingly, nor would there seem to be any doubt about the matter." [116] And in *A New Voyage Round the World* (1830), Otto von Kotzebue reports that one of the Samoans allowed on board his ship "was so tempted by the accidental display of a sailor's bare arm, that he could not help expressing his horrible appetite for human flesh; he snapt at it with his teeth, giving us to understand by unequivocal signs, that such food would be very palatable to him." This manifestation of cannibal appetite served "to complete our disgust and aversion, and to accelerate the expulsion of the remaining savages from our vessel." [117] It should be obvious that neither this sign, nor any of the others, was as "unequivocal" as Kotzebue suggests. When we take into consideration the frequency of the interrogators' "eager and earnest" pantomimes of cannibalism (Cook and King, *Pacific*, 3:133) and the tactical advantages that could be gained from the interrogators' "disgust and aversion," such scenes begin to look very much like intentional acts of terrorism.

Those intentions are particularly evident in a pair of encounters involving one of the principal chiefs of the Nootka, a tribe occupying the Nootka Sound region on the northwest coast of America. In 1786, a commercial expedition led by James Strange was horrified to find that the Nootka customarily preserved the severed hands of their enemies. Assuming, on this basis, that the Nookta were cannibals, they began buying up the hands, inveighing, as they did so, against the practice of eating human flesh. According to Alexander Walker, the Nootkas' typical response to this obviously mixed message was to declare that they did indeed eat their enemies, and that they liked it: "They would testify their pleasure by stroking their bellies, and licking their lips; exclaiming 'klookh, klookh,' 'good, good.' " Whenever the members of the expedition would attempt to reeducate a particularly powerful chief named Maquilla, the chief would recite, "as we told him, that it was bad food, a wicked custom, and the like, but having in this way repeated all our arguments, he would laugh aloud, and thrust his hand into his mouth." [118] The lesson of these intervention sessions, for Maquilla, was that the English were strangely attracted to the signs of cannibalism, but that they would shrink back when confronted with them. Two years later, when John Meares's expedition came into the Sound, he put this lesson to good use. Having accidentally cut his leg while ascending Meares's ship, he

> sucked himself the blood which flowed freely from it: and when we expressed our astonishment and disgust at his conduct, he replied, by licking his lips, patting his belly, and exclaiming *cloosh*,

cloosh; or good, good. Nor did he now hesitate to confess that he eat human flesh, and to express the delight he took in banquetting on his fellow creatures. Nay, he not only avowed the practice of which he had been accused, but informed us, as we stood shuddering at the story, that, a very short time before, the ceremony of killing and eating a slave had taken place even in Friendly Cove.[119]

As the historian Christon Archer has observed, Maquilla was in competition with other local chiefs for "the coveted role as middleman between the Europeans and other bands." [120] By putting on this hyperbolic, autocannibalistic show before Meares and his crew, who were "absolutely haunted" by "the idea of being eaten by the Americans," Maquilla seems to have intended to exhibit himself as a man of power, on the Englishmen's terms, to get them to funnel their trade through him.[121]

As we might expect, the post-Enlightenment travelers and reviewers who denied the existence of lustful cannibalism regularly commented on these aspects of the cannibal encounter. In the course of his 1803 argument that "[t]he Africans have been very unjustly branded with the title of anthropophagists," for example, Timothy Winterbottom takes issue with the accounts of Dahomean cannibalism in the narratives of William Snelgrave and Robert Norris on the grounds that "in the present instance, where ocular demonstration alone, not vague report, is to be depended on, we have reason to suspect that they were imposed upon, as they no where affirm that they were eye witnesses of the transaction." [122] With respect to the cannibalism that followed their human sacrifices, Snelgrave "readily gave credit to whatever was told him" (162), and Norris's only evidence of the act is that "*if report may be credited,* the carcase of the human victim is almost wholly devoured" (163). But these reports should *not* be credited, Winterbottom argues. Snelgrave and Norris have not sufficiently weighed the possibility that they may have been "imposed upon" in this transaction—that the Dahomeans may have been posing as cannibals to make themselves more imposing in their visitors' eyes.

These kinds of readings of the encounter do not fit neatly into the ordinary rhetorical mode of the deniers, however. As a rule, writers like Winterbottom were inclined to emphasize, in William Wales's words, "how far we are liable to be misled by Signs, report, & prejudice" in the encounter with supposed cannibals.[123] In doing so, they generally took it for granted that the sole distorting factor in the encounter was the prejudice of the interrogator, who wrongly construed the innocent signs and reports of "humane" savages. Committed to establishing the baseline humanity of savages and desiring to reestablish the supremacy of the editor function over the author function, they needed to characterize savages as honest producers of signs of their humanity while characterizing travelers as unskilled and biased readers of those signs. It was a little uncomfortable, therefore, to consider that the verdict of cannibalism that resulted from such encounters might be doubly distorted, signifying not only the credulity of the traveler but also the imposition of the savage. If that was so, then what they had in these narratives of encounter was not a failure to communicate, but a remarkably successful communication of unreliable information. These deceptive communications could be cited as a satire on the credulity of the traveler, but if that satire were to be pressed too far, it would suggest that no one, neither author nor editor, could be a privileged reader of the signs of savagery, because those signs pointed to the savage's contingent interests and not to the eternal truths of his nature. The deniers of cannibalism had some interest in using the deceptiveness of the savage informant as a satirical dramatization of the traveler's credulity, but they had an even greater interest in keeping that satire from going too far.

This may help to explain why the tone of those passages in which reviewers call attention to the potential deceptiveness of cannibal informants is very often light. After quoting at length from John Anderson's account of cannibalism among the Battas of Sumatra, John Barrow declares that he "cannot help thinking that the Malays, who are a shrewd people, and the Batta chiefs, who are by no means wanting in intelligence, on discovering Mr. Anderson's anxiety about men-eaters, indulged him with the above, and many other similar stories contained in his narrative, by way of quizzing and laughing at his credulity." [124] The *Athenaeum* reviewer I mentioned earlier performs a similar deflation of Joel Polack's account of cannibalism in New Zealand. He points out that Polack specifically *asks* a Maori to produce a piece of cooked human flesh, and that the Maori's subsequent display of a small, pale piece of meat is somewhat ostentatious. The reviewer quotes Polack as saying, among other things, that "[t]he sight of this piece of mortality afforded the chief some pleasure, for he stretched out his tongue, pretending to lick the food, and gave other significant signs, indicative of the excessive delight he felt in partaking of human flesh." As far as the reviewer is concerned, this passage offers "nothing to convince those who are disposed to incredulity. The native who showed our author the meat, which was probably pork, was obviously a wag, and well inclined to tickle the white man's prurient sensibility." [125]

I do not mean to suggest that these accounts are not funny, or that the native informants are not taking pleasure in their cannibal performances. But in their emphasis on the humor of these scenes, Barrow and the *Athenaeum* reviewer have effectively contained their potential disruptiveness. If they had represented the Maoris and Battas as something more than "wags" getting a laugh out of their visitors' horror and prurience, the politics of colonialism might have begun to infiltrate their reading of these encounters. And if they had taken the further step of interpreting these encounters as particularly vivid instances of a dynamic that pervades all transactions between self and other on the borderlands of the empire, something even more unsettling might have followed from this masquerade—something like the postcolonial crises of knowledge and authority that we are becoming so familiar with today. That these readers did not take those steps does not mean that those steps could not be taken; it simply means that it was very difficult to take them without the prompting of a translator, a transmitter of low-frequency signals. Only when those signals were sufficiently strengthened would it be possible for a significant number of Westerners to read the cannibal encounter in the way that I have described here.

Here lies the significance, as well as the insignificance, of Melville's engagement with the discourse on cannibalism. To have become this kind of translator, under these circumstances, is a stunning achievement. It was made possible in part by an extraordinary experience: a four-week residence in the summer of 1842 among the Typees, one of the last Polynesian tribes to use the open avowal of cannibalism as a deterrent to colonial intrusion. It was made possible, too, by his repeated description of these experiences to shipmates and family members, an exercise that schooled him in the expectations that listeners brought to such narratives and made those expectations objects of interest in their own right. Finally, it was made possible by his thoughtful reading of other travelers' accounts of cannibalism, including several of the ones I have mentioned in this chapter.[126] Perhaps because he harbored literary ambitions, and because he identified literary work with the revelation of ambiguity, he was more attentive than most to the anxieties and disavowals implicit in those texts. All of these circumstances, taken together, put him in a discursive position so singular that he could not count on much of an audience. He could certainly hope for one; as I have tried to show, the post-Enlightenment discourse on cannibalism was noticeably fractured, and its "point of impossibility" was unusually visible. But the business of ideology is to cover up such gaps and points, and in the absence of a concerted project of discursive disruption, that business tends to remain

in operation. Accordingly, it was Melville's fate to become an electri-
fyingly postcolonial writer in search of an answering "shock of recognition" from readers who gave it to him only rarely, or not at all. My
hope, in retransmitting that current, is that it is still capable of producing such a shock, and that this shock will be able to run, in our more
overtly postcolonial world, "the whole circle round" (*PT*, 249).

2 ✋ THE TERROR OF THEIR NAME:
REFLECTIONS ON *TYPEE*

In an essay first published almost thirty years ago, William Charvat argues that the most distinctive feature of *Moby-Dick,* whether considered within the Melville canon or within mid-nineteenth-century literature more generally, is its pedagogical method. The novel's operatic meditations on elements, animals, texts, laws, characters, and colors share a common structure, he says, and taken as a whole, they suggest that Melville had very consciously "worked out a system to train the reader in imaginative, exploratory thinking."[1] This system involved "first, identifying himself with the reader; second, getting the reader interested in a fact or object, the nature of which invites speculation; third, 'priming' the reader's mind by putting suggestions in the form of questions; fourth, sometimes stopping short after opening up a possibility and inviting the reader to draw the inference himself" (246). The point of the system was to "break down stock responses to images and types," a difficult task at any time, but particularly when writing for "a generation of readers still predominantly governed by Scottish common sense with its official catalogues of approved responses to poetic stimuli" (247). What makes this system so exceptional, Charvat says, is that it combines a spirit of inquiry with a spirit of collaboration; in chapters like "Loomings" and "The Whiteness of the Whale," Melville rises above the self-indulgence of *Mardi* and the audience indulgence of *Redburn* and *White-Jacket* to imagine, for once, the possibility of meeting his readers on a ground that is both theirs and his own. Never before had he been so committed to the project of taking those readers through the stages of an extended thought at the proper speed, and after the relative failure of *Moby-Dick,* he would never be so committed again.

But *Moby-Dick* is not, in fact, the only book in which Melville engages in a systematic effort to draw the reader into his own paths of reflection. Consider the concluding paragraph of the chapter in *Typee* called "The Social Condition and General Character of the Typees":

> The reader will ere long have reason to suspect that the Typees are not free from the guilt of cannibalism; and he will then, perhaps, charge me with admiring a people against whom so odious a crime is chargeable. But this only enormity in their character is not half so horrible as it is usually described. According to the popular fictions, the crews of vessels, shipwrecked on some barbarous coast, are eaten alive like so many dainty joints by the uncivil inhabitants; and unfortunate voyagers are lured into smiling and treacherous bays; knocked in the head with outlandish war-clubs; and served up without any preliminary dressing. In truth, so horrific and improbable are these accounts, that many sensible and well-informed people will not believe that any cannibals exist; and place every book of voyages which purports to give any account of them, on the same shelf with Blue Beard and Jack the Giant-Killer; while others, implicitly crediting the most extravagant fictions, firmly believe that there are people in the world with tastes so depraved that they would infinitely prefer a single mouthful of material humanity to a good dinner of roast beef and plum pudding. But here, Truth, who loves to be centrally located, is again found between the two extremes; for cannibalism to a certain moderate extent is practised among several of the primitive tribes in the Pacific, but it is upon the bodies of slain enemies alone; and horrible and fearful as the custom is, immeasurably as it is to be abhorred and condemned, still I assert that those who indulge in it are in other respects humane and virtuous. (205)

In itself, this passage does not perfectly exemplify the collaborative speculation that Charvat is talking about. It does move the reader through multiple stages of possible responses, but it does so much more rapidly than a similar passage from *Moby-Dick* might, and it tends to occupy and relinquish successive stages by means of assertion, not proposition. What makes it worth our attention is what it encapsulates and draws us toward: the complex process of speculation on cannibalism that takes place in the book as a whole. Its purpose is to provide the reader with a map of the field within which Melville's narrator, Tommo, has been attempting to locate his changing opinions about the extent of cannibalism among the Typees, a secluded and reportedly dangerous tribe on the Marquesan island of Nukuheva. At the beginning of the book, Tommo is largely under the influence of the "popular fictions" that ascribe cannibalism to an epicurean lust. After having spent some time among the Typees, he briefly drifts over to the opinion of the "sensible and well-informed people" who deny the existence of cannibalism, only to split the difference between these extremes by declaring that the cannibalism of this tribe is "moderate," prompted by vengeance. But as the book approaches its climax, the security of this position begins to erode; he becomes increasingly aware of the peculiarities of Typee "custom," and increasingly anxious about his inability to come up with anything more definite than a "reason to suspect" that they are cannibals. That is to say that *Typee* as a whole does with cannibalism what "Loomings" does with water, or what "The Whiteness of the Whale" does with whiteness. In each of these cases, Melville calls up a commonsense perception of an object, raises the reader's interest in that object by subjecting it to close examination, and finally draws the reader, if he is successful, into sharing the discovery that the commonsense perception of the object has insensibly decayed, and that the subject and the object of this examination can no longer be found in their accustomed places.

Once we have identified the sequence and content of this pedagogical project, it should be possible for us to recognize just how postcolonial *Typee* really is. Not content to expose, as others before him had, the murderous self-interest of the French, British, and American projects of Pacific colonization, Melville attempts to expose the ambivalence at the heart of the *discourse* of colonialism, as embodied in the discourse on cannibalism. In twentieth-century criticism of *Typee*, Tommo's intermittently paralyzing fear of cannibalism has almost always been considered to be the symptom of some other, more pressing fear: of the law, of commodification, of a "devouring maternal power," of an "egalitarian homosexual relationship," of an impulse "to cannibalize the internalized corpse of his father," or, most often, of "culture."[2] But these readings do not account for the ways in which Tommo's explanation of cannibalism changes over the course of the book, shifting from lust to denial to vengeance and then, when superstition has been set aside, to terror. By means of this pedagogical strategy, Melville attempts to redirect our attention from the symbolic meaning *of* cannibalism to the antisymbolic implications of the discourse *on* cannibalism. Using nothing but explanations of cannibalism that are already in circulation, he takes us down a path of reflection that ends at the moment when the perception of cannibalism as a romantic act of vengeance gives way to the perception of cannibalism as a kind of stage effect, the function of certain exterior signs that are activated in the name of terror. He invites us to enter into the spirit of the vengeful cannibal and then, once he has us imagining ourselves united with this spirit, suggests that it may be nothing more than a specter, a shadow cast by certain players on the colonial stage. In the chill of that sudden exile from intimacy, we experience, if only for a moment, the climate of the postcolonial world.[3]

"Popular Fictions"

Captain ——— , a Scotchman of respectable character, who commanded one of the government vessels of New South Wales a few years since, has told me that while he was lying at the Marquesas many years ago, he had seen human viscera hung up for use in the same way as a sheep's or bullock's are frequently seen in England; and that, on inquiring on one occasion of an elderly woman what had become of a little orphan boy she seemed to be rearing, and to which he had himself got somewhat attached, he was horrified to learn that the boy had been killed and eaten. Nay, he once assured me that he was once offered a human finger himself as a peculiar delicacy. — John Dunmore Lang (1834)

When Captain Vangs orders the sea-weary *Dolly* turned toward the Marquesas islands for "refreshing" (*T*, 3) — a nineteenth-century sailor's term that embraced food, wood, water, and sex — Tommo is instantly put in mind of a series of "outlandish things" conjured up by "the very name" of those islands: "Naked houris — cannibal banquets — groves of cocoa-nut — coral reefs — tatooed chiefs — and bamboo temples; sunny valleys planted with bread-fruit-trees — carved canoes dancing on the flashing blue waters — savage woodlands guarded by horrible idols — *heathenish rites and human sacrifice*" (5). As he goes on to say, these are "strangely jumbled anticipations." The naked bodies of the islanders first appear as feminized objects of lust, then instantly reappear as masculinized agents of lust. The coconut groves and coral reefs of the naturalist's account give way to the tattooed chiefs and bamboo temples of the ethnographer's account, and the image of pagan temples eventually leads up to the missionary's italicized horror of heathenish rites, sacrificial and otherwise. The images "haunt" him, but not in an unpleasant way; he feels "an irresistible curiosity to see those islands which the olden voyagers had so glowingly described" (5). There is no indication, at this point, that he means to criticize the inconsistency of these anticipations or to undermine the conventional association of the name Marquesas with any one of these "outlandish things." The prospect opened up by this passage is purely touristic, involving nothing more than the narrator's desire to repeat, successively, an inconsistent jumble of previously represented experiences. All he wants to do is to see the islands—the *same* islands—"which the olden voyagers had so glowingly described."

Another way of saying this is that *Typee* presents itself to its readers as an "Orientalist" narrative, one that promises to explore what Edward Said describes as an "imaginative geography."[4] The region it turns toward in this passage is purely textual, consisting of nothing but "that collection of dreams, images, and vocabularies available to anyone who has tried to talk about what lies east of the dividing line" (*Orientalism*, 73). And in at least one respect, the book does indeed land us squarely within that textual region. Just a chapter after the incantatory reference to "naked houris," the *Dolly* is boarded by a group of barely clothed Marquesan women who are so "[u]nsophisticated and confiding" that they interpose no barriers "between the unholy passions of the crew and their unlimited gratification" (*T*, 15). Less explicitly sexual glimpses of these same houris later help to pass the time during Tommo's stay in the Typee valley; bosoms repeatedly heave beneath fortunately arranged hair, and entirely naked women repeatedly bound up from pools of water.[5] One way of reading the subtitle of the book—*A Peep at Polynesian Life*—is as a promise to the reader that the book will deliver exactly these kinds of Playboy-mansion images of Polynesian women. But if the word *peep* implies the salacious reseeing of an already-seen image, it also implies that the vision of this image is brief and partial. There is, accordingly, a necessary tension between the satisfaction of the peep and the partiality of that satisfaction. With respect to the "naked houris," this tension is low level and easily transcended; though the peep must indeed be endlessly repeated, the fetishistic objects of that peep are unfailingly available. But with respect to the second item on the list of anticipations, the "cannibal banquets," the object of the anticipated peep is not so forthcoming. In this case, the only reason Melville identifies himself with the Orientalist desire of his readers is so that he can bring them to see, in the failure of his voyeuristic desire, the failure of theirs.

To heighten this desire without actually satisfying it, he provides his readers with a series of secondhand accounts of Marquesan cannibalism, all of which emphasize that the cannibalism of these islanders is motivated by an ingrained animal lust. Shortly before jumping ship, Tommo learns of the existence of a tribe that "appear[s] to inspire the other islanders with unspeakable terrors. Their very name is a frightful one; for the word 'Typee' in the Marquesan dialect signifies a lover of human flesh" (24). Given that "the natives of all this group are irreclaimable cannibals," Tommo thinks, the name can only "denote the peculiar ferocity of this clan," indicating that these people have an even more irresistible desire to eat other people than the average Marquesan. This piece of information is subsequently corroborated by the islanders he meets in Nukuheva Bay, who denounce "their enemies—the Typees—as inveterate gormandizers of human flesh" and attempt to frighten visiting sailors "by pointing to one of their own number, and calling him a Typee, manifesting no little surprise that we did not take to our heels at so terrible an announcement" (25). Though these "revolting stories" fill Tommo with "a particular and most unqualified repugnance to the aforesaid Typees," they do not detract from the anticipation that originally accompanied the thought of cannibal banquets. He tells us that as the *Dolly* passed the bay leading to the Typee valley, a crewmate named Ned, "pointing with his hand in the direction of the treacherous valley, exclaimed, 'There— there's Typee. Oh, the bloody cannibals, what a meal they'd make of us if we were to take it into our heads to land! but they say they don't like sailor's flesh, it's too salt. I say, maty, how should you like to be shoved ashore there, eh?'" "I shuddered at the question," Tommo says, little thinking "that in the space of a few weeks I should actually be a captive in that self-same valley" (25–26). Although his shudder is certainly intended to indicate the involuntariness of his "unqualified repugnance," his teasing allusion to the imminent appearance of these lovers of human flesh suggests that this heightened repugnance is perfectly compatible with heightened attraction, both in himself and in his readers.

The source of this attraction is not difficult to discover. Like the prospect of "naked houris," the prospect of "bloody cannibals" promises to confirm that savagery is just what previous travelers had said it was, and thereby to confirm that the civilized identity defined in opposition to savagery has a permanent ground. The desire expressed in Tommo's shudder is a desire to come into contact with what Captain Delano will call "naked nature," that timeless substance that "humane" beings tend to think of themselves as emerging from. The sense of timelessness ordinarily attached to the repeatable stereotype is intensified, in this case, by the conventional association of lustful cannibalism with instinct. The Typees are "irreclaimable" and "inveterate" gourmands, so thoroughly addicted to cannibalism that it has become a biological trait. Protected from the incursions of Westerners by their remoteness and their reputation, they "are in every respect unchanged from their earliest known condition," retaining all the artless behaviors that are associated with the "state of nature" (11). For someone who hates artificial forms and lost time as much as Tommo does, there is something almost irresistibly seductive about the idea that cannibalism is natural to the Typees, that it has been since the darkness of prehistory, that it will be until the end of time. As Said has said, what makes Oriental stereotypes most appealing to the Orientalist is that "[t]hey are all declarative and self-evident; the tense they employ is the timeless eternal; they convey an impression of repetition and strength; they are always symmetrical to, and yet diametrically inferior to, a European equivalent, which is sometimes specified, sometimes not. For all these functions it is frequently enough to use the simple copula *is*" (*Orientalism*, 72). Whether an object of desire, like naked houris, or an object of dread, like cannibal banquets, the stereotypes associated with savagery are almost inevitably objects of anticipation, insofar as they promise the certain and constant presence of the substance that makes a civilized, humane identity possible.

Not surprisingly, as Tommo's attraction to the primitive becomes more intense, his visions of cannibalism become increasingly racist. At one point, while envisioning himself free of the *Dolly* and surrounded by natural abundance in the mountains of Nukuheva, Tommo suddenly recalls "one rather unpleasant drawback to these agreeable anticipations— the possibility of falling in with a foraging party of these same bloody-minded Typees, whose appetites, edged perhaps by the air of so elevated a region might prompt them to devour one" (31). He confesses that this is "a most disagreeable view of the matter," and seems about to leave it at that, but the specter of "prowling cannibals" continues to haunt him. "Just to think of a party of these unnatural gourmands taking it into their heads to make a convivial meal of a poor devil," he exclaims in the next paragraph, before repressing it again. This vision of predatory beasts in human form suggests that Tommo has read or heard some version of an especially nasty story about the Nukuhevans that first appeared in the Russian admiral Adam Krusenstern's *Voyage Round the World* (1813). Though Krusenstern admits that his personal encounters with these islanders left him with "a most favorable impression," the stories of two renegade Europeans he met there convinced him that the Nukuhevans were in fact "very much addicted to cannibalism," and "that the appearance of content and good humour, with which they had so much deceived us, was not their true character."[6] Among other things, the renegades had told him that "in their art of war, there is a perfect similarity between the character of these savages and of wild beasts. They seldom meet in large parties on the field; but their usual mode of warfare is, to be constantly watching for and secretly seeking to butcher their prey, which they devour on the spot" (1:167–68). Krusenstern's final assessment is that the Nukuhevans must be ranked "with those men who are still one degree below the brute creation" (1:182–83). By providing his readers with these visions of "prowling cannibals," Tommo has made that conclusion available to them, as he well knows. Late in the narrative, he will declare that "[t]here are no wild animals of any kind on the island, unless it be decided that the natives themselves are such" (*T*, 212).

But if he opens up this racist territory to his readers, in the interest of meeting the majority of them on their own ground, he also does his best to keep them from occupying it. After a journey through the Nukuhevan mountains, in which his anticipations of a "frightful death at the hands of the fiercest of cannibals" (66) become increasingly intense, he finds himself trapped in the heart of a remote valley, surrounded, as promised, by the notorious Typees. Nothing particularly gruesome happens to him in his first two days in the valley; the tribespeople feed him and his companion Toby, treat his wounded leg, bathe him, and seem generally devoted to his well-being. On the evening of the third day, however, he and Toby fall asleep in the Ti, the all-male quarters in the Taboo Groves, and wake around midnight to see flames rising from the depths of the groves and silhouetted figures "dancing and capering about" (93). When Tommo asks Toby what this might mean, Toby tells him that the Typees are preparing "the fire to cook us, to be sure. . . . Depend upon it, we will be eaten this blessed night, and there is the fire we shall be roasted by." "I shuddered," Tommo says, "when I reflected that we were indeed at the mercy of a tribe of cannibals, and that the dreadful contingency to which Toby had alluded was by no means removed beyond the bounds of possibility." At that moment four islanders are seen approaching the Ti, and the anticipations that Tommo has built up throughout the early chapters of the narrative hit their highest pitch: "They came on noiselessly, nay stealthily, and glided along through the gloom that surrounded us as if about to spring upon some object they were fearful of disturbing before they should make sure of it. — Gracious heaven! the horrible reflections which crowded upon me that moment. — A cold sweat stood upon my brow, and spellbound with terror I awaited my fate!" (94).

As it turns out, the tribesmen have not come to eat their visitors, but to offer them the contents of "a large trencher of wood, containing some kind of steaming meat." With this unexpected puncturing of his anticipations, Tommo's dread instantly recedes. Toby remains spellbound, however, and in the conversation that follows, he succeeds in at least temporarily introducing a new version of those anticipations into Tommo's mind:

"But I say, Tommo, you are not going to eat any of that mess there, in the dark, are you? Why, how can you tell what it is?"

"By tasting it, to be sure," said I, masticating a morsel that Kory-Kory had just put in my mouth, "and excellently good it is too, very much like veal."

"A baked baby, by the soul of Captain Cook!" burst forth Toby, with amazing vehemence; "Veal? why there never was a calf on the island till you landed. I tell you you are bolting down mouthfuls from a dead Happar's carcass, as sure as you live, and no mistake!"

Emetics and lukewarm water! What a sensation in the abdominal region! Sure enough, where could the fiends incarnate have obtained meat? But I resolved to satisfy myself at all hazards; and turning to Mehevi, I soon made the ready chief understand that I wished a light to be brought. When the taper came, I gazed eagerly into the vessel, and recognised the mutilated remains of a juvenile porker! "Puarkee!" exclaimed Kory-Kory, looking complacently at the dish; and from that day to this I have never forgotten that such is the designation of a pig in the Typee lingo. (95)

This twin set of false alarms, pulled one right after the other, sets the narrative going in an entirely new direction. What looked like a fire they would be spitted over turns out to have been a sign of festiveness; what looked like predatory stealth turns out to have been a courteous desire to wake them gently; what tasted like it could have been human flesh turns out to have been *puarkee*. The anticipations that Tommo has steadily heightened over the course of the narrative suddenly look comically excessive, inflated out of all proportion to the actual situation. When Toby exclaims that the mystery meat is "baked baby," he is referring to a rumor that cannibals were particularly fond of the tender flesh of infants, just as Ned had invoked the authority of previous travelers in telling Tommo that cannibals didn't like the taste of salty white flesh.[7] But this time around, it is quite clear that the rumor does not signify the epicurean excesses of Pacific islanders so much as it signifies the rhetorical excesses of white men; Toby himself quickly drops this figure of speech to declare, more seriously, that Tommo is masticating an adult warrior from an enemy tribe. When he invokes the soul of Captain Cook, too, he is aligning his own response to an indeterminate piece of flesh with the equally exaggerated conclusion that Cook's crew drew from the circumstances of their captain's death. As Tommo tells us near the end of the book, after Cook was killed by Hawaiians in 1778, the islanders returned a ten-pound piece of flesh that they said came from Cook's body, though there was no way of verifying that it had. Tommo's opinion is that this supposed fragment of the explorer "was no such thing; and that the whole affair was a piece of imposture which was sought to be palmed off upon the credulous Europeans" (234). Though Cook's career in the Pacific generally embodied the Enlightenment conviction that the uncertainties surrounding the existence and extent of cannibalism could be resolved, the circumstances of his death were more often used by later writers to represent the permanence of those uncertainties.[8] In the context of wildly excessive visions of baked babies, the allusion to the late Captain Cook serves as a reminder that Tommo and Toby are not the first travelers to treat "doubtful" (234) pieces of flesh as confirmations of their worst fears.[9]

Once the contents of the vessel have turned out to be something far more benign that Tommo had anticipated, the meaning ordinarily attached to the name Typee begins to seem partially, if not entirely, in error. "[D]espite the apprehensions I could not dispel," Tommo says at the beginning of the next chapter, "the horrible character imputed to these Typees appeared to me wholly undeserved." He continues to believe that they are cannibals, but now insists in conversation with Toby that "a more humane, gentlemanly and amiable set of epicures do not probably exist in the Pacific" (97). He lapses occasionally into the former mood of apprehension and disgust, referring to the Typees at one point as "nothing better than a set of cannibals" (118), but with those rare exceptions, the initial equation of the name Typee with the love of human flesh is never again taken at face value. Beginning here, Tommo is haunted less by anticipations than by doubts; the source of his discomfort is not so much the thought that his awful expectations will soon be realized as it is the thought that he is now deprived of the Orientalist equation that had enabled him to expect with certainty the repetition of the same. If *Typee* does not signify cannibal lust, what *does* it signify? Who *are* the Typees? The readers of the book are now invited to continue turning the pages not out of a desire to see the foreseen, but out of a desire to discover the unforeseen—not out of a desire to assure themselves that the signification of the name Typee partakes of the timelessness of the symbol, but out of a desire to discover the true contents of that mysterious semiotic vessel. This is the point in the process of collaborative speculation that Charvat calls "priming," in which, rather than simply unveiling the endpoint of inquiry, Melville chooses to "[put] suggestions in the form of questions." To open up a field of discourse that has been so far confined to a single position, he alerts us to the existence of a position at the other end of that field, not because he means to occupy it, but because the process of entertaining this possibility will better prepare us to explore the full range of positions available within the discourse as a whole.

"Sensible and Well-Informed People"

[T]hose inhabiting the Valley in Comptroller's Bay, are called Typees, who are said to be the most warlike in the Island, as well as being a species of the Anthropophagi, but I am yet to learn, how they gained this unnatural reputation, for when I made an incursion into the interior of their country, I could not perceive the least trace of cannibality among them, or aught, to authorize my drawing so horrible a conclusion. — John Shillibeer (1817)

The chapter in which Tommo begins to consider a wider range of discursive possibilities is, appropriately, the one in which he first begins to "ramble about the valley." Liberated from the imprisoning effects of a mysterious leg ailment that flares up whenever his "dismal forebodings" get the best of him, he experiences a new freedom of movement, and with it, a new "elasticity of mind" (*T*, 123). One of the consequences of this elasticity, he says, is that

> I began to distrust the truth of those reports which ascribed so fierce and belligerent a character to the Typee nation. Surely, thought I, all those terrible stories I have heard about the inveteracy with which they carried on the feud, their deadly intensity of hatred, and the diabolical malice with which they glutted their revenge upon the inanimate forms of the slain, are nothing more than fables, and I must confess that I experienced something like a sense of regret at having my hideous anticipations thus disappointed. I felt in some sort like a 'prentice boy who, going to the play in the expectation of being delighted with a cut-and-thrust tragedy, is almost moved to tears of disappointment at the exhibition of a genteel comedy.
>
> I could not avoid thinking that I had fallen in with a greatly traduced people, and I moralized not a little upon the disadvantage of having a bad name, which in this instance had given a tribe of savages, who were as pacific as so many lambkins, the reputation of a confederacy of giant-killers. (128)

The position he is edging toward in this passage is the one he will later describe as the outpost of those "sensible and well-informed people [who] will not believe that any cannibals exist; and place every book of voyages which purports to give any account of them, on the same shelf with Blue Beard and Jack the Giant-Killer." The subsequent skirmish between the Typees and the Happars, which ends without any "materials for the cannibal entertainment which I had heard usually terminated every engagement," only reinforces the appeal of this idea. In the last sentence of the chapter, he again declares that he is "much inclined to believe that such shocking festivals must occur very rarely among the islanders, if, indeed, they ever take place" (130).

From that point on, however, he will never again give any serious consideration to this idea. As the above passage indicates, he has already begun to favor the idea that cannibalism is an act of revenge, and, before long, he will snap back to that "moderate" position. This peculiar treatment of the element of the discourse on cannibalism that I have labeled denial prompts two immediate questions. First, if it is to be so brief, why is it necessary to bring it up at all? And second, if it is necessary to bring it up, why is it so brief? I have already suggested part of an answer to the first question: Melville needs to introduce this radical alternative to the lust explanation to stretch his readers' minds wide enough to accommodate less radical possibilities. When stated in those terms, however, that answer is too likely to imply that his evocation of this alternative was a wholly original act of defamiliarization. In fact, as he well knew, there were "many sensible and well-informed people," such as the skeptical reviewers for the *Quarterly Review* and the *Athenaeum,* who had already established denial as a recognizable element of the discourse on cannibalism. By means of that subsequent allusion to the armchair philosophers who have classified all accounts of cannibalism as fairy tales, he makes it clear that there is nothing particularly new about his suggestion that the Typees might not be cannibals. He has not made an inductive breakthrough; he has simply shifted from one established discursive position to another. Just as he observes that in his excursions through the Typee valley, "there were limits set to my wanderings" (123), so does he ask us to see that in his excursions through the discourse on cannibalism, he never says anything that exists outside the region of the already-said. By insisting on the conventionality of the denial of cannibalism, Melville turns our attention from the private narrative of Tommo's conflicts and resolutions to the public discourse that is the condition of its possibility. The complete answer to this question, then, is that the introduction of denial is necessary because it enables the reader to see the discourse on cannibalism not as a single authoritative point but as a differentially authorized field. In the discourse on cannibalism, as in the valley of cannibals, Tommo is neither confined to one place nor perfectly free.

The importance of the second question—why the suggestion of this alternative is so brief—might not be immediately apparent. To get a sense of its significance, it will be helpful to look at another late passage in which Tommo retrospectively surveys his progress from the lust explanation to denial. He asks us to recall that after "entering their valley, as I did, under the most erroneous impressions of their character, I was soon led to exclaim in amazement: 'Are these the ferocious savages, the blood-thirsty cannibals of whom I have heard such frightful tales! They deal more kindly with each other, and are more humane, than many who study essays on virtue and benevolence, and who repeat every night that beautiful prayer breathed first by the lips of the divine and gentle Jesus'" (203). What he wants us to notice here is that in passing from the lust explanation to denial, he has passed from a vision of the Typees as transcendently savage to a vision of the Typees as transcendently humane. Given that one of the principal goals of *Typee* is, as Tommo says at one point, to alter the "low opinion" of "the moral character of the islanders" that "the reader of South Sea voyages is too apt to form" (201), why then does he choose to evacuate a position that had allowed him to entertain such a remarkably high opinion of their character? The answer that may suggest itself first is that Melville knows this position will soon be made obsolete by Tommo's discovery of a vessel full of human bones. As we will see, however, that discovery offers nothing but a "reason to suspect" the existence of cannibalism; it is still possible to imagine, at the end of the narrative, that the Typees are not cannibals at all. Under these circumstances, the question revives with additional force: Why not offer a longer and louder defense of a position that would have so dramatically offset the negative stereotyping of Pacific islanders?

The answer to this question has at least three parts. First, Melville is anxious throughout *Typee* to avoid the taint of "theory." As David Simpson has shown, theory was a dirty word in early-nineteenth-century England and America, connoting the simultaneously effeminate and dangerous idealism of those philosophers who were thought to have spurred on the French Revolution.[10] In saying a good word for the moral character of Pacific islanders, Melville knew he was setting himself up to be attacked as a Rousseauian throwback, unwilling or unable to accept that savages were savage. Moreover, he knew that his decision to omit some of the most widely recognized marks of generic authenticity—dates, systematized explanations of customs, and numbingly plain speech—made it possible for critics to dismiss his narrative as untrustworthy not only in its conclusions but also in its data. To ward off the expected attacks on his data, he studded the book with insistences that it is entirely "based upon facts admitting of no contradiction, and which have come immediately under the writer's cognizance" (xiv). On at least eighteen occasions, he declares to us that his descriptions are drawn from memory and that his memory is perfectly exact, untainted by the colorings of imagination.[11] Similarly, to ward off the expected attacks on his conclusions, he takes pains to assure us that "[t]he conclusions deduced from these facts are unavoidable" (xiv). Insofar as they are perfectly spontaneous—he insists at one point that they "arose in my mind as I gazed upon the novel spectacle before me" (29)—his conclusions are as factual as the facts they arise from, unlike those anticipatory theories that are produced at a distance from the phenomenon. To emphasize that these conclusions arise on the spot and after the fact, he calls them "reflections," a word that shows up in this context at least twenty times.[12] Eager to engage his readers in the process of speculation, but well aware that they would be spooked by the specter of "theory," Melville ostentatiously represents *Typee* as a manly, practical, commonsensical text, consisting of nothing but first-person experiences and spontaneous reflections, both of which were perfectly preserved in the amber of memory before being transferred to the page.

Accordingly, it would have been strange if he *had* attempted an extended defense of the idea that cannibalism might not exist. As we saw in the last chapter, those writers who denied the existence of cannibalism were very often stigmatized as deskbound theoreticians, incapable of accepting the fact that the world contained more than had been dreamed of in their philosophies. To avoid that stigma, Melville both backs away from this theory after suggesting it and, in the passage I began with, gently ridicules the theorists himself. In part, then, the brevity of his suggestion is a sign of the demands that the market for travel narratives was making on him. But it also seems to have proceeded from his own discomfort with the dogmatism of this position. The speculative process that he is trying to initiate in his readers is explicitly opposed to theories that totalize, whether they do so by insisting that a propensity to cannibalism is inherent in the bodies of dark-skinned people, or by insisting that a propensity to avoid cannibalism is inherent in the bodies of all people. Throughout most of the book, unlike most "writers of travels among barbarous communities," he refrains, when describing customs, "from entering into explanations concerning their origin and purpose" (xiii). Even in his accounts of events that "will be sure to appear strange, or perhaps entirely incomprehensible, to the reader," he records them "just as they occurred, and leaves every one to form his own opinion concerning them" (xiv). It is not surprising, then, that when he actually does enter into explanations of origin and purpose, in the case of cannibalism, he steers clear of a mode of explanation that aspires to the condition of a grand unifying theory. If he were to proclaim without qualification that cannibalism did not exist, he would be as much of an absolutist as those "senseless sceptics" who would soon be doubting the truth of *Typee*—"men," he says in an 1846 letter, "who go straight from their cradles to their graves & never dream of the queer things going on at the antipodes" (C, 65–66).

My argument, at this stage, is that Melville introduces the denial of cannibalism because he wants to make the entire discursive field an object of critical attention, and that he backs away from it because it is incompatible with his project of processual speculation and potentially damaging to the book's reception. But there is at least one more reason he backs away from this idea, one that helps to make sense of the fact that the false alternatives of lust and denial quickly give way to the dream of vengeance. If the men of Typee were indeed too humane to be cannibals, they would be, for all practical purposes, indistinguishable from the women of Typee. Like the women, they would be embodiments of classical virtues, allegorical emblems of Temperance, Symmetry, and Harmony. In his moods of middle-class "propriety," which come over him at intervals throughout the book, Tommo does indeed appear to value these virtues above all else.[13] The man whose physical appearance he praises most loudly is Marnoo, whose "matchless symmetry of form" leads Tommo to envision him "standing for the statue of a Polynesian Apollo" (135). In Marnoo's body, Apollonian balance is explicitly associated with femininity; his untattooed cheeks are of a "feminine softness," and the "oval of his countenance and the regularity of every feature" recall Fayaway's "rounded oval" face and "perfectly formed" features (135, 85).[14] Insofar as the body social of Typee is characterized by this same "harmony and smoothness" (200), it is similarly gendered in feminine terms. In his declaration that "[t]he natives appeared to form one household, whose members were bound together by the ties of strong affection" (204), Tommo's rhetoric bears a striking resemblance to the language of domesticity. At those times when Tommo is his own "proper" self, the Typees' "Happy Valley" (124) could very often be taken to be an allegorical reproduction of the "separate sphere" of nineteenth-century American women.

His moods of propriety are only passing, however; his lasting attraction is to the idea of men who are "governed by no fixed principles"

(151). As we saw above, when he first considers the idea that Typee men are not cannibals at all, but are in fact as "genteel" as Typee women, he is "almost moved to tears." Having anticipated a "cut-and-thrust tragedy," a melodramatic opposition of metaphysical principles, he is painfully disappointed to discover what appears to be a theater of lawful and familiar action. His subsequent return to the vengeance explanation is largely motivated by his impatience with "the proprieties of time and place" (151)—the same impatience that initially drove him away from the *Dolly,* whose feminine designation is most meaningful when considered in this context. As a result of this conflict between his sentimental admiration of (feminine) regularity and his romantic attraction to (masculine) irregularity, a double standard begins to take shape. Although the men are generally "amiable and forbearing" (191), he neither expects nor wants them to be as consistently amiable and forbearing as the women. He is glad to see, for instance, that when they are threatened by invasion, the men are not forgiving enough "to sit down under their grievances, and to refrain from making any reprisals" (128). Instead, they are transformed into melodramatic avengers, animated by gusts of vengeful passion that sweep over them and then vanish, like the tropical storms that pass over the island. Tommo considers this to be a noble trait, a spontaneous expression of sincere feeling that parallels the perfect self-evidence of Marquesan females. The difference between the two is that whereas Tommo's ideal woman is necessarily constant and symmetrical, his ideal man is necessarily inconstant and disproportionate. Once we understand that he is working within the logic of this particular double standard, it should be clear that the denial of cannibalism is not, in fact, the most appealing of the images of savagery made available within the discourse as a whole. As far as he is concerned, it is better to have been a vengeful cannibal, expressing an uncompromising and unpredictable resistance to external rule, than never to have been a cannibal at all.

"A Certain Moderate Extent"

That [the Nukuhevans] are cannibals is well ascertained. They form distinct factions, and make war upon the ruling chief; the rebels are denominated the Typees; and the opposing parties are horribly sanguinary towards each. . . . A native man belonging to Port Anna Maria, who was not tatooed, and in consequence prohibited from the eating of human flesh, on pain of death, impatient of the restraint, fell upon one of the murdered bodies, and darting his teeth into it in all the madness of a voracious fury, exhaled the crimson moisture, which had not yet coagulated. — *The Salem Advertiser* (1817)

When Tommo describes vengeful cannibalism, in the passage I began with, as cannibalism taken only to "a certain moderate extent," he means that the islanders are cannibals only on the special occasion of war, and that the passion that moves them is not animal but moral. As we have seen, this was an ordinary way of staking out a middle ground between the extremes of lust and denial. In *Travels in New Zealand* (1843), for instance, the naturalist Ernest Dieffenbach writes that "[t]he savage, passionate and furious with the feeling of revenge, slaughtering and devouring his enemy and drinking his blood, is no longer the same being as when cultivating his fields in peace; and it would be as unjust to estimate his general character by his actions in these moments of unrestrained passion, as to judge of Europeans by the excesses of an excited soldiery or an infuriated mob." [15] In this context, there is nothing contradictory about Tommo's statement that although "several of the primitive tribes in the Pacific" are indeed vengeful cannibals, they "are in other respects humane and virtuous." As he has already said, savages are "proverbial" for their "inconstancy" (*T*, 76); he is simply asking his readers to apply that proverbial fact in a way that enables them to treat the islanders' behavior at war as something other than an index of their character. And like Dieffenbach, who argues that vengeful cannibalism is disconnected not only from the character of the Maori at peace, but also from "the pleasure of eating human flesh" (*Travels*, 128), Tommo goes out of his way to insist that "this only enormity in their character is not half so horrible as it is usually described." The idea "that there are people in the world with tastes so depraved that they would infinitely prefer a single mouthful of material humanity to a good dinner of roast beef and plum pudding" (205) is nothing more than one of those "extravagant fictions" that have falsified the real condition of the world outside the West.

But if vengeful cannibalism is moderate when considered together with their ordinary humaneness or in relation to the extravagant fiction of lustful cannibalism, it is not moderate in itself. It was conventionally thought to take place in what Dieffenbach calls "moments of unrestrained passion," blackouts of humanity in which nothing is impossible. In the passage in which Tommo first doubts the existence of cannibalism, he makes it clear that this convention of representation is both familiar and attractive to him; he is saddened by the possibility that "all those terrible stories I have heard about the inveteracy with which they carried on the feud, their deadly intensity of hatred and the diabolical malice with which they glutted their revenge" might be untrue. Like the lust explanation and denial, the vengeance explanation is explicitly characterized as the product of "stories," not as an original reflection

91

on novel experience. What these stories have taught him, above all else, is that when cannibals devour "the bodies of slain enemies," they do so with a "deadly intensity." At times, this expectation is obviously a source of horror; after the Typees fiercely reject Marnoo's suggestion that they release Tommo, he exclaims, "How strongly rooted, then, must be the determination of the Typees with regard to me, and how suddenly could they display the strangest passions!" (143). He takes the episode to be a sign of "the danger of trifling with the wayward and passionate spirits against whom it was vain to struggle, and might even be fatal to do so" (144). But this aspect of their character is just as clearly a source of their appeal, a sign of what he calls, in another context, "that glorious principle inherent in all heroic natures—the strong-rooted determination to have the biggest share of the pudding or to go without any of it" (137). The true romance of *Typee* has as its object this immoderate masculine sensibility, consisting of a strong-rooted determination that manifests itself in wayward explosions of passion.

Tommo's admiration of these qualities is most vividly apparent in his descriptions of Toby. He is both a man of "dauntless courage" and "a strange wayward being, moody, fitful, and melancholy—at times almost morose. He had a quick and fiery temper too, which, when thoroughly roused, transported him into a state bordering on delirium." Tommo defends this trait as a sign of how "big-hearted" Toby is; in such "paroxysms," he says, Toby "vented the bile which more calm-tempered individuals get rid of by a continual pettishness at trivial annoyances." When he is in these bile-venting moods, moreover, even the largest man will "quail before this slender stripling," a phenomenon that testifies to "the power that a mind of deep passion has over feebler natures" (32). The peculiar admiration of delirium that emerges from these passages has at least three sources. First, Tommo imagines excesses of mood to signify, by reason of their intensity, a spiritual depth. Waywardness is in this sense entirely compatible with rootedness, insofar as excessive expressions of feeling can create the impression that there exists, beneath the realm of representation, a great and permanent source of feeling. Second, the deliriousness of these moods promises that there is no mediation between feeling and expression, but that the signified feeling is actually present in the signifying expression. Even in less extreme moods, Toby tends to be a transparent vessel of being; when the solution to a problem comes into Toby's mind, for instance, he signals it by springing to his feet, "while his eyes lighted up with that gleam of intelligence that marks the presence of some bright idea" (56). Finally, and perhaps least obviously, the purgative nature of these moods suggests the presence of a spiritual substance that is worth maintaining in its original purity. By preventing his shipmates from learning anything about his past and raging at even minor insults, Toby displays a protectiveness that can be taken to signify not only the presence, but also the value, of an interior essence.

It may be more difficult to recognize Tommo's romanticization of these same qualities in the men of Typee, because his attraction is so thoroughly mixed with fear. But the attraction is unquestionably there; nothing in their character is more appealing to him than the aura of authentic being that is generated by their excessive, unmediated, and purgative expressions of feeling. Even before Toby shows up, he is singing the praises of the Typee warriors in precisely these terms. Aware that the only existing impression most American readers will have of the Typees comes from U.S. Navy Capt. David Porter's account of his assault on their valley during the War of 1812, Tommo goes out of his way to say that the "hard fighting" of the Typees, which ultimately "obliged their assailants to retreat and abandon their design of conquest," was an admirably passionate act of self-defense. He acknowledges that their defense was indeed marked by a spirit of excess, signaling "the deadly hatred of the Typees to all foreigners," but argues that this must be understood as an expression of feeling no less natural than the excessive hospitality with which all Pacific islanders "rush down to the beach in crowds, and with open arms stand ready to embrace the strangers." When the strangers greet them with "unprovoked atrocities," he says, "the instinctive feeling of love within their breast is soon converted into the bitterest hate" (26). He cites the notorious reports that Fijians massacred and ate several American sailors in 1834 as an example of how far this bitter hate has led some islanders, "who, after all, have but avenged the unprovoked injuries which they have received."[16] The islanders' vengeance is as infinite as their original love, is unmediated by technology or law, and is an attempt to purge themselves of the elements of corruption. It is an error, accordingly, to give them the name of "savages," since that name implies an originally "cruel and bloodthirsty disposition" (27). Because they have been "exasperated into savages" by the cruelty of Europeans, their violence must be understood as the spontaneous and sincere expression of a distinctly moral passion.

To a certain degree, then, *Typee* can be thought of as a defense of anticolonial violence on Fanonian grounds. In *The Wretched of the Earth*, Frantz Fanon similarly argues that the unmediated, excessive violence of the decolonization process is "a cleansing force. It frees the native from his inferiority complex and from his despair and inaction; it makes him fearless and restores his self-respect." [17] It takes place, he says, in "lightning flashes of consciousness which fling the body into stormy paths or which throw it into an almost pathological trance where the face of the other beckons me on to giddiness" (139). With this delirious assault on the colonialist, who was the original "bringer of violence into the home and into the mind of the native" (38), the character of the colonized subject undergoes a "total, complete and absolute substitution" (35). Vengeful violence "brings a natural rhythm into existence, introduced by new men, and with it a new language and a new humanity. Decolonization is the veritable creation of new men" (36). The crucial difference between the two books is that Melville's romance of anticolonial violence is far more attitudinal than Fanon's. Very often, his critique of colonialism is more a plea for improved methods than it is a vision of its apocalyptic end. "Let the savages be civilized, but civilize them with benefits, and not with evils," he says at one point, later adding that "[l]est the slightest misconception should arise from anything thrown out in this chapter, or indeed in any other part of the volume, let me here observe, that against the cause of missions in the abstract no Christian can possibly be opposed: it is in truth a just and holy cause" (T, 195, 197). And when he does take sides with the forces of native resistance, he frequently sounds as if he is doing nothing more than assuming a glamorous pose. "All hail, therefore, Mehevi, King of the Cannibal Valley, and long life and prosperity to his Typeean majesty," he declares, shortly before the passages I have just quoted. "May Heaven for many a year preserve him, the uncompromising foe of Nukuheva and the French, if a hostile attitude will secure his lovely domain from the remorseless inflictions of South Sea civilization" (189). Although we should acknowledge the potential force of Tommo's anticolonial rhetoric, we should also acknowledge that he seems to be more interested in shedding the aura of authenticity on the warriors of Typee than in actually praying for the advent of Fanon's New Man.[18]

His conception of rage as an admirably authentic expression of masculine sensibility quite clearly informs the two places in the narrative in which he explicitly attributes the cannibalism of the Typees to vengefulness. First, in the midst of an extended appreciation of Typeean virtues, he interrupts himself to observe:

> it will be urged that these shocking unprincipled wretches are cannibals. Very true; and a rather bad trait in their character it must

be allowed. But they are such only when they seek to gratify the passion of revenge upon their enemies; and I ask whether the mere eating of human flesh so very far exceeds in barbarity that custom which only a few years since was practised in enlightened England: —a convicted traitor, perhaps a man found guilty of honesty, patriotism, and suchlike heinous crimes, had his head lopped off with a huge axe, his bowels dragged out and thrown into a fire; while his body, carved into four quarters, was with his head exposed upon pikes, and permitted to rot and fester among the public haunts of men! (125)

Unlike Western retribution, which is mediated by both law and technology, Typeean cannibalism is instantaneous and radically intimate, the natural language of rage. Rather than straining to make the retaliation appear natural by appealing to what he will later call "arbitrary codes" (201), the Typees simply allow a pressing moral passion to exteriorize itself. And rather than extending the punishment over time, embodying the power of the state in the instruments that are successively brought to bear on the body of the victim, the Typees fulfill the demands of that passion in a single moment of delirium. Unmediated vengeance is at least spontaneous and sincere; vengeance disguised by justifying narratives and prolonged by instruments of power leads to calculating excesses such as the U.S. Exploring Expedition's slaughter of Fijians, which "are enough of themselves to distinguish the white civilized man as the most ferocious animal on the face of the earth" (125). Just as he considers life imprisonment to be less natural and more cruel than the death penalty, in that it destroys criminals "piece-meal, drying up in their veins, drop by drop, the blood we are too chicken-hearted to shed by a single blow" (125), so does he suggest that the collapsed time of vengeful cannibalism is preferable to the monstrously distended time of Western retribution.[19]

The second explicit attribution of cannibalism to vengefulness comes in the passage I quoted at the beginning of this chapter, where Melville limits the extent of the act to "the bodies of slain enemies alone." Melville sets up this passage by mounting two separate explanations of the Typees' hatred of outsiders, distinguishing their hostility toward white men from their hostility toward other Nukuhevan tribes. In the case of white men, he says, "[t]he cruel invasion of their country by Porter has alone furnished them with ample provocation; and I can sympathize in the spirit which prompts the Typee warrior to guard all the passes to the valley with the point of his levelled spear, and, standing upon the beach, with his back turned upon his green home, to hold at bay the intruding

European" (205). With that final image, which he draws from the illustration that I discussed in the previous chapter, he reemphasizes a point he has made more than once already: that Typeean aggression against white men is animated by a strongly rooted desire to preserve their original integrity. But in the case of the Typees' aggression against tribes such as the Happar, he cannot be sure; because he does not know "the origin of the enmity of this particular clan towards the neighbouring tribes," he cannot confidently "say that their foes are the aggressors." It could be that this is simply a case of "evil passions" finding "vent" (205), the unplanned release of a spirit of rage that is beyond control, but seems to gravitate naturally, if left unchecked, toward strangers. It could be, then, that like Toby's delirious venting of rage, the Typees' "excess of animosity" (128) toward the Happars simply expresses a waywardness of spirit, a tendency to veer sharply out of bounds that is common to "minds of deep passion." When he finally says, in the next paragraph, that the Typees cannibalize "the bodies of slain enemies alone," that act has been made to connote the presence of some indeterminate mixture of a spirit of fixity and a spirit of unpredictability. By mingling these two explanations, he leaves us in a position in which we can only speak of the spirit of cannibalism in the most general and mythical terms; all we can safely say, at this point, is that it signifies a fundamentally masculine capacity for rage that is deeply rooted and expressed without mediation or bounds.

One of the things that the discursive history of cannibalism can teach us is that this particular mode of representation was "available," both to Melville and to his readers. But it also teaches us that by the 1840s, the association of cannibalism with vengefulness, and thereby with the dream of an authentic manhood, had become somewhat tenuous. If one wanted to argue that cannibalism was motivated by vengeance, clearing away the extreme alternatives of lust and denial was not enough; one had to contend, once that was over, with the increasingly powerful and equally "moderate" argument that it was motivated by superstition. Beyond that argument, moreover, lay the less prominent but far more disconcerting suggestion that cannibalism was motivated by a desire to terrorize—a suggestion that threatened to explode the dream of savage authenticity, just as the suggestion of superstition, with its connotations of cowardice, threatened to explode the dream of savage manhood. Both of these anxieties are present in the passage I began with. When Tommo declares that "horrible and fearful as the custom is, immeasurably as it is to be abhorred and condemned, still I assert that those who indulge in it are in other respects humane and virtuous," he is raising the possibility that the vengeful spirit might not be free of the taint of "custom," that it might refer not to its own independent origin, but to an external system of traditions. Similarly, when he says that "[t]he reader will ere long have reason to suspect that the Typees are not free from the guilt of cannibalism," he is alerting us to the fact that our evidence of cannibalism will not consist of unmediated expressions, but of equivocal signs. Vengeful cannibalism might at first appear to be the place where Tommo finally comes down, after bouncing between the extremes of lust and denial. But the process continues: in the same way that he spends the first half of the book occupying lust, only to push it to the point at which it turns into something else, he spends the second half of the book occupying vengeance, only to bring us to the awareness of a world that lies just beyond the edges of that dream.

"Fearful as the Custom Is"

In point of morals, the Marquesans must be classed with the lowest of our species. . . . [T]hey can kill and devour each other and yet think they are doing God service. — Richard Armstrong (1838)

The first allusion to what missionaries tended to call "the system of superstition" comes in Tommo's preliminary list of anticipations, in which he dwells on the thought of "savage woodlands guarded by horrible idols—*heathenish rites and human sacrifice.*" As with his anticipation of "cannibal banquets," he begins the process of intervening in his readers' conventional expectations by first introducing those expectations and identifying himself with them. And although he does not reiterate his anticipations of heathenish rites nearly as often as his anticipations of cannibal banquets, he does return to them one more time. On his second day in the valley, just before the midnight meal of pork, he and Toby arrive for the first time at the Taboo Groves, which he describes as

> the scene of many a prolonged feast, of many a horrid rite. Beneath the dark shadows of the consecrated bread-fruit trees there reigned a solemn twilight—a cathedral-like gloom. The frightful genius of pagan worship seemed to brood in silence over the place, breathing its spell upon every object around. Here and there, in the depths of these awful shades, half screened from sight by masses of overhanging foliage, rose the idolatrous altars of the savages, built of enormous blocks of black and polished stone, placed one upon

another, without cement, to the height of twelve or fifteen feet, and surmounted by a rustic open temple, enclosed with a low picket of canes, within which might be seen, in various stages of decay, offerings of bread-fruit and cocoa-nuts, and the putrefying relics of some recent sacrifice. (91)

There is at least a suggestion here of cannibalism motivated by superstition, in the linking of "horrid rites" with "prolonged feasts." But the associative connection is very loose, as Melville intended; the recently discovered draft manuscript of *Typee* shows that he initially described the groves as "the scene of many a *sensual* feast, of many a horrid rite," a formulation that must have subsequently struck him as too flagrant an association of cannibal banquets with idolatrous rituals.[20] All he wants to give us is the hint of superstitious cannibalism, together with the slightly stronger but still uncertain suggestion that the "putrefying relics of some recent sacrifice" are human, as his original anticipations of the Marquesas might lead us to expect.

The Gothic gloom of these expectations is partially dispelled by the comic scene that follows, which is as free of any sign of superstitious ritual as it is of any sign of cannibalism.[21] And several chapters later, after we have become accustomed to our new vision of the Typees as vengeful cannibals, if they are cannibals at all, the conventional association of savagery with "horrid rites" is more directly challenged. At the celebration that Tommo calls the Feast of Calabashes, he observes that the only flesh laid on the altars belongs to "baked hogs, laid out in large wooden trenchers." The not-particularly-horrid contents of these vessels clearly undermine Tommo's anticipations of human sacrifice, suggesting that his earlier glimpse of decaying flesh had been, like this, nothing but a glimpse of pork. There is still some evidence, however, that these offerings could form part of a regulated system of idolatrous worship. Beneath the altars he notices poles planted "at regular intervals," beneath which are "two parallel rows of cumbersome drums" that are "[a]t regular intervals . . . bound round by a species of sinnate" (167). These drums are beaten with equal regularity, and their "incessant din" (167) is accompanied by the "uninterrupted monotonous chant" of old men sitting in pulpits and keeping fans "in continual motion" (168). But these signs of organized ritual activity do not appear to signify. "[N]o attention whatever seemed to be paid to the drummers or to the old priests," Tommo says. "For all the observation it attracted, or the good it achieved, the whole savage orchestra might, with great advantage to its own members and the company in general, have ceased the prodigious uproar they were making." The "individuals who composed the vast crowd" were "entirely taken up in chatting and laughing with one another, smoking, drinking arva, and eating." Upon questioning some of these individuals "as to the meaning of the strange things that were going on," he received nothing but a "mass of outlandish gibberish and gesticulation" and "gave up the attempt in despair" (168).

The casualness of this event becomes the occasion for a critical reflection on the discourse of missionary narratives, which had led him to anticipate *"heathenish rites and human sacrifice"* at all the islands of the Pacific. "As a religious solemnity," Tommo declares, the Feast of Calabashes "had not at all corresponded with the horrible descriptions of Polynesian worship which we have received in some published narratives, and especially in those accounts of the evangelized islands with which the missionaries have favoured us." One of these narratives is especially offensive in this regard.

> In a certain work incidentally treating of the "Washington, or Northern Marquesas Islands," I have seen the frequent immolation of human victims upon the altars of their gods, positively and repeatedly charged upon the inhabitants. The same work gives also a rather minute account of their religion, — enumerates a great many of their superstitions, — and makes known the particular designations of numerous orders of the priesthood. One would almost imagine from the long list that is given of cannibal primates, bishops, archdeacons, prebendaries, and other inferior ecclesiastics, that the sacerdotal order far outnumbered the rest of the population, and that the poor natives were more severely priest-ridden than even the inhabitants of the papal states. These accounts are likewise calculated to leave upon the reader's mind an impression that human victims are daily cooked and served up upon the altars; that heathenish cruelties of every description are continually practised; and that these ignorant Pagans are in a state of the extremest wretchedness in consequence of the grossness of their superstitions. (169–70)

The narrative he refers to is the Reverend Charles Stewart's *A Visit to the South Seas* (1831), which contains, as Tommo indicates, a description of human sacrifice and ritual cannibalism among the Nukuhevan priesthood. On the basis of his own observations on the religious habits of the islanders, Tommo unequivocally rejects Stewart's account of priests who perform ceremonies over human victims before offering them in sacrifice, and who "alone have the privilege of eating of any thing offered in sacrifice to the gods." [22] "In all my excursions through the valley of Typee," he says, "I never saw any of these alleged enormities. If any of them are practised upon the Marquesas Islands they must certainly have come to my knowledge while living for months with a tribe of savages, wholly unchanged from their original primitive condition, and reputed the most ferocious in the South Seas" (170).

Tommo's refusal to accept the existence of cannibalism motivated by superstition may seem strange to twentieth-century readers, who are used to thinking that the truest and friendliest thing one can say about the practices of "natives" is that they are meaningful on their own terms. But in the era before the development of the culture-concept, such a refusal was logically consistent with the refusal to accept the existence of cannibalism motivated by lust. Like the lust explanation, the superstition explanation tended to suggest that the people in question existed in "a state of the extremest wretchedness." Though the Nukuhevans may be "free from the restraints of civil and military power," Stewart warns, "they are notwithstanding under the dominion of an iron-handed tyranny—the tyranny of superstition, over the darkness of minds and hearts lost in ignorance and sin" (1:266). In his rejection of the lust explanation and the superstition explanation—as in his omission of the famine explanation, which had once been a popular way of accounting for Marquesan cannibalism [23]—Tommo is denying that savagery is a condition in which humanity has been displaced by a deterministic force. As far as he is concerned, the only deterministic force that we need to worry about is the one that substitutes algebraic signs like "savage" and "pagan" for an inconsistent assemblage of human beings. Once that substitution has been made, it is virtually inevitable that westerners will begin reading the destruction of colonized societies by "disease, vice, and premature death" (T, 195) as a welcome sign that "[t]he abominations of Paganism have given way to the pure rites of the Christian worship,—the ignorant savage has been supplanted by the refined European!" (196). "The Anglo-Saxon hive have extirpated Paganism from the greater part of the North American continent," he says, "but with it they have likewise extirpated the greater portion of the Red race. Civilization is gradually sweeping from the earth the lingering vestiges of Paganism, and at the same time the shrinking forms of its unhappy worshippers" (195).

In the place of these fixed and therefore dangerous designations,

Tommo offers the vision of savagery that accompanies the vengeance explanation: savagery as the unmediated and unbounded expression of a natural human sensibility. The Typees are not, as Stewart would have it, miserably priest-ridden and superstition-driven; they are simply "a community of lusty savages, who are leading a merry, idle, innocent life." Like other travelers with ethnographic pretensions, Stewart has replaced this easygoing community with "a very circumstantial and learned narrative of certain unaccountable superstitions and practices, about which he knows as little as the islanders do themselves." The truth beneath that systematized abstraction, Tommo says, is that the Typees "are either too lazy or too sensible to worry themselves about abstract points of religious belief" (171). In fact, as a result of the "unbounded liberty of conscience" that prevailed among them, "religious affairs in Typee were at a very low ebb" (171, 174). In a parodic litany of declensions, he declares that the Typees are "a back-slidden generation. They are sunk in religious sloth, and require a spiritual revival. A long prosperity of bread-fruit and cocoa-nuts has rendered them remiss in the performance of their higher obligations. The wood-rot malady is spreading among the idols—the fruit upon their altars is becoming offensive—the temples themselves need re-thatching—the tattooed clergy are altogether too light-hearted and lazy—and their flocks are going astray" (179). To him, these rotting symbols of obligation are signs of good health and spirits, an indication that "[t]he 'independent electors' of the valley were not to be brow-beaten by chiefs, priests, idols, or devils"—that, in fact, they "submitted to no laws human or divine" (177). Like Said, Tommo reacts to the "antihuman and persistent" nature of colonial stereotypes (*Orientalism,* 44) by positing the existence, beneath those stereotypes, of a "humanity" defined against all forms of fixity. If it is the work of the Orientalist "to be always converting the Orient from something into something else" (67), Tommo and Said take it to be the work of the social critic to reverse that process of algebraic substitution, replacing it with what Said calls "ordinary human reality, Yeats's 'uncontrollable mystery on the bestial floor,' in which all human beings live" (230).

Once he has left behind the idea that the Typees are subject to "the tyranny of superstition," Tommo ascends to the high point in his romance of spontaneous masculine sensibility. Customs do exist among the Typees—he does not want to go to the "theoretical" extreme of saying that their existence is entirely unpatterned—but these conventionalized forms of social expression do not compromise the uncontrollable mystery of their inner lives. Customs are things that the Typees simply play with, he argues, things that are fundamentally exterior to them, and can therefore be picked up and set down without a second thought. When the chiefs perform a ceremony in honor of Moa Artua, the tiny idol reputed to be "the 'crack' god of the island," the ceremony is primarily intended "for the entertainment of those who believe in him" (175). The ceremony is inspired by the chiefs' boredom after their noontime nap, and its mood is the raucousness of low theater; when the priest whacks Moa Artua on the head and stuffs him in a box, the chiefs "loudly applaud" (175), and when the priest relays the chastened idol's messages, one chief "claps his hands in a rapture; another shouts with merriment; and a third leaps to his feet and capers about like a madman" (176). Following David Porter, whose narrative furnished the basis of this scene, Tommo declares that "[t]he whole of these proceedings were like those of a parcel of children playing with dolls and baby houses" (176).[24] Among the Marquesans, idols are idols only in the moment of play; the first white woman on the Marquesas is revered as a new divinity only until the islanders determine her sex, and Kory-Kory is respectful of a leaning wooden idol only until it falls on his back. In each of these cases, idolatry is quickly transformed into "contempt" (6, 179), and the power to originate meaning returns to those who had temporarily surrendered it. Though Tommo seems to want to make fun of this tendency, observing at one point that "in the celebration of many of their strange rites, they appeared to seek a sort of childish amusement" (174), he also makes it clear that in his own sentimentally poetic moods, he does exactly the same thing. In the scene that immediately precedes the ceremony of Moa Artua, we learn that he is in the habit of sinking into a reverie before an effigy of a rowing chief and seeing, "with the eye of faith," the spirit of the chief approaching the "dimly looming shores of Paradise." In yielding himself up "to the fanciful superstition of the islanders" (173), he is behaving like a Typee—temporarily surrendering to a superstition that is understood to be "fanciful," for the sake of the pleasure that accompanies the blurring of a sign with its signified.[25]

In the context of this representation of Typeean superstition, the word *custom* in the passage I began with is disarmed of its power to suggest an enslavement to tradition. Insofar as custom is radically exterior to the self, it does not impose on its autonomy, and insofar as it reflects the mercurial interiority of the self, it does not question its authenticity. As long as we are willing to grant both of these propositions, it remains possible to combine the idea that cannibalism is a customary practice with the idea that cannibalism is the effect of an occasional gust of vengeful passion. The customary nature of vengeful cannibalism contributes to our impression that this act lies outside the sphere of the Polynesians' real existence, and the vengeful nature of customary cannibalism contributes to our impression that the act glows with the truth of that real existence. Taken together, custom defined as play and vengeance defined as delirium make up a vision of savagery that is so coherent and appealing that it would seem to bring Tommo's process of reflection to a halt. After drawing us first into and then past the vision of savagery as an enslavement to lust or superstition, he has now raised in its place a vision of savagery as a sublime independence from all forms of externally imposed rule. But the most extraordinary thing about *Typee,* the thing that makes it appropriate to speak of its pedagogical method as an early version of the pedagogical method of *Moby-Dick,* is that the process of reflection does not stop here. As he says in the opening sentence of this passage, we will soon discover that we have nothing more than a "reason to suspect" the existence of cannibalism among the Typees. In giving us this warning, he is not returning us to the outright denial of cannibalism; he is simply alerting us to the fact that the signs of cannibalism we will encounter will be markedly opaque. Beneath the cover of colonial discourse, he has hoped to find the shimmering symbols of true savage nature. But when he lifts that lid, all he will find will be another dulled cover, one that will face him with the terrible reflection of a self that has neither autonomy nor authenticity, because it has no interior.

"Reason to Suspect"

A young Spaniard, about eighteen years of age, formerly a midshipman in the Peruvian service, but now residing upon Nuuhiva, is reported by his fellow renegades to have partaken of one of these diabolical feasts. When I questioned him upon the subject, he stoutly denied any participation, but said that he was present and saw the body cooked and eaten. [If] we depend upon such testimony the subject might rest forever; but the universal testimony of natives is alike conclusive and painful. Each person or tribe, when accused, invariably deny the charge as referring to themselves, but accuse their neighbours, and add that formerly it was practised by themselves, but not now. So little dependence can we place upon the statements of the natives, that we are at a loss what to say on the subject.—Robert Thomson (1841)

We begin our descent into that moment of inverse revelation—the revelation that there is nothing to reveal—soon thereafter. On one of his "strolls with Kory-Kory," Tommo comes across a native artist engaged

in tattooing the eyelids of an old man. The artist is bent over his subject, "working away for all the world like a stone-cutter with mallet and
chisel," and though the old man has assumed a "forced composure," he is
evidently "suffering agony" (*T*, 217). Spread out beside the artist is an array of "curious black-looking little implements" (217), several of which
are curved in a way that suggests they are "intended to be introduced
into the orifice of the ear, with a view perhaps of beating the tattoo upon
the tympanum" (218). This pun on "tattoo"—signifying both the indel-
ible inscription of shapes and the monotonous repetition of sounds—is
not incidental. The artist is not "engaged on an original sketch," as it
turns out, but is "merely employed in touching up the works of some of
the old masters of the Typee school, as delineated upon the human canvas before him." For Tommo, the most horrible aspect of this repetitive
sketching is that it is being performed on the "shutters to the windows
of the soul," whose "exquisite sensibility" is signified, in spite of all the
old man's assumed stoicism, by "sundry twitchings and screwings of
the muscles of the face" (218). His horror is infinitely increased when
the artist, whose name is Karky, discovers his presence, and is suddenly
taken with "[t]he idea of engrafting his tattooing upon my white skin."
As Karky's finger "swept across my features, in laying out the borders of
those parallel bands which were to encircle my countenance," Tommo
says, "the flesh fairly crawled upon my bones" (219). His shudder, like
the old man's twitching, is intended to signify the involuntary resistance
of "humanity," defined as an originality and sensibility of soul, to the
imposition of a surface as repetitious as a drum beat and as insensible
as a stone.

"This incident opened my eyes to a new danger," he declares. "I now
felt convinced that in some luckless hour I should be disfigured in such a
manner as never more to have the *face* to return to my countrymen, even
should an opportunity offer." The heavily emphasized pun on "face,"
signifying both countenance and character, makes it clear that Tommo's
resistance to tattooing is driven not only by a fear that it will blot out
the sign of his soul, but also by a fear that it will blot out a highly visible
sign of his social privilege: his white skin. In describing his face as something that he has, something that can be alienated, he is suggesting that
the tattooing of his face would not transform him from a natural subject into an artificial object so much as it would transform him from one
kind of object into another. This is a subdued suggestion, however, and
he quickly backs away from it. When he subsequently exclaims, "What
an object he would have made of me!" (219), he is again characterizing

the prospect of Karky's assault as an unprecedented interference with the natural transparency of his " 'face divine,' as the poets call it" (220). As a result, he begins to imagine that he can get away from this conception of humans as repetitiously inscribed objects by getting away from the Typees. After several days punctuated by monotonous requests to choose a design for his face, he says, "my existence became a burden to me; the leisures I had previously enjoyed no longer afforded me delight, and all my former desire to escape from the valley now revived with additional force" (220). This statement marks a crucial transition in the narrative; it reverses his earlier pronouncement that Polynesians are humane in relation to Western savagery, leaving us in the grip of something like his original anticipation that Polynesians would be savage in relation to Western humanity. But the definition of savagery has changed. Whereas the heart of Typeean darkness was once cannibal lust, an animalistic instinct that neither acknowledged nor created signification, it is now signification itself, understood as pervasive and persistent, that sends Tommo backpedaling away from the object of his romance.

The fact that the Marquesans are fond of ornamentation and display is not surprising in itself; Tommo has frequently commented on the pleasure that both women and men take in adorning themselves with objects and assuming alien roles. Before now, however, he has been able to conceive of these traits as essentially innocent and irrelevant. At the end of the first chapter, for instance, a Marquesan queen breaks up an official ceremony on board an American man-of-war by first pausing to admire the exposed surfaces of "an old *salt,* whose bare arms and feet, and exposed breast were covered with as many inscriptions in India ink as the lid of an Egyptian sarcophagus," and then lifting up her skirt "to display the hieroglyphics on her own sweet form" (8). Soon after their arrival in the valley, Tommo and Toby are invited to participate in a similarly reciprocal display of signs; a long line of Typees "introduced themselves to us by pronouncing their respective names, and retired in high good humor on receiving ours in return. During this ceremony the greatest merriment prevailed . . . which induced me to believe that some of them at least were innocently diverting the company at our expense, by bestowing upon themselves a string of absurd titles, of the humor of which we were of course entirely ignorant" (72). Just as the queen's encounter with the sailor indicates nothing more than her innocent love of exhibition, the arbitrariness of the names the Typees assign to themselves indicates nothing more than their innocent love of play. In their love of simple ornamentation for its own sake, Tommo declares, the

Marquesans are superior to those Westerners who use coded ornaments as instruments of power. If one were to place the women of the valley, whose only ornaments are floral, beside "our fashionable ladies in dress," it would be like "the Venus de' Medici placed beside a milliner's doll" (161). This is because middle-class American women, bedecked in "[t]heir jewels, their feathers, their silks, and their furbelows," are engaged in a social competition marked by "stiffness, formality, and affectation" (161), whereas Typee women are "not filled with envyings of each other's charms, nor displaying the ridiculous affectations of gentility, nor yet moving in whalebone corsets, like so many automatons, but free, inartificially happy, and unconstrained" (126–27). The same is generally true of Typee men, he says, in that their ornamental necklaces, earrings, and tattoos leave them for the most part "in all the nakedness of nature," still exhibiting the "original magnitude" of "the mere creature," still opposed to any effort to convert them into "the semblance of all that is elevated and grand" (29).

But with respect to the men, he has occasionally noticed that their simple ornaments are capable of being systematically oriented toward the creation of "semblance." On Tommo's first morning in the valley, an imposing figure appears before him, ornamented with such "barbaric trinkets" (77) as hair bracelets, whale-tooth earrings, and, around his neck, "several enormous necklaces of boar's tusks, polished like ivory" (77). Even more remarkable "was the elaborate tattooing displayed on every noble limb. All imaginable lines and curves and figures were delineated over his whole body, and in their grotesque variety and infinite profusion I could only compare them to the crowded groupings of quaint patterns we sometimes see in costly pieces of lacework" (78). The most noteworthy aspect of this "extraordinary embellishment," however, is the striped tattooing on his face, which "may possibly have denoted his exalted rank." The islander turns out to be the chief Mehevi, who, after being recognized, "seemed to enjoy not a little the effect his barbaric costume had produced upon me" (79). Like the French in Nukuheva Bay, who perform military exercises in uniforms that are "resplendent with gold lace and embroidery, as if purposely calculated to dazzle the islanders" (17), Mehevi has assumed his formal regalia for the sake of its effect on his visitor. But Mehevi's creation of "semblance" goes deeper than that of the French sailors. Although it remains possible to envision, beneath the French regalia, the presence of a naturally signifying body, Mehevi's self-display merges the ornamented body with the body as ornament. In light of the continuum that Tommo establishes between the bone and hair appended to Mehevi's body and the "lacework" shapes tattooed on it, that body is not so much the metaphorical expression of Mehevi's inner being as it is one more metonymic appendage to it. As long as Tommo is able to convince himself that these kinds of append-ages are ultimately playful, and therefore inessential, he finds it bearable to think about bodies in this way. In the aftermath of Karky's assault, however, the habit of ornamenting the self with signs begins to seem far more consequential than he had ever allowed himself to imagine. As this metonymic mode of expression rises from a hum in the background to an unnerving roar, the innocently metaphorical expression of the "mere creature" diminishes to a remembered echo; the exception and the rule trade places, confronting Tommo with a field that suddenly consists of almost nothing but margin.

His immediate response is to reconsider the significance of one of the elements of Typeean life that he had previously dismissed as a rela-tively unimportant appendage to their real character. In one of his more rhapsodic moments, he had declared himself "almost tempted to say" that the Typees were not governed by "any general rule or standard of conduct," given that the only apparent standard of conduct among them, other than their innate moral sense, was "the mysterious 'Taboo' " (200). He now believes, however, that though the taboo, like the tat-too, is confined to the most superficial plane of Typeean existence, this plane of existence is far more important than he once thought. "I per-ceived every hour the effects of this all-controlling power," he says of the taboo, "without in the least comprehending it. Those effects were, in-deed, wide-spread and universal, pervading the most important as well as the minutest transactions of life. The savage, in short, lives in the con-tinual observance of its dictates, which guide and control every action of his being" (221). It has been difficult for Tommo to recognize the existence of this "all-controlling power" because he has tended to asso-ciate power with an identifiable agent. But given "the slight disparity of condition among the islanders—the very limited and inconsiderable pre-rogatives of the king and chiefs—and the loose and indefinite functions of the priesthood," the "authority which regulates this potent institu-tion" must be of a different kind. Because the taboo is so contingent, existing apart from any authoritative source of meaning, it is markedly "capricious": "[i]t is imposed upon something to-day, and withdrawn to-morrow; while its operations in other cases are perpetual" (224). And because the word "is used in more than one signification" (224), as most other Polynesian words are, its meaning is strikingly dependent on its context, "the particular meaning being shown chiefly by a variety of gestures and the eloquent expression of the countenance" (225). Like every other Typeean custom, that is, the taboo is external to individuals but not tyrannically imposed on them. Each of the Typees repeatedly *chooses* to observe the taboo, occasionally changing or reinflecting it in the process, for no other reason than that, as Tommo discovered earlier, it is pleasurable to yield oneself up to the repetitive rhythm of a "fanciful superstition." Because this is the case, the taboo must generate its power to "guide and control" in the same way that fetishes like Moa Artua do: by seducing the subject into picking it up and putting it down, over and over again.[26]

The fetishistic nature of Typeean custom becomes particularly clear two chapters later, when Tommo turns to yet another practice that once seemed superficial and irrelevant, but now seems superficial and fundamental: the taking of trophies. Tommo has frequently observed that from the ridgepole of Marheyo's house hang several large packages, containing things "held in high estimation" (82). He has also let us know that "[t]he heads of enemies killed in battle are invariably preserved and hung up as trophies in the house of the conqueror" (194). It is not particularly surprising, then, that he comes home one day to find the inhabitants of the house examining their collection of packages and, despite their best efforts, catches "a glimpse of three human heads, which others of the party were hurriedly enveloping in the coverings from which they had been taken" (232). But in Tommo's current mood, it becomes a thing of unusual horror. One of the sources of its horror is that it provides yet another example of the degree to which the Typees are invested in ornamentation. As he has already said, every house has packages suspended in it, and the contents of these packages signify the household's "relative wealth" (202). What these packages contain, for the most part, are ornaments, such as festival dresses, earrings, and white men's shoes. Though the trophy heads are not worn, they are clearly ornaments, items of "personal property" (201) that can be made to constitute personhood by being put on display. In discovering that the members of Marheyo's household like to take their heads down for a fetishistic glimpse, that is, Tommo discovers that the custom of trophy taking is, like tattooing and tabooing, more important to his hosts than he had once thought. Still more horrifying, for him, is the fact that one of the heads "was that of a white man" (233). The fearful prospect of being made into someone else's personal property, by having his head hung from a ridgepole, is simply a more Gothic version of his ongoing fear that he will be made into his own personal property, by being tattooed. In each case, he fears that he will be made to enter the social economy of savagery, now understood as a mode of existence based on the continual display and recognition of "face."

In the context of this new and terrifying vision of savagery, the specter of cannibalism suddenly reappears. It was not only "the murder of the stranger that overcame me with gloom," Tommo admits. He also "shuddered at the idea of the subsequent fate his inanimate body might have met with. Was the same doom reserved for me? Was I destined to perish like him—like him, perhaps, to be devoured, and my head to be preserved as a fearful memento of the event? My imagination ran riot in these horrid speculations, and I felt certain that the worst possible evils would befal me" (233). In part, this passage is simply a restatement of the established theory of Typee cannibalism—that it follows naturally from the enraged murder of strangers—with the twist that Tommo now understands himself to be, at least potentially, one of those strangers. But there is more to it than that; in this new formulation, cannibalism involves not only the singular moment of rage but also the repeatable moment of report. Previously, while still skeptical of the existence of cannibalism, Tommo had asked why Mehevi had not followed up on a successful repulsion of the Happars by descending into their valley and bringing back "some trophy of his victory—some materials for the cannibal entertainment which I had heard usually terminated every engagement" (130). There, the trophy corpse referred to the victory only, and was obliterated by "the diabolical malice with which they glutted their revenge upon the inanimate forms of the slain" (128). In the later passage, only part of the body is eaten, and what remains is strategically preserved as a "memento of the event," referring more to the act of cannibalism than to the victory. Cannibalism is a two-part movement, that is, consisting of enraged conquest and the public signification of that conquest. As Marnoo will later tell Tommo, if the Typees "get mad," they will "kill you, eat you, hang you head up there, like Happar Kannaka" (241). Though it is still true that cannibalism cannot be divorced from the rage against strangers, it now also seems true that it cannot be divorced from the desire to exhibit the sign of its consummation.

The threat that this new logic of cannibalism offers to Tommo's romance of masculinity is identical to the one that is offered by the tattoo and the taboo. In all these cases, he can conceive of the self-expression of Typee warriors as unmediated and boundless only as long as he can think of the desire to repeat and preserve as a trivial supplement to their otherwise spontaneous modes of feeling and acting. That distribution of relative significance has already shifted in the cases of the tattoo and the taboo, and his account of the Typeean penchant for fetishizing trophy heads has made it seem that it is in danger of shifting in the case of cannibalism. He emphasizes that danger in the digression that follows, a carefully placed reminder that Western accounts of cannibalism are notorious for consisting not of the authentic descriptions of the authentic act, but of the reports of its reports. "It is a singular fact," he says, "that in all our accounts of cannibal tribes we have seldom received the testimony of an eye-witness to the revolting practice. The horrible conclusion has almost always been derived either from the second-hand evidence of Europeans, or else from the admissions of the savages themselves, after they have in some degree become civilized" (234). If Westerners' encounters with cannibalism have never been anything other than encounters with the reports of cannibalism, which can never do anything more than suggest the departed presence of the thing itself, how can we continue to believe in the existence of that thing? If, for instance, the conviction that the Hawaiians wreaked on Cook's body "the vengeance they sometimes inflicted on their enemies" rests on nothing more than the belated confession of an old chief who is "actuated by a morbid desire for notoriety," how can it possibly be sustained? One of the implications of this digression is that the experience of being confined to the plane of simulation can weaken one's faith in the subterranean existence of the original. But Tommo's faith is not yet dead; the only thing standing in the way of an encounter with this original, he thinks, is the "craft peculiar to savages," who "are aware of the detestation in which Europeans hold this custom" and therefore "endeavour to conceal every trace of it" (234). By suggesting that Tommo still believes that the spontaneously enacted custom exists apart from its scripted simulation or dissimulation, and that its vengeful spirit can be authoritatively witnessed, the digression helps to establish the context that we need in order to feel the shock of what he actually discovers.

The scene of that discovery immediately follows. After another battle with the Happars, the Typee warriors return to the Taboo Groves bearing "three long narrow bundles" (235) that apparently contain enemy corpses, though "their thick coverings prevented my actually detecting the form of a human body" (236). The Typees immediately hold another festival in the groves, but this time Tommo is banished, and for a full day so are all the islanders but the chiefs and priests. This circumstance "strengthened my suspicions with regard to the nature of the festival they were now celebrating; and which amounted almost to a certainty. While in Nukuheva I had frequently been informed that the whole tribe were never present at these cannibal banquets; but the chiefs and priests only, and everything I now observed agreed with the account." With this report of socially exclusive banqueting reverberating in his mind, the sound of the Typees' drumming, "falling continually upon my ear," fills him with "a sensation of horror which I am unable to describe." Though he had been able to relegate the relentless tattoo of the drums to the realm of the insignificant during the Feast of Calabashes, he now takes it for granted that it is intimately related to the act of cannibalism; upon "hearing none of those noisy indications of revelry," he concludes "that the inhuman feast was terminated" (237). Possessed by a "morbid curiosity to discover whether the Ti might furnish any evidence of what had taken place" (237), he enters the groves, accompanied by Kory-Kory, and "looked fearfully round in quest of some memorial of the scenes which had so lately been acted there" (238). At first he finds nothing, but on his way out, he notices "a curiously carved vessel of wood, of considerable size, with a cover placed over it, of the same material, and which resembled in shape a small canoe. It was surrounded by a low railing of bamboos, the top of which was scarcely a foot from the ground." Driven "by a curiosity I could not repress," he takes a peep at the contents of the vessel: "[I]n passing it I raised one end of the cover; at the same moment the chiefs, perceiving my design, loudly ejaculated, 'Taboo! taboo!' But the slight glimpse sufficed; my eyes fell upon the disordered members of a human skeleton, the bones still fresh with moisture, and with particles of flesh clinging to them here and there!" (238).

What has he seen? Though Kory-Kory tries to convince him that it is nothing more than the remains of another pig feast, and though he never actually saw enemy bodies being brought into the groves, the most likely answer is that he has indeed caught a quick glimpse of moist human bones. But even if we accept that there are human bones in the vessel, we cannot take it for granted that the flesh missing from these bones has been eaten. As I will demonstrate at greater length in chapter 4, it was widely recognized throughout the early nineteenth century that the discovery of human remains did not count as evidence of cannibalism. Speaking only of the Nukuhevan custom of preserving skulls, the Russian explorer Urey Lisiansky declares in *A Voyage Round the World* (1814) that "neither their wearing them as trophies, nor offering them for sale, proves cannibalism: like other savages, they may cut off the heads of their vanquished enemies, without the idea occurring to them of eating their flesh." [27] And speaking more generally of the Nukuhevan custom of preserving entire skeletons, David Porter notes in his *Journal of a Cruise Made to the Pacific Ocean* (1815), "Their fondness for their [enemies'] bones as trophies, is evident to every person. Their skulls are carefully preserved and hung up in their houses. Their thigh bones are formed into harpoons, and sometimes are richly ornamented with carvings; their smaller bones are formed into ornaments to be hung round their necks, representing figures of their gods: they are also converted into fan-handles, form a part of the ornaments of their war conchs, and in fact compose part of every description of ornament where they can possibly be applied." When the Nukuhevans say that they eat human flesh, Porter argues, they are probably using the word *eat* in an extended sense, and mean only that they keep the bones of enemies as trophies. [28] This is why Tommo warned us that we would ultimately have only a "reason to suspect" the existence of cannibalism, and why he told us earlier in the chapter that all he saw in the vessel was the presence of something "which *indicated* the existence of the practice" (233; my emphasis). All he actually discovers, at the end of the quest for the thing itself, is another one of its traces. [29]

This does not mean that nothing can be concluded from this scene. Given the description of the vessel—ornamented with carvings, larger than normal, and surrounded by a miniature, purely decorative fence— it is highly probable that its contents are not trash, the unsignifying residue of a maddened feast, but souvenirs, the signifying products of a significant event. In Tommo's words, they are the "memorial of the scenes which had so lately been acted there," just as the heads strung up in Marheyo's house are "fearful memento[s] of the event." But they are also something more than souvenirs, in that they are intended to do something more than preserve a private memory for the chiefs and priests alone. Concealed in plain sight under a ceremonial cover, like the heads wrapped in cloth and hung inside houses, the bones are coded as objects of "high estimation," metonymically conferring a high social estimation on their owners. They are in this sense monuments, signifying not only the worth of the tribe in relation to its enemies, but also the worth of the chiefs and priests in relation to the rest of the people of Typee. With his discovery of the bones, that is, Tommo confirms the truth of the story he remembers hearing while at Nukuheva Bay, in which it was emphasized that Typeean cannibalism was confined to the aristocracy. In doing so, he implicitly throws his support behind the explanation of cannibalism I discussed at the end of the previous chapter: that it is motivated by a desire to create terror in others, in order to establish and maintain the social distinctions that structure relations between and within societies. The skeleton wakes him from his dream of a king without a scepter, a society in which representations of status are either nonexistent, as he suggests in his remarks on the absence of money, or insignificant, as he suggests in his discussion of the Feast of Calabashes. It is now quite obvious that inequalities of power among the Typee are real, and that they depend not only on gender—a fact he had noticed earlier, with some dismay[30]—but also on class. The source of those inequalities, just as obviously, is the complex and shifting system of distinctions that is put into play every time a Typee gets a tattoo, observes a taboo, or puts a trophy on display.

One of the next steps we could take would be to declare that Type-ean cannibalism doesn't exist at all. But as we have seen, Tommo considers that to be an unjustifiably absolute conclusion. The point where he leaves us is the point at which his dream of vengeful cannibalism, governed by a spirit of spontaneity and sensibility, has stiffened into the nightmare of terrorist cannibalism, governed by a spirit of ostentation and rigidity. What Melville wants to get across to his readers, above all else, is the horror of this moment of transition. It is the same horror that Tommo feels whenever the ordinarily "lively countenances of these people," which "are wonderfully indicative of the emotions of the soul," are masked by a "peculiarly stern expression" (142). Upon being escorted into Marheyo's house for the first time, he and Toby are confronted by a group of men who "regarded us with a fixed and stern attention." One of these men sets himself before them and looks at Tommo "with a rigidity of aspect under which I absolutely quailed. . . . Never before had I been subjected to so strange and steady a glance; it revealed nothing of the mind of the savage, but it appeared to be reading my own" (71). The rigid face seems to detach itself from the being behind it and to become an agent in its own right—a relationship between being and semblance that Tommo conceives of as the polar opposite of his own naked expressiveness. It is only temporary—the mask soon relaxes into the solicitous face of Mehevi—but as with tattoos, taboos, and trophies, it is repeated more often than Tommo would like. When he attempts to leave the Taboo Groves upon hearing that Toby has returned, Mehevi's face again takes on "that inflexible rigidity of expression which had so awed me on the afternoon of our arrival at the house of Marheyo" (119). As he pushes past Mehevi, the rest of the men in the groves arrange themselves around him, with the same expression on their faces. "It was at this moment," he says, "when fifty savage countenances were glaring upon me, that I first truly experienced I was indeed a captive in the valley. The conviction rushed upon me with staggering force, and I was overwhelmed by this confirmation of my worst fears. I saw at once that it was useless for me to resist, and sick at heart, I reseated myself upon the mats, and for the moment abandoned myself to despair" (119–20).

This response is precisely echoed in his response to the vessel full of bones. In the aftermath of that discovery, he says, "the full sense of my condition rushed upon my mind with a force that I had never before experienced" (238). As before, the realization that rushes in on him is that there is not "the slightest prospect of escape" (238), and his reaction is to conclude "that nothing remained but passively to await whatever fate was in store for me" (239). In this reaction, he again differentiates his own "humanity" from a "savagery" that he now conceives of as rigid and artificial. In the same way that his horror at the prospect of having his face tattooed allows him to identify himself with "humane" characteristics like sensibility and sincerity, his passive despair at the realization that he is a captive allows him to suggest the existence of an ontological gulf between himself and his savage captors. The essence of captivity, as he has told us at the beginning of this chapter, is the feeling that there is "no one to whom I could communicate my thoughts; no one who could sympathise with my sufferings" (231). The sign of his humanity is that he longs for an audience that will make it possible for him to offer up sincere expressions of thoughts and feelings; the sign of the Typees' savagery is that they are too oriented toward masking to provide him with such an audience. As he had suggested earlier, however, not all the Typees are as "rigid" as the members of the aristocracy. When his injured leg again swells up, confining him to Marheyo's house, it again becomes clear that the less privileged tribespeople are more capable of a humane response to his misery. In Marheyo's house, rather than being surrounded by the terrorist insignias of Typeean chiefs and priests, he is surrounded by solicitous islanders like Marheyo, Fayaway, and Kory-Kory, who express nothing but "deep commiseration" (243–44). In a reversal of his earlier expressions of preference for the apparently unfettered life of the men who frequented the bachelor's hall in the Taboo Groves, he now aligns himself with the sphere of "Home" and "Mother," the two English words that he teaches Marheyo (248). No longer able to believe in the sincerity and sensibility of those men, he divides the Typees into two camps—the savagely rigid elites and the humanely pliant masses—and places his sympathies on the "feminine" side.

This division of the tribe constitutes his final word on the character of the Typees. In the last chapter, when he finally makes his escape, the conflict between these two camps is what makes it possible for him to get to the boat that will take him to a waiting whaleship. Out of the blur of this escape, two diptychic images have imprinted themselves on his mind. While the intratribal conflict was taking shape, "old Marheyo came to my side, and I shall never forget the benevolent expression of his countenance" (248). And in the final moment of the escape, after thrusting a boat hook into Mow-Mow, the one-eyed chief, he sees him "rise to the surface in the wake of the boat, and never shall I forget the ferocious expression of his countenance" (252). In Tommo's memory, the face of Typeean society has two expressions—the unforgettably benevolent and the unforgettably ferocious—and each of them belongs to a distinct class of people. But because the benevolent expression remains constant throughout the book, and because it is already a familiar feature of domestic iconography, Tommo has given it relatively little attention, even though he ultimately decides in its favor. His more sustained interest lies in the other expression, which had once seemed to stand for a "waywardness" that stereotypes of Polynesian behavior could not contain. By bringing us to an awareness of the falseness of these stereotypes, he has tried to initiate the Saidian project of discovering the true nature that lies beneath the false name. The result, however, has been the discovery that beneath the false name that Westerners have given to the Typees lie the false names that they give to themselves. This is the lesson of his discovery of the bones, and it is also the lesson of Mow-Mow's face, bobbing up in the wake of his boat. The last object that Tommo sees in the territory of the Typees is this mutilated face, its features frozen in the stiff, hyperbolic expression that he now thinks of the deepest, truest essence of "savagery."

"The Terror of Their Name"

[Marnoo] related circumstantially the aggressions of the French—their hostile visits to the surrounding bays, enumerating each one in succession—Happar, Puerka, Nukuheva, Tior,—and then starting to his feet and precipitating himself forward with clenched hands and a countenance distorted with passion, he poured out a tide of invectives. Falling back into an attitude of lofty command, he exhorted the Typees to resist these encroachments; reminding them, with a fierce glance of exultation, that as yet the terror of their name had preserved them from attack. . . . (*T*, 137–38)

If the argument of this chapter were to be reduced to a single sentence, it would be this: *Typee* is a book about the terror of savagery, understood as the strategic and ceaseless ornamentation of one's self with signs. As Marnoo reminds the Typees in the above passage, this strategy of ornamentation has been their most powerful weapon in their resistance to colonialism. Because "[t]heir very name is a frightful one" (24), the Typees have been scrupulously avoided by most Westerners, and those who have visited have not stayed long enough "to gain any insight into their peculiar customs and manners" (6). The anticolonial implications of their strategy of self-naming run even deeper than this, however. What Tommo ultimately learns is that their deployment of ornamentation is so pervasive that it screens out even the well-intentioned visitor in search of "insight." There is no authentic interior visible within the name Typee; it is simply an object they metonymically append to themselves, like a tattoo, for the sake of its effects. With this rotation away from the possibility of insight, Tommo begins to sound less like a precursor of Said or Fanon than like a precursor of Homi Bhabha. As I noted in the introduction, Bhabha makes the same kind of half-turn away from the vision of colonialism as the totalized imposition of false names on subjects whose names are originally and ultimately true. The truly terrifying fact about these "savages," Bhabha says, is that although they repeatedly suggest to the colonialist that the names and places he has assigned to them are false, they do so "in the mocking spirit of mask and image" (*Location,* 62). For both Melville and Bhabha, the discursive authority of the colonialist is more anxious than we might think, and the subjectivity of the native more opaque.

I want to conclude by directing a final question of evidence at my own argument. If this is indeed the point that Melville intends to make in *Typee,* and if this point is indeed made in the language of a popular discourse, we might expect to find it corroborated by the responses of contemporary reviewers. As far as I have been able to tell, however, no such corroboration exists. In their readings of the narrative's violent end, the reviewers of *Typee* tended to follow one of two approaches, neither of which is identical to my own. For most of these reviewers, the conclusion signified a belated acknowledgment that savagery is indeed different from and inferior to humanity. By cannibalizing the Happars, and by assaulting Tommo and his rescuers, the Typees betray themselves: "however gentle or good-natured" they may at first appear, they are "savages after all."[31] In his reaction to the discovery of their savagery, moreover, Tommo betrays himself as well. Though he has portrayed Typeean society as the realization of "the Pantisocracy which Southey, Coleridge, and others, fancied the perfection of society during the phrensy of the French Revolution," his intense desire to escape makes it clear that "his theory and practice were different." [32] In two ways, then, this group of reviewers represented the violence of the narrative's conclusion as the return of the repressed; although the Typee valley *appears* to be a place where the visitor "need not fear the single rap at the door which dissipates his day-dreams" (Higgins and Parker, *Reviews*, 29), we are in fact awakened in the end to a real and unavoidable distinction between savagery and humanity. And while Tommo *appears* to long "for the cannibal condition of innocence and non-civilization . . . [t]he truth is, he felt himself a prisoner" (12), so much so that he was willing to risk killing a man in order to escape. For these reviewers, as for most later critics, the dramatic development of *Typee* terminates with the interruption of the ideal by the actual, at which point fiction falls away from fact and theory falls away from practice.

The major alternative to this approach was the argument that *Typee* exists entirely in the realm of the ideal; even in the conclusion, when we would appear to have touched down in fact, we again lift off into fiction. To those reviewers who considered the book to be less a travel narrative than a melodrama, every aspect of Typeean savagery, including the threat of cannibalism, was nothing more than a stage device. The London *Spectator* cites as an example of Melville's "tendency to make too much of things" his account of "the cannibal feast, which he is sure took place after a fight with the inhabitants of a neighbouring valley, when bundles consisting of human bodies wrapped in leaves were, as he infers, brought in" (Higgins and Parker, *Reviews*, 7). Another reviewer asserts that "all the conduct of the natives towards him, both in his stay and at his escape, is involved in such mere mystery as appears to us the voluntary resort of the story-teller only, who chooses, by the vague horror of cannibalism, to keep to the last what young ladies and the magazines written for them entitle the 'thrilling interest' of the tale" (75). From this perspective, *Typee* tells us nothing about the relative merits of savagery and civilization; the combination of the nightmare image of cannibalism and the dream image of primitive bliss tells us only that Melville is interested in producing a sensational effect on his audience. As far as Evert Duyckinck was concerned, there was nothing wrong with this. In his review of the book, he declared himself pleased by its "rose colored account of a tropical race which seems pictured to us cold northerners like the performers in some rich ballet rather than as actual inhabitants of this labor stricken earth," and even *more* pleased by the repeated threats of savagery, which "impart that pleasing horror of melodrama without which the enjoyment of a mere picture of happiness is entirely ineffective" (Higgins and Parker, *Reviews*, 17). In this tradition of reading, the tension between pleasure and threat does not inspire moral or social analyses; it simply prompts the observation, favorable or otherwise, that this tension is produced by the self-consciously theatrical machinations of the author, who has chosen to throw in "a dash of romantic Rousseauism, with now and then a shadow of the Cannibal as a corrective" (18).

My case would obviously be stronger if some reviewer had noticed a link between these two interpretive positions, which we can loosely define as the ethnographic and the melodramatic. Rather than reading the disarticulated bones ethnographically, as an authentic expression of savage nature, this reviewer would have suggested that their display is an example of narrative's pervasive theatricality. And rather than reading this theatricality as an expression of the author's fondness for melodrama, he or she would have suggested that it proceeds, at least in part, from the Typees themselves. But though the absence of this kind of definitive corroboration is less than ideal, it does not invalidate, in itself, the argument that I have made. Those who review books are not the only ones who read them; it remains possible that some of Melville's contemporaries made the same connection between *Typee* and the discourse on cannibalism that I have made here. More important, the coexistence of the ethnographic and melodramatic interpretations suggests that the only thing standing in the way of such a reading was the reviewers' inability or unwillingness to reflect on the implications of the points where those interpretations crossed. As Charvat reminds us, the reason Melville had to make such an effort to "get readers to entertain propositions with him rather than to accept commitments" is that his readers were inclined to seek out the places that shored up their existing commitments, not the places that compromised or eroded them (*Profession*, 246). Most important, perhaps, the reading I have offered is borne out by Melville's subsequent work; in *Moby-Dick,* "Benito Cereno," and elsewhere, he would continue to use cannibalism as the emblem of a "savagery" in which the illusion of transparency shades into the truth of pretense.[33] These are not smoking guns; they are just pieces of circumstantial evidence, assembled into a more or less compelling approximation of proof. But as *Typee* itself suggests, that is all we can ever hope to have.

Would that a man could do something & then say—It is finished.—not that one
thing only, but all others—that he has reached his uttermost, & can never ex-
ceed it. But live & push—tho' we put one leg forward ten miles—its no reason
the other must lag behind—no, *that* must again distance the other—& so we go
till we get the cramp & die.—*Correspondence*

Within two years of the publication of *Typee*, Melville was
sick of it. This is not a particularly surprising fact; as
he would write in the margins of his *Complete Poetical
Works of John Milton*, purchased in 1849, "He who thinks
for himself never can rema[i]n of the same mind."[1] All the same, if
we want to address the relationship between *Typee* and Melville's later
work, we need to have some way of explaining *why* he became sick of it.
He told the English publisher of *Mardi* that "[u]nless you should deem
it *very* desirable do not put me down on the title page as 'the author of
Typee & Omoo.' I wish to separate '*Mardi*' as much as possible from
those books" (C, 114–15). While waiting to go ashore at Dover in late
1849, he observed in his journal, "This time tomorrow I shall be on land,
& press English earth after the lapse of ten years—then a sailor, now
H. M. author of 'Peedee' 'Hullabaloo' & 'Pog-Dog'" (J, 12). And most
famously, in a letter to Hawthorne written while in the last stages of
composing *Moby-Dick*, he complained, "What 'reputation' H. M. has is
horrible. Think of it! To go down to posterity is bad enough, any way;
but to go down as a 'man who lived among the cannibals'! When I speak
of posterity, in reference to myself, I only mean the babies who will probably be born in the moment immediately ensuing upon my giving up the
ghost. I shall go down to some of them, in all likelihood. 'Typee' will be
given to them, perhaps, with their gingerbread" (C, 193). Taken together,
what these remarks imply is that Melville had come to think of *Typee* as

both juvenile—a "Peedee," fit for toddlers gumming gingerbread—and sordidly spectacular—a "Hullabaloo," trumpeting the exotic adventures of "a man who lived among the cannibals." Together with its sequel, it now signified his own youthful bondage to the "narrative of *facts*" and necessitated his subsequent efforts to prove to himself and to "those who may take any interest in the matter, that a *real* romance of mine is no Typee or Omoo, & is made of different stuff altogether" (C, 106).

One reason for his distaste, surely, was that the version of *Typee* that he expected to go down to posterity was the revised American edition, issued in late 1846 after the first edition had been accused of being immoral and fraudulent. When putting the best face on these revisions, in an 1846 letter to his English publisher John Murray, Melville declared that the new edition pared away "those parts not naturally connected with the narrative," imparting "a unity to the book which it wanted before." Having been "pursuaded that the interest of the book almost wholly consists in the *intrinsick merit of the narrative alone*," he suggested that it would be better to remove not just the passages referring to the missionaries, but all passages "foreign to the adventure," in order to assist "the wide & permanent popularity" of a work he considered to be "calculated for popular reading, or for none at all" (C, 56). In the preface to the revised edition, which he appears to have enclosed with the above letter to Murray, he repeats this argument in very similar terms, explaining that "as the interest of the book chiefly consists in its being the history of a remarkable adventure, in revising it, several passages, wholly unconnected with that adventure, have been rejected as irrelevant. . . . Thus revised, the book is simply a record of the adventure, interspersed with accounts of the islanders, and occasional reflections naturally connected with the subject" (T, 361). The purpose of the revision was to remove all those "reflections" that were not "naturally connected" to the story line, in order to leave the "adventure" relatively uninterrupted. These two descriptive terms would return in an 1854 letter to the American publisher George Putnam, in which he promises that *Israel Potter* "shall contain nothing of any sort to shock the fastidious. There will be very little reflective writing in it; nothing weighty. It is adventure. As for its interest, I shall try to sustain that as well as I can" (C, 265). It is hard to mistake the tone of these comments. As far as Melville is concerned, narratives of adventure are both lighter and safer than reflective writing: they are the kinds of literary commodities that publishers demand and that he himself disdains. In shearing *Typee* of its unconnected reflections, he is succumbing to the persuasion that it is, in essence, a lower-order work, "calculated for popular reading, or for none at all."[2]

Accordingly, whereas his subsequent contempt must be considered to be directed at the revised edition, it should be clear that the act of revising implied an element of contempt for the original edition. In declaring that "the interest of the book almost wholly consists in the *intrinsick merit of the narrative alone*" — that is, in "adventure" — he is pronouncing *Typee* to be nothing more than a commodity. It is because he is newly aware of the niche that his book occupies in the literary marketplace that he suggests to Murray, later in the same letter, that the title of the English edition ought to be changed from *A Narrative of a Four Months' Residence among the Natives of a Valley of the Marquesas Islands* to *Typee*. He gives two reasons for this change: first, " 'Typee' is a title *naturally suggested by the narrative itself*"; second, its "very strangeness and novelty, founded as it is upon the character of the book — are the very things to make 'Typee' a popular title" (*C*, 57). In light of the argument of the previous chapter, it might seem that by insisting on the name *Typee* he is attempting to point up the degree to which that name operates in the context of the narrative as a destabilizing, anticolonial force. In fact, what it reveals is his understanding that in the context of the marketplace for exotic travel narratives, the "strangeness and novelty" of the name "are the very things to make 'Typee' a popular title." When Murray agrees to the change, Melville writes back to say that he is rejoiced "that the magic, cabalistic, *tabooistic* 'Typee' will hereafter grace the title-page of all subsequent English editions of the book" (*C*, 65). In the letter in which he offers Murray the manuscript of *Omoo,* moreover, he is even more explicit about his conviction that the sales of an exotic travel narrative can only benefit from a title that can be construed as a kind of fetish object. "The title of the work, may be thought a curious one," he says, but he would like it "to remain untouched — its oddity, or uniqueness, if you please conveys some insight into the nature of the book. It gives a sort of Polynesian expression to its 'figure-head' " (*C*, 78). Given this understanding of his early titles as tabooistic figureheads, marking the books they named as objects whose value derived from their capacity to conjure up strange and novel scenes — much like the Polynesian paddles he brought back from his voyages and gave as presents to friends — it should be no surprise that it was the titles in particular that embarrassed him later.[3] They signified the degree to which those books, no matter what else they might be said to do, were articulated within the context of the literary marketplace as exotic curios; they signified the degree to which he had been complicit in the process of articulating them as commodities; and they signified the degree to which the reputation that these books had brought him had made him into an exotic curio as well.

The consideration of the marketplace context of *Typee* obviously complicates the argument I made at the end of the previous chapter. There, I suggested that the terror of savagery, especially as expressed in the opacity of the name Typee, presents an obstacle to both humanist and racist accounts of its essence. But as Melville's subsequent response to *Typee* should indicate, if the book is considered in terms of its status as a popular travel narrative, addressed to readers in search of a succession of comfortably distanced experiences of novelty, the terror that dominates the end of the book reappears—uncomfortably, from the standpoint of the postcolonial writer and reader—as titillation. This is something that is not sufficiently emphasized in Homi Bhabha's landmark analyses of colonial discourse: the recognition that the terror-effect of what he calls "colonial mimicry" is by no means inevitable. As Gayatri Spivak has pointed out in an essay called "Marginality in the Teaching Machine," the unsettling conception of marginality that emerges from a postcolonial strategy aimed at the "displacing and seizing of a previous coding of value" can be quite easily stabilized and familiarized within a teaching machine where "ethnicist academic agendas make a fetish of identity." Inside and outside the classroom, the project of "tampering with the authority of storylines" is for the most part "retranslated into the autonomy of the art object or its status as ethnic evidence, the particular voice of the marginal."[4] Even an act conceived of as a pure disarticulation can itself be disarticulated, in other words; though Bhabha occasionally insists that the native's strategy of mimicry "poses an immanent threat to both 'normalized' knowledges and disciplinary powers" (*Location*, 86), there is never anything "immanent" about the meaning of a sign. Upon being set down in the literary or academic marketplace, a postcolonial displacement is all too likely to be displaced in turn, retranslated into the erotic discourse of the inscrutable.

By bringing this realization home, the critical reception of *Typee* and *Omoo* contributes in no small degree to Melville's famous shift, in *Mardi*, from the travel narrative to the romance. In a book whose only organizational principle seems to be the idea of escape, one of the things that Melville himself is most desperately trying to escape is his growing reputation as the marketer of titillating images of savagery.[5] Shortly after the book has gotten underway, he openly declares his new creed: "All things form but one whole; the universe a Judea, and God Jehovah its head. Then no more let us start with affright. . . . Let us welcome even ghosts when they rise. Away with our stares and grimaces. The New Zealander's tattooing is not a prodigy; nor the Chinaman's ways an enigma.

No custom is strange; no creed is absurd; no foe, but who will in the end prove a friend" (*M*, 12–13). In doing so, he does not mean to suggest that the world of this book will be a world without wonders; *Mardi* is still, in the broadest sense, a narrative of travel, punctuated by repeated encounters with strangeness and novelty. The difference is that the "new world" our narrator seeks "is stranger far than his, who stretched his vans from Palos. It is the world of mind; wherein the wanderer may gaze round, with more of wonder than Balboa's band roving through the golden Aztec glades" (557). In a move that is a necessary by-product of the effort to disarticulate novelty and wonder from the discourse on savagery and rearticulate them within the discourse on mind, Melville attempts to establish intuition, rather than familiarity with discursive conventions, as the ground on which author and reader will meet: "The universe is all of one mind" (428). At the same time, however, he is aware that the announcement of the universality of the mind is no guarantee of that universality, insofar as "fiery yearnings their own phantom-future make, and deem it present" (557). In fact, what the pursuit of wonder in the mind reveals to us is that this mind can only be defined by what escapes it. In Babbalanja's climactic dream, we learn that even gods grope after something missing in them, that the only thing that is "universal and eternal" is loss, that it is sadness that "makes the silence throughout the realms of space" (636). After asking us to advance from divisive curiosity to unifying insight, that is, Melville asks us to recognize that the object of that insight, the mind, is not in fact a universal ground. The truly universal object is the thing that always escapes the mind, gliding just beyond the wondering gaze; a thing that is somehow always "behind thee, not before" (694).

Though *Mardi* was an extraordinarily important step in Melville's artistic and intellectual development, he was well aware that it was an awkwardly executed step. Accordingly, after earning some much-needed cash with a pair of adept but relatively inconsequential travel narratives, he went at it again. In the product of those labors we encounter a second and far more powerful engagement with the issues that were raised by the writing, marketing, and reception of *Typee*. Whereas the distinction between the curiosities of experience and the wonders of the mind was merely proclaimed in *Mardi*, it is dramatized at length in *Moby-Dick*, in a concerted effort to draw readers beyond their desire for the most vulgar forms of novelty. What he draws his readers toward, at least initially, is an idealized vision of savagery very much like the one he had offered in the middle chapters of *Typee*, embodied this time in a cannibal named Queequeg. But Queequeg soon fades from sight, and our attention is redirected toward Ishmael's doomed effort to represent the whale and Ahab's equally doomed effort to kill it. By means of these two failures, Melville dramatizes more effectively than before that though the mind may be a more humane horizon of experience than discourse, both horizons are nevertheless constituted by what must forever lie beyond them. As Ishmael says at one point, if the world were "an endless plain, and by sailing eastward we could for ever reach new distances, and discover sights more sweet and strange than any Cyclades or Islands of King Solomon, then there were promise in the voyage. But in pursuit of those far mysteries we dream of, or in tormented chase of that demon phantom that, some time or other, swims before all human hearts, while chasing such over this round globe, they either lead us on in barren mazes or midway leave us whelmed" (*MD*, 237). The "beyondness" that Tommo discovered in his encounter with savagery in *Typee* was not the accidental effect of unusual circumstances, in other words, and should be neither dismissed as an irrelevance nor stared at as a curiosity. If *Typee* asked us to feel the terror of the object that cannot be brought into a body of knowledge—the terror that lay at the dark heart of the discourse on cannibalism—*Moby-Dick* asks us to recognize this object as a constitutive absence, the blind spot in relation to which all vision is defined.

Sights

Among the various ships lying in Prince's Dock, none interested me more than the Irrawadday, of Bombay. . . .

Every Sunday, crowds of well-dressed people came down to the dock to see this singular ship: many of them perched themselves in the shrouds of the neighboring craft, much to the wrath of Captain Riga, who left strict orders with our old ship-keeper, to drive all strangers out of the Highlander's rigging. It was amusing at these times, to watch the old women with umbrellas, who stood on the quay staring at the Lascars, even when they desired to be private. These inquisitive old ladies seemed to regard the strange sailors as a species of wild animal, whom they might gaze at with as much impunity, as leopards in the Zoological Garden.—*Redburn*

Moby-Dick begins with a reverie that reminds us of where we left off in *Mardi*. Whenever he has fallen into a fit of depression, Ishmael tells us, he longs to go to sea. In case we might be inclined to take this as a sign of eccentricity, he insists that "[t]here is nothing surprising in this. If they but knew it, almost all men in their degree, some time or other, cherish very nearly the same feelings towards the ocean with me" (*MD*, 3). In water, we all see the same thing that Narcissus did: a reflection that splits the self into subject and object, initiating our desire for an unconditional and therefore unattainable reunion. The "tormenting, mild image" that Narcissus tried to grasp is the image that "we ourselves see in all rivers and oceans. It is the image of the ungraspable phantom of life; and this is the key to it all" (5). The ground where Ishmael asks his reader to meet him is not discourse but mind, and the object he asks us to focus on is not savagery but an insubstantial, unstable phantom. That phantom does not exist only in water, moreover; for Ishmael, it also looms in "the overwhelming idea of the great whale himself. Such a portentous and mysterious monster roused all my curiosity." He confesses that the supplementary wonders of a whaling voyage—"all the attending marvels of a thousand Patagonian sights and sounds"—did play some part in his decision, insofar as he is "tormented with an everlasting itch for things remote." But his desire "to sail forbidden seas, and land on barbarous coasts" is decisively subordinated to his desire to grasp that dream image of the whale: "one grand hooded phantom, like a snow hill in the air" (7).

Critics have been rightly puzzled by the turn the narrative takes at this point. Rather than immediately launching us in our pursuit of this phantom-whale, Melville ushers us through a series of preliminary chapters in which Ishmael makes the acquaintance of a Pacific islander named Queequeg. As Ishmael loiters toward the beginning of his metaphysical quest in the pleasant company of this cannibal, it begins to seem that we have unaccountably swerved from the end of *Mardi* back to the middle section of *Typee*. Even more surprisingly, once Ishmael finally does board the *Pequod*, his good friend Queequeg simply drops out of the narrative, reappearing only as an allegorical marker of savagery, virtually indistinguishable from the other harpooners. This peculiar circumstance has generally been explained in one of two ways: either Queequeg is less important than he appears to be in the first fifth of the book, or Queequeg is more important than he appears to be in the last four-fifths of the book. In the first case, the argument is that the book does not begin in earnest until Ahab shows up; in the second, the argument is that the memory of the friendship between Ishmael and Queequeg persists throughout the book as an alternative to Ahab's vision of self, world, and God.[6] But Ishmael's characterization of Ahab cannot be so easily separated from his characterization of Queequeg, and Queequeg cannot be so easily reduced to his status as Ishmael's "bosom friend." In at least two ways, Queequeg prepares us for the advent of Ahab: first, by drawing us away from a mode of interpretation that Melville now feels he did not sufficiently fend off in *Typee,* and second, by embodying an ideal "savagery" against which Ahab, among others, will be measured. That ideal is emphatically not a relational humanism; it is, instead, a more fully elaborated version of the masculinist ideal we encountered in the middle chapters of *Typee.* More important, as Queequeg's disappearance should suggest, this ideal is nothing more than a "phantom-future" conjured up by "fiery yearnings." Once we have taken a close look at the ways in which Queequeg prepares us for Ahab's quest, we will have to take an equally close look at the ways in which Ahab's quest helps us to revise our understanding of the ideal that Queequeg embodies. If Queequeg sets up the impossible pursuit of that "grand hooded phantom," that pursuit resituates our perspective on Queequeg in the most fundamental of ways.

The problem with Ishmael's initial way of seeing, as we discover in the chapter called "The Spouter-Inn," is that he is too willing to content himself with the cheap thrill of a conventional exotic sight. Much has been made of his attention to the "boggy, soggy, squitchy picture" in the entryway of the inn, and the "long, limber, portentous black mass of something hovering in the centre" (12), which he ultimately takes to be another version of that phantom image of the whale that is towing him out to sea. But when he is done looking at this "portentous something," he immediately turns to face the opposite wall of the entryway, which "was hung all over with a heathenish array of monstrous clubs and spears. Some were thickly set with glittering teeth resembling ivory saws; others were tufted with knots of human hair; and one was sickle-shaped, with a vast handle sweeping round like the segment made in the new-mown grass by a long-armed mower. You shuddered as you gazed, and wondered what monstrous cannibal and savage could ever have gone a death-harvesting with such a hacking, horrifying implement" (13). As in the earlier passage in which he distinguishes between the concentrated attraction of the singular whale image and the more diffuse appeal of "a thousand Patagonian sights and sounds," Ishmael hereby establishes a contrast between higher and lower forms of curiosity, and makes it clear that he is liable to be drawn in either of these directions. Though he is capable of prolonged efforts to sharpen his vision of half-seen things, he also likes to look at the kinds of exotic objects that allow him to conjure up some shudder-provoking image. When he gets to the bedroom he will soon be sharing with a strange harpooner, his attention is quickly drawn to one of the harpooner's possessions, something that looks like "a large door mat, ornamented at the edges with little tinkling tags something like the stained porcupine quills round an Indian moccasin." After slipping his head through the hole in the middle, he says, he "went up in it to a bit of glass stuck against the wall, and I never saw such a sight in my life. I tore myself out of it in such a hurry that I gave myself a kink in the neck" (20). Unlike Narcissus's water image, which prompts a desperate pursuit, Ishmael's image of himself as a white man gone native prompts a thrill of horror and an instantaneous backing away. As long as he retains his obvious attachment to these kinds of racially charged spectacles, it will be impossible for him to take up the metaphysical inquiry that lies ahead.

The scene that follows is, accordingly, much more than an incidental moment of comic relief: it is a conscious effort to propel the reader into and through this voyeuristic interest in savage sights by first inciting it and then making it an object of mockery. Ishmael has been informed by the landlord, Peter Coffin, that he will have to share his bed with an unnamed harpooner, and after some teasing banter about the harpooner's desire to "sell his head," Coffin has let him know that this harpooner "has just arrived from the south seas, where he bought up a lot of 'balmed New Zealand heads (great curios you know), and he's sold all on 'em but one, and that one he's trying to sell to-night" (19). Late that night the harpooner enters the room, carrying a light and the embalmed Maori head that he has been trying to peddle around town—"a ghastly thing enough," Ishmael tells us. From his concealed position in the bed, Ishmael waits with "eagerness" for the light to fall on the harpooner's face; when it finally does, "good heavens! what a sight! Such a face! It was of a dark, purplish, yellow color, here and there stuck over with large, blackish looking squares." Operating under the assumption that the harpooner is a white man, he concludes that he must have "fall[en] among the cannibals" and "been tattooed by them" (21). But when the harpooner undresses, revealing a purplish-yellow body marked all over with the black stains of tattooing, it is at last "quite plain that he must be some abominable savage or other" (22). Rather than interrupt this private spectacle of savagery, Ishmael watches him go through some ceremonial devotions before a small black idol, unable "to break the spell in which I had so long been bound." The harpooner himself brings the show to an close; after lighting his tomahawk-pipe, he extinguishes the lamp. With that, "this wild cannibal, tomahawk between his teeth, sprang into bed with me. I sang out, I could not help it now; and giving a sudden grunt of astonishment he began feeling me." Rolling toward the wall, Ishmael pleads with him "to keep quiet, and let me get up and light the lamp again." When the harpooner begins flourishing his tomahawk around him, saying things like "you no speak-e, dam-me, I kill-e," Ishmael screams for the landlord. "Stop your grinning," he shouts, when Coffin finally appears, lamp in hand. "[W]hy didn't you tell me that that infernal harpooner was a cannibal?" (23). "I thought ye know'd it," the landlord answers. "[D]idn't I tell ye, he was a peddlin' heads around town?" (23–24).

The humor of the scene derives from Ishmael's bombastic horror, which derives, in turn, from his naïve and vulgar desire for what he will later call "curious sight[s]" (30). When Coffin assures him that "Queequeg here wouldn't harm a hair of your head" (23), and when Queequeg tells him to get back in the bed in "a really kind and charitable way" (24), it becomes clear that Coffin and Queequeg are the insiders in the world of New Bedford, and that Ishmael is the exotic. To his credit, Ishmael recognizes this almost immediately: "What's all this fuss I have been making about, thought I to myself—the man's a human being just as I am: he has just as much reason to fear me, as I have to be afraid of him. Better sleep with a sober cannibal than a drunken Christian" (24). Because he now realizes the laughableness of his behavior, he does not protest when the landlord meets him with a grin the next morning, declaring instead that "if any one man, in his own proper person, afford stuff for a good joke to anybody, let him not be backward, but let him cheerfully allow himself to spend and be spent in that way" (29). As he spends and is spent, sharing in laughter directed at his own inexperience, he begins to align himself with the values of the experienced residents of New Bedford. Upon taking a walk down the street, he is even more impressed with how foolish he was to be "astonished at first catching a glimpse of so outlandish an individual as Queequeg circulating among the polite society of a civilized town." Here, "actual cannibals stand chatting at street corners; savages outright; many of whom yet carry on their bones unholy flesh. It makes a stranger stare" (31). Now that he is less of a stranger, however, the sight that is "still more curious, certainly more comical," is the sight of the staring strangers themselves, the "bumpkins" from rural New England who are "as green as the Green Mountains whence they come" (31–32). His critical perspective on these bumpkins marks the distance he has traveled since the previous evening, when he too acted as though he were "but a few hours old" (32), so innocent of the world that he transformed a fellow human with an unfamiliar appearance into the object of what Ahab will call "a doltish stare" (164).

In his critique of this way of seeing, Melville anticipates the modern critique of the racist gaze.[7] It is somewhat stunning that this has gone unremarked, but when Ishmael complains to Coffin that he was not told that his bedmate was a cannibal, he has no way of knowing anything about Queequeg's dietary history. His complaint is that he did not know that his bedmate was *not white*. Contemporary readers would have had little or no difficulty cracking this code; in the mid-nineteenth century, "cannibal" was a relatively common racial epithet, applied to "savages" in general and Pacific islanders in particular.[8] It is explicitly used in that sense, in fact, by two of the other characters we meet in the opening chapters. On the *Moss*, the packet that Ishmael and Queequeg take from New Bedford to Nantucket, the captain warns Queequeg against throwing his passengers into the air by saying, "I'll kill-e *you*, you cannibal, if you try any more of your tricks aboard here; so mind your eye" (61). And as soon as Captain Peleg of the *Pequod* catches sight of Ishmael with Queequeg, he "loudly hailed us from his wigwam, saying he had not suspected my friend was a cannibal, and furthermore announcing that he let no cannibals on board that craft, unless they previously produced their papers" (87). Like Ishmael, these two men have no way of knowing if Queequeg has in fact eaten human flesh; they are applying the word *cannibal* to this Pacific islander in precisely the same way that they would apply the word *nigger* to a black person. Melville had already spoken out against this habit of speech in *Omoo*; in *Moby-Dick*, he takes the further step of characterizing it as a sign of juvenile vision, in which one directs "a doltish stare" at a superficial mark of difference and comfortably defines one's identity against it.[9] In a subsequent interchange between Ahab and the captain of the *Bachelor*, it is quite clear that the unlovely effects of this kind of prejudice against Pacific islanders include the infantilization of the subject and the dehumanization of the object. After asking if the captain has seen the white whale, and learning that he doesn't even believe in him, Ahab uncharacteristically asks him, "Hast lost any men?" "Not enough to speak of," replies the captain, hands thrust in pockets "in self-complacent testimony of his entire satisfaction." "[T]wo islanders, that's all" (495).[10]

The most interesting aspect of Melville's critique of the racist gaze is that it is linked, in at least two ways, to a critique of institutions that support that gaze. To begin with, the image of Ishmael hidden in the darkness of the room, spellbound by the lamp-lit striptease of the harpooner, is clearly intended to suggest the relationship of audience to theatrical spectacle. This suggestion is reinforced by the fact that when

Ishmael is trying to decide whether Queequeg is a tattooed white man or an abominable cannibal, he is choosing between two figures who were familiar presences on the popular stage. In Melville's day, white men bearing tattoos and tales of adventures among cannibals were the unlettered versions of travel narratives, drawing curious crowds throughout Europe and America.[11] Like the war instruments that Ishmael stares at in the entryway of the Spouter-Inn, these tattooed men allowed their viewers to conjure up and shudder at a distanced vision of the "savages" who must have hammered those marks into that helpless white body. Though this spectacle is pleasurable enough, Ishmael's absorption becomes even more profound when he discovers that Queequeg is not just the metonymic trace of savagery but savagery incarnate. With the exposure of Queequeg's chest, it becomes clear to Ishmael that he is getting a free performance of an even more titillating kind of stage show, the exhibition of a "cannibal" resembling those who could be seen in such Manhattan venues as Peale's Museum in the 1830s and P. T. Barnum's American Museum in the 1840s. In late 1831 and early 1832, the patrons of Peale's Museum were treated to the sight of "two Cannibals of the Islands of the South Pacific," an exhibition that helped to inspire a play by Samuel Woodworth called *The Cannibals,* which was successfully produced at the Bowery Theater in 1833.[12] In 1842, around the same time that General Tom Thumb and the Fiji Mermaid were making him famous, Barnum exhibited a reportedly cannibalistic Fijian chief named Vendovi at the American Museum, and in 1845, his customers had the pleasure of staring at Harrewaukay, the Cannibal Chief of New Zealand. One of the things that this context suggests is that when Ishmael calls his theatrically displayed Pacific islander a "wild cannibal," he is operating under the influence of a brand of racism that has been shaped by the tradition of the public exhibition. This suggests in turn that when Queequeg douses the light and jumps into bed with Ishmael, erasing the distance between audience and theatrical spectacle, Melville is intervening not only in the racist gaze as such, but more specifically in that gaze as it has been conditioned by the institution of the exotic spectacle.[13]

The second form of Melville's institutional critique has to do with the embalmed Maori head that Queequeg is trying to sell. Another important but unremarked feature of the bedroom scene is the fact that Ishmael is surprised when the head peddling harpooner turns out to be a Pacific islander. The reason for his surprise is that head peddling was a *white man's* business, so much so that it had become established as a conventional sign of the "savageness" of the white market for exotic curiosities. The trade had been in existence since the 1770s, at first supplying museums, fairs, and private collectors with the occasional "curio," and then, beginning around 1820, with a flood of them. With the sudden increase in the number of local buyers, made possible by the missionaries' establishment of a relatively safe trading environment, the process of supply was transformed. Prior to European contact, the Maori had apparently preserved the heads of their friends as memorial objects and the heads of their enemies as trophies of victories, to be exchanged once hostilities had ended. But as the British ensign Alexander McCrae noted in 1820, "since Europeans have shown a disposition to procure them they have become like everything else an article of commerce."[14] One effect of this transformation was an alteration of the goals and methods of Maori warfare. The whaling captain Frederick Beechey reported in 1832 that Hongi, a Maori chief who had been "educated in England, was availing himself of the superiority he had acquired, and was making terrible ravages amongst his countrymen, whose heads, when dried, furnished him with a lucrative trade."[15] This mercantilization of warfare irrevocably transformed whatever meaning might originally have been attached to the preservation of heads. The missionary William Yate stated a few years later that this "inhuman traffic" had been carried on to such a "great extent" that "the natives have ceased altogether to preserve the heads of their friends, lest by any means they should fall into the hands of others and be sold; which, of all ideas, is the one most horrible to them" (*Account,* 131). Instead of referring to some supposedly authentic context of supply, the heads had begun to refer primarily to the "inhuman traffic" that now produced them. What the heads now signified was the white demand for heads and, to a certain extent, even the white supply; Charles Wilkes would later observe, "It is generally thought that many of the heads thus sold have been prepared by the white runaway convicts, who have learned the mode of doing this from the natives" (*Narrative,* 2:399).

By 1830, the head trade was widely recognized to be an embarrassing sign of the vulgar curiosity and contemptuous possessiveness animating Europeans and Americans in New Zealand. In a particularly ugly incident in early 1831, a British captain who had purchased heads from one Maori tribe went on to trade with the tribe from which those heads had come. While he had some members of this tribe on board, he "went into his cabin, and brought out a bag which contained the heads, and emptied them out, in the presence of the natives: some recognised their fathers—others their sons—some their brothers, and others near friends and relations. The weeping and lamentation caused by the indignity thus put on the relics of the departed were appalling; and all on board vowed revenge" (Yate, *Account*, 131). After the news of the incident reached the colonial governor in Sydney, he issued a proclamation outlawing the importation of embalmed heads, both because "there is strong reason to believe that such disgusting traffic tends greatly to increase the sacrifice of human life among savages" and because of "the scandal and prejudice which it cannot fail to raise against the name and characters of British traders, in a country with which it has now become highly important for the merchants and traders of this Colony, at least to cultivate feelings of mutual goodwill" (Elder, *Letters and Journals*, 500). The problem with the head trade was not just that it led to the deaths of Maoris, that is, but that it interfered with the material interests of the mother country by defaming "the name and characters of British traders." As James Busby would observe a year later, after being appointed British Resident to New Zealand, the profitable trade in flax could only be pursued if the Maoris had "a respect for the character of the English, and a dread of their power," and both of these things were diminished by the sordid enterprises of "persons not having authority from the British Government, to trade in the Islands" (*Authentic Information*, 67, 69). By all accounts, the efforts to suppress this delegitimating trade had a quick and permanent effect. Following his visit to New Zealand in 1839, Charles Wilkes reported, "The trade in native curiosities is not so great as it used to be, particularly in tattooed heads. . . . So effectually has the fine prevented the traffic, that it is an extremely difficult matter to obtain a head; they are as rare now as they have been common heretofore" (*Narrative*, 2:399–400).

Once we have these facts at our disposal, the conversation between Ishmael and Coffin at the end of the bedroom scene begins to make more sense. In declaring that he expected Ishmael to know that the head-peddler was a cannibal, Coffin is quite obviously "skylarking" (29), as Ishmael will later say. The reason he had such a "diabolically funny" expression on his face when he first informed Ishmael that his prospective bedmate was a head-peddler was that he could expect Ishmael to assume that this "dark complexioned chap" (15) was a white man; this is the necessary basis of the joke that he is playing on him. The principal point of the joke, as I have suggested above, is to raise Ishmael's curiosity to the point of terror and then turn a mirror on him, revealing to him his own "greenness." But there is another point to it as well; at the same time that it is intended to shock Ishmael into a recognition of his own inexperience, it is also intended to shock him into reflection on the implications of something he already knows. In his punch line—I thought you'd know that anyone carrying a head around would have to be a cannibal—Coffin is assuming, in mockery, a "greenness" so intense that it outgreens Ishmael; as his actions have demonstrated, even Ishmael knows enough of the world to assume that a head-peddler is a white man. Ishmael's problem is that he has not reflected sufficiently on his understanding that there are white men in the world who are "engaged in such a cannibal business as selling the heads of dead idolators" (19). If one operates under the assumption that there are white men in New England who ply a "cannibal business"—meaning a business fit only for cannibals, characterized by an inhumane contempt for the body—there is no good reason to get worked up by the sight of "actual cannibals." This lesson is brought still further home when Ishmael himself goes out peddling and succeeds in "disposing of the embalmed head to a barber, for a block" (58). Besides being infantile and dehumanizing, the gaze that seeks out and stops at the signs of racial difference also denies the secret knowledge that this difference is constructed, that Christians are just as likely to treat bodies with contempt as cannibals are. By reminding his readers of the white control of the New Zealand head trade in the 1820s and 1830s, Melville is initiating the book-long process of calling out his readers' secret knowledge that whites are as "savage," if not more so, than the racial others they define themselves against.

The conclusions that follow from this are simple but profound. By dramatizing the personal and social fixation on the sign of the cannibal, Melville allows us to see that the word *cannibal* names a fantasy object against which self and society are defined. In Ishmael's panicked reaction, we witness the "greenness" of those whose curious gaze stops too short; in the visual allusions to the spectacle of savagery—the theatrical display of tattooed men, cannibals, embalmed heads—we are reminded that Ishmael's private neurosis is tied to a very public social fantasy. Though these opening chapters may seem at first to be "light," they in fact represent what Slavoj Žižek calls "[t]he crucial step in the analysis of an ideological edifice," which is

> to detect, behind the dazzling splendour of the element which holds it together ("God", "Country", "Party", "Class" . . .) this self-referential, tautological, performative operation. A "Jew," for example, is in the last resort one who is stigmatized with the signifier "Jew"; all the phantasmic richness of the traits supposed to char-

acterize Jews (avidity, the spirit of intrigue, and so on) is here to conceal not the fact that "Jews are not really like that," not the empirical reality of Jews, but the fact that in the anti-Semitic construction of a "Jew," we are concerned with a purely structural function. (*Sublime Object*, 99)

By means of Ishmael's hysteria and subsequent mortification, Melville suggests that the spectacle of savagery is indeed a "purely structural function," holding down a place in the structures of self and society in order to keep those interrelated structures from blowing away. Like the "Jew," the "cannibal" is nothing more than a fetish, an object used to distract one's attention from the thing for which it substitutes and from the structure that produces it. Now feeling that he at least partially participated in that process of fetishization in *Typee*, Melville asks us to let the spectacle of the cannibal "wane," a word he uses in *Moby-Dick* to denote the dying down of wonders into commonplaces. When "lit up by the preternatural light" of the corpusants, Queequeg's tattooing burns "like Satanic blue flames on his body" — but that vision of demonic savagery "waned at last with the pallidness aloft; and once more the Pequod and every soul on her decks were wrapped in a pall" (506).

The question that faces us now is this: What are we left with once the dazzling spectacle of savagery has waned? One answer that has been very popular among critics of *Moby-Dick* is that we are left with the real Queequeg, the one with his arm thrown over Ishmael on the morning after their first encounter, lit only by the ordinary light of day. Just as Ishmael will later warn us not to trust "the artificial fire, when its redness makes all things look ghastly," but to view our world by the light of "the natural sun," so (the argument goes) does he intend us to proceed from an inauthentic perception of savagery, conditioned by the artificial light of the spectacle, to the authentic perception that begins to emerge once that light has begun to die. But in at least two ways, this celebration of the authentic perception of savagery stops too short. First, when it comes time to say exactly what that authentic perception consists of, critics have tended to do little more than offer variations on the standard readings of *Typee:* it is either a humanistic recognition of the identity of self and other, or a precocious anticipation of "cultural relativism." We can and should be much more specific in our descriptions of what Ishmael learns to see in Queequeg. Second, as I suggested earlier, when it comes time to address the fact that Queequeg fades rather suddenly into the margins of the text, most critics fall back on a quasi-theological conception of Queequeg as a symbolic figure shedding goodness without end, even at those times when Ishmael seems to have forgotten that he exists. It makes much more sense, however, to recognize in this disappearance a second waning. The values of savagery, as revealed by the light of the "natural sun," are simply an attractive prospect; as Queequeg's disappearance suggests, and as Ahab's quest will demonstrate, our only true ground is the fact that light and life wane. Watching the "final wanings" of a dying whale, accompanied by "that strange spectacle" of "the turning sunwards of the head," Ahab observes that "here, too, life dies sunwards full of faith; but see! no sooner dead, than death whirls round the corpse, and it heads some other way" (496–97).

Insight

One night I was returning to the ship, when just as I was passing through the Dock Gate, I noticed a white figure squatting against the wall outside. It proved to be one of the Lascars who was smoking. . . .

Finding that he spoke good English, and was quite communicative, like most smokers, I sat down by *Dallabdoolmans,* as he called himself, and we fell into conversation. So instructive was his discourse, that when we parted, I had considerably added to my stock of knowledge. Indeed, it is a God-send to fall in with a fellow like this. He knows things you never dreamed of; his experiences are like a man from the moon—wholly strange, a new revelation. If you want to learn romance, or gain an insight into things quaint, curious, and marvelous, drop your books of travel, and take a stroll along the docks of a great commercial port.—*Redburn*

Upon waking the next morning to find himself in Queequeg's embrace, Ishmael experiences a brief, hallucinatory feeling of strangeness. He describes the feeling as something like one he had experienced as a child, when, in the moment of waking, he had felt in his hand "a supernatural hand," and next to his bed, "the nameless, unimaginable, silent form or phantom, to which the hand belonged." If you "take away the awful fear," he says, "my sensations at feeling the supernatural hand in mine were very similar, in their strangeness, to those which I experienced on waking up and seeing Queequeg's pagan arm thrown round me." But that sense of Queequeg as a friendly version of that childhood "phantom" gradually wanes, as "at length all the past night's events soberly recurred, one by one, in fixed reality" (26). By the sober light of day, Queequeg is not a nameless, unimaginable phantom, not the exotic "sight" that Ishmael had made him out to be. This waning leads to two changes

in the way that Ishmael sees his bedmate. First, he now thinks of Queequeg as an autonomous subject who should by rights be immune from
the curious stare of a stranger. Although Ishmael is subsequently "guilty
of great rudeness" in "staring at him from the bed, and watching all
his toilette motions," he makes it clear that this is not a sanctioned way
of seeing, but a sign of "my curiosity getting the better of my breed-
ing" (27). Second, as a consequence of granting Queequeg an interior
that is properly his own, he begins to want to gain access to that interior, to advance from inauthentic sight to authentic insight: "Wild he
was; a very sight of sights to see; yet I began to feel myself mysteriously
drawn to him" (51). Though he is "hideously marred about the face—
at least to my taste—his countenance yet had a something in it which
was by no means disagreeable." That "something" is the soul of masculine savagery: "Through all his unearthly tattooings, I thought I saw the
traces of a simple honest heart; and in his large, deep eyes, fiery black
and bold, there seemed tokens of a spirit that would dare a thousand
devils" (49–50).

These "strange feelings" (51) signal a decisive shift away from the
mode of relation governed by the logic of the spectacle. Caught up by
what Jean Baudrillard has called "the system of collection," Ishmael has
until now been unable "to grasp the partner, the supposed object of
desire, as that singular totality we call a person"; in his accumulation of
exotic "sights," he has been "collect[ing] and eroticiz[ing] his own being,
evading the amorous embrace to create a closed dialogue with himself."[16] Considered in this light, the "amorous embrace" of Queequeg
would seem to offer the possibility of an open dialogue with the other,
conceived of as a "singular totality." That is to say, the sense of touch,
with its connotations of unstructured intimacy, would seem to have become newly privileged over the sense of sight, with its connotations of
distance and hierarchy. For those critics who argue that the Ishmael-
Queequeg relationship provides a salvific alternative to the Ahab-whale
relationship, these kinds of moments, when Melville seems to privilege
touch over sight, constitute the moral heart of the novel.[17] The most
famous of these moments occurs in the chapter called "A Squeeze of the
Hand," when "a strange sort of insanity" comes over Ishmael as he and
his coworkers are squeezing lumps of spermaceti into fluid, and he finds
himself "continually squeezing their hands, and looking up into their
eyes sentimentally." "Come," he envisions himself saying to them, "let us
squeeze hands all round; nay, let us all squeeze ourselves into each other;
let us squeeze ourselves universally into the very milk and sperm of kind-

ness." While in this state, he imagines that it is possible not just to shake hands but to "*splice* hands" (88), in the words of Captain Peleg: to make of self and other a single organic being. As an image of idealized inter-subjective relations, the squeezing of spermy hands is often compared to the images we are presented with in "The Monkey-Rope," where Ishmael and Queequeg are "wedded" by "an elongated Siamese ligature"; in "The Log and Line," where Ahab tells Pip that "thou art tied to me by cords woven of my heart-strings"; and in "The Grand Armada," where Starbuck sees a whale cub "tethered to its dam" by "long coils of the umbilical cord." In all these cases, the model of selfhood structured by sight appears to give way to a model of selfhood in which the other joins with the surface of the body, rather than phantasmatically entering the eye.

But if Ishmael's willingness to "splice" with others can be said to signal an alteration of his mode of perception, it does not necessarily follow that he *does* splice with others, or that splicing is, in itself, a viable alternative to the spectacle. The distinction is crucial: though it is clear that he *desires* intersubjective connectedness and that this desire signals a repudiation of the spectacle, it is not at all clear that this desire is *realized,* or even that it is realizable. In the monkey-rope passage, for instance, the cord that ties Ishmael to Queequeg signifies a relationship characterized by nothing other than the principle of causality: if Queequeg does x, Ishmael will experience y. If this is, as Ishmael suggests, "the precise situation of every mortal that breathes" (320), then the effect of this chapter is to *diminish* the prospect of a selfhood based on intersubjective connection, insofar as it indicates that the desire to splice is continuously liable to be obstructed and disrupted by forces beyond one's control. Ahab's announcement that Pip has touched his "inmost centre" (520) also becomes less appealing upon further inspection; the effect of this bond, as Ahab delights in observing, is that Pip is as obedient to Ahab's will "as the circumference to its centre" (535). The bond between mother and child represented by the whale's umbilical cord signifies a similar imbalance of power, and like the bond between Ahab and Pip, it is ultimately severed, leaving the cub with a trailing cord that can become, "in the rapid vicissitudes of the chase" (388), the instrument of its death. Even if we have recourse to "A Squeeze of the Hand," the place in the book where the ethic of touch is taken most seriously, we find that the dream of "squeezing that sperm forever" is explicitly represented *as* a dream. Though Ishmael is now "ready to squeeze case eternally," he acknowledges that this could only be possible in heaven; in this world, "attainable felicity" inevitably consists of a discontinuous succession of a variety of love objects: "the wife, the heart, the bed, the table, the saddle, the fire-side, the country." In his vision of paradise, moreover, he sees not a circle of angels around a tub of sperm, but "long rows of angels . . . each with his hands in a jar of spermaceti" (416). Though sperm squeezing may be pleasurable, it is in the end a solitary pleasure, in which the squeezer is left alone with his (or her) incommunicable sensations and sentiments.

The implication of these facts is that touch operates in *Moby-Dick* more as the rhetorical negation of the ethic of the spectacle than as a separate ethic in itself. By expressing a willingness to splice with Queequeg, Ishmael indicates that he has overcome the dread that was conventionally associated with the experience of being touched by a cannibal, a dread inseparable from the conditions of the spectacle. This dread was generally composed, in early-nineteenth-century travel narratives, of equal parts "homosexual panic" and "cannibalistic panic." [18] Jacques de Labillardiere reports in 1802 that during an encounter with the natives of New Caledonia, some of them "came up to the most robust of us, and felt the muscular parts of our arms and thighs, exclaiming *Kapareck!* with an air of admiration, and even something more, which was not very pleasant to our feelings." The inference "that these people considered the most musculous parts a very agreeable dish" made it "easy for us to explain why they frequently felt our arms and legs, manifesting a violent longing." [19] The sexual overtones of this "violent longing" are even more evident in a scene from the 1831 narrative of the missionaries George Bennet and Daniel Tyerman, in which they and the crew of their ship are suddenly overpowered by visiting Maoris. From his captive position on the other side of the deck, Bennet sees that the Maoris surrounding Tyerman "were, from time to time, handling his arms, his sides, and his thighs, while, from the paleness of his countenance—though he remained perfectly tranquil—it was evident that he was not unaware of the meaning of such familiarities; namely, that they were judging, with cannibal instinct, how well he would cut up, at the feast which they anticipated." [20] In this context, it is not surprising that when Ishmael is first touched by the strange Pacific islander, he invests that touch with the "something more" that offends Labillardiere's sensibilities and causes Tyerman to go pale and still; only when Queequeg has begun to grope him does he call him a "wild cannibal" (23), and only after Queequeg has pantomimically promised not to "touch a leg of ye" (24) does he get back into bed. It *is* surprising that by the next morning, Queequeg's touch has lost its power to provoke this kind of "awful fear." Though Ishmael does inform Queequeg of "the unbecomingness of his hugging a fellow male in that matrimonial sort of style" (27), this is essentially an invocation of the fastidiousness of others. He himself no longer seems to share the inclination to recoil from the touch of a fellow male, any more than he shares the inclination to treat the sight of interracial intimacy as a freakish spectacle; he has nothing but contempt for the people who "stared" when he and Queequeg walked down the street together, "not at Queequeg so much—for they were used to seeing cannibals like him in their streets,—but at seeing him and me upon such confidential terms" (58).

It would certainly be possible for Ishmael to proceed from this critique of the spectacle to an affirmation of a subjectivity based on the privileging of touch over sight. As I have already suggested, however, what he actually affirms—initially, at least—is a subjectivity based on the privileging of insight over sight. In the scene in which he experiences those "strange feelings" about Queequeg, this sensation does not result from the experience of touch but from his careful "scanning" of the "soothing savage" (50, 51). This reformed way of seeing, oriented toward Queequeg's hidden interior rather than his curious surface, is what leads Ishmael to "try a pagan friend"; in the process of scanning, he gains insight into aspects of Queequeg's being that act on him like "magnets" (51). The bonding experience that begins here reaches its culmination in another highly visual scene, in which Ishmael watches Queequeg save a bumpkin from drowning, and then, watching him casually lighting his pipe, imagines him saying, "It's a mutual, joint-stock world, in all meridians. We cannibals must help these Christians" (62). Most important, once Ishmael has acquired this ability to read the signs of Queequeg's inner being, their physical intimacy comes to an end; on the *Pequod*, they are very rarely even in the same scene with one another. If we accordingly take insight, defined as a sympathetic perception of the interior life of the other, to be the principal alternative to the curious stare, we find ourselves confronted by a problematic that is fundamentally at odds with the one that is generated by the opposition between sight and touch. When touch is taken to be the privileged term, readers are able to treat the book as the romance of a form of knowledge that exists outside Ahab's vortex of interpretation. But when insight is taken to be the privileged term, the opposition is not so stable, and the attention that both Melville and Ishmael give to Ahab, the man of "lower layer[s]" (163), is more explicable. Beginning from the problematic of the sight/insight opposition, therefore, I want to try to answer two questions: What does Ishmael learn to see in Queequeg, and to what extent is the content of that insight capable of serving as the narrative's ethical foundation?

The short answer to the first question is that he sees the same thing that Tommo sees in the middle chapters of *Typee:* an idealized masculine savagery, characterized by an absolute sincerity and spontaneity. In the Christian world, Ishmael sees only "hollow courtesy"; in Queequeg, he sees "a nature in which there lurked no civilized hypocrisies or bland deceits." If Queequeg were like the Christians Ishmael has known, his "sudden flame of friendship would have seemed far too premature, a thing to be much distrusted; but in this simple savage those old rules would not apply" (51). Despite his exposure to the Western world, which has led to degeneracies like head peddling, Queequeg remains, in the fullest sense of the word, aboriginal. In *Omoo,* Melville tells us that though the Polynesian "habit of making bosom friends at the shortest possible notice" seems to have "had its origin in a fine, and in some instances, heroic sentiment," the "sophisticating influences" of Westerners have since caused it to decay "into a mere mercenary relation" (*O,* 152). But Queequeg knows nothing of such "civilized hypocrisies"; immediately after becoming Ishmael's bosom friend, he divides all his money with him and gives him his embalmed head. The same distinction between coloniality and precoloniality is implicit in the later scene in which Queequeg reminisces about "a great battle wherein fifty of the enemy had been killed by about two o'clock in the afternoon, and all cooked and eaten that very evening" (*MD,* 85). Insofar as Queequeg's confession of cannibalism is not motivated by a desire to terrorize, but by an innocent and disinterested sincerity, it is yet another sign that he is not quite of our world. Here as elsewhere, Queequeg appears to turn back the colonial clock, restoring the lost ideal of a spontaneous, sincere, and masculine savagery.

But though spontaneity and sincerity are useful terms, they do not quite capture the essence of Melville's ideal of savagery. In the discussion that follows, I have broken that ideal down into what seem to me to be its three major components: the Queequegian virtues of inconsistency, irreverence, and gameness, arrayed in opposition to the excesses of consistency, reverence, and heedlessness that characterize Ahab, Starbuck, and Stubb. It is worth taking some time to get this right, both because it clearly matters to Melville and because it can help us learn how to distinguish this form of the discourse on savagery from humanism, racism, and culturalism, as those terms are ordinarily understood. The Melville of *Moby-Dick* is not a humanist, if by a humanist we mean someone for whom all gaps between and within people are illusory; as I tried to suggest above, the notion that such gaps are mere accidents of circumstance, and that experience as such is essentially holistic, is never presented to us in this book as a positive, unqualified basis of thought or behavior. Neither is he a racist, if by a racist we mean someone who believes in a hierarchical ordering of human types in which his or her type is preeminent, and consequently disavows all signs that this ordering is constructed and that he or she is constituted on its basis. As in *Typee,* Melville works very hard in *Moby-Dick* to bring these kinds of unacknowledged disavowals to light. Finally, he is not a culturalist, if by a culturalist we mean someone who attributes human differences to the incompatibility of the various thought-worlds that structure the experiences of social groups, an incompatibility that is either permanent or relatively permanent. Though he calls attention to the gaps covered up by the discourses of humanism and racism, he has no interest in reconstructing the blueprints of the mechanisms with which various peoples make sense of their world. The discursive position he occupies is one for which we have as yet no proper name, a position based on the relatively common nineteenth-century idea that there is an imperfect fit between the socioevolutionary opposition of savagery and civilization and the moral opposition of savagery and humanity. To name and evaluate this position, we must learn how to specify what Melville means by inconsistency, irreverence, and gameness—which is to say, what he means by Queequeg, as seen in the sober light of day.

Inconsistency. This aspect of Queequeg's character is evoked most vividly in Ishmael's description of his bedmate's arm, which is "tattooed all over with an interminable Cretan labyrinth of a figure, no two parts of which were of one precise shade—owing I suppose to his keeping his arm at sea unmethodically in sun and shade, his shirt sleeves irregularly rolled up at various times" (25). The arm is a sign, for Ishmael, of Queequeg's unmethodical, irregular, and therefore interminable mode of self-expression; because he always obeys his spontaneous impulses, Queequeg's actions constitute a series without any visible pattern or end. Queequeg's cheek, too, is "barred with various tints" (30), a sight that leads Ahab to refer to Queequeg and his fellow harpooners as the "Pagan leopards" with "cheeks of spotted tawn," and to characterize them accordingly as "unrecking and unworshipping things, that live, and seek, and give no reasons for the torrid life they feel!" (164). Such perfectly spontaneous beings necessarily express themselves "disjointedly" (162): Queequeg may be seen giving "his undivided attention to beefsteaks, done rare," at one moment, but Ishmael finds him "sitting there quietly digesting and smoking" in the next (30); he may have "brained his foes" with his tomahawk-pipe, but with that same instrument he subsequently "soothed his soul" (100). It is no surprise that in the chapter called "The Mat-Maker," the man with whom Ishmael intends to "boldly dip into the Potluck of both worlds" (57) becomes an allegorical emblem of this principle of randomness. When Queequeg slices the weave of the mat, he does so "carelessly and unthinkingly" (214), his "impulsive, indifferent sword, sometimes hitting the woof slantingly, or crookedly, or strongly, or weakly, as the case may be." If the warp and woof of the mat may be said to represent the intersections of fate and free will, Ishmael thinks to himself, then Queequeg's "easy, indifferent sword must be chance" (215).

In such inconsistency, Ishmael declares, we encounter an image of our natural and ideal state. The most exhilarating fact about the sea, to him, is that it "will permit no records" (60), that it is a place "where to traditions no rocks furnish tablets" (497). This recordlessness is what he assumes has driven Bulkington back to sea; away from "the treacherous, slavish shore," Bulkington has discovered a mode of existence that approaches "the highest truth, shoreless, indefinite as God" (107). His response to the sea is not unusual, Ishmael thinks: anyone who lives long enough in "the varying outer weather" will "inhale its fickleness" and become "capricious and unreliable" (212); anyone who is adrift long enough in "exiled waters" will lose "the miserable warping memories of traditions and towns" (190); anyone who takes "all nature's sweet and savage impressions fresh from her own virgin, voluntary, and confiding breast" will be "led to think untraditionally and independently" (73). This is what he has in mind when he says, "Long exile from Christendom and civilization inevitably restores a man to that condition in which God placed him, *i.e.* what is called savagery. Your true whale-hunter is as much a savage as an Iroquois. I myself am a savage, owning no allegiance but to the King of the Cannibals; and ready at any moment to rebel against him" (270). To be a savage is to be, like the weather, consistent only in one's inconsistency: without allegiance, mostly; loyal to one being, at least for now. It is to assume the position assumed by Daggoo in the whaleboat, where "the noble negro to every roll of the sea harmoniously rolled his fine form," thereby "sustaining himself with a cool, indifferent, easy, unthought of, barbaric majesty" (221). Though Flask, mounted on Daggoo's shoulders, stamps with impatience to see the whale, Daggoo's harmonious rollings are undisturbed. "So I have seen Passion and Vanity stamping the living magnanimous earth," Ishmael says, "but the earth did not alter her tides and seasons for that" (222).

To a certain degree, Ahab's spirit of vengefulness may be thought of as a natural expression of this "savage" spirit of inconsistency. Immediately after insisting to Starbuck that he *could* strike the sun if it insulted him, "since there is ever a sort of fair play herein," Ahab makes a point of disavowing the apparent implication that he himself is answerable to the rule of reciprocity: "But not my master, man, is even that fair play. Who's over me? Truth hath no confines" (164). By scorning fair play, Ahab liberates himself from what Pierre Glendinning's mother will call the "chain and ball" of "that vile word Propriety" (*P,* 195). Justice and propriety demand that our actions be recountable in a publicly acceptable manner, and Ahab will have none of that. The origin of his rage, after all, was his discovery of a gap between the scene of his experience and the scene of its narration; he first gives way to an "inflamed, distracted fury" at the whale *before* his leg is bitten off, when he swims from a wrecked whaleboat "into the serene, exasperating sunlight, that smiled on, as if at a birth or a bridal" (*MD,* 184). The appeal of an act of vengeance carried out in this spirit of "fury" is that it bypasses the logical deadlock of justice. That deadlock, stated briefly, is that there can be no such thing as an absolutely just sentence, insofar as it commits itself to proving something that it is impossible to prove: that nonidentical events—the transgressive act and the retributive act—are in fact identical. As Melville would later observe, because avengers refuse the impossible task of naturalizing the relationship between crime and punishment, their "retaliation is apt to be in monstrous disproportion to the supposed offense; for when in anybody was revenge in its exactions aught else but an inordinate usurer?" (*BB,* 80). What the appearance of such "monstrous disproportion" signifies, accordingly, is that one has freed oneself from the false principle of equivalency embodied in the scales of justice. Rather than attempting to close the gap between his private experience of loss and the publicly recognizable forms of narration, Ahab tries again and again to shape the world to his own private experience by means of acts and words that are essentially blasphemous, in that they refuse to acknowledge the established proportions of Justice and Providence.

But to hold himself free, forever, from all tradition and proportion, Ahab must hold himself perfectly still. Because he places such a tremendous value on the spirit of inconsistency, he must become monstrously consistent; because he takes pleasure in conceiving of himself as "[t]hat wild madness that's only calm to comprehend itself" (*MD,* 168), he must avoid all the things that might restore the ordinary mutations of mood: his pipe, sunny weather, Pip's love, the image in Starbuck's eye. Ahab may be free from the constraints of propriety, in other words, but he is nonetheless fixed in place by his attachment to the idea of himself as the demonic assaulter of Providence. Though he was the one who had that blasphemous idea, initially, that blasphemous idea now has him, so much so "that it all but seemed the inward mould of every outer movement" (160). Having yielded up "all his thoughts and fancies to his one supreme purpose[,] that purpose, by its own sheer inveteracy of will, forced itself against gods and devils into a kind of self-assumed, independent being of its own" (202). The paradox that emerges from passages like this is that the rejection of all external impositions of consistency engenders a purely independent self that is doomed to obey its own principle of consistency: "Ahab is for ever Ahab" (561). When he says "I now prophesy that I will dismember my dismemberer," he sets in motion a self-authored determinism that tows him along with it, no longer as an agential subject but as an instrumental "fulfiller" (168). In one of Ahab's last moments of introspection, he seems to recognize, however briefly, that absolute and permanent freedom, sought in a spirit of vengeance, is identical to determinism: " 'What is it, what nameless, inscrutable, unearthly thing is it; what cozening, hidden lord and master, and cruel, remorseless emperor commands me; that against all natural lovings and longings, I so keep pushing, and crowding, and jamming myself on all the time; recklessly making me ready to do what in my own proper, natural heart, I durst not so much as dare? Is Ahab, Ahab? Is it I, God, or who, that lifts this arm?' " (545). By setting and meeting a standard of consistency so steadfast that it has become self-existent, a "purpose" so grand that it has assumed sovereignty not only over Justice and Providence, but also over the inconsistent longings of his "proper, natural heart," he has destroyed the seat of selfhood that he initially set out to defend.

Irreverence. While scanning Queequeg in the aftermath of Father Mapple's sermon, Ishmael observes "a certain lofty bearing about the Pagan, which even his uncouthness could not altogether maim. He looked like a man who had never cringed and never had had a creditor" (50). He looks nothing like Mapple's Jonah, in other words, a man whose status as a "God-fugitive" is made evident "[i]n all his cringing attitudes" (46); nor does he look like the sailors on the *Jeroboam,* who "cringed" before the mad Shaker named Gabriel, "sometimes rendering him personal homage, as to a god" (315). Though Queequeg does worship a pocket idol named Yojo, Ishmael is repeatedly struck by the fact that Queequeg considers this idol to be nothing more than "a rather good sort of god, who perhaps meant well enough upon the whole, but in all cases did not succeed in his benevolent designs" (68). When first witnessing the spectacle of this worship, Ishmael notices that at its conclusion, Queequeg "took the idol up very unceremoniously, and bagged it again in his grego pocket as carelessly as if he were a sportsman bagging a dead woodcock" (23). Upon entering the Spouter-Inn after Mapple's sermon, Ishmael finds Queequeg "gently whittling away at [Yojo's] nose" (49), and upon bursting into their room at the Try-Pots, he finds him squatting with Yojo on his head, but remaining, in spite of this, "altogether cool and self-collected" (83). Like Tommo praising the Typees for their ability to play with their customs, Ishmael makes it clear that he admires Queequeg's cool refusal to become caught up in the logic of propitiation. The sight of the squid may be to Starbuck "a thing of portents," but "to Queequeg it was quite a different object" (282)—nothing more than the metonymic sign of the sperm whale who feeds on it, announcing the nearness of their prey. And though Queequeg does hold up a lamp when he and the rest of his boat's crew are stranded by storm and darkness, he does not do so in any spirit of supplication, but in the same uncringing spirit in which he holds Yojo on his head: "There, then, he sat, holding up that imbecile candle in the heart of that almighty forlornness. There, then, he sat, the sign and symbol of a man without faith, hopelessly holding up hope in the midst of despair" (225).

In his characterization of Queequeg, Melville quite clearly means to repeat one of the central propositions of *Typee*: that savages do not believe unconditionally in their gods. In *Omoo*, he had identified that spirit of faithless faith as a quality "more akin to hypocrisy than any thing else. It leads [the Polynesians] to assume the most passionate interest, in matters for which they really feel little or none whatever; but in which, those whose power they dread, or whose favor they court, they believe to be at all affected" (O, 175). Though Queequeg's attitude toward Yojo and the lamp pole is indeed akin to hypocrisy, in that he clearly thinks of these forms as nothing more than forms, it is not hypocritical in the ordinary sense of the term, insofar as it has as its aim the preservation of private space, rather than the securing of public status. It is an attitude that allows him to remain "entirely at his ease"; even when "thrown among people as strange to him as though he were in the planet Jupiter," he is "content with his own companionship; always equal to himself" (MD, 50). Though Ishmael's sermon on "the rare virtue of interior spaciousness" takes whales as its text, Queequeg could just as easily have been its point of reference: "Oh, man! admire and model thyself after the whale! Do thou, too, remain warm among ice. Do thou, too, live in this world without being of it. Be cool at the equator; keep thy blood fluid at the Pole. Like the great dome of St. Peter's, and like the great whale, retain, O man! in all seasons a temperature of thy own" (307). What these two passages suggest, taken together, is that Queequeg's admirable ability to remain "equal to himself" is a product of his "savage" predisposition to live ironically, to be in the world but not of it. Though Ishmael makes it clear that such perfect coolness is an unattainable ideal—"how easy and how hopeless to teach these fine things!"—he also makes it clear that it *is* an ideal. He himself is no Queequeg, "[b]ut even so, amid the tornadoed Atlantic of my being, do I myself still for ever centrally disport in mute calm" (389). Only by refusing the persuasions of "orthodoxy," defined as the "obstinate survival of old beliefs never bottomed on the earth" (309), can one enjoy, however imperfectly or intermittently, such interior spaciousness.

If the obverse of Queequeg's inconsistency is Ahab's paradoxical excess of consistency, the obverse of Queequeg's irreverence is Starbuck's paradoxical excess of reverence. Starbuck is introduced to us as a man unusually capable of maintaining "a temperature of his own": he seems "prepared to endure for long ages to come, and to endure always, as now; for be it Polar snow or torrid sun, like a patent chronometer, his interior vitality was warranted to do well in all climates" (115). But this interior vitality is doomed to decay, Ishmael warns us, precisely because Starbuck is so concerned with interiority as such. That concern manifests itself in two closely related ways, which can best be stated as follows: to preserve his sense of his own interior purity, he reads the surfaces of others as indices of interior horrors that are not properly his own. Listening to the howling crew and the silence of Ahab's cabin, he cries, "Oh, life! 'tis now that I do feel the latent horror in thee! but 'tis not me! that horror's out of me! and with the soft feeling of the human in me, yet will I try to fight ye, ye grim, phantom futures!" (170). To maintain his superstitious belief in the purity of his own humanity, that is, he gives way to a superstitious belief in "phantom" horrors "latent" in the world outside him. The consequence of this, Ishmael says, is that he is vulnerable to the influence of "[o]utward portents and inward presentiments" (116), and especially vulnerable to those "spiritual terrors, which sometimes menace you from the concentrating brow of an enraged and mighty man." Ishmael is deeply pained by the lesson of Starbuck's case—that an excessive attachment to the ideal of self-containment leads to the derealization of that ideal—because he feels that "man, in the ideal, is so noble and so sparkling, such a grand and glowing creature." Though he does go on to offer a testimonial to "that democratic dignity which, on all hands, radiates without end from God," it is a somewhat melancholic song of praise, insofar as it is prompted by his contemplation of the *loss* of dignity in Starbuck, "the fall of valor in the soul" (117). Starbuck's "fall" has made two things particularly clear: first, that "immaculate manliness" cannot actually be understood as an essential quality, because it depends for its existence on the spectacle of its absence; second, that the conscious effort to assure oneself of the stable presence of this "immaculate manliness" both exposes and exacerbates that embarrassingly superstitious dependence. What makes Queequeg so appealing, in this context, is that he doesn't attempt to define and conserve his interiority by generating an "orthodox" reading of it; his essentially ironic understanding of external forms suggests to Ishmael that "to be true philosophers, we mortals should not be conscious of so living or so striving" (50).

That is to say that Ishmael's ideal is a distinctly *unself-conscious* irreverence, one that is ultimately inseparable from the ideal of inconsistency. Taken together, these two ideals could be thought of as the constitutive obverse of Ahab's stony authority and the crew's cringing submission, which are equally inseparable phenomena: just as Ahab's projection of a superhuman consistency is an effect of enchanted attention, so is the subhuman reverence of the crew an effect of Ahab's theatrical use of forms. Especially toward the end of the book, the horror of Ahab's consistency is explicitly paired with the horror of the crew's tendency to "crouch abased before the tremendous centralization" (148). With the exception of the pagan harpooners, who are "unappalled" by projections of supernatural power (523), the members of the crew uniformly respond to such projections with "[a]bashed glances of servile wonder" (518). When "awestruck by the aspect of their commander," they gather "in one thick cluster" (501); in a parallel instance, the apparition of St. Elmo's fire reveals the spectacle of several sailors who, "arrested by the glare, now cohered together, and hung pendulous, like a knot of numbed wasps from a drooping, orchard twig. In various enchanted attitudes, like the standing, or stepping, or running skeletons in Herculaneum, others remained rooted to the deck; but all their eyes upcast" (507). If we consider these representations of the horror of superstitious reverence in relation to the horror of Ahab's constructed consistency, they may seem to suggest that the ideal of inconsistent irreverence is diametrically opposed to any form of identity that participates in the logic of the spectacle. They may seem to suggest, in other words, that the only way of avoiding the rootedness of both actor and audience in the glare of the spectacle is to avoid all potentially spectacular—which is to say, all properly social—relationships. For this reason, it might be thought that Ishmael's ideal is ultimately quietistic, a cowering avoidance of all thoughts and acts and selves that threaten to interrupt the free play of his own inaccessible being. But if Ishmael himself occasionally seems susceptible to this critique, his "savage" ideal, especially as represented in Queequeg, clearly includes the element of engagement. Wherever Melville speaks seriously of savagery, he means to evoke a state of being characterized not only by inconsistency and irreverence, but also by the quality we will turn to now, the one he defines in *Moby-Dick* as "gameness."

Gameness. When Queequeg seems about to die from his fever, Pip cries, "Oh for a game cock now to sit upon his head and crow! Queequeg dies game!—mind ye that; Queequeg dies game!—take ye good heed of that; Queequeg dies game! I say; game, game, game!" (479–80). Queequeg is so game, in fact, that he simply chooses not to die; by the force of "his own sovereign will," he recovers from his illness, and only a few days later, "pronounce[s] himself fit for a fight" (480). In its ideal form, gameness consists of a masculine fortitude that manifests itself in the play of provocation, in an instant readiness to give oneself up to the risk of the contest.[21] To a greater extent than anyone else in the book, Queequeg typifies this "desperate dauntlessness" (56). Once he has "vowed a vow" to leave his island for a whaler, for instance, only death will prevent him from fulfilling it; after leaping from his canoe to the side of the whaler and climbing to the deck, he grabs a ringbolt and swears "not to let it go, though hacked to pieces" (55, 56). Whenever there is an occasion that calls for the expression of an "ambitious soul," from the rescuing of the drowning bumpkin to the rescuing of Tashtego from the head of the whale, he rises to it without a moment's hesitation. Critics have occasionally suggested that these scenes characterize Queequeg as the representative of the principle of self-sacrifice and, as such, the more or less Christian alternative to Ahab's killing quest. But Queequeg's willingness to put his honor and his life at risk is anything but Christian; it is expressive, instead, of a "savage" bravado, a desire to be measured by one's ability to overcome great opponents or great odds. When the captain of the *Moss* berates him for assaulting a staring bumpkin, Queequeg assumes "an unearthly expression of disdain" and says, "ah! him bery small-e fish-e; Queequeg no kill-e so small-e fish-e;

Queequeg kill-e big whale" (61). Here as elsewhere, it is quite clear that one of the side effects of his desire to be measured against creatures of similar magnitude is a disdain for "small fish." He calls the buttocks of the sleeping rigger his "face," and when Ishmael chides him for sitting there and consequently "grinding the face of the poor," he explains that on his island, "the kings, chiefs, and great people generally, were in the custom of fattening up some of the lower orders for ottomans." Though it would be "[p]erry easy, kill-e," he says, waving his tomahawk-pipe over the head of the rigger, it would not be worth the trouble (60). The only things worth attempting to kill are the things not easy to kill; the only acts capable of reflecting and extending one's gameness are those that occur on distinctly elevated fields of competition.

Another way of saying this is that Queequeg is a man of honor. Honor, in the anthropological sense, denotes a way of thinking about the self that is characterized by an attention to "external form and effect" and a consequent devotion to "the proving of prowess."[22] The game of honor is, in Pierre Bourdieu's words, "a competition of merit played out before the tribunal of public opinion"; it is the provisional space within which the relative magnitudes of external forms are made visible.[23] One of the results of this emphasis on visibility is that these games of honor necessarily assume "an intimate relation between honour and the physical person," if we take the physical person to mean both the body and its most immediate adornments.[24] Societies structured around the principle of honor are characterized, accordingly, by bodily exhibitions designed to express the magnitude of one's own living form and by a "terror of mutilation after death, defilement, and denial of honorable burial."[25] With these theories of honor in mind, it may be easier to recognize the relationship between the way Queequeg conceives of prowess and the way he conceives of the body and its ornaments. When he decorates himself with haphazardly assumed articles of Western clothing, he intends not to symbolize his inner being, but to reflect and extend his external form; in his indifference to what Melville describes in *Omoo* as "the relation subsisting between the various parts of a gentleman's costume" (*O*, 182), he evinces an understanding of adornment as nothing more than the aggregation of visibility. His tattooing similarly presents, in the words of Susan Stewart, "not depth but additional surface."[26] When he copies a tattoo from his body onto the papers of the *Pequod*— a practice of self-signification popularly associated with Maoris[27]—he is doing nothing more than extending, metonymically, a field of display. And when he copies his tattooing onto the lid of his coffin, he is not attempting to achieve "the illusion of consistency" generated by what John Irwin has described as "the scenario of hieroglyphic doubling"; rather, in a spirit of "wild whimsiness," he is supplementing himself with "all manner of grotesque figures and drawings," signs that are not intended to signify an absent presence so much as they are intended to accumulate, in all their resolute materiality.[28] It would be a mistake, then, to assume that he "shudder[s]" at the thought of being "tossed like something vile to the death-devouring sharks" (MD, 478) because he conceives of the body as the holistic symbol of the soul. He is anguished at the thought of having his body treated "like something vile" because he conceives of it as the surface of his honor, with which and on which he has inscribed his presence in the world.[29]

This reading of Queequeg's body is reinforced by the connections that Ishmael establishes between cannibalism and the signification of magnitude. Upon first sighting the Pequod, he is struck by the fact that the ship is "apparelled like any barbaric Ethiopian emperor, his neck heavy with pendants of polished ivory. She was a thing of trophies. A cannibal of a craft, tricking herself forth in the chased bones of her enemies" (70). In yoking together the word cannibal and the practice of ornamenting the body with the chased, or engraved, bones of enemies, Ishmael is drawing on two closely related nineteenth-century assumptions about savages in general and cannibals in particular. The first assumption is that savages express and recognize identity in terms of quantity.[30] This is the implication of the last lines of "Etymology," in which we are told that in the languages of Fiji and Erromanga—islands famous for being the habitats of cannibals[31]—the words for whale are "pekee-nuee-nuee" and "pehee-nuee-nuee" (xvi). The word pekee or pehee signifies "fish," and as Melville informs us in Omoo, "the word 'nuee' is significant of quantity. Its repetition is like placing ciphers at the right hand of a numeral; the more places you carry it out to, the greater the sum" (O, 157). The same assumption underwrites the scene in which Queequeg finds a large book in the Spouter-Inn, and rather than reading it, simply counts its pages, pausing "at every fiftieth page" to deliver "a long-drawn, gurgling whistle of astonishment" (49). He simply takes it for granted that the most important fact about any given object is its "nuee-nuee-ness," just as he takes it for granted that his own tattooed body, described elsewhere as a "wondrous work in one volume" (481), is not there to be read but to be admired. The second assumption is that ornamental display, understood as an extension of one's surface, is an essentially savage practice.[32] This is the point of the paragraph in which Ishmael declares that "[l]ong exile from Christendom" results in a reversion to "what is called savagery"; it sets up his subsequent argument that white men who are at sea long enough begin to share the typically "savage" obsession with decoration. One of the better-known features of savagery, he says, is that "wonderful patience of industry" that enables Hawaiians to produce an art object that "in its full multiplicity and elaboration of carving, is as great a trophy of human perseverance as a Latin lexicon." Because the scrimshawed whalebones of long-exiled sailors are characterized by a "miraculous intricacy" and "maziness of design," they should be classified along with Hawaiian spear paddles and the engravings of Albrecht Dürer as "savage," an adjective that signifies, in this context, a form of inscription in which marks are like trophies (270).

One of the things we can say about Melville's characterization of Queequeg, then, is that it draws on a conventional distinction between the metonymically elaborated surfaces of savages and the metaphorically expressive surfaces of "humane" beings. It should already be obvious, however, that he introduces this distinction only to break it down. Just as he asks us to come to terms with the implications of the assumption that white men peddle human heads, so does he ask us, in the passages quoted above, to consider the significance of the bone trophies on the *Pequod* and the bone ornamentation of "the white sailor-savage" (270). Critics have frequently quoted these particular passages as signs of Melville's capacity to see beyond conventional distinctions between the West and its others, but they have inevitably overlooked the specificity of the distinction Melville is addressing in these cases—a distinction between an interior dignity that is expressed by means of organic symbols and an exterior honor whose surface is extended by means of artificial signs. The same is true of a passage from *Israel Potter* in which Melville again invokes and subverts the distinction between "humanity" and "savagery." In Paris during the Revolutionary War, the American captain John Paul Jones is dressed in broadcloth and ruffles, and his hand is "ornamented with several Parisian rings." But when he rolls up his sleeve, he reveals a patch of tattooing so "deep blue, elaborate, labyrinthine, [and] cabalistic" that it reminds Israel Potter of tattoos seen "on the arm of a New Zealand warrior, once met, fresh from battle, in his native village." The contrast between these two modes of adornment is only apparent, however, for Jones is "a sort of prophetical ghost, glimmering in anticipation upon the advent of those tragic scenes of the French Revolution which levelled the exquisite refinement of Paris with the blood-thirsty ferocity of Borneo; showing that broaches and finger-rings, not less than nose-rings and tattooing, are tokens of the primeval savageness which ever slumbers in human kind, civilised or uncivilised"

(*IP*, 62–63). This passage is usually said to embody Melville's awareness that there is a spirit of murderous violence inherent in all human beings. But what he is specifically emphasizing here is that both "civilized" and "savage" peoples ornament the body, and that this metonymic form of self-elaboration suggests a desire to enter into contests of magnitude—a "gameness" that is appealing when it appears in the form of Queequeg, and less so when it becomes fixed as the mode of identity and recognition that governs an entire society. Taken to that extreme, as in "those tragic scenes of the French Revolution," it becomes the principle of a world much like the world of the "Whale Song" that ends "Extracts," where "the rare old Whale, mid storm and gale / In his ocean home will be / A giant in might, where might is right, / And King of the boundless sea" (*MD*, xxviii).

Once the contests of magnitude that are ordinarily confined to the realm of the game become the characteristic features of the social sphere as such, we find ourselves confronted by what Ishmael calls the "full awfulness of the sea." Not merely "a foe to man who is an alien to it," the sea "is also a fiend to its own offspring . . . . Like a savage tigress that tossing in the jungle overlays her own cubs, so the sea dashes even the mightiest whales against rocks" (273, 274). When Ishmael asks us to "[c]onsider, once more, the universal cannibalism of the seas, all whose creatures prey upon each other, carrying on eternal war since the world began" (274), he means to evoke the horror of that kind of heedlessness, the heedlessness of beings for whom all others are aliens. In this context, the force of the phrase "universal cannibalism" derives less from the word "cannibalism" than from the word "universal"; the principles of gameness are compatible with cannibalism, but they are not at all compatible with universalism. The "full awfulness of the sea" is that it presents us with a competitive struggle without sidelines or clock, a struggle so thoroughly generalized that it seems, in the case of the shark, to continue even after death. This is what differentiates "the universal cannibalism of the seas" from Queequeg's brand of cannibalism, as Queequeg himself suggests in the scene in which he almost loses his hand to the postmortem snap of a shark's jaw: " 'Queequeg no care what god made him shark,' said the savage, agonizingly lifting his hand up and down; 'wedder Fejee god or Nantucket god; but de god wat made shark must be one dam Ingin' " (302). As a "game" cannibal, Queequeg is provisionally heedless; faced with a creature whose heedlessness is eternal, he makes it clear that he considers both it and its maker to belong to a sphere of being apart from his own. Though he retains an irreverent indifference as to the origin of the shark, neither here nor elsewhere does he allow that indifference to slide into a sharkish abandonment of "common regardings" (127), an unconditional insensibility to "that common decency of human recognition which is the meanest slave's right" (245).

Whereas Queequeg assumes that this spirit of universalized heedlessness cannot be definitively linked either to Fijian cannibals or Nantucket Christians, Ishmael is inclined to think that Westerners are nearer than non-Westerners to the undifferentiated and unending aggression of the shark. "Go to the meat-market of a Saturday night," he says, "and see the crowds of live bipeds staring up at the long rows of dead quadrupeds. Does not that sight take a tooth out of the cannibal's jaw? Cannibals? who is not a cannibal? I tell you it will be more tolerable for the Fejee that salted down a lean missionary in his cellar against a coming famine; it will be more tolerable for that provident Fejee, I say, in the day of judgment, than for thee, civilized and enlightened gourmand, who nailest geese to the ground and feastest on their bloated livers in thy pate-de-foie-gras" (300). All humans may be "cannibals," in the sense that we are all at some time or another heedless, but Westerners carry that spirit much farther than Fijians, "adding insult to injury" (300) in countless uncounted ways. As Melville will later write in *Israel Potter*, in light of the ferocity of the battle between the *Serapis* and the *Bonhomme Richard,* "one may well ask—What separates the enlightened man from the savage? Is civilization a thing distinct, or is it an advanced stage of barbarism?" (*IP*, 130). Ishmael's most detailed study of this "advanced" or "acute" spirit of heedlessness is his characterization of Stubb, whose "gamesome" spirit too often rises to a feverish pitch. After killing a whale, Stubb is "flushed with conquest," and being "intemperately fond of the whale as a flavorish thing to his palate," he orders the black cook, Fleece, to cook him a whale steak (*MD*, 292). That night, while sharks are feasting on the carcass of the *Pequod*'s freshly killed whale, Stubb does the same, and is so engaged in his meal that at first he "heeded not the mumblings of the banquet that was going on so nigh him, no more than the sharks heeded the smacking of his own epicurean lips" (293). He is similarly heedless of Fleece, corralling him into a minstrel routine to satisfy his racist longings for spectacularized entertainment. Fleece gets the last word, however; leaving the deck, he says to himself, "Wish, by gor! whale eat him, 'stead of him eat whale. I'm bressed if he ain't more of shark dan Massa Shark hisself" (297). Like the sharks, Stubb is never "in gayer or more jovial spirits" (293) than when banqueting on the fruit of his conquest, and once in those spirits, he is almost incapable of recognizing the presence of a subjectivity other than his own. Just as the too jolly men of the *Bachelor* ignore the presence of the *Pequod*, "never heeding their gaze for the lively revelry they were in" (495), so does Stubb's feverish gamesomeness usher him into an endless, universal, and ultimately solitary feast.

If Queequeg embodies the virtues of inconsistency, irreverence, and gameness, then, the antitheses of these virtues—the excesses of consistency, reverence, and heedlessness—are embodied in Ahab, Starbuck, and Stubb. And just as these virtues are interdependent in Queequeg, so do their antitheses cohere in a single, dystopian complex. Melville makes this point explicit in a scene late in the book in which Stubb, Starbuck, and Ahab come together in their status as allegories of what Queequeg is not. Seeing Ahab pausing before his ruined whaleboat, Stubb attempts "to evince his own unabated fortitude" by laughing, while Starbuck calls it "a solemn sight, an omen, and an ill one." "Begone!" says Ahab. "Ye two are the opposite poles of one thing; Starbuck is Stubb reversed, and Stubb is Starbuck; and ye two are all mankind; and Ahab stands alone among the millions of the peopled earth, nor gods nor men his neighbors! Cold, cold—I shiver!" (553). Stubb and Starbuck are "the opposite poles of one thing" in that strained heedlessness and reverential heedfulness are each in excess of what Ahab considers to be the proper attitude when facing a wreck: a silent indifference. But though Ahab's indifference may free him from the mechanical heedlessness of Stubb and the superstitious heedfulness of Starbuck, his relentless effort to maintain that perfect indifference leaves him alone and cold. By means of this tableau, Melville makes it abundantly clear that he intends these characters to constitute a composite allegory of the nightmare state that the example of Queequeg invites us to escape. The essence of this contrast is best expressed in the chapter called "Fast-Fish and Loose-Fish," in which Ishmael reflects on the implication of the two-section whaling code which states that "[a] Fast-Fish belongs to the party fast to it" and "[a] Loose-fish is fair game for anybody who can soonest catch it" (396). To be "fast" is to be marked as the possession of another; to be "loose" is to be free from such marking. In carrying the spirits of consistency, reverence, and heedlessness to excess, Ahab, Starbuck, and Stubb have become "fast," in that they have been possessed by those spirits. Queequeg remains "loose," conversely, because he is able to live *in* the world—in a fully spontaneous and responsive manner—without being *of* it.

If we were to stop here, *Moby-Dick* would be a relatively conservative book, both epistemologically and ethically. Its epistemology would consist of the assumption that close and careful observation will reveal the truth behind appearances, and its ethics would consist of the injunction to "be loose, not fast." Its world would be one in which it would be possible to imagine that the true nature of all things will be uncovered in time, and that what is uncovered will inevitably fall into place within the master opposition of looseness and fastness. What we would have, in other words, would be one more reading of *Moby-Dick* capable of being slotted within what Donald Pease has called "the Cold War paradigm." As Pease observes, the standard critical reading of the book, in which "Ishmael is said to recover . . . the free play of indeterminate possibility in a world forced to reflect Ahab's fixed meanings," is a reading that shares the epistemology and ethics of the cold war.[33] The end of the cold war does not seem to have interfered in any way with this habit of reading; readers continue to take it for granted that the ethical opposition between freedom and totalitarianism is never called into question by the radical spirit of inquiry embodied in Ishmael, the all-American hero. But if this reading is correct, if Melville's resistance to humanism and racism really does ground itself in the unexamined assumption that pure insight will always reveal a pure, preexistent opposition between looseness and fastness, *Moby-Dick* would have to be characterized as little more than a masculinist retrenchment of the humanist ground. There can be little doubt that at least part of the reason Melville rearticulates "humanity" with the image of the male savage is that he is uncomfortable with the conventional linkage between "humanity" and the image of the white, Christian female; at the same time that he defines the humanity of the savage against the "real" savagery of fastness, he also defines it against the lack of gameness in all those who do not publicly struggle against the manifestations of fastness. If he does indeed mean us to understand these defining oppositions as natural, he is not only reproducing the basic assumptions of humanism—the preexistence of epistemological and ethical oppositions—but also deploying those questionable assumptions in the service of an unmistakably antifeminine assault on the liberal-Christian model of humanism that was dominant in its day.[34]

But to stop here would be to stop too short. As the above discussion should already have suggested, Melville is well aware that looseness depends on fastness, that the ethical opposition he is attempting to articulate is neither neat nor natural. In the flyleaf of one of his Shakespeare volumes, sometime shortly before writing *Moby-Dick*, he jotted down a few lines drawn from an 1823 *Quarterly Review* essay called "Superstition and Knowledge," one of which reads, "Madness is undefinable—It

& right reasons extremes of one." In the original, the idea is expressed as follows:

> In considering the actions of the mind, it should never be forgotten, that its affections pass into each other like the tints of the rainbow: though we can easily distinguish them when they have assumed a decided colour, yet we can never determine where each hue begins. It has been said that
>   "Great wit to madness nearly is allied,
>   And thin partitions do the bounds divide."
> The truth of this observation may be extended beyond the letter of the observation. Madness is almost undefinable. Right reason and insanity are merely the extreme terms of a series of mental action, which need not be very long.[35]

It is possible to locate madness at the far end of a spectrum of "mental action," in other words, but it is impossible to identify the point on that spectrum where rationality shades into insanity. Melville repeats that argument in precisely those terms in *Billy Budd,* in which he asks, "Who in the rainbow can draw the line where the violet tint ends and the orange tint begins? Distinctly we see the difference of the colors, but where exactly does the one first blendingly enter into the other? So with sanity and insanity" (*BB,* 102). Ethical oppositions like madness and reason are not discovered in nature, in other words, but are the radically contingent resolutions of an essentially unresolved field. This is the understanding that informs Melville's treatment of the opposition between looseness and fastness; after a string of examples that are intended to suggest that perfect looseness and perfect fastness are unrealizable ideals, he concludes the chapter on that subject by asking, "what are you, reader, but a Loose-Fish and a Fast-Fish, too?" (*MD,* 398). Like the allegorical meanings that Sophia Hawthorne finds in *Moby-Dick,* fixed terms like looseness, fastness, madness, reason—even, as we will soon see, violet and orange—are, in Melville's words, "things which while you think you but humbly discover them, you do in fact create them for yourself" (*C,* 219). To do justice to the position Melville asks us to occupy in *Moby-Dick,* we have to recognize that the forceful injunction to "be loose" is supplemented by the equally forceful reminder that this injunction imposes a resolution on an unresolved field of experience, and that in all such processes of imposition, there is always some aspect of the field that eludes us. This, as Ishmael has told us from the beginning, is "the key to it all."

But not yet have we solved the incantation of this whiteness, and learned why it appeals with such power to the soul. . . .

[I]s it, that as in essence whiteness is not so much a color as the visible absence of color, and at the same time the concrete of all colors; is it for these reasons that there is such a dumb blankness, full of meaning, in a wide landscape of snows—a colorless, all-color of atheism from which we shrink? And when we consider that other theory of the natural philosophers, that all other earthly hues—every stately or lovely emblazoning—the sweet tinges of sunset skies and woods; yea, and the gilded velvets of butterflies, and the butterfly cheeks of young girls; all these are but subtle deceits, not actually inherent in substances, but only laid on from without; so that all deified Nature absolutely paints like the harlot, whose allurements cover nothing but the charnel-house within; and when we proceed further, and consider that the mystical cosmetic which produces every one of her hues, the great principle of light, for ever remains white or colorless in itself, and if operating without medium upon matter, would touch all objects, even tulips and roses, with its own blank tinge—pondering all this, the palsied universe lies before us a leper; and like wilful travellers in Lapland, who refuse to wear colored and coloring glasses upon their eyes, so the wretched infidel gazes himself blind at the monumental white shroud that wraps all the prospect around him. And of all these things the Albino whale was the symbol. Wonder ye then at the fiery hunt?—*Moby-Dick*

The above passage, which concludes "The Whiteness of the Whale," has been quoted and analyzed so often in discussions of *Moby-Dick* that it can be difficult to recapture its disorienting effect. But as Ishmael says at the beginning of this excursion into the theory of color, if the reader does not come to understand why "[i]t was the whiteness of the whale that above all things appalled me," then "all these chapters might be naught." He prepares for this passage with great care, laboriously attempting to convince the reader that he does not fear whiteness simply because he is "green," to borrow a term from an earlier part of our discussion, but because he has acquired an insight into those "nameless things" signified by whiteness, those "invisible spheres" that "were formed in fright" (194–95). By means of this argument, he reaffirms the stability of the two polarities that underwrite so much of his account of Queequeg: the epistemological distinction between uninformed sight and informed insight and the ethical distinction between innocent goodness and "the demonism in the world" (194). Accordingly, when this argument takes a last-minute turn—"But not yet have we solved the incantation of this whiteness"—there is a great deal at stake. That is what makes it particularly surprising that the turn is less a supplement than a revision, presenting us with three new propositions that are intended to prepare the way for an entirely new conclusion. The propositions are as follows: (1) whiteness is visible absence; (2) all other colors are not inherent in substances but produced by light; (3) light, the agent of color, is colorless in itself. The conclusion that proceeds from these propositions is that the universe is ultimately a visible absence—that the only stable insight is the one that perceives this absence, and that the only essential opposition is the one between the fact of absence and the illusion of presence. If we are not capable of reorienting our epistemological and ethical suppositions in the light of this conclusion, the quest of the *Pequod* will never be anything more to us than an object of "[w]onder," the curious but ultimately insignificant repudiation of a stable epistemological insight and a stable ethical injunction. If we do reorient ourselves, however, we are suddenly operating in a world very much like the one that Lacan and others like him have taught late-twentieth-century readers to see.

Before moving on to address some of the implications of this shift, I want to emphasize that this family resemblance between Melville's whiteness and Lacan's Real does not demand the conclusion that Melville is a genius working above and beyond the limitations of space and time. All it means is that the Lacanian Real has an antecedent in the post-Kantian theory of vision that developed in the early nineteenth century and that Melville obviously encountered in some form. If there was a single source, it was probably Goethe's *Theory of Colours,* which was published in German in 1810 and translated into English in 1840; it was the best-known articulation of this "theory of the natural philosophers," and all three of Ishmael's propositions about color may be found in it.[36] In the case of the first proposition, Goethe's argument is that although it is theoretically possible to conceive of space as purely transparent, we encounter it in practice as a "light-transmitting semi-transparent medium."[37] As this medium accumulates, it becomes less transparent, and our perception of color undergoes successive changes. When the medium has attained "[t]he extreme degree of this accumulation," the color we perceive "is white; the simplest, brightest, first, opaque occupation of space" (61). This conception of color as a spectrum ranging from a dark transparency at one end to an opaque whiteness at the other leads to the second proposition, that the so-called primary colors are, in Ishmael's words, "not actually inherent in substances, but only laid on from without." If we direct light through a semitransparent medium onto an object, "by increasing the degree of opacity in the medium, we can deepen a bright object from the lightest yellow to the intensest ruby-red. Blue, on the other hand, increases to the most beautiful violet, if we rarefy and diminish a semi-opaque medium, itself lighted, but through which we see darkness" (212). The final proposition simply rounds out the previous two: if whiteness is the accumulation of a semitranspar-ent medium, and if the spectrum of the "primary" colors is produced by light acting on the incremental thicknesses of this medium, it fol-lows that light itself is either "colourless" or "in its full force . . . purely white" (38). With the addition of this final proposition, it becomes pos-sible to argue, as Goethe does, that the complex phenomenon of color may be reduced to "a primordial vast contrast between light and dark-ness, which may be more generally expressed by light and its absence" (296). The whole "visible world of light, shade, and colour" (296) is the result of the interplay between the degrees of light and the degrees of semitransparent space, in which space is understood to be, in essence, the absence of light.

But the horror of unrelieved whiteness, for Ishmael, is not simply that it bears witness to a world that consists of nothing but the interplay be-tween light and its thickened absence. The deepest horror of whiteness is that it represents the point at which that play ends, the point at which the sliding reel of colors tapers into an infinity of light without space or space without light. That is to say that whiteness is to the eye as death is to the organism, an analogy supported by Goethe's observation that although "[e]verything living tends to colour . . . [e]verything in which life is extinct approximates to white, to the abstract, the general state, to clearness, to transparence" (234). It is not hard to see Ishmael's anxiety about whiteness as a version of his much-remarked anxiety about death; in each case, he fears that his experience of himself and his world as richly colored essences may be illusory, dependent on the continuous disavowal of an encroaching absence. From his own perspective, then, the "primordial" opposition is not so much the contrast between light and its absence as it is the contrast between his own richly colored sub-jectivity and its absence, signified by the idea of whiteness or the idea of death. Goethe addresses this contrast in the section of his treatise de-voted to the "physiological colours," in which he argues that images that "last for some time, even when the external cause is removed" (7), are not "illusions of sight" but the products of a "healthy and duly efficient eye" (74–75). The "after-vision" (20) of these images is purely subjec-tive; after the initial stimulus, such images "belong to the eye" (xli), and unfold without any reference to the object itself. As in the case of the physical colors, moreover, though we may ascribe to the physiological colors "a certain objective character, their distinctive quality still consists in their being transient, and not to be arrested" (56). One of the effects of Goethe's characterization of the retinal afterimage as an ordinary element of experience is that the sufficiency of vision is thrown into question. As he himself observes, colors that belong to the eye are "less than the light, inasmuch as they are a repetition of an impression of light, nay, at last they leave this impression quite as a dark" (230–31). The retinal afterimage is "less than the light" in that it is an attenuated representation of the illuminated object, and its procession of colored images can be no compensation for that inability to capture the object itself, insofar as these images steadily dim and ultimately leave the initial impression "quite as a dark." To the degree that visual experience belongs to the eye, it consists of nothing more a transient succession of images, founded on a loss and proceeding toward a darkness.[38]

Without this understanding of visual experience, Ishmael says, the book "might be naught." If he does not succeed in forcing his readers to question the Enlightenment understanding of vision, in which the mind receives and judges perfect impressions of everything outside it, the quests to know and destroy the whale will seem merely curious. If, however, he can bring his readers to understand visual experience in terms of what it lacks—the object that cannot be brought into view—and to perceive the massive white whale as the symbol of the fullness that always escapes us, they may begin to feel that they have a stake in the outcome of this "fiery hunt." In the failure of that hunt, moreover, they may be brought to recognize something that on some level they already know: that there is an objectivity permanently remote from the subject, a "dead, blind wall" that "butts all inquiring heads at last" (MD, 521). This is the "demon phantom that, some time or other, swims before all human hearts" (237), the "gliding great demon of the seas of life" (187) that drags Ahab and his crew on their quest, the "shadow in the water" that sinks beneath Ahab's gaze "the more and the more that he strove to pierce the profundity" (543). If we feel in ourselves the agony of its infinite deferral, its ceaseless incitement and denial of our desire "to feel something in this slippery world that can hold" (470), then it will be possible to comprehend both the heroism and the horror of Ahab's fixed pursuit. Melville clearly wants us to feel that Ahab is acting in our stead, that he is motivated by the same "intellectual and spiritual exasperations" that have plagued the "whole race from Adam down" (184). But he also wants us to recognize that the desire to establish wholeness is, in its projection of a permanently arrested slipperiness, the desire for the stillness of death. The desire to take into the self the thing it is lacking is an irreducible component of human experience, but that desire must be tempered by the willingness to recognize that each thing we take in is a specter, through which we perceive, with greater or lesser but never total exactness, the object itself.

The name that Melville gives to this phantasmatic object, composed of illumination superimposed on opacity, is "truth." When he says in "Hawthorne and His Mosses" that "the things that make Shakespeare, Shakespeare" are "those deep far-away things in him; those occasional flashings-forth of the intuitive Truth in him," he is referring to things that are only virtually present, flashing forth but still far away. Even when characters such as Lear speak "the sane madness of vital truth," for instance, Shakespeare is providing us with nothing more than "indices" of those "terrifically true" things that it is impossible "for any good man, in his own proper character, to utter" (*PT*, 244). Like Shakespeare, Melville argues, Hawthorne is one who constantly "seek[s] for Truth" but remains "a seeker, not a finder yet" (250); though his tales are intended to illuminate certain moral truths, the allegorical mode of that illumination draws attention to the impossibility of embodying meaning in a fully realized symbol. This is what Melville means when he says that in "spite of all the Indian-summer sunlight on the hither side of Hawthorne's soul, the other side—like the dark half of the physical sphere—is shrouded in a blackness, ten times black" (243). The light of the allegorical sign is always set off against the "infinite obscure" of the thing it cannot signify, and though this light may be an "evermoving dawn" (243), continually bringing new truths to light, it is always preceded and pursued by a shadow. If we lose sight of the inevitable distance between the signifier and its remainder, we become like Ahab, grimly determined to live in world that lacks nothing, a body that lets nothing in or out. "[W]hat plays the mischief with the truth," Melville writes to Hawthorne in 1851, "is that men will insist upon the universal application of a temporary feeling or opinion" (*C*, 194). Insofar as truth is constituted by the relationship between the accounted for and the unaccounted for, those who deny the existence of the unaccounted for necessarily lose the truth in the attempt to gain it.

For this reason, *Moby-Dick* keeps asking us to conceive of truth as a thing that is not exhausted by the signs of its presence. After a careful exposition of the nature of Ahab's madness, for instance, Ishmael tells us, "This is much; yet Ahab's larger, darker, deeper part remains unhinted. But vain to popularize profundities, and all truth is profound." That unhinted part is like the statue of a king in the Roman ruins that lie beneath a Parisian hotel, a forever silent thing whose archaeological priority makes it suggestive of lost origins: "Wind ye down there, ye prouder, sadder souls! question that proud, sad king! A family likeness! aye, he did beget ye, ye young exiled royalties; and from your grim sire only will the old State-secret come" (MD, 185). As Ahab himself momentarily recognizes, the tension between the known surface and the unknowable depths suggests that "[t]here is no steady unretracing progress in this life; we do not advance through fixed gradations, and at the last one pause" (492). That is to say, in Lacan's terms, the dialectic of a body of knowledge and the truth outside it is not "convergent," in that it does not attain "the conjuncture defined as absolute knowledge." If truth was "no more than that which is lacking for the realization of knowledge," we could look forward to the day when we all will live in a world from which "there is nothing more to be expected," in which each subject will be "fulfilled in his identity to himself." The reason we should not expect that day, Lacan says, is that the pursuit of truth marks a *constitutive* lack in knowledge.[39] "Where lies the final harbor, whence we unmoor no more?" asks Ahab. "In what rapt ether sails the world, of which the weariest will never weary? Where is the foundling's father hidden?" The answer to these questions is suggested by the simultaneous nearness and remoteness of the truth that would complete our body of knowledge: "Our souls are like those orphans whose unwedded mothers die in bearing them: the secret of our paternity lies in their grave, and we must there to learn it" (MD, 492). Like Ahab's missing leg, this truth is "uninterpenetratingly" present; though we feel its "tingling life" (471), it will never be a part of our being.

We should recognize in this "truth" the principal source of the terror that haunts the end of *Typee*, the terror of a condition—cannibalism—that is both present and resolutely absent, in that its climactic signification does not secure the knowledge of its existence and meaning. The crucial difference is that in *Moby-Dick*, Melville makes it quite clear that the experience of this not-quite-present presence is not merely an effect of the Westerner's attempt to know the savage, but an inescapable element of knowledge as such. In a revisiting of Babbalanja's dream, Ishmael tells us that "the ancestry and posterity of Grief go further than the ancestry and posterity of Joy," and that when we "trail the genealogies of these high mortal miseries," we are forced to conclude "that the gods themselves are not for ever glad. The ineffaceable, sad birth-mark in the brow of man, is but the stamp of sorrow in the signers" (464). Sadness is universal because it is impossible for us to be "fulfilled in [our] identity to [ourselves]," and that fulfillment is impossible because objectivity—nature and nature's God—necessarily disappoints our expectations. There is a "general stolidity discernible in the whole visible world; which while pauselessly active in uncounted modes, still eternally holds its peace, and ignores you, though you dig foundations for cathedrals" (467). This visible stolidity that "hears no mortal voice" (450) is what Ishmael discovers in the deafening grove in the Arsacides, and what Pip discovers when abandoned at sea, where he learns, "among the joyous, heartless, ever-juvenile eternities" to be "uncompromised, indifferent as his God" (414). Though it is madness to respond to this stolidity, as Pip does, by making no further demands on it, it is equally insane to make absolute demands on it, as Ahab does. There is, however, a middle ground between these extremes: the attempt to fill out the self by illuminating obscurities, accompanied by the afterthought that all such illuminations leave a shadowy remainder. Even Ahab, in the midst of a diatribe against the god responsible for thunderstorms, is capable of recognizing that this god is, after all, no more than a "personified impersonal" (507). With this recognition, he attains at least a partial distance from his madness; though he continues to address this god as a person, he is nonetheless aware that "[t]here is some unsuffusing thing beyond thee, thou clear spirit, to whom all thy eternity is but time, all thy creativeness mechanical. Through thee, thy flaming self, my scorched eyes do dimly see it" (508). He attains an even greater distance from his madness in a brief moment earlier on, when he seems to recognize that this "personified impersonal" is simply a projection of his own "deeper part," which similarly partakes "more of significant darkness than explanatory light" (464). Insofar as the world on which we make demands is a personified world, he says, it is, like the doubloon, "a magician's glass," which "to each and every man in turn but mirrors back his own mysterious self. Great pains, small gains, for those who ask the world to solve them; it cannot solve itself" (431).

In this denial of the idea that we can be solved by what lies outside us, we arrive at an epistemology that is strikingly different from the one I identified earlier. When we advance beyond the misrepresentation of the spectacle, we do not attain a perfect insight into the object itself—only another representation of it, consisting of a phantom-image and an unsuffusing thing beyond it. This is the phenomenon that Goethe calls *Abklingen,* translated as "after-vision" in the English edition of 1840, but better translated, I think, as "aftersight," a word that suggests its relation to but distinctness from the phenomena of "sight" and "insight." As Jonathan Crary has said, by characterizing this aftersight as the normal activity of the healthy eye, Goethe "allowed one to conceive of sensory perception as cut from any necessary link with an external referent" and introduced "temporality as an inescapable component of observation. . . . The shifting processes of one's own subjectivity experienced in time became synonymous with the act of seeing, dissolving the Cartesian ideal of an observer completely focused on an object."[40] Both of these implications—the "cut" between perception and referent and the temporality of perception—are very much alive in *Moby-Dick,* as two particularly famous examples should indicate. The discontinuity of perception and referent is most evident in "The Doubloon," in which Pip, after observing several different efforts to interpret the meaning of the coin, advances to the mast and says, "I look, you look, he looks; we look, ye look, they look" (434). The relationship between this discontinuity and the temporality of perception is, in turn, the subject of a passage at the end of "The Mast-head," in which Ishmael's Platonist lookout

> takes the mystic ocean at his feet for the visible image of that deep, blue, bottomless soul, pervading mankind and nature; and every strange, half-seen, gliding, beautiful thing that eludes him; every dimly-discovered, uprising fin of some undiscernible form, seems to him the embodiment of those elusive thoughts that only people the soul by continually flitting through it. In this enchanted mood, thy spirit ebbs away to whence it came; becomes diffused through time and space; like Wickliff's sprinkled Pantheistic ashes, forming at last a part of every shore the round globe over. (159)

Because this reflective process is strictly interior, it leaves us alienated from objectivity, but because it is also strictly physiological, it leaves us vulnerable to the interruptions of that alienated objectivity: "move your foot or hand an inch; slip your hold at all; and your identity comes back in a horror" (159). As Melville says in a letter to Hawthorne, the good thing about his life since his return from the sea is that "[t]hree weeks have scarcely passed, at any time between then and now, that I have not unfolded within myself." The bad thing about this intensely interior life is that afterimages of experience always dim as they unfold, finally decaying to a dark: "I feel that I am now come to the inmost leaf of the bulb, and that shortly the flower must fall to the mould" (C, 193).

It would be too easy to dismiss as nihilistic an epistemology grounded in the propositions that subjectivity is alienated from objectivity and that the process of interior development is identical with the process of interior decay. It is not nihilistic in itself, and it most certainly does not lead to nihilistic conclusions in *Moby-Dick*. In itself, it simply prompts us to remember that the act by which we bring an unknown object into the realm of the known is always insufficient to the object itself, in that it neither captures the object in its fullness nor produces a durable substitute for it. Only by remembering this do we keep ourselves from imagining, like Ahab, that the end point of knowledge is the end of knowing, the whiteness of space cleansed of the disturbing element of light, or light cleansed of the disturbing element of space. As a book that is most fundamentally about the survival of its object—the whale that escapes both the wrath of Ahab and the inquiry of Ishmael—*Moby-Dick* affirms the value of a subjectivity that is squarely but loosely oriented toward the object that eludes it. The subjectivity constituted in relation to that object cannot offer us the consolations of stability or multiplicity; the curious sight is not succeeded by insight but by aftersight, and the variable interior experience of the subject is not a sign of plenitude but of an always encroaching lack. But it is nonetheless a vital and deeply ethical subjectivity, with its own peculiar rewards. "[T]hrough all the thick mists of the dim doubts in my mind," Ishmael says, "divine intuitions now and then shoot, enkindling my fog with a heavenly ray. And for this I thank God; for all have doubts; many deny; but doubts or denials, few along with them, have intuitions. Doubts of all things earthly, and intuitions of some things heavenly; this combination makes neither believer nor infidel, but makes a man who regards them both with equal eye" (374). Only because he has "dim doubts" does he receive such intuitions, for "rainbows do not visit the clear air; they only irradiate vapor" (374). More important, only because he is capable of regarding intuitions *in their relation* to the dim doubts beyond them is he able to witness the full spectrum of color, a spectrum that does not inhere in the substances themselves but in our living relation to them.

Once we have made this epistemological shift, it becomes possible to understand why Queequeg disappears from the story so soon and with so little fanfare. Simply put, the reason his absence is unremarked is that he is never really present to begin with. Like Fedallah, he is explicitly characterized as a phantom of the mind, "a creature [such] as civilized domestic people in the temperate zone only see in their dreams, and that but dimly" (231). This air of unreality is most powerfully suggested by the chapter called "Biographical," in which he is introduced to us as "a native of Kokovoko, an island far away to the West and South. It is not down in any map; true places never are" (55). The use of the word *true* in this passage is telling; as elsewhere, it indicates a flashing forth of a resolutely faraway thing, an allegorical illumination trailed by a shadowy remainder. It implies, moreover, a justification for introducing a blatantly imaginary figure into a book in which every other character is from a place that *can* be found on a map. As Melville will write in *The Confidence-Man*, the advantage of the romance is that its imaginative excesses provide us with "more reality, than real life itself can show. . . . It is with fiction as with religion: it should present another world, and yet one to which we feel the tie" (*CM*, 183). By ostentatiously introducing Queequeg as a man from a place that does not exist, Melville signifies that this is a character whose "reality" is to be judged not in terms of his fidelity to "real life," but in terms of his fidelity to the dreams of "civilized domestic people." His "looseness" is not intended to be measured against the "real life" of Pacific islanders, that is, but to be received as a heavenly intuition of the nobleness of savagery, irradiating our "[d]oubts of all things earthly." By continuing to remind us of Queequeg's fictiveness, moreover, he prompts us to regard his looseness with "an equal eye." To see Queequeg correctly is to see his ideality in relation to his nonexistence, in the same way that we see a phantom—or, to use a more modern analogy, a hologram—in relation to the empty space it occupies.[41]

We are reminded of the hollowness of his presence in several ways. In his stories of Kokovoko, for instance, we repeatedly find ourselves sliding back into the gratuitous silliness of *Mardi*. The most ludicrous of these stories is his assertion that the great people of Kokovoko buy up fattened commoners for use as household furniture, but his accounts of Kokovokans modeling their worship on the behavior of ducks and of his father sticking parsley in the mouths of roasted corpses also situate his character in the realm of obvious exaggeration. Another example, one that would have been more obvious to Melville's contemporaries than it is to us, is the tale I mentioned earlier of a "great feast given by his father the king, on the gaining of a great battle wherein fifty of the enemy had been killed by about two o'clock in the afternoon, and all cooked and eaten that very evening" (85). In the basic outline of this story—a cannibal king who hosts a feast in which fifty corpses are eaten in a single day—contemporary readers would undoubtedly have caught the echo of an extraordinarily popular song called "The King of the Cannibal Islands." The third verse of the song goes like this:

One day this King invited most
All of his subjects to a roast,

For half his wives gave up the ghost,
The King of the Cannibal Islands:
Of fifty wives he was bereft,
And so he had but fifty left,
He said with them he would make shift,
So for a gorge all set off swift,
The fifty dead ones were roasted soon,
And all demolished before the noon,
And a lot of chiefs vowed to have soon
The King of the Cannibal Islands.[42]

Melville was clearly familiar with the song; it is the song the French band strikes up when greeting the king and queen of Nukuheva in *Typee* (7), and the phrase "King of the Cannibals" shows up in both *Omoo* (8) and *Moby-Dick* (270). And there is no question that he could have expected his audience to be familiar with it; as Anthony Bennett has demonstrated in a recent essay on the song, it enjoyed a "runaway popularity" in the 1830s and 1840s, and its fame was still great enough in the 1860s that Mayne Reid could introduce a discussion of the Fijians by asking, "Have I a reader who has not heard of the 'King of the Cannibal Islands'?"[43] At the same time that the story of the cannibal feast is intended to dramatize the depth of Queequeg's spontaneity and sincerity, then, it is also intended to prevent us from taking him as seriously as we otherwise might.[44]

But as I have been suggesting all along, the clearest evidence of Queequeg's phantasmatic status is his virtual disappearance from the text after the *Pequod* has set sail. At sea, the only chapters in which Ishmael and Queequeg appear to be "bosom friends" are "The First Lowering" and "The Monkey-rope," and in each of these, the point of bringing Queequeg back into the story is to make him an allegorical emblem of Chance. Otherwise, their rare simultaneous appearances are purely incidental, and in moments when we might expect them to reaffirm their bond, as when Queequeg is dying, they make no contact whatsoever. Toward the end of the book, Ishmael habitually blurs the distinctions between Queequeg, Tashtego, and Daggoo, referring to them on five occasions as "the pagan harpooners"—the thoroughly deindividualized markers of an abstract condition. And when Ishmael is ultimately saved by the lifebuoy that had once been Queequeg's coffin, he does not even mention that the coffin had once been Queequeg's, much less suggest that Queequeg's love has been the agent of his rescue. What the coffin-lifebuoy represents above all else is a sign that is temporally discontinuous with itself; as Ahab says, it is "the very dreaded symbol of grim death, by a mere hap, made the expressive sign of the help and hope of most endangered life" (528). This is the only sense in which it could be said to signify Queequeg's agency in Ishmael's rescue. As Ishmael has said all along, and with increasing passion as the book approaches its climax, we are only saved from the static extremes of mental action by the recognition of the temporal relation between signs of hope and symbols of death; dim doubts are eventually irradiated by rainbow intuitions, and radiance eventually dies down to a colorless mist. The connection with Queequeg should be clear: just as his radiance, as an emblem of looseness, is an irradiation of our initial image of him as a grim and deadly cannibal, so is his subsequent waning a reminder that rainbows are not burned into the texture of the sky. At the end point of this waning, all that is left of him is a laboriously personalized coffin without a body to enclose, a shadow whose substance is elsewhere. If Queequeg is connected to Ishmael's survival in any way, it is in the sense that Ishmael stays up after the *Pequod* goes down because the tattooed vessel, the sign of the cannibal, is both sealed and vacant.

"[T]hat mortal man who hath more of joy than sorrow in him," Ishmael says at the end of "The Try-works," "that mortal man cannot be true—not true, or undeveloped. With books the same. The truest of all men was the Man of Sorrows, and the truest of all books is Solomon's, and Ecclesiastes is the fine hammered steel of woe. 'All is vanity.' ALL" (424). To be true, as he goes on to say, is to realize the vanity of experience, the inevitable hollowness of everything we grasp, without giving ourselves up to the "woe that is madness" (425). What makes *Moby-Dick* a true book, in Melville's terms, is that it drives us in the direction of this doubled realization. By asking us to see that it is necessary both to fill out our emptiness with desire and to realize that our desire masks an emptiness, Melville means to drive us *against* our inclination to stop short, to end before the end. In the case of Queequeg, there are several places along the way where we could conceivably stop short, the most prominent of which are the conclusions that he is a curiosity, an emblem of intersubjectivity, or an emblem of looseness. As I have argued, however, if we are satisfied with any of these conclusions, we are ending before the end. The complete narrative of Ishmael's shifting perception of Queequeg goes something like this: After pushing past the representation of the cannibal as a sight and the dream of intersubjective touch, he arrives at an insight into the ideality of savagery; but even as he promotes that insight, he asks us to see that the truest form of looseness requires the recognition that all such visions are in fact aftersights, provisional resolutions of an unresolved field. The only serious response to the criticism that Melville's vision of looseness is an intensely masculinist vision may be found precisely here, in the fact that Melville supplements it with the insistent reminder that it is not grounded in nature. Though Queequeg is the character in *Moby-Dick* represented with the most affection and invested with the deepest ethical significance, he is nonetheless a "vanity," a phantom hovering momentarily in a space that is forever empty. If we are nostalgic for him in his absence, we miss the point that an ethics of looseness cannot, after all, reside in a figure on whom we are expected to model our behavior. It must instead reside, as Slavoj Žižek has said, "in the distance we are obliged to assume towards our most 'authentic' dreams, towards the myths that guarantee the very consistency of our symbolic universe." [45]

Out of the heart of mirthfulness, this shadow had come forth to him. Encircled by bandelets of light, it had still beamed upon him; vaguely historic and prophetic; backward, hinting of some irrevocable sin; forward, pointing to some inevitable ill. One of those faces, which now and then appear to man, and without one word of speech, still reveal glimpses of some fearful gospel. — *Pierre*

L ess than a week after the American publication of *Moby-Dick,* Melville told Hawthorne that he had found a new literary subject: "[L]et us add Moby Dick to our blessing, and step from that. Leviathan is not the biggest fish;—I have heard of Krakens" (*C,* 213). Just as *Typee* and *Mardi* had made *Moby-Dick* possible, so had the process of writing *Moby-Dick* called up an object of reflection that was, like those mythical sea beasts, more terrible and more spectral than the whale. In *Pierre,* published nine months later, that object appears before the protagonist, Pierre Glendinning, in the form of a "shadow": the face of Isabel, who may or may not be his illegitimate half-sister. The meaning of this sight is never clarified by a subsequent insight, as it is, at least temporarily, in the case of Ishmael's encounter with Queequeg. Though Isabel eventually tells the murky story of her life to Pierre, that story does not explicate the "fearful gospel" of her face, and he does not expect it to. This is because "his profound curiosity and interest in the matter—strange as it may seem—did not so much appear to be embodied in the mournful person of the olive girl, as by some radiations from her, embodied in the vague conceits which agitated his own soul. *There,* lurked the subtler secret: *that,* Pierre had striven to tear away." Believing that "[f]rom without, no wonderful effect is wrought within ourselves, unless some interior, responding wonder meets it" (*P,* 51), he chooses to pursue the subjective meaning of his reaction to her face more vigorously than the objective meaning of the face itself. In *Moby-Dick,* the shock of the new inspires Ishmael to take up the necessarily impossible projects of ethnographic, biographical, and cetological illumination; in *Pierre,* it inspires our hero to linger in the shadow of Isabel's face, so that he might use it as a conduit into the equally shadowy realm of his own psyche.

I want to use this shift from leviathans to krakens — from worldly objects that encourage objective analysis to otherworldly objects that encourage subjective analysis — as a way into the haunted, twilight world of "Benito Cereno." We begin that story with an image of birds skimming low over the water, their trailing shadows "foreshadowing deeper shadows to come" (46). When the American captain Amasa Delano boards the *San Dominick,* he finds that the suddenly disclosed spectacle of Spanish sailors and African slaves has on him "something of the effect of enchantment. The ship seems unreal; these strange costumes, gestures, and faces, but a shadowy tableau just emerged from the deep, which directly must receive back what it gave" (BC, 50). After the Americans have at last discovered that the Africans, not the Spaniards, are in control of the *San Dominick,* and that the slaves' former master, Don Alexandro Aranda, has been killed, stripped of his flesh, and nailed to the ship's prow, they see the slave ship come "round to the wind; the prow slowly swinging into view of the boats, its skeleton gleaming in the horizontal moonlight, and casting a gigantic ribbed shadow upon the water. One extended arm of the ghost seemed beckoning the whites to avenge it" (102). And when Delano fails in his efforts to cheer up the nominally restored Spanish captain, Benito Cereno, he cries, "You are saved . . . you are saved: what has cast such a shadow upon you?" (116). Cereno's response — "The negro" — sheds no direct light on the story's shadows; it merely names Babo as their agent and suggests that a more general "darkness" is their ultimate principle. If the shadow of Isabel's face is the kraken of *Pierre,* the shadow of the "negro" is unquestionably the kraken of "Benito Cereno" — a spectral, voiceless image that is meant to "overthrow in us all foregone persuasions, and make us wondering children in this world again" (*P,* 43).

The power of such images depends, to a great degree, on their silence. It is because Pierre recognizes that Isabel's interiors are "lidded" and "locked" (*P,* 141) that he begins to search himself for the cause of the image's significance. What he finds there, ultimately, is a silence no less deep. "He saw that human life doth truly come from that, which all men are agreed to call by the name of *God;* and that it partakes of the unravelable inscrutableness of God" (208). Though "impostor philosophers" claim that it is possible to hear and do God's will, "Silence is the only Voice of our God" (204). It is "absurd" to imagine that one can "get a Voice out of Silence" (208), to imagine that material and spiritual phenomena have an assignable origin in either the divine or the human will: "[T]he wisest man were rash, positively to assign the precise and incipient origination of his final thoughts and acts. Far as we blind moles can see, man's life seems but an acting upon mysterious hints; it is somehow hinted to us, to do thus or thus. For surely no mere mortal who has at all gone down into himself will ever pretend that his slightest thought or act solely originates in his own defined identity" (176). Having recognized that he cannot seek for the origin of his self outside himself, Pierre begins peeling off layers of inessentials within himself, looking for his "unlayered substance." But like an Egyptologist who mines into the central room of the pyramid, opens the sarcophagus, and finds "no body," Pierre finds no primitive essence in himself—only "surface stratified upon surface" (285). In its depiction of Delano's and Cereno's responses to the figure of Babo, "Benito Cereno" asks us to make the same discovery. The lesson of the kraken, in each case, is that the appearance of substance is always an illusion—a presence projected into the place of a lingering absence, a sound that is "preceded and attended by Silence" (P, 204).

Though this reading of "Benito Cereno" has become increasingly widespread in recent years, it is by no means the "standard" reading. The reading that has dominated the criticism of the story for over sixty years, and continues to be one of the most powerful influences on modern interpretations, is the one that finds in the silences of the story the voice of savagery. "As a projection of the unknown in man," writes Ruth Mandel, "the blacks in 'Benito Cereno' symbolize his buried, disguised drives for power, self-gratification and violence."[1] For Barry Phillips, "Babo is the mysterious subterranean potential lurking beneath all natural human surface"; for Max Putzel, "there can be no doubt" that Babo "represents primitive man in a cyclical world where time and history do not exist."[2] In this reading, the point of "Benito Cereno" is to lead us into "the farthest recesses of depravity in their primordial dusky beginnings," to confront us with "the 'prehistoric man' moving in the blackness behind the 'double,' at the primal sources of being," and thereby to remind us that "to ignore evil is a dangerous thing to do, for whether it is in the wilderness without or the even murkier one within, the beast in the jungle eventually leaps."[3] The place where the link between blacks and savagery is clinched, for most critics, is the hull of the ship, where Aranda's body is stripped of its flesh. Beginning with Sidney Kaplan in 1957, at least twenty-one critics of "Benito Cereno" have declared, suggested, or simply presumed that this flesh was not only removed but also eaten.[4] The hull, as the site of cannibalism, literalizes these critics' metaphorical descriptions of savagery as "underground stuff," "buried, disguised drives," or "subterranean potential." And cannibalism, as an image of radical primitiveness, emphasizes the temporal component of that vertical stacking, suggesting that what lies beneath is also what lies behind, in our "primordial dusky beginnings." Once readers perceive that Melville has forced them to be detectives, in other words, the contests of signification on the deck of the *San Dominick* melt away to reveal, below decks, the unlit realm of truth and the untamed realm of demand. The interiors of the hull may then be used to decode the interiors of Babo's skull, which ends the story on a pole in the Plaza of Lima, staring out at the churches where Aranda and Cereno have been buried. Like the unexplored hull, the region behind Babo's eyes becomes the lair of that savagery that has been in existence since the beginning of time and continues to lie, concealed and impatient, beneath all appearances of humanity.

Although I disagree with the conclusions of these critics, I think that they raise a crucial question, one that has been too often ignored in poststructural and postcolonial criticism of the story. If "Benito Cereno" is, like *Pierre* and *The Confidence-Man,* a story about the sources and consequences of uncertainty, then why does Melville make it pivot around the discovery of Aranda's skeleton? What could be more certain, as a sign of savagery, than that murdered, fleshless man, revealed with such a flourish at the climax of the story? If we don't have a way of answering that question, the efforts to elevate "Benito Cereno" into the canon of "post-" texts will inevitably, and rightly, stall. I think, though, that we *do* have an answer at hand. As we have seen, the visual evidence of cannibalism was widely recognized to share, at least potentially, the epistemological status of Othello's "ocular proof." More specifically, we have seen Melville present the discovery of disarticulated human bones at the end of *Typee* as nothing more than a "reason to suspect" that a Happar has been cannibalized. In several of the works that followed *Typee,* Melville again represented the sign of the cannibal in a way that turns our attention to the broadly "colonial" inclination to overread such signs. In *Mardi,* to take only one example, Yoomy asks Media why the inhabitants of Verdanna (Ireland) are aggrieved by the rule of King Bello of Dominora (England).

> "They are arrant cannibals, Yoomy," said Media, "and desire the privilege of eating each other up."

"King Bello's idea," said Babbalanja; "but, in these things, my lord, you demi-gods are ever unanimous." (*M*, 493)

Considered in this context, the display of Aranda's skeleton cannot be said to force us to the conclusion that the blacks on board the *San Dominick* symbolize the lurking presence of savagery. It may instead be said to represent the culmination of Melville's career-long effort to get his readers to see the spectacle of savagery *as* a spectacle—to get them to plunge, in an instant, from the warmth of the savage symbol to the coolness of the savage sign.[5]

To make that case, we will need to descend from the general crisis of "ocular proof" to the very specific crises of interpretation that accompanied the display of human bones. Once we know more about the complex evidentiary status of such displays, it will be easier for us to see Babo's performance as a savage as the mirror image of his more famous performance as a childlike slave; in each of these roles, he masterfully enacts the mode of anticolonial subjectivity that we now associate with the work of Homi Bhabha. But though this may be the principal reason the story is worthy of our renewed attention, it is not the only reason. By showing us exactly how Delano manages to misrecognize the implications of Babo's masquerade, Melville asks us to see that this performative subjectivity is radically dependent on the interpretive work of the colonialist, and that it is not easy to interfere with the colonialist's desire "to fix cultural difference in a containable, *visible* object" (Bhabha, *Location,* 50). In addition, by means of Cereno's mournful and generalized reflections on Babo's masquerade, Melville indicates that if we push past Delano's misrecognitions, we will find that not only on the colonial stage, but in every imaginable social environment, the knowledge of difference is only *apparently* fixed and visible. He shows Cereno sinking under the weight of this recognition not because he wants his white readers to think themselves to death, nor because he wants them to swing back in the direction of Delano, but because he wants them to act otherwise: to learn how to live in a world where meaning is the product of ungrounded decisions, and where acts of illumination are always shadowed by the darkness they displace. In spite of his deepening pessimism about the prospect of teaching anyone anything, Melville clearly hopes that at least some of those readers will take account of the mode of "black" subjectivity exemplified by Babo's masquerade, and imagine, on that basis, a mode of "white" subjectivity that forges past the dead ends of Delano's misrecognition and Cereno's melancholy.[6]

* * * that, during the three days which followed, the deponent, uncertain what fate had befallen the remains of Don Alexandro, frequently asked the negro Babo where they were, and, if still on board, whether they were to be preserved for interment ashore, entreating him so to order it; that the negro Babo answered nothing till the fourth day, when at sunrise, the deponent coming on deck, the negro Babo showed him a skeleton, which had been substituted for the ship's proper figure-head—the image of Christopher Colon, the discoverer of the New World; that the negro Babo asked him whose skeleton that was, and whether, from its whiteness, he should not think it a white's; that, upon his covering his face, the negro Babo, coming close, said words to this effect; 'Keep faith with the blacks from here to Senegal, or you shall in spirit, as now in body, follow your leader,' pointing to the prow; * * * that the same morning the negro Babo took by succession each Spaniard forward, and asked him whose skeleton that was, and whether, from its whiteness, he should not think it a white's; that each Spaniard covered his face; that then to each the negro repeated the words in the first place said to the deponent; * * *. . . .

. . . Some months after, dragged to the gibbet at the tail of a mule, the black met his voiceless end. The body was burned to ashes; but for many days, the head, that hive of subtlety, fixed on a pole in the Plaza, met, unabashed, the gaze of the whites; and across the Plaza looked towards St. Bartholomew's church, in whose vaults slept then, as now, the recovered bones of Aranda; and across the Rimac bridge looked towards the monastery, on Mount Agonia without; where, three months after being dismissed by the court, Benito Cereno, borne on the bier, did, indeed, follow his leader. — "Benito Cereno"

Upon being brought to face Aranda's skeleton, the Spaniards on the *San Dominick* invariably cover their eyes. With that image lingering in front of them, as a shifting, fading aftersight, they are suddenly invaded by the sound of Babo's voice, telling them where their resistance to his authority will lead. This transition from unbearable sight to unbearable sound, repeated daily, complicates the meaning of the phrase chalked on the pedestal supporting the new figurehead: *Follow your leader.* In the final paragraph of the story, there is no way of telling whether the "leader" that Cereno follows to death is Aranda's skeleton or Babo's still-potent skull; by that time, the two have become virtually interchangeable. The answer to the question at the heart of the story—What is the source of the shadow that has fallen over Cereno?—is not just "the negro," in other words, but "the negro" *as projected in the skeleton.* Once we recognize that Cereno's "leader" is a combination of Babo and Aranda, actor and prop, we are left with two related questions: What lesson has Cereno drawn from this performance, and what lesson does

Melville expect his readers to draw from it? In this section, I want to open up these questions by placing Babo's display within the context of the post-Enlightenment discourse on preserved and exhibited bones. Here as elsewhere, I do not mean to suggest that the reconstruction of a discourse can solve, by itself, the interpretive problems raised by a work of literature. Because there was a range of potential explanations within that discourse, just as there was in the more general discourse on cannibalism, anything that we say about the specific meaning of the bones displayed in "Benito Cereno" still has to be grounded in a close and argumentative reading of the text. But with that discourse at our disposal, we should be able to produce a reading of the story that will do as much as any reading can do—which is, simply, to bring us *nearer* to the sense that Melville is interested in making and that his readers are capable of taking.

The best points of entry into this discursive history are the scenes of the first encounters between Enlightenment voyagers and Pacific islanders. While visiting New Zealand in January 1770, James Cook writes, he "got from one of them the bone of the fore arm of a Man or a Woman which was quite fresh and the flesh had been but lately pick'd off which they told us they had eat. . . . [T]here was not one of us that had the least doubt but what this people were Canabals, but the finding this Bone with part of the sinews fresh upon it was a stronger proof than any we had yet met with" (Beaglehole, *Journals,* 1:236). On the same visit, the naturalist Joseph Banks found two gnawed bones in a basket belonging to some Maoris, and "[o]n asking the people what bones are these? they answerd, The bones of a man.—And have you eat the flesh?—Yes.—Have you none of it left?—No." "We were pleased," Banks says, "at having so strong a proof of a custom which human nature holds in too great abhorrence to give easy credit to" (1:455). The artist Sydney Parkinson similarly concluded that these kinds of encounters constituted "adequate proof that they are CANNIBALS," adding, "We also found human bones in the woods, near the ovens, where they used to partake of their horrid midnight repasts: and we saw a canoe the baler of which was made of a man's skull. The natives seemed even to take pride in their cruelty as if it was the most laudable virtue."[7] The possibility that the Maoris' avowal of cannibalism was motivated by something other than the pressure of a hidden truth does not seem to have entered into the calculations of these writers. And though Banks does suggest that the crew's conclusions on this subject are not particularly trustworthy, for "they only know a few words of the language, and eating people is now always the uppermost Idea in their heads" (Beaglehole, *Journals,* 1: 462), he does not allow this consideration of the effects of preconceived beliefs and equivocal signs to endanger the conclusions of the educated members of the expedition. To a man, the members of the expedition came away from New Zealand confirmed in their belief that the possession of human bones was a strong indication of cannibalism, and that the addition of native testimony raised it to the status of a proof.

But not all of those who heard or read these stories upon the voyagers' return to England were equally convinced. In his journal of his second voyage, Cook writes that he was dismayed to find that because his first account of cannibalism was "partly founded on circumstances," it was "discredited by many people. I have often been asked, after relateing all the circumstance, if I had actualy seen them eat human flesh my self" (Beaglehole, *Journals,* 2:294). Cook's consequent frustration was one of the motives behind the famous experiment on the *Resolution,* which both countered those objections and validated their basis: that "ocular proof," not bones and sign language, was the standard of evidence for cannibalism. Throughout the first half of the next century, this standard would continue to haunt those writers who convicted people of cannibalism on the basis of preserved or displayed body parts. In a review of John Anderson's *Mission to the East Coast of Sumatra* (1826), Sir John Barrow observes that Anderson's "main proof" of cannibalism among the Battas is that some members of the tribe presented him with the head "of a victim which they said they had just devoured. . . . A Batta, who had seen the human heads which no long time ago were stuck upon Temple Bar, would have just as good proof for saying that the people of London were cannibals" ("Anderson's *Mission,*" 108). Elsewhere, Barrow chastises a French surgeon who "mistook the bones of a kangaroo for those of a young girl, and set down the harmless people of Van Dieman's Land for cannibals," and the Russian admiral Adam Krusenstern, who "believes the inhabitants of the Marquesas to delight in human flesh; a fact which he considers to be corroborated by human skulls being offered for sale, and human bones being attached to various parts of their furniture" ("Porter's *Cruize,*" 367, 368). Not surprisingly, this ongoing critique had a noticeable effect on the way early-nineteenth-century travelers assessed the significance of the bones they found. While on the northwest coast of America in 1816, Camille de Roquefeuil reported that one of the members of his crew "found some human bones, which, with other indications, led us to imagine that they were the remains of a repast of Cannibals." But after a native tells him that the bones belonged "to bodies unburied by the bears, which often disturbed the graves," Roquefeuil admits the possibility of a mistake: "The idea of an abominable repast, suggested by the accounts of [John] Meares," might have "possessed my mind, and cast a gloom over all this scene." [8] In addition to being a sign of his own capacity for self-criticism, Roquefeuil's quick reevaluation of his initial conclusion is an indication of how weak the link between bones and cannibalism had become.

Under these circumstances, it is not at all surprising that this mode of criticism began to be applied to the account of cannibalism that initiated the modern history of the discourse. It was well known, in the early nineteenth century, that the word *cannibal* was a corruption of Carib, the name of the tribe that Columbus's reports had so powerfully associated with the practice of "anthropophagy." It was equally well known, moreover, that Columbus had based his enormously consequential conclusion that the Caribs were cannibals on nothing more than poorly translated native testimony and the discovery of human bones. William Sheldon, writing in 1823, was particularly dismissive of the historical evidence for Carib cannibalism. "If Columbus found bones and skulls of men," he says, "they were probably those of their ancestors and relations, whose bodies were carefully preserved and buried in the carbets where they died." [9] As for "the roasted arm of a man, mentioned in the voyage of Columbus, that was a trophy of victory among the Caraibs, and continued to be so two hundred years after his time" (418). Like the practice of preserving relics of dead relations, Sheldon says, "this practice of making trophies of the limbs of those they had slain, is not positive evidence of their being cannibals—it has rather a tendency to prove the contrary" (423). He concludes that the Spaniards, in an attempt "to justify their own enormous and unexampled cruelties . . . have, doubtless, slandered the much injured people of that quarter of the world," and that the worst offender in this regard is "Columbus, the origin and cause of the evils the Indians have suffered, and the perpetrator of many of them, particularly in the conquest of St. Domingo" (423–24).

The connection between the accusation of cannibalism and "the evils the Indians have suffered" is spelled out even more clearly in Alexander von Humboldt's widely read *Personal Narrative of Travels to the Equinoctial Regions of America,* originally published in English in 1822 and republished, in a new translation, in 1853. Like Sheldon, Humboldt observes that though the fifteenth-century Spanish accounts of the Caribs "have rendered the names of cannibals, Caribbees, and anthropophagi, synonymous," these accounts were plainly "exaggerated by the early travellers." [10] He then goes on to provide an especially detailed exposition of the historical fact that "[t]he first idea of attacking this nation, and depriving it of liberty and of its natural rights, originated with Christopher Columbus, who was not in all instances so humane as he is represented to have been" (3:86). Columbus's 1494 letter arguing for the enslavement of all New World cannibals was a major influence on the Spanish court's decision to issue "the celebrated *Provision Real* of the 30th of October, 1503, by which the Spaniards are permitted to make slaves of the anthropophagic Indians of the archipelago of San Bernardo, opposite the mouth of the Rio Sinu, the Isla Fuerte, Isla Bura (Baru), and Carthegena" (3:213). Once the Spanish prohibition of slavery was thereby cracked open, it was only a matter of time before it was broken to bits. In Rodrigo de Figueroa's *El Auto de Figueroa,* commissioned by the Spanish court and published in 1520, "every [South American] nation that could be accused of having devoured a prisoner after a battle, was arbitrarily declared of Carib race. . . . All the tribes designated by Figueroa as Caribs were condemned to slavery; and might at will be sold, or exterminated by war" (3:87). By that time, the circles spreading from the stone Columbus had cast had already touched the shores of Africa; the first black slaves had arrived in the New World in 1517.

Both of these aspects of the discourse associating Columbus with the unfounded imputation of cannibalism—the ambiguity of bones and the use of cannibalism as a justification for slavery—are taken up in Washington Irving's *History of the Life and Voyages of Christopher Columbus,* an extraordinarily popular biography first published in 1828. The only physical evidence suggesting that the Caribs were cannibals, Irving notes, was the presence among them of human bones. When Columbus's sailors entered a deserted Carib village for the first time, they were horrified by "the sight of various human bones, vestiges, as they supposed, of the unnatural repasts of the savages. . . . These dismal objects convinced them that they were now at the abodes of the Cannibals, or Caribs, those roving and ferocious warriors, whose predatory expeditions and ruthless character rendered them the terror of these seas." [11] But Irving insists that these "dismal objects" are not evidences of "cannibal propensities" so much as they are evidences of "the careless and inaccurate observations of seafaring men, and the preconceived belief of the fact [of cannibalism], which existed in the minds of the Spaniards" (2:30–31). He notes:

> It was a custom among the natives of many of the islands, and of other parts of the New World, to preserve the remains of their de-

ceased relatives and friends. Sometimes the entire body; sometimes only the head, or some of the limbs, dried at the fire; sometimes the mere bones. These, when found in the dwellings of the natives of Hispaniola, against whom no prejudice of the kind existed, were correctly regarded as relics of the deceased, preserved through affection or reverence; but any remains of the kind found among the Caribs, were looked upon with horror as proofs of cannibalism. (2:83)

Like Humboldt and Sheldon, Irving goes on to demonstrate that these "proofs" served as useful excuses for Spanish atrocities. After repeating the story of Columbus's 1494 letter recommending the enslavement of the Caribs, Irving justly observes that though Columbus might have deluded himself into thinking "that he was obeying the dictates of his conscience . . . he was in reality listening to the incitements of his interest"; he "feared the disappointment of the sovereigns in respect to the product of his enterprises, and was anxious to devise some mode of lightening their expenses until he could open some ample source of profit" (2:18). In the "revolting" practice of cannibalism, he had discovered an ideal justification for establishing possession of the Indians' bodies, as well as their land.

As these accounts should suggest, there was more than one way of rearticulating the meaning of bones once they had been disarticulated from the presumption of cannibalism. One argument, employed by both Sheldon and Irving, was that displayed bones were in fact objects of reverence. In the early nineteenth century, this argument surfaced most frequently in discussions of the meaning of bones discovered among Hawaiians. In reaction against the popular belief that Hawaiians had cannibalized Cook, the British captain George Anson Byron pointed out that those who subscribed to this belief had not adequately distinguished between the practice of preserving human bones and the practice of consuming human flesh. In paying their respects to dead nobility, Byron wrote in 1826, the Hawaiians sometimes "consumed the flesh by fire, or sometimes allowed the first process of putrefaction to take place under a bed of leaves, and then separated the flesh from the bones with wooden saws and scrupulously burned it, and, in all cases, carefully collected the bones, wrapped them in cloth, and deposited them in some safe and sacred place."[12] The missionaries George Bennet and Daniel Tyerman offer a slightly different account of this procedure, but one that reinforces its main points. While on a tour of the island of Hawaii in 1822, their guide pointed out the hollow, in the volcanic mass, where the body of Captain Cook was roasted, and a little further on, the place where his arms and legs were submitted to the same process. This was, in fact, the highest honor that his murderers (with the inconsistency of savages) could show to his remains; the corpses of their kings and chiefs being prepared in a similar manner, that the flesh might be more easily separated from the bones, and the skeleton afterwards be put together and preserved, as an object not only of reverence, but even of religious homage. (*Journal*, 1:376)

Cook's body was cooked not for the sake of its meat, in other words, but for the sake of its bones, which were then treated as sacred relics, and "annually carried in procession" (J. Martin, *Account*, 306).

The other argument is the one we find near the end of Sheldon's defense of the Caribs: that bones are not the residue of an unthinking feast, nor objects imbued with superstitious meaning, but "trophies." We have already encountered two examples of this argument: Urey Lisiansky's insistence that although the Marquesans do preserve human skulls, "neither their wearing them as trophies, nor offering them for sale, proves cannibalism" (*Voyage*, 87–88), and David Porter's argument that when the Marquesans "informed me that they sometimes ate their enemies," they were merely expressing "[t]heir fondness for their bones as trophies" (*Journal*, 2:46). In a similar vein, the American trader Benjamin Morrell remarks upon nearing a New Zealand harbor in 1830 that Captain Vancouver had here "lost a boat's crew, upon whose bodies, it is generally supposed, that the natives feasted; but from the account I received from one of the chiefs on the north side of the strait, I am led to believe that the flesh was thrown away, and the bones worn as ornaments by the principal chiefs" (*Narrative*, 369). Like the argument that the Hawaiians preserved the bones of Cook as sacred objects, the argument that the Marquesans and Maoris preserved the bones of their enemies as trophies asks us to see those bones not as the symbols of a desire to devour, but as the signs of a desire to signify. There is, however, a crucial difference between the ways in which these two arguments characterize that desire. In the first case, the islander is cast as a victim of superstition, viewing the bones through the medium of tradition as symbols of a power that is beyond him. In the second, the islander is cast as a strategist, turning objects to the use of turning away enemies. This doubled turning is embedded in the word *trophy*, from the Greek *tropos*; by misusing, or troping, the bones of an enemy, the islander attempts to coerce the surviving enemies into averting their gaze, reversing their vengeful direction. A particularly telling evocation of this dynamic is a passage from the missionary Charles Stewart's 1831 narrative of a visit to Nukuheva, in which he and his companions come upon a Happar canoe with "the skull of a murdered Taipii . . . lashed on each corner of the platform elevated at the stern — proclaiming the prowess of the victor in past engagements, and designed, by their spectral gaze, to throw intimidation and terror upon the enemy hardy enough to approach in another conflict. Not having met any thing of the kind before, the unexpectedness of the sight was accompanied by a feeling, that made us sensible of being in one of those 'dark places of the earth,' that are 'full of the habitations of cruelty' " (*Visit,* 1:327). For Stewart, a man devoted to the production of a world that brims with the symbolic presence of the sacralized object, the "spectral gaze" of these trophies is the emblem of the antihuman. By inserting, between the self and its others, the screen of the contingent sign, it destroys the illusion of transparency that all symbols require.

This leaves us with three ways of looking at a skeleton displayed by "savages": first, as a symbol of cannibal desire; second, as an object sacralized by superstition; and third, as a trophy designed "to throw intimidation and terror upon the enemy." Of these interpretive categories, only one is radically at odds with the presentation of the skeleton in "Benito Cereno": it is hard to imagine anyone concluding that the bones were preserved as objects of devotion, signifying that the blacks thought of Aranda as a hero or a god. It is, however, entirely possible to imagine readers leaning toward the first or the third interpretation of the scene: that it reveals the savage's transparent expression, or that it reveals the savage's spectral gaze. That said, we must immediately add that for readers leaning toward the first explanation, the textual support is unusually shaky. By revealing the skeleton immediately after Delano has finally seen the blacks "with masks torn away, flourishing hatchets and knives, in ferocious piratical revolt" (99), Melville does indeed enable us to decide that the skeleton symbolizes the presence of an instinctual savagery. But at the same time that he makes it possible for us to use this decision as the ground of all subsequent interpretation, he alerts us to the fact that "every inch" of this ground is "mined into honeycombs" beneath us (115). One of the ways he does this is by refusing to authorize the conclusion that the slaves have cannibalized their former master. Because bones were such an uncertain sign of cannibalism, their unsupplemented presentation could not provide, in itself, a secure basis for that conclusion. To remind us of this uncertainty, moreover, Melville conjures up the historical context in which those doubts were most acute. By juxtaposing the skeleton of the slaveholder with the figurehead of Columbus on a ship named the *San Dominick,* he offers the legions of readers who were familiar with the history of Columbus's voyages an indirect but emphatic warning: If you conclude on the basis of bones that a group of people are cannibals, you will be repeating Columbus's monumentally self-interested mistake.

But his most powerful challenge to the idea that the blacks are inherently cannibalistic is his repeated evocation of the third interpretive option. As we learn in the deposition, Babo's decision to macerate and exhibit Aranda's body is the product of a strategy session, in which he and Atufal conclude that the best way "to keep the seamen in subjection" is "to prepare a warning of what road [the Spaniards] should be made to take did they or any of them oppose him" (106). The unmistakable implication of this statement is that for Babo and Atufal, the skeleton is nothing more than a device, an emblematic object consciously intended to produce a certain effect on its audience. This implication is reinforced by the theatrics that accompany the skeleton's presentation to the Spaniards, and by the fact that when the scene shifts, the props shift with it. Upon discovering the *Bachelor's Delight* in the bay of Santa Maria, Babo and Atufal confer again, and Babo decides that he must devise new emblems, "uniting deceit"—the illusion of Spanish power— "and defense"—the threat of black power. The skeleton is covered with canvas, and is replaced by such things as "the device of the six Ashantees," stationed "as if to clean certain hatchets" but in reality to use them at Babo's signal, and "the device of presenting Atufal, his right hand man, as chained, though in a moment the chains could be dropped" (109). These devices are more complex than the device of the skeleton, insofar as they must influence two radically different audiences at once, but they are not categorically distinct from it. Neither are these African devices, taken as a whole, distinct from the Spanish devices that precede and succeed the revolt, like the figurehead of Columbus and the exhibition of Babo's severed head. The world of "Benito Cereno" is a world governed by the logic of the device, as Melville suggests in his depiction of the *San Dominick*'s stern-piece, "medallioned about by groups of mythological or symbolical devices, uppermost and central of which was a dark satyr in a mask, holding his foot on the prostrate neck of a writhing figure, likewise masked" (49). And what all such devices signify, when considered from a sufficient distance, is the condition of their production: the struggle for command, conceived of not as an encounter of essences but as a mutual masquerade.

As in *Typee* and *Moby-Dick,* then, Melville is asking us to think of the encounter with the "savage" as a compound process of recognition and misrecognition. In this case, of course, the process is more condensed; whereas those earlier works move us from racism through a masculinist humanism to their haunting afterthought, "Benito Cereno" contents itself with naturalizing and denaturalizing the racist perspective on savagery. Rather than projecting a substitute vision of the blacks as romantically "game" savages and then calling the substantiality of that vision into question, Melville centers all his attention on the racist vision, so that we might feel as fully as possible the effects of the transition from the fully constituted symbol of racial otherness to its destitute sign. These effects are, at least potentially, quite traumatic. In the social realm, Homi Bhabha has observed, "the displacement from symbol to sign creates a crisis for any concept of authority based on a system of recognition"; in the personal realm it destroys "the *depth* associated with the sign of symbolic consciousness" (*Location,* 114, 53). With that in mind, it is easier to understand why Babo chooses not to terrorize the Spaniards with an explicit account of the "fate [that] had befallen the remains of Don Alexandro." By confining himself to asking each sailor brought before the skeleton "whether, from its whiteness, he should not think it a white's," he simultaneously holds out and withholds the prospect of resolution, indicating both that the skeleton is a sure indication of Aranda's fate and that, as the cosmopolitan in *The Confidence-Man* will later say, "[y]ou can conclude nothing absolute from the human form" (*CM,* 226). Considered in this light, Babo's anticolonial strategy is identical to that of the bearers of menace who populate Bhabha's essays. Like them, Babo enacts "that ambivalent 'turn' of the discriminated subject into the terrifying, exorbitant object of paranoid classification" (*Location,* 113).

If we return now to the basic problem of the story—What is the unnamed thing that is emblematized by "the negro" and the skeleton?—it should be clear that the answer is not savagery, in the sense of a timeless instinct. The thing that Cereno recognizes, and Delano does not, is savagery in the sense of an identity-effect, a stiff and staring specter produced by overacting on the one hand and overreading on the other. Like all performative gestures, Babo's presentation of the skeleton "creates its signification behind it," and is, for this reason, "distinct from what might be called an *itself* that is behind" (Lacan, *Concepts,* 116, 99). From this perspective, "Benito Cereno" is neither a racist slipup nor an expression of "humanity"; it is, to the contrary, one of the most powerful nineteenth-century explorations of the postcolonial condition. In *Typee,* the terror of savagery did not ultimately interfere with the readers' predilection to think of savagery as a substance and to establish their humanity in a pleasurable sensation of horror. In *Moby-Dick*, Melville succeeded in accentuating the unsettling hollowness of savagery, but did so at the cost of making the novel's principal savage an explicitly fictional creation. The extraordinary thing about "Benito Cereno" is that the blacks on the *San Dominick* are entirely of this world *and* entirely inaccessible. Without assimilating them to the overly exotic domain of curious objects, and without assimilating them to the overly familiar domain of "humanity," Melville represents them as a company of actors on the colonial stage, neither present enough to provide us with the Otherness necessary to the constitution of our selves, nor absent enough to be safely ignored.

It would be a mistake, however, to limit the sphere of this inverted revelation to the colonial stage. Although it is obviously one of the locations most conducive to this revelation, it is not the only such location; as Robert Young has observed, it is hard to see why Bhabha's theory of the colonial encounter cannot be said to encompass every kind of encounter in which power is unequally distributed.[13] One of the virtues of "Benito Cereno" is that it encourages us to draw exactly this kind of connection between the colonial and noncolonial production of significance, between the truth of savagery and truth *as such.* By examining the connections that Melville establishes between the discourse on savagery and "the world of Mind" in his characterization of Delano and Cereno, we will see that to sever racial politics from theories of knowledge in our analyses of Melville's work is to cut ourselves off from a process of reflection that is essential to our understanding of Melville's literary development. We will see, moreover, that we are going to have to modify the preceding claim that the blacks on the *San Dominick* have succeeded in using the existing arrangements of the Western discourse on savagery as the conditions of their emergence as subjects. Bhabha is absolutely right to say that in our readings of these kinds of texts, "the point of intervention should shift from the ready recognition of images as positive or negative, to an understanding of the *processes of subjectification* made possible (and plausible) through stereotypical discourse" (*Location,* 67). But as Melville recognized after writing *Typee,* and as he dramatized in his creation of Delano, those "savages" who wish to subjectify themselves within the terms of the colonial encounter cannot count on the thoughtful attention of the "humane." If "the negro" is for Cereno the darkness that trails the sun around the globe, he is never anything more to Delano than a passing shadow.

Considering the lawlessness and loneliness of the spot, and the sort of stories, at that day, associated with those seas, Captain Delano's surprise might have deepened into some uneasiness had he not been a person of a singularly undistrustful good nature, not liable, except on extraordinary and repeated incentives, and hardly then, to indulge in personal alarms, any way involving the imputation of malign evil in man. Whether, in view of what humanity is capable, such a trait implies, along with a benevolent heart, more than ordinary quickness and accuracy of intellectual perception, may be left to the wise to determine. — "Benito Cereno"

The herb-doctor was silent for a time, buried in thought. At last, raising his head, he said: "I have considered your whole story, my friend, and strove to consider it in the light of a commentary on what I believe to be the system of things; but it so jars with all, it is so incompatible with all, that you must pardon me, if I honestly tell you, I cannot believe it." — *The Confidence-Man*

In one of the best recent studies of "Benito Cereno," James Kavanagh has suggested that the story "can be read as a discourse about discourse, about how the mind of a certain type of social subject *talks to itself,* giving itself the evidence with which to feel and live its own ruthlessness as 'innocence' and 'moral simplicity.'"[14] Like the herb doctor in *The Confidence-Man,* Amasa Delano insists on interpreting everything he sees as a commentary on what he believes to be "the system of things," seizing on all the pieces of evidence that fit, or seem to fit, his preexistent system of belief, and discarding all the ones that do not. But as Kavanagh has noted, most critics have not seen Delano in this light. Just as they have thought of Babo as a symbol of a universal savagery, so have they thought of Delano as a foolishly benevolent figure who will not acknowledge "the problem of the blacks" or "the problem of evil."[15] In the case of the first epigraph to this section, they have read Delano's resistance to "the imputation of malign evil in man" as a commentary on his overly "benevolent heart," which will not allow him to see that our common nature is irredeemably savage. If choosing against Delano's reading really did require us to assert that Babo is the embodiment of an immanent savagery, we would have to characterize the story as an accessory to the process that Frantz Fanon has described as the "fixing" of the black subject, "in the sense in which a chemical solution is fixed by a dye."[16] As I have already suggested, however, the story does not in fact present us with that initial choice between a world of perfect benignity and a world of lurking evil. Though a relative unwillingness to believe in the existence of "malign evil" may be one of the potential *effects* of Delano's "good nature," the most important *quality* of that nature is that it is "singularly undistrustful," incapable of processing the suggestion that things are not as they seem.

Consider, for example, the long passage in which Delano first begins to meditate on the "singular alternations of courtesy and ill-breeding in the Spanish captain." As he revolves that "unaccountable" behavior in his mind, he is suddenly possessed by the conviction that "[t]he man was an imposter":

> The alleged Don Benito was in early manhood, about twenty-nine or thirty. To assume a sort of roving cadetship in the maritime affairs of such a house, what more likely scheme for a young knave of talent and spirit? But the Spaniard was a pale invalid. Never mind. For even to the degree of simulating mortal disease, the craft of some tricksters had been known to attain. To think that, under the aspect of infantile weakness, the most savage energies might be couched—those velvets of the Spaniard but the silky paw to his fangs.
>
> From no train of thought did these fancies come; not from within, but from without; suddenly, too, and in one throng, like hoar frost; yet as soon to vanish as the mild sun of Captain Delano's good-nature regained its meridian.
>
> Glancing over once more towards his host—whose side-face, revealed above the skylight, was now turned towards him—he was struck by the profile, whose clearness of cut was refined by the thinness incident to ill-health, as well as ennobled about the chin by the beard. Away with suspicion. He was a true off-shoot of a true hidalgo Cereno. (64–65)

Most readers have taken this passage to be an expression of Delano's inability to come to terms with the reality of "savage energies." If we look more closely, however, it should become obvious that the truly indigestible element in Delano's "system" is not savagery, but deception. For one thing, the "fancy" that initiates this reflection is the thought of "wicked imposture" (64)—the idea that Cereno is not actually Cereno, but a lower-class "trickster" who is "simulating" aristocratic behavior. For another, the notion that allows Delano to say "Away with suspicion" is the revived conviction that we can read the character of others in their faces—that we all have an internal counterfeit detector that allows us to distinguish between true and false appearances. When "the mild sun of

Captain Delano's good-nature regain[s] its meridian," what it dispels, first and foremost, is the shadowy thought that Cereno is an impersonator.

This interplay of hesitation and resolution, in which thoughts of imposture troop into his consciousness and are immediately driven out, is repeated throughout the story. While waiting for his boat to arrive with food and water, Delano finds "his eye falling continually, as from a stage-box into the pit, upon the strange crowd before and below him," and suffers a "relapse" of suspicion (78). As he watches Babo slide the shaving razor across Cereno's throat and listens to Cereno retell, with "more than usual huskiness," the history of the voyage, the same notion returns:

> To Captain Delano's imagination, now again not wholly at rest, there was something so hollow in the Spaniard's manner, with apparently some reciprocal hollowness in the servant's dusky comment of silence, that the idea flashed across him, that possibly master and man, for some unknown purpose, were acting out, both in word and deed, nay, to the very tremor of Don Benito's limbs, some juggling play before him. . . . But then, what could be the object of enacting this play of the barber before him? At last, regarding the notion as a whimsy, insensibly suggested, perhaps, by the theatrical aspect of Don Benito in his harlequin ensign, Captain Delano speedily banished it. (87)

The crucial detail of these passages is the source of Delano's unease: the hollowness of apparently theatrical behavior. But it is also worth noting the chronic recurrence of this unease, "one of those antic conceits, appearing and vanishing in a breath, from which, perhaps, the best regulated mind is not always free" (85). What this recurrence suggests is that even the most "credulous good-nature" cannot entirely eliminate its "distrusts" (96); even the most "singular guilelessness" cannot prevent the "return of involuntary suspicion" (67). "[T]his is like the ague," Delano thinks to himself immediately after one of these episodes; "Because it went off, it follows not that it won't come back" (78). The only way for him to maintain his sense of himself as the "good captain" is to actively and continually defend his understanding of "the system of things" from the "enigmas and portents" that surround him (67).

One of the ways he wards off such sights is by "exerting his good-nature to the utmost" and reaching an internal compromise: "this is a strange craft; a strange history, too, and strange folks on board. But— nothing more" (78). More often, however, he attempts to occupy his attention with a "spectacle of fidelity" (57), an image that offers him the illusion of perfect self-evidence. At one point, he spies "a slumbering negress, partly disclosed through the lace-work of some rigging," with a child "[s]prawling at her lapped breasts." When the woman sees Delano watching her, she acts as if she is "not at all concerned at the attitude in which she had been caught," simply lifting the child to her body and "covering it with kisses." "There's naked nature now," thinks Delano, "pure tenderness and love" (73). As when he subsequently watches Babo performing his valet work with "a certain easy cheerfulness, harmonious in every glance and gesture" (83), it is the apparent spontaneity and sincerity of these "maternal transports" (73) that puts him "at ease with respect to exterior things," and allows his nature to remain "not only benign, but familiarly and humorously so" (84). The same may be said of his response to the long-awaited "sight" of his "household boat," the *Rover*, "not as before, half blended with the haze, but with outline defined, so that its individuality, like a man's was manifest" (77). By leaving him with the impression that the interior essence of each object is visible on its surface, these sights have the effect of "somehow insensibly deepen[ing] his confidence and ease" (73). The fact that they are spectacles of benign domestic relations is less important than the fact that they are *transparent* spectacles, enabling him to be "at ease with respect to exterior things" by dissolving that exteriority.

Nowhere is this more obvious than in his response to the sight of a Spanish sailor with "a face which would have been a very fine one but for its haggardness." As Melville observes, "Whether this haggardness had aught to do with criminality, could not be determined; since, as intense heat and cold, though unlike, produce like sensations, so innocence and guilt, when, through casual association with mental pain, stamping any visible impress, use one seal—a hacked one" (71–72). But this is not the idea that occurs to Delano, that supposedly "charitable man." "Rather another idea. Because observing so singular a haggardness combined with a dark eye, averted as in trouble and shame, and then, again recalling Don Benito's confessed ill opinion of his crew, insensibly he was operated upon by certain general notions which, while disconnecting pain and abashment from virtue, invariably link them with vice" (72). By allowing us to see Delano positively *welcoming* the "imputation of malign evil in man," Melville asks us to recognize that the indeterminacy of exterior things is Delano's profoundest horror. What Delano cannot bear to acknowledge is that innocence and guilt use the same hacked seal, that the signs of "pain and abashment" do not necessarily signify either virtue or vice. To repress the indeterminacy of the sailor's haggard face, he pairs it with other uncertain signs—the sailor's dark eye, Cereno's "ill opinion of his crew"—and in doing so, calls up a set of powerful assumptions that precede him and work through him. Without knowing it, he is "operated on by certain general notions" that treat haggardness as a sure symbol of vice. Here, more than anywhere else, the story does indeed become "a discourse about discourse." We are all susceptible to these kinds of "general notions," Melville suggests, and the most we can do to escape their insensible operations is to establish ourselves at a distance from them—to recognize that the seemingly natural links between signs and meanings are in fact arbitrary, and that the range of meanings that can be ascribed to each sign is broader than we might at first imagine.

In part, then, Melville may be said to be dramatizing Ishmael's observation that "there is no Champollion to decipher the Egypt of every man's and every being's face. Physiognomy, like every other human science, is but a passing fable" (*MD*, 347). In his ironization of Delano's desire to establish the origin and significance of every "visible impress," he may be said to be continuing a meditation on causation that he had pursued more explicitly in *Pierre*:

> In their precise tracings-out and subtile causations, the strongest and fieriest emotions of life defy all analytical insight. . . . The metaphysical writers confess, that the most impressive, sudden, and overwhelming event, as well as the minutest, is but the product of an infinite series of infinitely involved and untraceable foregoing occurrences. Just so with every motion of the heart. Why this cheek kindles with a noble enthusiasm; why that lip curls in scorn; these are things not wholly imputable to the immediate apparent cause, which is only one link in the chain; but to a long line of dependencies whose further part is lost in the mid-regions of the impalpable air. (*P*, 67)

But the virtues of his characterization of Delano extend beyond its contribution to his more general critique of physiognomic thinking. As John Haegert has recently observed, the structure of the story forces the first-time reader to travel *through* Delano's consciousness before traveling *past* it, in an inevitably belated recognition of its limitations.[17] Before reading against Delano, and acknowledging the ultimate impossibility of "analytical insight," we are asked to read with him, to some degree, in order to experience what it is like to have the continuity of one's identity depend on the repression of that impossibility. If we identify even in part with Delano's desire for physiognomic certainty, we will be better able to feel how much is lost when the face of sincere and transparent expression gives way to the face of the kraken. And if we have felt how much is at stake in the reproduction of discursively conditioned assumptions, we will be better able to understand both how difficult and how important it is to recover the questions of evidence that are repressed in the moment of discursive closure.

One of the things that makes that process of recovery so difficult is the seductiveness of the book's climactic moment, in which Delano suddenly figures out who has been mastering whom. After first Cereno and then Babo have leaped from the *San Dominick* into Delano's boat, Delano sees Babo raising a dagger to strike Cereno:

> That moment, across the long-benighted mind of Captain Delano, a flash of revelation swept, illuminating in unanticipated clearness his host's whole mysterious demeanor, with every enigmatic event of the day, as well as the entire past voyage of the San Dominick. . . . [G]lancing up towards the San Dominick, Captain Delano, now with the scales dropped from his eyes, saw the negroes, not in misrule, not in tumult, not as if frantically concerned for Don Benito, but with mask torn away, flourishing hatchets and knives, in ferocious piratical revolt. (99)

Most readers have taken this scene to be the long-awaited solution to the drawn-out problem of the *San Dominick,* and it is easy to see why: we are used to thinking of clarity as a good thing. But far from being an illumination of the thing he most feared—the savagery in man—this "flash of revelation" provides Delano with exactly what he has been wishing for all along: a certainty so perfect that all preceding doubts and prospective afterthoughts are gathered into the present moment and incinerated. "In the cold courts of justice," Melville writes in *Pierre,* "the dull head demands oaths, and holy writ proofs; but in the warm halls of the heart one single, untestified memory's spark shall suffice to enkindle such a blaze of evidence, that all the corners of conviction are as suddenly lighted up as a midnight city by a burning building, which on every side whirls its reddened brands" (*P*, 71). As far as Delano is concerned, all the shadows that had previously been lurking in "the corners of conviction" are now no more. In that moment of illumination, in which "past, present, and future seemed one" (BC, 98), he has obliterated every piece of recalcitrant evidence, every potential testimony to the ongoingness of misrecognition. What appears to be the story's moment of clearest vision is, paradoxically, its ultimate moment of repression.[18]

This is the point that Cereno tries to make in his last recorded conversation with Delano. After reminding Delano of the mistake he had made in reading him as the villain, Cereno begins to "generalize" more "mournfully" on how easily it is to be mistaken "in judging the conduct of one with the recesses of whose condition he is not acquainted" (116, 115). Your case is actually a special one, he tells Delano, for two reasons: "you were forced" to your conclusion by the imposition of fictional devices, and "you were in time undeceived" (115). If the only things intervening between uncertainty and certainty were these kinds of forcefully imposed fictions, there would be little to be mournful about; it would be possible to imagine that we could expose the true recesses of another's condition by clearing those fictions away. But in the final sentence of his speech—"Would that, in both respects, it was so ever, and with all men"—Cereno suggests that these fictions are both more structural and more tenacious than Babo's temporary deception of Delano might suggest. In most cases, we are not forced into errors by the devices of an outside agent; our anxieties and "general notions" are capable of generating a world of errors all by themselves. In most cases, moreover, we are never "undeceived." We sleepwalk through a ghostly landscape of our own imagining, and we never wake up. Not surprisingly, Delano rejects this reading, insisting that, like the "bright sun . . . and the blue sea, and the blue sky," we must "[turn] over new leaves," and that the presence of the trade winds, those "steadfast friends," means that there is no cause for concern (116). But as Cereno well knows, the fact of the sun does not abolish the fact of darkness, and the trade winds are anything but steadfast. For Delano, the day's events are bathed in the brilliant light of his climactic recognition; for Cereno, they are plunged in the shadow of all the misrecognitions that came before.

One of the potential effects of Cereno's gnomic pronouncements in this scene is to transform him, in the reader's eyes, into the subject-who-knows. After traveling in and above Delano's consciousness over the course of the story, readers generally come to see him as the subject-who-does-not-know, the paranoid and violent rehabilitator of social and discursive order. In opposing Cereno's melancholy awareness to Delano's blithe repressiveness, Melville appears to be suggesting that the title character is, indeed, the preeminent figure of narrative authority, the principal source of insight into the hidden regions of the story. By de-emphasizing the significance of the climactic revelation, Cereno enables us to see how fleeting all such revelations are, and how distant the effects of things ordinarily are from their causes. By "generaliz[ing]" the implications of Babo's masquerade, he enables us to see the colonial encounter as a local embodiment of a larger phenomenon; by generalizing "mournfully," he enables us to recognize that the essential aspect of all such encounters is remoteness. For an implicitly "white" readership, unwilling to take their lead from the figure of Babo, Cereno offers the most obvious alternative to the way of being that is modeled by the good captain.[19] But in encouraging us to share Cereno's recognition of the significance of "the negro," Melville is not encouraging us to fall, like Cereno, into a suicidal depression. Instead, he is asking his "white" readers to make a pair of related choices: to choose Cereno's open, empty realm of Mind over Delano's closed, complete realm of Discourse, and then to choose *against* Cereno's conduct: to learn how to live with the loss that he has so narcissistically refused.

Melancholy

And here it may be randomly suggested, by way of bagatelle, whether some things that men think they do not know, are not for all that thoroughly comprehended by them; and yet, so to speak, though contained in themselves, are kept a secret from themselves? The idea of Death seems such a thing. —*Pierre*

[T]he cable of the *San Dominick* had been cut; and the fag-end, in lashing out, whipped away the canvas shroud about the beak, suddenly revealing, as the bleached hull swung round towards the open ocean, death for the figure-head, in a human skeleton; chalky comment on the chalked words below, "*Follow your leader.*"

　　At the sight, Don Benito, covering his face, wailed out: " 'Tis he, Aranda, my murdered, unburied friend!" —"Benito Cereno"

At the moment when the canvas is swept away from the bow of the *San Dominick*, revealing "death for the figure-head, in a human skeleton," we encounter the allegorical signification of the object *before* we encounter the object itself. The peculiar phrasing of this passage calls our attention first to the "idea of Death" that is encrypted in us all, and only secondarily to the skeleton that represents it. It is no accident of syntax; Melville has hinted, throughout the early part of the narrative, that the *San Dominick* is an allegorical Ship of Death. We hear, for example, that the ship seems "launched from Ezekiel's Valley of Dry Bones" (48); that its roll is "hearse-like" (49); that the old Africans' chant sounds like a "funeral march" (50); that the ship's bell has a "dreary grave-yard toll" (61); that the dead-lights on the quarter-gallery are "closed like coppered eyes of the coffined" and that the state-cabin door is "calked fast like a sar-cophagus lid" (74). In his repeated allusions to the inscription below the skeleton, moreover, he evokes an old American funerary practice: the tradition of engraving skeletons or death's-heads on grave markers, ac-companied by a somber written reminder of the viewer's own inevitable demise. One of the most common of these epitaphs was "Prepare for death and follow me." [20] By the turn of the nineteenth century, such me-mento mori had been generally rejected as gloom-producing Puritanisms and replaced, in cemeteries and in the literature of death and mourn-ing, by images and inscriptions that memorialized the personality of the departed.[21] Viewed in this light, the appearance of the skeleton may be said to represent the recursion of a pre-sentimental understanding of the relationship between body and spirit. No longer the symbol of person-ality, the corporeal self has become, once again, a purely indifferent sign.

We may say of "Benito Cereno," then, what Walter Benjamin has said of the *Trauerspeil:* that it presents us with a world where characters die not so that we can witness their passage into immortality, but so that we can witness their existence as corpses. When a body becomes a corpse, Benjamin says, it enters "the homeland of allegory"; no longer mistak-able for a hieroglyphic symbol of an individual spirit, an organic whole that is always itself, it now stands revealed as "a fragment, a rune. . . . The false appearance of totality is extinguished." [22] Once the illusory light of an immanent presence has been blown out, we are confronted by a body that signifies only what we make it signify through the opera-tions of allegory. A symbol has been collapsed into "a signature, only the monogram of essence, not the essence itself in a mask." [23] In its represen-tation of this collapse, "Benito Cereno" reintroduces one of the central questions of *Pierre:* "How can lifelessness be fit memorial of life?" After discovering that his carefully preserved souvenirs have not retained their original significance, Pierre declares himself an apostate from the senti-mental cult of the symbol: "Hitherto I have hoarded up mementoes and monuments of the past; been a worshiper of all heirlooms; a fond filer away of letters, locks of hair, bits of ribbon, flowers, and the thousand-and-one minutenesses which love and memory think they sanctify:— but it is forever over now!" Mocked by the sight of memorials that have collapsed into memento mori, he resolves never again to "play the vile pigmy, and by small memorials after death, attempt to reverse the de-cree of death, by essaying the poor perpetuating of the image of the original" (*P,* 197–98). Through his presentation of Aranda's skeleton, Melville tries to get his readers to share Pierre's recognition that ob-jects are incapable of holding onto the meaning that has been assigned to them—that souvenirs are always en route to becoming what Susan Stewart calls "antisouvenirs," the "mere material remains of what had possessed human significance" (*On Longing*, 140).

In the world of the story, the character who models this recognition for us is Cereno. Prompted by what Melville calls, in "The Encantadas," the "strong persuasions of [the] Romish faith, which sets peculiar store by consecrated urns" (*PT*, 155), Cereno did his best to protect the integrity of Aranda's remains in the days following his murder; he "frequently asked the negro Babo where they were, and, if still on board, whether they were to be preserved for interment ashore, entreating him so to order it" (BC, 107). In the context of these requests, the parodic resurrection of the corpse on the morning of the fourth day is deeply wounding; nothing could be further from Christ's risen body than those unsanctified, indefinite bones. This is the wound that Delano reopens when he tells Cereno that

> "by a sympathetic experience, I conjecture, Don Benito, what it is that gives the keener edge to your grief. It was once my hard fortune to lose, at sea, a dear friend, my own brother, then supercargo. Assured of the welfare of his spirit, its departure I could have borne like a man; but that honest eye, that honest hand—both of which had so often met mine—and that warm heart; all, all—like scraps to the dogs—to throw all to the sharks! It was then I vowed never to have for fellow-voyager a man I loved, unless, unbeknown to him, I had provided every requisite, in case of a fatality, for embalming his mortal part for interment on shore. Were your friend's remains now on board this ship, Don Benito, not thus strangely would the mention of his name affect you."
>
> "On board this ship?" echoed the Spaniard. Then, with horrified gestures, as directed against some spectre, he unconsciously fell into the ready arms of his attendant, who, with a silent appeal toward Captain Delano, seemed beseeching him not again to broach a theme so unspeakably distressing to his master. (61)

After suffering the mutilation and likely disposal of parts that Delano unthinkingly describes, Aranda's remains can no longer serve as an assurance of "the welfare of his spirit." In their resolute materiality, they can only point to the *absence* of the spirit that had once animated them, and thereby to the allegorical idea of Death that Cereno has tried to secrete within himself.

As a similar reaction in a later scene should suggest, Cereno's fear of the skeleton, understood as the antisouvenir of human presence, corresponds to his fear of "the negro," understood as the antisouvenir of colonial presence. While explaining again to Delano how the *San Dominick* had arrived in the harbor, Cereno's "sane memory of the past seemed replaced by insane terrors of the present. With starting eyes he stared before him at vacancy. For nothing was to be seen but the hand of his servant pushing the Canary over towards him" (90). To Cereno, Babo is indeed "nothing"; the "hand of his servant" is as evacuated of meaning as the body of his friend. This is why his responses to Delano's efforts to engage him in a discussion of physiognomy are so dulled; he can no longer believe, with Delano, that the "expression and play of every human feature" are "impossible to . . . counterfeit" (69). When Delano observes that the physiognomy of the mulatto Francesco is "more regular than King George's of England," and asks Cereno to confirm his inference that the slave is "a king, indeed—the king of kind hearts and polite fellows," he receives a "phlegmatic" response. Undeterred, Delano goes on to allude to the countervailing theory that the blood of mulattos is naturally "vitriolic." After half-heartedly observing that he has heard similar stories, Cereno says, "I know nothing about the matter" (89). Just as the key hanging from Cereno's neck and the padlock at Atuful's groin are not "significant symbols" of Cereno's "lordship over the black" (63)—just as his "silver-mounted sword, apparent symbol of despotic command," is in fact the "ghost" of a sword in an "artificially stiffened" scabbard (116)—so are the bodies of the blacks not the expressions of their beings. When Cereno ascribes his melancholy to "the negro," one of the things he means is that Babo's masquerade has led him to see every "apparent symbol" as an "artificially stiffened" sign, and to conclude that he "know[s] nothing" about the relationship between form and character.

In this sense, Cereno represents the point of contact between Melville's treatments of the discourse on savagery and his explorations of the "world of Mind": the image of "post-Enlightenment man tethered to, *not* confronted by, his dark reflection, the shadow of colonized man, that splits his presence, distorts his outline, breaches his boundaries, repeats his action at a distance, disturbs and divides the very time of his being" (Bhabha, *Location,* 44). Once he realizes that "the negro" is a shadow divorced from its substance, Cereno loses faith in the real presence of all forms of substance, including his own. Asked by Delano to explain the significance of his ceremonial interrogation of Atufal, he replies:

> "It means that that negro alone, of all the band, has given me peculiar cause of offense, I have put him in chains; I—"
> Here he paused; his hand to his head, as if there were a swim-

ming there, or a sudden bewilderment of memory had come over him; but meeting his servant's kindly glance seemed reassured, and proceeded:—

"I could not scourge such a form." (62)

The word he stumbles over, as if unable to imagine what could possibly come after it, is "I." It is this inability to articulate the nature of his self, in the midst of a discourse on his other, that makes Cereno such an archetypal example of the colonialist in the process of becoming post-colonial. As Bhabha has said, when "the self that develops in the symbolic consciousness of the sign" is mocked by the simulated presence of the other, "*The real Me* emerges (initially as an assertion of the authenticity of the person) and then lingers on to reverberate—*The real Me?*— as a questioning of identity" (*Location,* 49). By focusing our attention on the spectacle of Cereno "painfully turning in the half embrace of his servant" (56), Melville asks us to see that the "white" subject is not himself without the presence of the other, and therefore never quite himself.

But though the story does ask us to share Cereno's perception of Babo's masquerade, it does not ask us to share his response to that perception. Immediately after the retaking of the *San Dominick,* Cereno shows "some sign of regaining health with free-will," but soon, "agreeably to his own foreboding," he becomes "so reduced as to be carried ashore in arms" (103). Declaring himself "broken in body and mind" (114), he retreats to a monastery on Mount Agonia, where he is attended by a monk named Infelez—"his one special guardian and consoler, by night and by day" (103)—until his death three months later. For a contemporary audience, it would have been abundantly clear that the brokenness of his body is a consequence of the brokenness of his mind. The disease that kills him is quite obviously tuberculosis; we hear early on that he has a "tendency to some pulmonary complaint [that] appeared to have been lately confirmed" (52) and that he repeatedly experiences "febrile and transient" fits of "hectic animation" that die away into "indifference and apathy" (58, 91). Throughout most of the nineteenth century, "consumption" was popularly represented as a "disease of extreme contrasts: white pallor and red flush, hyperactivity alternating with languidness. . . . The sufferer is wracked by coughs, then sinks back, recovers breath, breathes normally; then coughs again." [24] The cause of Cereno's illness is equally obvious; after one "fainting attack of his cough," we are told that the episode has been "brought on, no doubt, by his mental distress" (55). Prior to the establishment of the germ theory of tuberculosis in the 1880s, the standard medical opinion was that the disease had its origin in "long and grievous passions of the mind," and more particularly in "ungratified desires, the principal of which is nostalgia."[25] It was thought to be the disease of those who were "consumed" by the sense that some bright and necessary ideal was irretrievably lost, permanently unrealizable. In *Billy Budd,* for instance, we are told that as Billy lies in chains, awaiting his execution, "the skeleton in the cheekbone at the point of its angle was just beginning delicately to be defined under the warm-tinted skin." Though Billy shares the name of the man whose researches on African sailors in the 1850s helped to establish the germ theory of tuberculosis, Melville draws the old-fashioned moral: "In fervid hearts self-contained, some brief experiences devour our human tissue as secret fire in a ship's hold consumes cotton in the bale" (*BB,* 119).[26]

With this moralistic representation of Cereno's illness and death, Melville moves away from his usual critique of the logic of physiognomy. In doing so, however, he moves toward a crucial distinction between proper and improper forms of grief. By recognizing the implications of Delano's misrecognition, Cereno has demonstrated that "[t]he intensest light of reason and revelation combined, can not shed such blazonings upon the deeper truths in man, as will sometimes proceed from his own profoundest gloom" (*P,* 169). But by sinking into the deadly embrace of Unhappiness, Cereno demonstrates that "continual unchanging residence" in "the haunts of woe" will "bring on woe's stupor, and make us as dead" (*P,* 156). Unlike Eva's death-by-woe in *Uncle Tom's Cabin,* Cereno's expiration is not a sign that he is too good for this world, the embodiment of a set of moral values that must be aspired to here and realized elsewhere. It is, instead, a sign that he *thinks* he is too good for this world. At one point, as we observe Cereno in "the full indulgence of his morbid hour," Melville tells us, "Meantime the sound of the parted waters came more and more gurglingly and merrily in at the windows; as reproaching him for his dark spleen; as telling him that, sulk as he might, and go mad with it, nature cared not a jot; since, whose fault was it, pray?" (BC, 95). Not nature's; as Melville observes in *Pierre,* nature is "the mere supplier of that cunning alphabet, whereby selecting and combining as he pleases, each man reads his own peculiar lesson according to his own peculiar mind and mood" (*P,* 342). Far from being the natural reaction to the discovery that Cereno has made, sulkiness is a purely personal *reading* of that discovery, produced by a "moody man" (BC, 116). Because Cereno longs, like Macbeth, to be "Whole as the marble, founded as the rock, / As broad and general as the casing air," he cannot live with the recognition that he is in fact a "walking shadow," unfounded and transitory. Like Macbeth, he believes that a life without stability, expansiveness, and perfect presence is nothing better than "a tale / Told by an idiot, full of sound and fury, / Signifying nothing."[27]

But as Emily Dickinson so eloquently suggests, in one of her late, brief poems, there is nothing inherently depressing about the passing and repassing of shadows, and the signification of nothingness is not necessarily a cause for despair:

> By homely gift and hindered Words
> The human heart is told
> Of Nothing—
> "Nothing" is the force
> That renovates the World—

In this rereading of "nothing" lies the final step of the argument we have seen Melville making, with increasing assuredness, in his reflections on the sign of the cannibal. We are indeed walking shadows, but this inability to embody our essence in the act of willing is what makes communication both necessary and possible. We do indeed signify "nothing," but the emptiness at the heart of our being and behavior is what makes it possible for us to organize ourselves in new ways. Throughout his work, Melville has asked us to recognize that our encounters with the other, savage or otherwise, are frustrated by the "continual recession of the goal" (BC, 70); every time we think we are about to witness the revelation of an interior, it turns out to be, "upon its sudden and complete disclosure," nothing more than "a shadowy tableau" (50). In "Benito Cereno," more clearly than anywhere else, he asks us to see, in this deferral of presence, the engine of all anti-ideological intervention. Through the example of Cereno's final comments, he shows that the recognition of this negation can break the grip of Delano's ideology; through his criticism of Cereno's melancholy withdrawal, he suggests that we can and should survive it. Knowing ourselves to be shadows whose substance is Elsewhere, we can and should keep walking: awake, as opposed to Delano, alive, as opposed to Cereno, and hearing, with every step, the echo of nothingness, the only voice of our God.

AFTERWORD

Finding is the first Act
The second, loss,
Third, Expedition for
The "Golden Fleece"
Fourth, no Discovery—
Fifth, no Crew—
Finally, no Golden Fleece—
Jason—sham—too.
—Emily Dickinson

For the past two years, I have lived about twenty-five miles from Arrowhead, the farmhouse in Pittsfield, Massachusetts, where Melville wrote *Moby-Dick,* "Benito Cereno," and all his other fiction of the 1850s. It is now a museum that offers daily tours in the spring, summer, and fall; twice a week during the academic year, I drive by the sign advertising it. But in all this time, I haven't once visited the house. I think I know why. I have been building in my mind, in my notebooks, and on my computer screen, a "Melville." This Melville read many of the same obscure travel narratives and periodical reviews that I have read, and came, like me, to the conclusion that there was something peculiar and important about the ways his contemporaries talked about cannibalism. I am, for the most part, convinced of the existence of this Melville; I believe what I have said in the preceding chapters. But what if I were to go to the once-actual home of the once-actual Melville and experience no sense of confirmation there? Or, worse, a sense that Melville was emphatically *not* what I have imagined him to be? What if I have been making the whole thing up? What if this has been a kind of puppet show, in which I have created a stage called "the discourse on cannibalism," pulled the sock I call "Melville" over my fist, and started talking? And if there is indeed no Golden Fleece, if "finding" is only an illusion, is "Jason—sham—too"?

My desire to avoid the potential occasions of these doubts has not made them go away. Like all afterthoughts, they are structural, and no act of will is going to relieve me of them. Given the argument that I have been making in this book, there is no reason to keep them to myself, or to disguise with hyperbole the places where they have cropped up. But neither is there any reason to retract the argument that I have made in the face of these doubts. As I write this, I am reminded of something Hawthorne once said of Melville, that he could neither believe, nor be comfortable in his disbelief—and with that, I instantly find myself back where I began, projecting myself into the space of "Melville" and recoiling in embarrassment. One of the points of this book has been to show that there is no way out of those kinds of loops, and that the process of cycling through them does not necessarily lead to despair. What I have not stressed enough, perhaps, is that the moments when we find ourselves caught in them are, for all that, painful. In response to the experience of being doubled back on myself, all I can do is tell another story, one that has occasionally restored for me a measure of conviction. It will not erase any of the doubts that I have described here, but it will write in larger letters, and more firmly, my belief that Melville addressed the tensions within the discourse on cannibalism with more passion and subtlety than anyone else of his age.

In November 1820, Capt. George Pollard of the whaleship *Essex* brought his whaleboat back from an unsuccessful hunt in the equatorial Pacific to find that the *Essex* had disappeared. According to the first mate, Owen Chase, who had observed the disaster from his own whaleboat, the rowers in Pollard's boat uttered a "cry of horror and despair . . . as their looks were directed for [the ship], in vain, over every part of the ocean." Pollard himself

> had no power to utter a single syllable: he was so completely overpowered with the spectacle before him, that he sat down in his boat, pale and speechless. I could scarcely recognise his countenance, he appeared to be so much altered, awed, and overcome, with the oppression of his feelings, and the dreadful reality that lay before him. He was in a short time however enabled to address the inquiry to me, "My God, Mr. Chase, what is the matter?" I answered, "We have been stove by a whale."[1]

The ship was not yet altogether gone; while it lay just below the surface of the water, the crew managed to get some supplies from it. Then, as Pollard later told the missionary George Bennet, instead of pushing away for some port, so amazed and bewildered were we, that we continued sitting in our places, gazing upon the ship as though she had been an object of the tenderest affection. Our eyes could not leave her, till, at the end of many hours, she gave a slight reel, then down she sank. No words can tell our feelings. We looked at each other—we looked at the place where she had so lately been afloat—and we did not cease to look, till the terrible conviction of our abandoned and perilous situation roused us to exertion, if deliverance were yet possible. (213)

Having decided not to row with the wind to nearby Tahiti, because "we feared we should be devoured by cannibals," Pollard and his men attempted to row two thousand miles against the wind to South America. One of the three boats disappeared, and the remaining boats separated. On Pollard's boat, two men died from natural causes and were roasted in the bottom of the boat and eaten. Once this food was gone,

> [w]e looked at each other with horrid thoughts in our minds, but we held our tongues. I am sure that we loved one another as brothers all the time; and yet our looks told plainly what must be done. We cast lots, and the fatal one fell on my poor cabin-boy. I started forward instantly, and cried out, "My lad, my lad, *if you don't like your lot,* I'll shoot the first man that touches you." The poor emaciated boy hesitated a moment or two; then, quietly laying his head down upon the gunnel of the boat, he said, "*I like it as well as any other.*" He was soon despatched, and nothing of him left. I think, then, another man died of himself, and him, too, we ate. But I can tell you no more—my head is on fire at the recollection. I hardly know what I say. (215)

When their boat was finally spotted by a passing ship, only Pollard and a single "brother" were still alive. "Captain Pollard closed his dreary narrative," Bennet writes, "with saying, in a tone of despondency never to be forgotten by him who heard it—'After a time I found my way to the United States, to which I belonged, and got another ship. That, too, I have lost by a second wreck off the Sandwich Islands, and now I am utterly ruined. No owner will ever trust me with a whaler again, for all will say I am an *unlucky* man'" (215).

While whaling in the equatorial Pacific in the early 1840s, Melville read Chase's narrative. In a copy he later acquired, he would recall that "[t]he reading of this wondrous story upon the landless sea, & close to the very latitude of the shipwreck had a surprising effect upon me" (Heffernan, *Stove*, 191). Some aspects of that "effect" may be detected in *Mardi,* in which the narrator remarks on the fate of "the good craft Essex" (*M,* 40) just before he and his companion, adrift in the Pacific in an open boat, suffer through a four-day calm. As the calm deepens, a telling look comes into their eyes: "What sort of expression my own countenance wore, I know not; but I hated to look at Jarl's. When I did it was a glare, not a glance" (49). Before this time, the narrator has been so resolutely good-natured that he has barely entertained the thought that their supplies might run out. When he has entertained it, moreover, he has transformed it into an affirmation of his geniality: "if it came to the last dead pinch, of which we had no fear, however, I was food for no man but Jarl" (20). But now, he says,

> I wished I was alone. I felt that so long as the calm lasted, we were without help; that neither could assist the other; and above all, that for one, the water would hold out longer than for two. I felt no re-morse, not the slightest, for these thoughts. It was instinct. Like a desperado giving up the ghost, I desired to gasp by myself.
> From being cast away with a brother, good God deliver me! (49–50)

In that last cry, we hear the echo of Pollard's voice: "I am sure that we loved one another as brothers all the time; and yet our looks told plainly what must be done." Though the narrator and his companion discover a ship four days later, and leave the open boat, the narrator has been jarred by the onset of something that exists beyond his ordinary understanding of himself—not "savagery," which could be imaginatively transposed into his interior, but the unbudging materiality of a world "without help," in which Providence has failed.

Though this is a lesson that did not *depend* on a familiarity with the narratives of Bennet and Chase—it was an available element of the dis-course on shipwreck cannibalism—these narratives were, for Melville, the principal sources of his reflections on the subject. He borrows from Bennet and Tyerman's *Journal of Voyages and Travels* elsewhere in *Mardi,* he quotes from it in the "Extracts" to *Moby-Dick,* and he uses details drawn from Bennet's interview with Pollard in "The Affidavit."[2] The influence of Chase's narrative is even more obvious; Melville acquired a copy of it in 1851, as he was accelerating toward the conclusion of *Moby-Dick,* and left in it not just marginalia, but an extensive record of his response, written on blank pages bound into the front and back of the book. In this written record, he emphasizes above all else the *Essex's* "miserable pertinaciousness of misfortune" (Heffernan, *Stove,* 203): the horribly misinformed decision to steer away from Tahiti, the cannibalism on the boats, Pollard's subsequent shipwreck, and the infidelity of Chase's wife. In his marginalia, too, he lays particular stress on passages that address the mysteriousness and inescapability of that "misfortune." The most vigorously highlighted passage is one in which Pollard's boat suffers a shadowy repetition of the whale's attack. Hearing Pollard call out for help, Chase "made all haste to put about, ran down to him, and inquired what was the matter; he replied, 'I have been attacked by an unknown fish, and he has stove my boat.' It appeared, that some large fish had accompanied the boat for a short distance, and had suddenly made an unprovoked attack upon her, as nearly as they could determine, with his jaws; the extreme darkness of the night prevented them from distinguishing what kind of animal it was" (208). When Chase subsequently writes that "[t]here was not a hope now remaining to us but that which was derived from a sense of the mercies of our Creator" (209), Melville makes it quite clear that the narrative has not led him to share that belief. He underlines the words "mercies of our Creator" and adds, above them, a question mark.

As Henry Pommer long ago observed, Melville's reflections on the *Essex* material did not end with *Moby-Dick.* In July 1852, Melville traveled to Nantucket, where he met George Pollard, then working as a night watchman. Remembering their conversation late in his life, he wrote that "[t]o the islanders he was a nobody—to me, the most impressive man, tho' wholly unassuming even humble—that I ever encountered" (Heffernan, *Stove,* 195–96). Though Melville had already indicated that he thought of Pollard's reactions to his experiences as one of the most important elements of the *Essex* story, the retired, silently reflective captain would become, in the wake of this encounter, even more of an iconic figure. The "Agatha story" that Melville proposes to Hawthorne in August 1852 has in it "a man of the sea" who has been "early driven away from it by repeated disasters," and is now "subdued & quiet & wise in his life" (*C*, 237). In his characterization of Benito Cereno, he explores another version of this figure, with the crucial difference that Cereno does not succeed in becoming, like Pollard, an "unassuming" survivor of his disaster. But his most powerful and extensive reflection on Pollard would come twenty years later, in *Clarel.* Observing the chastened behavior of the pilgrim Nehemiah, Rolfe is reminded of the story of a captain who once believed in "man's free will" but was converted

to "Calvin's creed" by misfortunes at sea: a wreck followed by cannibalism, another wreck, caused by "a whale / Of purpose aiming," and
then a long, lonely endgame as a stigmatized "night patrolman." By this
time Melville too was "on the quay / Watching the bales," as an inspec-
tor of customs in Manhattan, and the question raised by Pollard's life —
How do we survive our disasters? — was even more urgent than it had
been before.[3] In returning, after all this time, to the subject of cannibalism, he allows us to see just how deep and prolonged his interest in that
subject could be, and how consistent he was in his treatment of it.[4]

Stranded in an open boat after being wrecked by a hidden rock, the
captain and his men row against the trade winds for South America.
After some weeks, their bread and water

> Ran low and lower — ceased. They burn —
> They agonize till crime abhorred
> Lawful might be. O trade-wind turn!
>> Well may some items sleep unrolled —
> Never by the one survivor told.
> Him they picked up, where, cuddled down,
> They saw the jacketed skeleton,
> Lone in the only boat that lived —
> His signal frittered to a shred.
>> "Strong need'st thou be," the rescuers said,
> "Who has such trial sole survived."
> "I *willed* it," gasped he.

Having apparently convinced himself that the crime of cannibalism is,
under the circumstances, "[l]awful," the captain interprets his survival
as a confirmation of his power "to effect each thing he would, / Did
reason but pronounce it good." Just as Billy Budd will overcome a paralyzing attack of stuttering by delivering an apparently spontaneous blow
to Claggart's forehead, so does the captain overcome the shipwreck,
which brings an "arrest to keel and speech," by means of a monumental
act of will. This is an understanding of famine cannibalism that brings
it close to the spirit of vengeful cannibalism; in moving from the realm
of "humanity" to the realm of "savagery," the captain imagines, he has
only occupied more fully the space of the naturally imperial and transcendently rational self.

But the captain changes his mind. After his second ship is destroyed
by a whale, he is labeled a Jonah, and never again granted the opportunity to command. While pacing the docks in the long after-years,

unbending into the grip of Calvinism, "[o]ft on some secret thing [he] would brood." This "secret thing" is, to all appearances, an altered repetition of the earlier secret: the unmentioned act of survival in the open boat. Now that he has converted to the "creed austere" of his mate, who believed that "heaven's over-rulings sway / Will and event," he can no longer think of this act, or any other act, as a sign of perfect self-possession. Far from being a transparent expression of will, famine cannibalism is, like the hidden rock, or the unfathomed "purpose" of the whale, an *interruption* of the will. In this sense, the captain's encounter, in memory, with his own act of cannibalism may be said to replicate the two-part structure of Melville's earlier treatments of the encounter with a cannibal outside the self. In each case, the dream-thought of presence gives way to the afterthought of absence, the subject's belated recognition that it has *produced* the objects and events that have provided it with the illusion of inevitability.

This is not to say that the captain responds to his recognition as Melville would; in surrendering himself to the God of Calvin, the captain identifies the force that interrupts the will with an all-encompassing Presence, something that Melville himself rarely, if ever, does. In spite of this fact, the story of the captain may still be said to take us to the heart of an essentially Melvillean drama. In encountering so often, and on such an epic scale, the moment of interruption, the fictionalized Pollard becomes one of Melville's most powerful representations of the subject who discovers himself to be only nominally self-possessed. After Rolfe finishes his tale, Nehemiah, the man who originally prompted it, draws near. But now the listeners seem uninterested in him; still thinking about the story of "the changed master," they scan him "absently." Disjoined from the fictional captain, but occupying his place, Nehemiah begins to waver before them like "[a] phantom . . . from zone / Where naught is real tho' the winds aye moan." These are the last words of the canto, and as they hang in the air, the very irrelevance of Nehemiah, in relation to the story of the captain, suddenly makes his arrival seem like the most appropriate conclusion to that story. Precisely because he is incommensurable with the tale that is told of him, he is the ideal embodiment of its moral.

NOTES

Preface

1   Lacan, *Concepts,* 55, 53.
2   Griffiths, "Myth of Authenticity," 76.
3   Laclau, *New Reflections,* 212.
4   *Othello,* 1.3.143–45.
5   Žižek, *Sublime Object of Ideology,* 126.
6   Silverman, *Threshold of the Visible World,* 81.

Introduction

1   *Journal of the* Resolution's *Voyage,* 94. Burney and his men subsequently drove a
    group of Maoris away from a fire further down the beach, and there "beheld the
    most horrible sight that ever was seen by any European; the heads, hearts, liver, and
    lights of three or four of their people broiling on the fire, and their bowels lying at
    the distance of about six yards from the fire, with several of their hands and limbs,
    in a mangled condition, some broiled, and some raw; but no other parts of their
    bodies, which gave cause to suspect that the cannibals had feasted and eaten all the
    rest" (95). Even here, we should notice, the evidence is said to give us only a "cause
    to suspect" that the Maoris are cannibals.
2   Earle, *Narrative of a Residence,* 112. Subsequent page references will be cited paren-
    thetically in the text.
3   The American historian Jared Sparks wrote in 1824 that although "[i]t was for a
    long time doubted whether there existed on the globe a race of men, addicted to the
    custom of devouring one another," the Cook expeditions furnished "occular [*sic*]
    proof of the fact" ("New Zealand," 344). In 1830, Robert Southey acknowledged
    that although he had not "the least doubt" that the Battas of Sumatra were canni-
    bals, "ocular proof by an European appears to be still wanting" ("*Life and Public
    Services,*" 435). And in 1853, the British captain John Elphinstone Erskine used the
    currency of the phrase in accounts of cannibalism as the basis of a joke, reporting
    that the sight of a Fiji islander eating an eye that he had plucked from a skull left
    members of the Wilkes expedition "fully satisfied with this ocular proof of canni-
    balism" (*Journal of a Cruise,* 259).

4 *Othello*, 3.3.359–60, 3.4.160–61.

5 Barrow, *"Expeditions,"* 19.

6 Todorov, *Conquest of America*, 160. Subsequent page references will be cited parenthetically in the text.

7 The same could be said of Todorov's more specific assumption that cannibalism signifies a destructive literalism. In a frequently cited monograph on the subject, Eli Sagan declares that "[t]he undeveloped imagination of the cannibal does not deal very adequately with metaphorical usage. He is compelled to take the urge for oral incorporation literally" (*Cannibalism*, 28). This belief ultimately underwrites Sagan's conclusion that "all subsequent forms of social aggression are related to cannibalism in some way. There is something of cannibalism in all subsequent, sublimated forms of institutionalized aggression" (109). Every time a critic like Sagan disparages a supposedly "civilized" practice by saying that it is "like cannibalism," he or she reproduces the damaging assumption that cannibalism exists entirely within the realm of the literal and overt, and may therefore serve as a reference point against which the implicitly progressive symbolic forms of "civilization" may be measured and found wanting. See, for example, Derrida's recent argument that everyone, not just cannibals, practices "denegation": "The so called nonanthropophagic cultures practice symbolic anthropophagy and even construct their most elevated socius, indeed the sublimity of their morality, their politics, and their right, on this anthropophagy" ("Eating Well," 115, 114).

8 I do not mean to suggest that my reading of these scenes *disproves* Todorov's reading of the Spanish-Aztec encounter—only that it calls the theoretical framework of his reading into question. Other scholars have, however, questioned both Todorov's assumptions *and* their application to the case of the Spanish conquest. Inga Clendinnen characterizes the Aztecs as notably "innovative" people, "alert to the possibilities of psychological warfare, capitalizing on the Spaniards' peculiar dread of death by sacrifice and of the cannibalizing of the corpse" (" 'Fierce and Unnatural Cruelty,' " 26–27). In the same vein, Gananath Obeyesekere reads Bernal Diaz's report of Aztecs eating Spanish prisoners in front of the Spanish army as "an excellent example of Aztecs manipulating a human sacrifice for political purposes, utilizing a conventional sign system to frighten the Spaniards, and no doubt succeeding" (*Apotheosis of Captain Cook*, 18).

9 Greenblatt, *Marvelous Possessions*, 122.

10 In associating this fetishistic tendency with "explorers" in general, I am obviously leaving myself open to questions of the kind recently posed by Stephen Slemon: "Can you look at 'colonial discourse' only by examining what are taken to be paradigmatic moments within colonialist history? If so, can you extrapolate a modality of 'colonialism' from one historical moment to the next? Does discursive colonialism always look structurally the same, or do the specifics of its textual or semiotic or representational manoeuvres shift registers at different historical times and in different kinds of colonial encounters?" ("Scramble for Post-Colonialism," 20). Although I do want to insist that postcoloniality is a generalizable condition, definitionally linked to every manifestation of colonialism, I do not want to pass over the very real differences among the forms and degrees of its emergence. My aim is to avoid the sterility of the universal and the historical, taken separately, by treating each of these modes of analysis as the supplement of the other. As Kaja

Silverman has said, with respect to the theory of the gaze, it is as wrong for Lacan to ignore "what is socially and historically relative about the field of vision" as it is for Jonathan Crary, a historian of optical techniques, to ignore "what persists beyond one social formation to the next" (*Threshold of the Visible World*, 131).

In that spirit, I want to observe very briefly that the two scenes I began with have not only a *generic* context in postcoloniality, but also a *specific* set of contexts deriving from the representational innovations of the Enlightenment. One of those contexts, as we will see, is the decertification of the discursive image of the cannibal, which took place in or around the 1730s. Another is the mid-eighteenth-century ascendance of the *tableau*, "the portable and self-sufficient picture that could be taken in at a glance, as opposed to the 'environmental,' architecture-dependent, often episodic or allegorical project that could not. . . . The primary function of the *tableau* . . . was not to address or exploit the visuality of the theatrical audience so much as to neutralize that visuality, to wall it off from the action taking place on stage, to put it out of mind for the dramatis personae and the audience alike" (Fried, *Absorption and Theatricality*, 89, 96). This formal isolation of the spectator was also taking place in Enlightenment narratives of murder; as Karen Halttunen points out, the new convention of the corpse-discovery scene emphasized "the sense of horror evoked by that discovery," a sensation that signified, within the logic of Lockean psychology, "a shutting down of those sensory faculties through which experience impinged upon the mind to become knowledge" ("Early American Murder Narratives," 89, 90). These insistences on the innocence of spectators would take their *most* insistent form in melodrama, a post-Revolutionary innovation in theater that produced "incessant struggle against enemies, without and within, branded as villains, suborners of morality, who must be confronted and expunged, over and over, to assure the triumph of virtue" (Brooks, *Melodramatic Imagination*, 15). In its anxious repetition of this "triumph," however, melodrama could not help raising a suspicion that tableaux and horror narratives were capable of raising as well: that "its plenitude may be a void" (200). The instability of the scenes I began with should be ascribed not just to the constitutive instability of colonial discourse, in other words, but also to their historically determined efforts to capture a real live cannibal in a melodramatic tableau of horror.

11 Lacan, *Concepts*, 107.

12 Bhabha, *Location*, 126. Subsequent page references will be cited parenthetically in the text.

13 Emerson, *Selected Essays*, 236.

14 One such critic is Neil Lazarus, who condemns Bhabha for parading "a reading of colonised elitism" as "a *general* theory of the constitution of subjectivity under colonialism," and thereby eliding "the vastly differential thrusts, effects, and modes of domination/subjection of colonialism as practised at different times by different powers in different parts of the world, or even within single but 'unevenly developed' colonies." He allows that Bhabha's work on mimicry is a "suggestive" reading of some forms of colonial subjectivity—"of the figure of Frantz Fanon as he presents himself in *Black Skin, White Masks*, perhaps." Beyond that line, however, Bhabha is a trespasser, invading a region of historical and geographical "differences" that Lazarus does not feel compelled to specify ("National Consciousness," 218).

15 In his strongest statement of this argument, Bhabha writes that "the encounters and

negotiations of differential meanings and values within 'colonial' textuality, its governmental discourses and cultural practices, have anticipated, *avant la lettre,* many of the problematics of signification and judgement that have become current in contemporary theory" (*Location,* 173).

16 Jan-Mohammed, "Economy of Manichean Allegory," 79. Jan-Mohammed is by no means the only critic who has made this argument. Aijiz Ahmad similarly dismisses Bhabha as a well-heeled poststructuralist, arguing that he "lives in those material conditions of *post*modernity which presume the benefits of modernity as the very ground from which judgements on that past of this *post-* may be delivered" (*In Theory,* 68). Robert Young is more sympathetic, but he too asks "what, if anything, is specific to the colonial situation if colonial texts only demonstrate the same properties that can be found in any deconstructive reading of European texts[?]" (*White Mythologies,* 153). Bhabha frequently attempts to counteract such readings, arguing that "[m]y use of poststructuralist theory emerges from this postcolonial contramodernity" (175) and that "the rule of empire must not be allegorized in the misrule of writing" (129). But in an essay called "The Commitment to Theory," the argument does in fact come out the other way around: "It is only when we understand that all cultural statements and systems are constructed in this contradictory and ambivalent space of enunciation, that we begin to understand why hierarchical claims to the inherent originality or 'purity' of cultures are untenable, *even before* we resort to empirical historical instances that demonstrate their hybridity" (37; my emphasis). There is clearly a space for questioning here, but as I indicated earlier, there is no reason for such questioning to progress, automatically, to the rejection or marginalization of Bhabha's claims.

17 Baker, "Scene," 41. Subsequent page references will be cited parenthetically in the text.

18 Baker, *Modernism,* 72. Subsequent page references will be cited parenthetically in the text.

19 DuBois, *Souls of Black Folk,* 74–75.

20 Douglass, *Narrative,* 58.

21 Fanning, *Voyages,* 180–81.

22 In an entry composed a few days later, Fanning declares that the Nukuhevans were indeed cannibals,

> or at least so far as the eating of the flesh of their enemies makes them such; as a proof of this I observed one day while trading with the canoes alongside, something wrapped up in some palm leaves, on board of one of them, the native in which did not offer it for barter. This was so unusual, that I examined it, and found the same to be a piece of human flesh, baked; surprised, I shrunk back with horror, and asked him what he was going to do with it. The fellow took my meaning, and replaced the leaves around it as formerly, only answering, that as it was a part of one of their enemies, it was therefore very good food for him, and whenever he was hungry, he was going to eat it. This, was the only evidence that came under my immediate observation: I endeavored to make him comprehend how wicked and awfully disgusting such a practice was; with what success, however, I know not. (Ibid., 212–13)

23 I am using the term *cannibal studies* to refer to all academic inquiry into the uses of cannibalism as a textual symbol and/or the meanings of cannibalism as a historical

practice. Though it is not a discipline, or even an entirely self-conscious field, it is unquestionably a booming academic industry. What follows is a rough count, by decade, of the number of English-language books and essays prominently applying one of these modes of inquiry within the fields of literary criticism, history, cultural studies, or anthropology. (Articles written for popular journals are excluded.) In the 1970s, there were 20 essays and 4 books; in the 1980s, there were 45 essays and 5 books; in the first seven years of the 1990s, there have been 80 essays and 8 books.

24 Hulme makes this point most forcefully in the course of a recent exchange with Myra Jehlen. In response to Jehlen's contention that his symptomatic analysis of the early European accounts of Carib cannibalism moves the discussion of cannibalism "into the realm of the European imaginary" and thereby "erases a particularly sure sign that the Caribbean might constitute a genuinely alternative culture" ("History before the Fact," 683, 684–85), he argues that there is no way to recover a pure culture, innocent of colonial overwritings, from colonial-era texts. "I remain skeptical," he says, "of the privileging of such a realm as in any way innocent of colonial projections or fantasies, a move that seems to bespeak a desire for some pure and uncontaminated evidence that can translate itself across the centuries without the elaborate machinery of our interpretive strategies" ("Making No Bones," 185).

25 In the British-Maori encounters, Obeyesekere suggests, the conspicuous emphasis on the subject of cannibalism indicates that "[c]annibalistic discourse . . . was a weapon, one might say, employed by all the parties" ("British Cannibals," 646). With respect to the Maori, who "are at great pains to prove that not only are they cannibals, but truly horrible ones" (647), the putatively "cultural" meaning of cannibalism cannot be divorced from "the context of domination and terror" (644).

26 In *Colonial Encounters*, Hulme declares that cannibalism, as a discursive object, allows nations to repress "the conflict at the root of their socio-political structure by projecting on to those outside the structure, those about perhaps to be devoured by it ('incorporated' into it) the violence on which that body politic is inevitably based, the exploitation inseparable from divided societies" (87). He is even more explicit in a later note: "cannibalism quite simply *is* nothing other than the violence of colonialism incarnate beyond the pale" (308 n. 76). In a similar vein, Obeyesekere argues that the British obsession with cannibalism marks their "latent wish" to consume human flesh ("British Cannibals," 635). It is perhaps logically consistent, but nonetheless odd, that Obeyesekere ascribes this "latent wish" to the Maori as well. It means that his insistence on the pragmatic rationality of Polynesians is, in the end, nothing more than a step on the way to the thoroughly conventional conclusion that "following Freud and Jung, one can say that what gives us all a common humanity is not only our higher nature but also a shared dark side of our being" (638).

27 Copjec, *Read My Desire*, 118, 119.

28 The classic statement of the first position may be found in Stern, *Fine-Hammered Steel;* the classic statement of the second may be found in T. W. Herbert, *Marquesan Encounters;* the classic statement of the third may be found in Dimock, *Empire for Liberty.*

29 Among those who link their critique of colonialism in Melville to a critique of his failure to be sufficiently humanist or culturalist are Wai-Chee Dimock, Malini Johar Schueller, and Dana Nelson. Dimock argues that Melville, influenced by contemporary American imperialism, strove for a language and an authorial identity that

would constitute "a self-enclosed universe, untouched by the barbaric world, untouchable to barbaric readers" (*Empire*, 212). In its "spectralization of the Other" (68), she says, this project forecloses the humanist/culturalist recognition that experience consists of "action and reaction between persons," a "process of reversals at once inevitable and interminable" (129, 130). My argument, of course, is that Melville *refuses* the logic of the self-enclosed universe, and that he does so not by substituting the idea that encounters between people are endlessly full of an unimaginably rich meaning, but by insisting that these encounters are *always* spectralized, and that this spectralization can be made to function as a threat to the imperial subject who depends on it. As opposed to Schueller, I am arguing that Melville *recognized* that "he could not disrupt the civilization/savagery dichotomy enough not to figure the natives as Other" ("Colonialism," 15); as opposed to Nelson, I am placing a positive value on his "ironic critique" of that dichotomy, even though he does not go on "to posit countervening antiracist possibilities for action/knowledge" (*Word in Black and White*, 110).

30 F. Marc Bousquet's recent study of the manuscript of "Hawthorne and His Mosses" suggests that Melville tended to add these kinds of hedgings during the process of revision. On leaf 15 of the fair copy manuscript, Melville originally wrote, "let America rather praise mediocrity in her children than the best excellence in the children of any other land." He then amended the passage to read "let America *first* praise *even* mediocrity in her own children, *before* she praises (*for anywhere, merit demands acknowledgment from every one*) the best excellence in the children of any other land" (my emphasis). As Bousquet observes, the revisions "convert a boldly chauvinist challenge . . . into something more like an appeal sharply qualified by a universalist sentiment" ("Mathews's Mosses," 623).

31 Morrison, *Playing in the Dark*, 69.

32 Delbanco, "Melville in the '80s," 723.

33 Hawthorne, *Marble Faun*, 10. I draw this argument from Nancy Bentley's *The Ethnography of Manners*.

34 Pearce, *Savagism and Civilization*, 244.

35 Parry, "Problems in Current Theories," 43.

36 Laclau, *New Reflections*, 245. When asked to describe the material form of a *"real* humanism," one "that acknowledges its radical historicity, and does not take any of the conditions of its arrival for granted" (245), Laclau suggests that the slow reformulation of humanism has already begun to allow for

> a more democratic vision of social demands. People do not now have to justify their demands before a tribunal of history and can directly assert their legitimacy on their own terms. Social struggles can thus be seen as "wars of interpretations" in which the very meaning of demands is discursively constructed through struggle. The demands of a lesbian group, a neighbours association or a black self-defence group are therefore all situated on the same ontological level as working class demands. In this way the absence of a global emancipation of humanity allows the constant expansion and diversification of concrete "emancipatory" struggles. (216)

Because Melville lived and wrote so long before these kinds of developments, his most immediate concern was the desubstantiation of the classic forms of humanism, rather than the construction of post-humanist subject positions. But he is, for all that, a contributor to the conditions within which those constructions are possible.

37 The quotation comes from the very end of *Paradise Lost:* "The world was all before them, where to choose / Their place of rest, and Providence their guide." On at least six occasions, Melville employs some version of the phrase "The world was all before them" (Pommer, *Milton and Melville,* 35). He never suggests that Providence, or anything else, will be our guide.

1   In the Wake of the Resolution:
The Post-Enlightenment Discourse on Cannibalism

1   Beaglehole, *Journals,* 2:293. Subsequent page references will be cited parenthetically in the text.

2   G. Forster, *Voyage,* 1:512. Subsequent page references will be cited parenthetically in the text.

3   Cook, *South Pole,* 1:243–44. Subsequent page references will be cited parenthetically in the text.

4   See also the *Journal of the* Resolution*'s Voyage,* whose author similarly declares that the Maori who "greedily" ate the piece of flesh did so "in presence of the whole ship's crew." This, the author says, made it "an incontestable proof of their eating human flesh, if any had been wanting to confirm the truth of so inhuman a practice" (103).

5   McNab, *Records,* 1:117, 539. Subsequent page references will be cited parenthetically in the text.

6   Because I have worked only with sources in English, I can speak with absolute certainty only of England and America. Several French, Russian, and German narratives were translated into English in the late eighteenth and early nineteenth centuries, however, and several more have been translated since then. Everything I have seen from these countries indicates that the travelers were fully aware of the controversies that conditioned the form of the post-Enlightenment discourse on cannibalism, and that they shared the same range of answers that the English and American travelers did.

7   Though we might expect to find that the answers the travelers selected depended on the practices of the tribes they encountered, the whole range of answers was applied to each of the major "cannibal" tribes in the Pacific and Indian Oceans — the Maoris, the Hawaiians, the Marquesans, the Fijians, and the Battas — as well as to the less clearly distinguished "Indians" and "Africans." I have documented this claim with respect to the Marquesans in the epigraphs to chapter 2; similar documentation could be adduced for each of the other groups I have mentioned above.

8   I do not mean to suggest that these answers were new; they had all been around, in some form, for centuries. What *was* new was their consistent articulation in a highly self-conscious and self-contained discourse.

9   The dominance of this explanation is reflected in the contemporary connotations of the word *cannibal.* The African traveler Robert Norris writes in 1789 that he does "not think the Dahomans are *anthropophagists,* in the full sense of that word; though they scruple not to eat a devoted victim at the public festivals," they do not eat human beings "as a familiar repast" (*Memoirs of Bossa Ahádee,* x). In his *History*

of the Conquest of Mexico (1843), William Prescott similarly insists that although the Aztecs did eat human flesh, they "were not cannibals, in the coarsest acceptation of the term. They did not feed on human flesh merely to gratify a brutish appetite, but in obedience to their religion. . . . This is a distinction worthy of notice" (1:84). The same rhetoric shows up in narratives of Pacific travel: Edmund Fanning reports that the natives of Nukuheva "were cannibals, or at least so far as the eating of the flesh of their enemies makes them such" (*Voyages*, 212), and Edward Belcher describes the same islanders as "half (if not entire) cannibals" (*Narrative*, 1:359). The fact that so many writers considered it necessary to distinguish between "entire" cannibals, who "feed on human flesh merely to gratify a brutish appetite," and "half" cannibals, who consume human flesh under the influence of superstition or vengeance, indicates the degree to which the word *cannibal* had become associated with lustfulness.

10 For a study of medieval accounts of cannibals in the East, see Guzman, "Reports"; for Africa, see Barker, *African Link;* for the Americas, see Hulme, *Colonial Encounters,* and Pagden, *Fall of Natural Man.*

11 Sparks, "New Zealand," 344, 345. As early as 1774, the elaborately racist Edward Long had supported his declaration that all Africans have a "custom of gormandizing on human flesh" with the footnoted observation that "[t]he existence of canibals or man-eaters is now unquestionably proved, by the late discoveries made by Mr. Banks and Dr. Solander, in their voyage to the South Sea; where they found, in the country called *New-Zealand,* a people who fed upon human flesh" (*History of Jamaica,* 2:381, 382).

12 Busby, *Authentic Information,* 62.

13 An essay in the 1810 *Eclectic Review* indicates just how conventional this coupling was. After praising the extensiveness of Robert Southey's account of cannibalism in South America, the reviewer "regret[s]" the absence of narratorial horror. It is unfortunate, he says, that "Mr. Southey has collected the particulars attending these soul-sickening scenes, and narrated them with a minute explicitness, too obviously for the sake of effect. There is not, or certainly there ought not to be, any thing inviting in the mere contemplation of such things; and, abstracted from every purpose of moral utility, the impression left upon the mind is, in our opinion, extremely undesirable" ("Southey's *History of Brazil,*" 797).

14 Nicholas, *Narrative,* 1:148. Subsequent page references will be cited parenthetically in the text.

15 Sparks, "New Zealand," 346.

16 Porter, *Journal of a Cruise,* 2:44; Oliver, *Wreck of the* Glide, 22.

17 "Prescott's *History*" (1844), 174.

18 Higgins and Parker, *Reviews,* 63.

19 Bolingbroke, *Voyage to Demerary,* 98–99.

20 Hegel, *Philosophy of History,* 95.

21 Russell, *Polynesia,* 264–65.

22 Priest, *Slavery,* 191, 199.

23 Defoe, *Robinson Crusoe,* 210, 213.

24 Patterson, *Narrative of the Adventures,* 100.

25 Langsdorff, *Voyages,* 141, 143. Subsequent page references will be cited parenthetically in the text.

26 Taylor, *Society,* 127; A. Thomson, *Story,* 141.

27 Craik, *New Zealanders*, 107. Subsequent page references will be cited parenthetically in the text.

28 Polack, *New Zealand*, 2:2–3.

29 Wilkes, *Narrative*, 3:101.

30 Barker, *African Link*, 129.

31 Chamerovzow, *New Zealand Question*, 17.

32 E. J. Wakefield, *Adventure*, 2.

33 Fox, *Colonization and New Zealand*, 7.

34 E. J. Wakefield, *Adventure*, 3. Once that project gets in full swing, we begin to encounter the occasional use of cannibalism as an image justifying colonialism. In an 1839 tract promoting colonial settlement, Patrick Matthew drafts a sample proclamation of British sovereignty over New Zealand, leaving a space near the bottom where Victoria could sign it, if she so chose. "Be it known to all men," he writes, that "whereas the inhabitants of these islands are in a state of murderous anarchy and cannibalism, shocking to humanity, and totally incapable of establishing social order among themselves," and because England is powerful enough "to establish a strong general government, to check the evils under which the natives are fast disappearing, and to bring these islands from being the haunts of roaming cannibals and banditti to a state of high prosperity . . . WE, THE QUEEN OF GREAT BRITAIN, VICTORIA, from this date, do take absolute sovereign possession of these regions" (*Emigrant Fields*, 173–74). Though this passage does suggest a connection between the image of lustful cannibalism and the prosecution of colonialism, its late date and its relative isolation should allow us to recognize that this connection is not *necessary*.

35 Atkins, *Voyage*, xxii. Subsequent page references will be cited parenthetically in the text.

36 Arens, *Man-Eating Myth*, 170. The similarities between Atkins and Arens are surprisingly extensive. Like *A Voyage to Guinea*, Arens's book is only nominally grounded in a study of the circumstantiality of accounts of cannibalism. It is, as he admits at one point, "deductive" (33); he is "dubious about the actual existence of this act as an accepted practice for any time or place" (9) because "it does not accord with a century of experience accumulated by anthropologists on the human condition" (33). If an anthropological narrative does not square with his sense of what is "human," he simply rejects it; in dismissing a particularly grotesque account of cannibalism among the Fore in New Guinea, he asks, "could Fore behavior . . . be so far removed from what we and the rest of the world accept as conforming to common standards?" (100).

37 Quoted in Barker, *African Link*, 131.

38 Fliegelman, *Declaring Independence*, 172.

39 Bancroft, *Essay*, 260.

40 Marsden, *History*, 390. Subsequent page references will be cited parenthetically in the text.

41 Beaglehole, Endeavour *Journal*, 1:455. Subsequent page references will be cited parenthetically in the text.

42 Locke, *Essay Concerning Human Understanding*, 71.

43 *Travels of Hildebrand Bowman*, 24, 25. See also the anonymous *Dialogue between Farmer Trueman and His Son George* concerning reports of cannibalism among the Battas of Sumatra. George is horrified to hear his father call the Battas fellow crea-

tures, saying, "Surely you do not put *us* upon a footing with such blood-hounds, do you?" His father's simultaneously pious and associationist response is yes: "You must be taught the humbling lesson, that had you been born in those parts you would have been in no wise better than they" (4).

44 See David Simpson, *Romanticism, Nationalism, and the Revolt against Theory*. A good example of this rhetorical strategy appears in the American translation of Jean François Galoup La Perouse's *Voyage Round the World* (1801). After a passage in which La Perouse declares that he cannot accept previous reports of Hawaiian cannibalism, because "a people so good, so mild, and so hospitable cannot be cannibals," the translator considers it necessary to insert the following disclaimer: "The English navigators appear to have established this fact, which it is so painful to believe, upon evidence too strong to be refuted. La Peyrouse, with a gentleness and benignity, which would gladly vindicate human nature from the charge of the most savage crime by which it can be degraded, has endeavoured too ineffectually to convince us that cannibalism here is unknown" (1:350).

45 Barrow, "Porter's *Cruize*," 367. Subsequent page references will be cited parenthetically in the text.

46 Barrow, "Dentrecasteaux," 38.

47 Barrow, "Cruise—*New Zealand*," 58. Subsequent page references will be cited parenthetically in the text.

48 Barrow, "*Expeditions*," 18. Subsequent page references will be cited parenthetically in the text.

49 Barrow, "Russian Embassy," 371.

50 "Prescott's *History* (1843)," 207.

51 Ellis, *Polynesian Researches*, 3:253-54.

52 Barrow, "Beechey's *Voyage*," 68.

53 Polack, *New Zealand*, 2:2.

54 "Polack, *New Zealand*," 581.

55 Polack, *Manners and Customs*, 1:29 n. 1.

56 "Polack, *Manners*," 288.

57 Polack, *Manners and Customs*, 1:29 n. 1.

58 Voltaire, *Candide*, 71.

59 Voltaire, *Philosophical Dictionary*, 87.

60 Pauw, *Selections*, 65.

61 Hawkesworth, *Account of the Voyages*, 447-48.

62 See Harner, "Ecological Basis of Aztec Cannibalism," and Harris, *Cannibals and Kings*.

63 Darwin, *Journal*, 214. Subsequent page references will be cited parenthetically in the text.

64 A. W. B. Simpson, *Cannibalism and the Common Law*, 145.

65 See Byron's *Don Juan*; Poe's *The Narrative of Arthur Gordon Pym*; Thackeray's "Little Billee"; Dickens's essay "The Lost Arctic Voyagers"; Whittier's "Snowbound"; and Twain's "Cannibalism in the Cars."

66 Dalyell, *Shipwrecks*, 2:16, 434, 497; 1:185. Subsequent page references will be cited parenthetically in the text.

67 See ibid., 2:15, 434; Duncan, *Chronicle*, 2:173, 336. Subsequent page references to the latter work will also be cited parenthetically in the text.

68 Parley, *Tales about Shipwrecks,* 313.

69 See Leviticus 26 and Deuteronomy 28; the phrase "the consequences of disobedience" is used as the heading to each of these chapters in the King James Version.

70 Saunders, *Narrative,* 12, 18.

71 Viaud, *Shipwreck,* 165. Subsequent page references will be cited parenthetically in the text.

72 I am referring to Dickens's "The Lost Arctic Voyagers," in which he fervently denies the reports that Sir John Franklin and the members of his Arctic expedition had sunk to cannibalism before dying. Because he associated famine cannibalism with lustfulness, he could not allow that a member of the nobility and his noble-by-association team were capable of transgressing the bounds of their humanity.

73 See, for example, Maggie Kilgour's representation of shipwreck cannibalism as a "horrifying image for the loss of human identity" (*From Communion to Cannibalism,* 149). Stories of shipwreck cannibalism "exert a lurid fascination," she says, because they indicate "how fragile the boundary between cannibal and Christian is, and how difficult it is to tell where communion stops and cannibalism sets in" (149–50). What I am suggesting is that when we examine the luridness of that fragility, rather than the fragility alone, the ultimately conservative implications of these stories begin to emerge.

74 Jameson, *Political Unconscious,* 68.

75 Taylor, *Natural History of Society,* 1:127.

76 Cooper, *Red Rover,* 336.

77 Byron, *Don Juan,* book 2, canto 72.

78 R. Thomas, *Interesting and Authentic Narratives,* 183.

79 Robertson, *History of America,* 81.

80 J. Martin, *Account,* 205. Subsequent page references will be cited parenthetically in the text.

81 Yate, *Account of New Zealand,* 129, 99–100.

82 Foucault, *Madness and Civilization,* 84. Subsequent page references will be cited parenthetically in the text.

83 J. Forster, *Observations,* 328–29. Subsequent page references will be cited parenthetically in the text.

84 It was fairly common, throughout this period, to suggest as Forster does here that Europeans were once cannibals themselves. In *Sartor Resartus,* for instance, Carlyle's Teufelsdrockh tells his reader that "thy own amber-locked, snow-and-rose-bloom Maiden . . . has descended, like thyself, from that same hair-mantled, flint-hurling Aboriginal Anthropophagus!" The spin that Carlyle puts on this fact is typical: "all that Mankind does or beholds, is in continual growth, regenesis and self-perfecting vitality" (150). Two writers on Polynesia, Edward Gibbon Wakefield and Michael Russell, approvingly reproduce a similar passage from Edward Gibbon's *Decline and Fall of the Roman Empire,* in which Gibbon uses a fifth-century account of cannibals in Scotland to argue that "[i]f in the neighbourhood of the commercial and literary town of Glasgow, a race of cannibals has really existed, we may contemplate in the period of the Scottish history, the opposite extremes of savage and civilized life. Such reflections tend to enlarge the circle of our ideas, and to encourage the pleasing hope, that New Zealand may produce, in some future age, the Hume of the Southern Hemisphere" (E. G. Wakefield, *British Colonization,* 263; Russell, *Polynesia,* 427).

85 Crawfurd, *History of the Indian Archipelago*, 1:65, 66.

86 Busby, *Authentic Information*, 62.

87 Cook and King, *Pacific*, 1:138. Subsequent page references will be cited parenthetically in the text.

88 La Perouse, *Voyage Round the World* (1799), 1:454.

89 Elder, *Letters and Journals*, 129. Subsequent page references will be cited parenthetically in the text.

90 Lang, *View*, 74. New Zealand is, of course, directly east of Australia.

91 Morrell, *Narrative*, 367–68.

92 Breton, *Excursions*, 150.

93 Taylor, *Natural History of Society*, 1:126–27.

94 Sanday, *Divine Hunger*, 36.

95 For a still-useful analysis of the function of "error" in Enlightenment discourse, see Frank Manuel, *The Eighteenth Century Confronts the Gods*.

96 As Nicholas Thomas observes, "[i]t particularly suited missionary discourse when the local religion could be characterized as idolatry, because this meant that 'idols,' as objectifications of the false religion, could be abstracted from their context in native worship and destroyed or displayed" (*Entangled Objects*, 153).

97 Herbert argues that several preanthropological social theorists, ranging from Adam Smith to Henry Mayhew, anticipated the point that Edward Tylor would broach and Bronislaw Malinowski would elaborate: "that a society's customs cannot be made intelligible if interpreted piecemeal—from which point of view they seem more nonsensical the longer we study them—but must be taken all together, as a 'complex whole,' " (*Culture and Anomie*, 88). But because late-eighteenth- and early-nineteenth-century writers so uniformly treat customs and superstitions as, in J. W. Burrow's words, "merely curious, disgusting, or tedious, or as useful ammunition in religious and political controversy" (*Evolution and Society*, 76), Herbert must read their texts "as if they were poems" and trace the prehistory of the culture-concept "[l]ike an astronomer tracking an invisible planet by studying deflections in the orbits of visible ones" (*Culture and Anomie*, 25, 24). It is a tremendously sensitive textual analysis, but it does not sufficiently address the question of who, at the time, read those texts as sensitively as Herbert does now. Nor, for that matter, does it sufficiently inquire into the ultimate truth and value of the culture-concept, understood as "a numinous reality . . . that lies beyond perception" (*Culture and Anomie*, 17).

98 Oliver, *Wreck of the* Glide, 21.

99 "Ashantee," 708.

100 Terry, *New Zealand*, 193–94.

101 Breton, *Excursions*, 151.

102 Bourdieu, *Outline*, 169, 168.

103 See Butler, *Gender Trouble*, and Copjec, *Read My Desire*.

104 Foucault, *History of Sexuality*, 100; my emphasis.

105 Žižek, *Sublime Object*, 183.

106 Quoted in Guzman, "Reports," 36.

107 Lery, *History*, 127.

108 Carver, *Travels*, 303–4.

109 Savage, *Some Account*, 35.

110 Raffles, *Memoir*, 2:92.

220   Notes to Chapter One

111 Reynolds, *Voyage*, 179.

112 Foucault, *Discipline and Punish*, 33, 49.

113 Bennet and Tyerman, *Journal*, 2:136. John Turnbull is more explicit about the source of that dread: "There is something of indiscribable horror in the apprehension of being murdered by cannibals! it is akin to that of being torn to pieces by wild beasts, where death is but the least consideration" (*Voyage*, 397).

114 Ledyard, *Journal*, 151.

115 In a similar scene, a Hawaiian informs the members of the third Cook expedition that a "small wooden instrument, beset with sharks teeth" was used "to cut out the fleshy part of the belly, when any person was killed" (Cook and King, *Pacific*, 210–11). When he was asked "if his countrymen eat the part thus cut out," he denied it; when asked again, he "shewed some degree of fear, and swam to his canoe," where an old man was waiting. The Englishmen then repeated the question to the old man, who "answered in the affirmative, and laughed, seemingly at the simplicity of such a question. He affirmed the fact, on being asked again; and also said, it was excellent food, or, as he expressed it, 'savoury eating' " (211). One of the implications of such scenes is that the cannibal encounter provides an occasion for two distinctly antagonistic forms of pleasure: for Westerners, the shudder that authenticates their "humanity," and for non-Westerners, the sight of intruders who shrink back in horror.

116 Barratt, *Bellingshausen*, 41.

117 Kotzebue, *New Voyage*, 263.

118 Quoted in Archer, "Cannibalism," 466.

119 Meares, *Voyages*, 257.

120 Archer, "Cannibalism," 468.

121 Meares, *Voyages*, 161.

122 Winterbottom, *Account*, 161. Subsequent page references will be cited parenthetically in the text.

123 Quoted in Barber, "Record of Maori Cannibalism," 256.

124 Barrow, "Anderson's *Mission*," 108.

125 "Polack, *New Zealand*," 581.

126 Among Melville's known sources for *Typee* were Ellis, Fanning, Krusenstern, Langsdorff, Porter, and Stewart; earlier reading took him to Chase, Cooper, Dana, Defoe, and Montaigne. We also know that after writing *Typee*, he consulted Bennet and Tyerman, Byron, Carlyle, Darwin, Duncan, Jacobs, Kotzebue, Morrell, Poe, Reynolds, Russell, and Wilkes, and that he read deeply in periodicals such as the *Quarterly Review*, to which his father-in-law, Lemuel Shaw, subscribed (Sealts, *Melville's Reading*, 16).

2 *The Terror of Their Name: Reflections on* Typee

1 Charvat, *Profession*, 246. Subsequent page references will be cited parenthetically in the text. Charvat is, of course, not alone in his attention to this aspect of Melville's style. In a discussion of "The Try-Works," R. W. B. Lewis argues that "one way to grasp this passage and Melville's achievement in general is to notice that Melville is not posing static alternatives but tracing a rhythmic progression in experience and

matching the rhythm as best he can in language" (*American Adam*, 133). In a more recent reading, Michael Gilmore argues that Ishmael establishes a bond with the reader "by constantly appealing for support, offering assistance, or joining forces to solve a problem. . . . His inquiries commonly begin with an invitation—'Let us, then, look at this matter'—and end with a collaborative statement such as 'thus we see' or 'we must conclude.' He is solicitous to prevent misunderstanding, and if he feels that an explanation has failed to satisfy, he will volunteer, 'I have another idea for you,' or interject, 'Explain thyself, Ishmael'" (*American Romanticism and the Marketplace*, 122). Charvat's account is more useful than these, however, in that he explicitly links the processual to the collaborative and just as explicitly characterizes this stylistic ideal as a project only, rather than an achieved poetic effect (Lewis) or an achieved experience of communion (Gilmore).

2 The first five examples I allude to are, in order, Harvey, "'Precepts Graven on Every Breast,'" 414; Rowe, "Melville's *Typee*," 271; Rogin, *Subversive Genealogy*, 48; Bergman, *Gaiety Transfigured*, 149; and Tolchin, *Mourning, Gender, and Creativity*, 52. Those who fall into the sixth category, treating Tommo's fear of cannibalism as a disguised fear of being assimilated into a crudely understood "culture," include Dimock, "*Typee*," 35; Breitwieser, "False Sympathy," 412; Samson, *White Lies*, 32; and Alberti, "Cultural Relativism and *Typee*," 339.

3 Some of my readers may have noticed that I am using the names *Tommo* and *Melville* interchangeably, in variance with the generally accepted dictum that "Tommo and Melville should not be confused" (Breitwieser, "False Sympathy," 396). My blurring of that distinction between author and narrator is quite conscious. Rather than looking beyond the text for what biblical exegetes call the "underthought" (M. B. Campbell, *Witness and the Other World*, 75), I am looking on the surface of the text for what DuBois calls the "afterthought"; rather than establishing a vertical distinction between the deluded Tommo and the prescient Melville, I am establishing a horizontal distinction between Tommo/Melville at the beginning of the book and Tommo/Melville at the end. By mapping that horizontal transformation on the preexistent structure of the discourse on cannibalism, moreover, I want to make it impossible to say either that Melville "[made] up an ideology as he wrote" (Bryant, *Melville and Repose*, 160) or that he "[repeated] cultural colonialism through strategies of difference" (Schueller, "Colonialism," 4). Both of those arguments are predicated on the notion that Melville is striving for containment and coherence—a triumph of "tense repose" for Bryant (145), and a sign of "the persistence of empire-building in the literary imagination of nineteenth-century America" for Schueller (14). I am suggesting, by contrast, that the book drives toward a moment that radically obstructs the desire for containment and coherence, and that the evocation of that moment is neither an act of transcendence nor an act of collusion.

4 Said, *Orientalism*, 71. Subsequent references will be cited parenthetically in the text.

5 The swimming pool descriptions are especially good examples of this prurient mode of representation. In one, he writes that "[f]rom the verdant surfaces of the large stones that lay scattered about, the natives were now sliding off into the water, diving and ducking beneath the surface in all directions—the young girls springing buoyantly into the air, and revealing their naked forms to the waist, with their long tresses dancing about their shoulders, their eyes sparkling like drops of dew in the sun, and their gay laughter pealing forth at every frolicsome incident" (90). In another, he ob-

serves that these women "might be seen gliding along, just under the surface, without apparently moving hand or foot—then throwing themselves on their sides, they darted through the water, revealing glimpses of their forms, as, in the course of their rapid progress, they shot for an instant partly into the air—at one moment they dived deep down into the water, and the next they rose bounding to the surface" (131).

6 Krusenstern, *Voyage,* 1:178, 179. Subsequent references will be cited parenthetically in the text.

7 The rumor regarding the tastiness of baby's flesh can be found in Langsdorff's *Voyages and Travels,* one of Melville's principal sources for *Typee.* Langsdorff declares, on the authority of those "people who feed upon human flesh merely on account of its delicacy, and as the height of *gourmandise*" that "the flesh of young girls and women, particularly of new-born children, far exceeds in delicacy that of the finest youths, or grown men" (141). The rumor regarding the aversion to eating white men's flesh can be found in several early-nineteenth-century accounts of New Zealand. The Reverend Samuel Marsden writes in 1819 that when he told some Maori chiefs that white people were afraid of being eaten by them, the chiefs said that "as we had done them no injury, they had no satisfaction to demand from us and no just feelings of retaliation to gratify, and observed with a smile that, if they naturally craved after human flesh, we might make ourselves easy on that head, as the flesh of New Zealanders was much sweeter than that of an European in consequence of the white people eating so much salt" (Elder, *Letters and Journals,* 214). The British captain Richard Cruise similarly reports in his *Journal of a Ten Months' Residence in New Zealand* (1823) that the Maoris "describe the flesh of a white man as tough and unpalatable when compared to that of their countrymen, and they attribute its inferiority to our universal practice of using salt with our food" (286–87). Two decades later, the Maoris were still telling their visitors the same thing and their visitors were still passing it on, though with a little less credulity. The naturalist Ernest Dieffenbach writes in *Travels in New Zealand* (1843) that several Maoris told him, "when conversing with me freely upon the subject," that "[t]he flesh of Europeans they consider salt and disagreeable—a curious physiological fact, if true" (129–30).

8 For more particulars on the doubts surrounding Cook's fate, see chap. 4.

9 Nor is Tommo the first traveler to discover that what he thought was human flesh was in fact pork. In the narrative of his third and final voyage, Cook writes that while at the island of Atiu in 1777, his Tahitian companion Omai saw that the natives "had dug a hole in the ground for an oven, which they were now heating; and he could assign no other reason for this, than that they meant to roast, and eat us, as is practised by the inhabitants of New Zealand." But this terror was only temporary, for "a pig which we saw, soon after, lying near the oven, which they had prepared and heated, removed Omai's apprehension of being put into it himself" (Cook and King, *Pacific,* 1:190, 191). Likewise, William Breton notes in *Excursions in New South Wales* that although the Maoris appear to be constantly at war with one another, "not unfrequently, when they pretend they are going to slay and devour their enemies, their arms have been miraculously converted into potatoes, and their implacable foes into a marvellous herd of fine hogs, both of which were cooked and consumed without compunction by the *soi-disant* combatants; or, to speak more soberly, they had gone to meet another and friendly tribe, in order to have a feast" (149). And in a particularly relevant example, Edward Belcher writes in his *Narrative of a Voyage Round*

the World (1843) that "[i]n the case of the captain and mate of a whaler, not many years since cut off by the natives of Comptroller's Bay, the Teii [Typee], said to be the most ferocious on the island, seldom communicating with their neighbours, and never with foreigners,—how did they act? They amused themselves by exciting their fears. Having made a fire sufficiently large to bake them, a hog was substituted, which, when cooked, they were invited to partake of" (2:317). Tommo's discovery of *puarkee* is, in other words, a conventional moment of cannibal bathos. It is one of the most pointed of several early suggestions that any attempt to determine the existence and extent of cannibalism among the Typees will have to contend with the fact that the signs of cannibalism come to Tommo by way of the Typees, and that the Typees may have their own reasons for exposing those signs to view.

10 See David Simpson, *Romanticism, Nationalism, and the Revolt against Theory*.

11 Some version of these phrases may be found on the following pages: "I can never forget," 9, 25, 40, 46, 95, 196, 248 (twice), 252; "the impression will never be obliterated" 28, 45, 207, 243; "I can recall even now" 29, 49, 86, 91, 244.

12 See pp. 29, 46, 76, 94, 103, 106, 108, 124, 142 (twice), 155, 199, 226, and 233, and the subheadings to chaps. 3, 4, 11, 14, 19, and 26.

13 On three occasions, Tommo characterizes himself as a man who is governed by a sense of "propriety" (77, 121, 167). Elsewhere, he describes himself as a "quiet, sober-minded, modest young man" (152), animated by severe "scruples" (191).

14 The pool that Tommo names "Fayaway's lake" (171) is the embodiment in the natural sphere of these same virtues. It is "miniature," "almost circular," and ornamented at its margins by "the symmetrical shaft of the cocoa-nut tree" (131).

15 Dieffenbach, *Travels*, 130-31. Subsequent page references will be cited parenthetically in the text.

16 Tommo gets many of the details of this story wrong—most noticeably the name of the ship, which he gives as the *Hobomok*—but he can be referring to nothing other than the *Charles Doggett* massacre. Wilson Heflin long ago discovered that official records and newspapers show "no mention of a massacre occurring aboard the *Hobomok*," and surmised that Melville was conflating his memories of massacres on the *Awashonks* and the *Sharon* ("Herman Melville's Whaling Years," 217, 224). Unlike the *Charles Doggett* incident, however, neither of these massacres involved Fijians and neither of them prompted any American naval retaliation. The *Charles Doggett* massacre was avenged in 1840 by Capt. Charles Wilkes of the United States Exploring Expedition, who heard while at Fiji that a chief named Vendovi was responsible for the 1834 murder and cannibalization of eight Americans preparing beche-de-mer on the island of Kantavu. Wilkes captured Vendovi and brought him back to America, where he soon died. In doing so, Wilkes was not acting in accordance with "written instructions," as Tommo suggests. Moreover, he did not burn down Fijian villages in retaliation for the *Charles Doggett* incident, but for the murders of two members of the Expedition on the island of Malolo. These retributive actions were reported in New England newspapers (Ward and Dodge, *American Activities*, 3:464-67) and described in detail in Wilkes's *Narrative* (1845).

17 Fanon, *Wretched*, 94. Subsequent page references will be cited parenthetically in the text.

18 Tommo makes the narcissistic nature of his attraction to the Typees especially evident when he represents them as being more nearly white than other Pacific

islanders. Two paragraphs before the passage I just quoted, he refers to the present king of Hawaii as "a fat, lazy, negro-looking blockhead" (189), and in the previous chapter, he describes the "dark-hued Hawiians and the woolly-headed Feegees" as being "immeasurably inferior" to the Typees, whose features have a markedly "European cast" (184). As Schueller rightly observes, such passages allow us to see that Tommo's "reflections on the beauty of the Typees"—a beauty whose masculine form, I am arguing, is a passionate vengefulness—"are, in effect, reinforcements of European norms" ("Colonialism," 11).

19 Tommo's rhetoric in this passage is pretty clearly influenced by Montaigne's essay "On Cannibals," in which Montaigne declares that although the Tupi of South America are indeed cannibals, "[t]hey do not do this, as might be supposed, for nourishment as the ancient Scythians did, but as a measure of extreme vengeance" (*Essays*, 113). Montaigne takes this to be less a sign of their "horrible savagery" (113) than a sign that "[t]hese people are wild in the same way as we say that fruits are wild, when nature has produced them by herself and in her ordinary way; whereas, in fact, it is those that we have artificially modified, and removed from the common order, that we ought to call wild" (109). He declares that it is "more barbarous to eat a man alive than to eat him dead; to tear by rack and torture a body still full of feeling, to roast it by degrees, and then give it to be trampled and eaten by dogs and swine—a practice which we have not only read about but seen within recent memory, not between ancient enemies, but between neighbours and fellow-citizens and, what is worse, under the cloak of piety and religion—than to roast and eat a man after he is dead" (113). For Montaigne as for Melville, vengeful cannibalism is the expression of a naturally masculine "[v]alour . . . of the heart and soul" (116), and less horrible, accordingly, than acts of retribution that are mediated and prolonged. And to make this point clear, both authors assert that superstition plays no part in the act of cannibalism; nothing they do, Montaigne insists, "is done out of simple and servile bondage to common usage, or under weight of the authority of their ancient customs" (118).

20 Leaf 3, box 309, the Gansevoort-Lansing Collection of the New York Public Library. For a more extended discussion of this portion of the *Typee* manuscript, see Bryant, *Melville and Repose*, 148–49.

21 One sign of Melville's desire to keep the reader from thinking of this feast as a "horrid rite" is his deletion of a paragraph near the end of this chapter in the draft manuscript. In his description of the islanders carrying the remains of the feast back to Marheyo's house, he had initially suggested that "[t]his picturesque procession carrying along such glorious specimens of tropical vegetation moving with wild chants through the sylvan defiles of the valley might have been taken for a throng of the ancient devotees of Ceres wending their way with votive offerings towards the altars of the goddess" (leaf 11). But in accordance with his general tendency to minimize even the suggestion of serious ritual activity, this passage was cut.

22 C. Stewart, *Visit*, 1:276, 266. Subsequent page references will be cited parenthetically in the text. Melville acknowledges Stewart as a source in the first chapter of *Typee*, and his reference in this chapter to "the Washington, or Northern Marquesas Islands" is, except for the comma, an exact quotation from Stewart (1:214).

23 Those who visited the Marquesans immediately after the Cook expeditions frequently reported that "the natives, when pushed by famine, would make use of all

the art they possessed, to get one of their enemies into their hands, for the purposes of food" (Fanning, *Voyages,* 145). Most famously, a resident Englishman named Roberts told Adam Krusenstern in 1804 that "during a famine, a Nukahiwer will murder his wife, to satiate his hunger with her flesh; and he butchers his child and devours it with the same voracity" (Krusenstern, *Voyage,* 1:166). This explanation was quickly overtaken by the others I have described here, however, and by the 1840s, it was rarely given any consideration.

24 For the details of this borrowing, see Anderson, *Melville in the South Seas,* 172–73.

25 This is a good example of what Tobin Siebers has described as the Romantics' "sentimental form of superstition" (*Romantic Fantastic,* 35). For writers like Sir Walter Scott, as long as superstition is "not arrayed in her full horrors, but laying a gentle hand only on her suppliant's head," it has "charms which we fail not to regret, even in those stages of society from which her influence is well-nigh banished by the light of reason and general education" (quoted in Siebers, 23). What is unusual about Tommo's celebration of this form of superstition is its suggestion that for the *Typees,* as well as for Romantics like himself, superstition never does anything more than lay its hand on its suppliant's head, insofar as it is always infused by the always transitory spirit of nostalgia.

26 My discussion of this fluid form of fetishism owes a great deal to David Simpson's argument, in *Fetishism and Imagination,* that the Typees are "freer in their para-theological customs than are their more civilized observers" (7). Aware that "[s]elf knows itself only by reflection upon what is other," and that this other is "a result of a perceptive mechanism in which the self has already played a creative part," the Typees engage, among themselves, in that "*continual* creation and reaction which save such gestures from inertia, and hence from fetishism," understood here as "a fixed form beyond the reach of time or change" (14, 15). Where I depart from Simpson is in my suggestion that in their interactions with Tommo, the Typees repeatedly *fix* their fluid cycling of forms, and thereby obstruct his desire to believe that all such forms are bottomed on an infinitely rich and variable consciousness.

27 Lisiansky, *Voyage Round the World,* 87–88.

28 Porter, *Journal of a Cruise,* 2:46.

29 This argument is reinforced, at a remove, by something that Elizabeth Melville wrote after her husband's death. In response to an essay in the September 1901 issue of the *Bulletin of the Society of American Authors* in which the Typees were described as "man-devouring," she declared that "whatever might have been [Herman's] suspicions, he never had evidence that it was the custom of the tribe" (Leyda, *Melville Log,* 1:37).

30 The dismay only enters, however, when the prohibitions laid on women get in the way of his own pleasure. When he declares that "for the life of me I could not understand why a woman should not have as much right to enter a canoe as a man," for instance, it is because he is aggravated by the fact that the taboo restricting women's contact with canoes has reduced his opportunities for "[b]athing in company with troops of girls" (133, 131).

31 "*Narrative of a Four Months' Residence,*" 220.

32 Higgins and Parker, *Reviews,* 7. Subsequent page references will be cited parenthetically in the text.

33 Outside of *Typee, Moby-Dick,* and "Benito Cereno," references to cannibalism ap-

pear frequently but incidentally, which means that the truly innovative aspect of Melville's treatment of the subject—his attention to the process of conviction's unraveling—is necessarily absent. These scattered allusions do confirm the argument I am making here, however, in that they show Melville thinking about cannibalism only in terms of the four absolutely crucial stages in that process: (1) vengeance, (2) terror, (3) humane horror, and (4) the mockery of that horror. I will give a representative example of each of these usages and cite the location of the rest.

1. Midway through *Israel Potter,* John Paul Jones explodes with rage at everyone who has ever slandered him, and swears vengeance on them all. In an explanation that echoes his analysis of Toby's character, Melville writes: "Men with poignant feelings, buried under an air of care-free self-command, are never proof to the sudden incitements of passion. Though in the main, they may control themselves, yet if they but once permit the smallest vent, then they may bid adieu to all self-restraint, at least for that time. Thus with Paul on the present occasion. . . . When it was gone by, he seemed not a little to regret it. But he passed it over lightly, saying, 'You see, my fine fellow, what sort of a bloody cannibal I am' " (91). See also Bembo's fury in *Omoo* (71, 88, 92–93), Babbalanja's self-torturing grief in *Mardi* (594), the vengeful temper of the dispossessed Redburn (*R,* 13, 15), and the maddened mobs in "Rich Man's Crumbs" (*PT,* 298) and "Naples in the Time of Bomba" (*CP,* 357).

2. In *Mardi,* Taji remarks on the book-smitten Babbalanja's desire to lunch by himself "and, like a cannibal, feed upon an author, though in other respects he was not so partial to bones" (387). The logic of the analogy is as follows: Babbalanja is *like* a cannibal in that he is "feeding" on the mind of an author, but *unlike* a cannibal in that cannibals are partial to the preservation and display of bones, whereas he is distinctly averse to these "emblem[s] of dominion over mankind" (253). This connection between cannibalism and the signification of dominion may also be found in *White-Jacket,* where the narrator compares naval floggings to the terrorism of cannibals (124, 387); in *Pierre,* where the worm is said to be "like a cannibal" in its perpetration of indignities on the corpse (198); in "Rich Man's Crumbs," where the narrator tells his guide that the banqueters contemptuously celebrating the victory at Waterloo might as well have had "Napoleon's head in a charger" (*PT,* 299); in an 1848 letter to Evert Duyckinck in which Melville refuses to review a book by Joseph Hart, asking "What has Mr. Hart done that I should publicly devour him?" (*C,* 113); and in "House of the Tragic Poet," in which the editor compares his hostile readership to the "tattooed savages" who "cooked and served up" Captain Cook (quoted in Sandberg, "Adjustment of Screens," 445).

3. In *White-Jacket,* the narrator declares that "as the whole matter of war is a thing that smites common sense and Christianity in the face; so everything connected with it is utterly foolish, unchristian, barbarous, brutal, and savouring of the Feejee Islands, cannibalism, saltpetre, and the devil" (315). Confronted by the horrors of war, understood as "cannibalistic," in that they are monstrously excessive significations of dominion, the narrator retreats into a wounded "common sense and Christianity," just as Tommo does in *Typee.* This is a rare gesture; these kinds of pronouncements are usually either ironized, as in the examples I will turn to next, or directed solely at white people who are described as being like cannibals but worse (see *R,* 293, and "The Encantadas," *PT,* 162–63).

4. In *White-Jacket,* a lieutenant on the *Neversink* pretends to be a cannibal in order

to "play upon [the] credulity" of the ship's surgeon, Cadwallader Cuticle. After sending the surgeon a piece of sago pudding labeled as "an uncommonly fine specimen of a cancer," the lieutenant sidles up to him and asks for a bite: "You know, I was in New Zealand last cruise, Cuticle, and got into sad dissipation there among the cannibals; come, let's have a bit, if it's only a mouthful" (250). Cuticle's enthusiasm for the morbid instantly kicks in; he calls the lieutenant an "infernal Feejee," gives the pudding to him, and then stands with his hands uplifted, watching him eat. When at last he realizes that he has been hoaxed, and that his obsession with "all species of morbid anatomy" has been mirrored back to him as a lusting after human flesh, he storms out of the room. Other examples of this "quizzing" of humane horror include Ishmael's self-consciously sermonic account of the "Fejee that salted down a lean missionary in his cellar against the coming famine" (MD, 300), Taji's similarly bombastic reveries on Hawaiian cannibalism (M, 206) and Batta cannibalism (M, 288–89), Taji's satire of sensational accounts of cannibalism and of their use in justifications of colonialism (M, 384, 493), and Redburn's boyish conviction that a notice reading "MAN-TRAPS AND SPRING-GUNS!" signifies the presence of cannibals (R, 210).

3   *The Aftersight:* Moby-Dick *and the Spectacle of Savagery*

1   Quoted in Parker, *Herman Melville,* 618.
2   Among the passages he cut were several that touched on the discourse on cannibalism, including the Montaignean defense of vengeful cannibalism in chap. 17 and the digression on the toe of Captain Cook in chap. 32. None of these expurgations affect the basic structure of the speculative process that I described in chap. 2; readers of the revised American edition can also trace Tommo's movement from lust to vengeance to terror. But they do deprive that process of much of its richness and seductiveness, thereby making it easier for readers to avoid entering it.
3   These paddles are on display in the Herman Melville Reading Room of the Berkshire Atheneum in Pittsfield, Massachusetts.
4   Spivak, *Outside in the Teaching Machine,* 64–65, 75.
5   In December 1847, a writer in the *Dublin Review* surmised that the author of *Typee* and *Omoo,* "for aught we know, may next turn up at the North Pole, and amuse the world and ourselves with adventures among the Esquimaux. Perchance he may be the identical man who has exhibited Tom Thumb, or the Bosjemans from Caffraria" (Higgins and Parker, *Reviews,* 164). On February 12, 1848, the following parody of Melville appeared in an American magazine called *The Elephant:*
      Cannibalism.—The following brief extract from a new work, entitled "Travels in the Cannibal Islands, by the author of Omoo," is highly illustrative of the manners and customs of the people of those benighted regions. Dining one day with the king he urged me to try a cut of cold clergyman, which lay on a side-table; this I declined, much to the King's surprise, with as good grace as I could, professing a great partiality for a dish of fricaseed mermaid then on the table before me. (Quoted in Yanella, " 'Seeing the Elephant,' " 111)
   Melville was well aware of the freak-show context within which his early works were being received; in *Mardi,* he includes in the collections of Oh-Oh, a luridly fetishistic lover of "*curios*" (379), a travel narrative entitled "A Sojourn among

the Anthropophagi, by One whose Hand was eaten off at Tiffin among the Savages" (384).

6 The history of the first argument, which presumes an abrupt redirection of intent midway through the composition of *Moby-Dick,* is summarized in the fifth section of the historical note at the end of the Northwestern-Newberry edition; the two possibilities it presents are that Queequeg is the vestige of an earlier, nonmetaphysical conception of the book, or a "humanizing" character hastily written into the early chapters during the final stages of composition. The effect of each of these arguments is to characterize Melville's creations of Queequeg and Ahab as entirely distinct activities, corresponding to antithetical phases of Melville's own personality. Although the second argument resists the questionable assumption that there are "two" or "three" distinct *Moby-Dicks,* it depends on the equally questionable assumption that the thing Ahab symbolizes emanates without end from one region of the book while the thing Queequeg symbolizes emanates without end from another. For recent examples of this reading, see Karcher, *Shadow over the Promised Land;* R. K. Martin, *Hero, Captain, and Stranger;* and Tolchin, *Mourning, Gender and Creativity.*

7 For a description and analysis of that gaze, see Frantz Fanon, *Black Skin, White Masks,* 109–40.

8 In the midst of his 1847 account of mercenary warfare in New Guinea, John Coulter notes that "[i]t appeared to be perfect gratification to our four seamen to be 'popping off the cannibals,' as they termed nearly all savages" (*Adventures,* 2:226). In a more restricted sense, the word could be used interchangeably with "Pacific islander," and in an even more restricted sense, with "Maori." Thomas Jefferson Jacobs observes in 1844 that his shipmates were in the habit of calling the islands of the southwestern Pacific the "Cannibal Islands" (*Scenes,* 246), and Arthur Thomson declares, a few years later, that "[t]he New Zealanders have obtained a disagreeable notoriety for this vice; and so much so that few persons can think of New Zealanders without thinking of cannibalism, or of cannibalism without thinking of the New Zealanders" (*Story,* 1:141).

9 In *Omoo,* Melville's narrator tells us that the crew of the *Julia* are in the habit of circulating "[h]ard stories" about the Maori harpooner, Bembo, including "something, in particular, concerning an hereditary propensity to kill men and eat them" (71). By characterizing these stories as "hard," he implies that they are both derogatory (without humane softness) and untrue (difficult to swallow). (Compare the "hard stories" of shipboard abuses told by the crew of the *Leviathan* at the end of *Omoo* [313], the "tough yarns" told by unscrupulous beachcombers in *Typee* [170], and Samoa's "tough . . . tales" of pig-to-man grafting in *Mardi* [299].) "True," he says, Bembo "came from a race of cannibals; but that was all that was known to a certainty" (71). When members of the crew stand over the fallen Bembo after a fight, "rating him in sailor style, for a cannibal and a coward" (88), they are calling him a cannibal not because it is "known to a certainty" that he is one, but because he is of a race conventionally associated with cannibalism, and because the epithet conventionally expressed contempt. As several contemporary travelers had noted, Pacific islanders were quite aware of the insult implicit in this epithet. Richard Henry Dana writes that the Hawaiians he met in San Diego did not like "to have anything said about Captain Cook, for the sailors all believe that he was eaten, and that, they cannot endure to be taunted with" (*Two Years before the Mast,* 206), and Samuel Martin

similarly reports that young Maori men are "so much ashamed of this savage custom, that nothing is calculated to offend them so much as to call them cannibals" (*New Zealand,* 283). Melville is critical of the use of this epithet against Bembo not only because it is baseless, then, but also because it is damaging, ultimately contributing to Bembo's enraged efforts to destroy the *Julia* by running it aground.

10 It is surprising, again, that none of the critics who have commented on both *Moby-Dick* and *Huckleberry Finn* have noticed the similarities between this scene and the famous moment in Twain's book when Aunt Sally asks if anyone was hurt in a supposed steamboat explosion and Huck answers, "No'm. Killed a nigger" (243). Because critics of American literature still tend to think of race in black and white terms, it continues to be difficult to recognize the exercises and critiques of racism that are carried out in other terms.

11 See Evelev, " 'Made in the Marquesas.' " Though Evelev discusses just two tattooed men, John O'Connell and Jean-Baptiste Cabri, his list could easily be extended. In *The New Zealanders,* George Craik includes a lengthy excerpt from the dictated narrative of John Rutherford, who was taken prisoner by the Maori in 1816 and tattooed over most of his body. Upon his return to England, Rutherford "occasionally maintained himself by accompanying a travelling caravan of wonders, shewing his tattooing, and telling something of his extraordinary adventures" (277–78). Craik met Rutherford in 1829, "when he was exhibited in London," and secured his permission to reprint parts of his narrative, together with a drawing of him stripped to the waist. Rutherford "greatly disliked being shown for money," Craik wrote, but submitted to it, as he submitted to his inclusion in Craik's history, so that he could get enough money to return to the Pacific. See also Barnet Burns's *Brief Narrative of a New Zealand Chief* (1844), which has as its frontispiece a portrait of the narrator with a thoroughly tattooed face and is similarly published for the sake of self-support. As Evelev correctly observes, Melville was anxious not to be confused with such characters. Largely because of this "fear of being turned into a kind of freak by fame," he would later refuse to supply a magazine with a daguerreotyped image of his head (" 'Made in the Marquesas,' " 35).

12 Odell, *New York Stage,* 3:591, 636–37. The two cannibals were exhibited together with conjoined twins, a living skeleton, an anaconda, and a mummy; the play was generally performed on the same bill with one of the greatest hits of that theater season, T. D. Rice singing "Jim Crow."

13 Melville had attacked this discourse in very direct terms once before, in "Authentic Anecdotes of 'Old Zack,' " published in the satirical magazine *Yankee Doodle* in 1847. In response to the "fabular anecdotes" concerning Gen. Zachary Taylor, which had been circulated solely "to titilate public curiosity," Melville's special correspondent promises to provide his readers with "authentic anecdotes" that "have been collected on the ground from the most reliable and respectable sources" (*PT,* 212, 213). The comedy of the piece derives in part from the triviality or ludicrousness of the "authentic anecdotes," which satirize the frivolity and credulity of "public curiosity." But it also derives from the conflict between the authorized correspondent and the unauthorized agent of Barnum, who is "anxious to secure every relic of General TAYLOR" for exhibition "at his Museum, for the satisfaction of the curious" (224, 229). The agent finally tells Taylor's servant that Barnum's ultimate aim is to have the general "grinning through the bars of a cage"; the next

day, Taylor receives a letter from Barnum offering him employment in his museum, where he "will be associated with all that is curious in art and nature," so long as he agrees to surrender himself "to the control and direction of the said Peter Tamerlane B———m, who will treat you no worse than he has the venerable nurse of our beloved Washington and the illustrious General Tom Thumb" (225). To be a public curiosity in a market context dominated by the figure of P. T. Barnum is to become an object under the control of both promoter and audience, who take their "satisfaction" from seeing you at a distance, behind literal or figurative bars.

14   McCrae, *Journal Kept in New Zealand*, 17.

15   Beechey, *Narrative of a Voyage*, 222.

16   Baudrillard, "System of Collecting," 19.

17   The romanticization of touch is most evident in Robert K. Martin, who argues that Queequeg leads Ishmael to "the discovery of the body as a source of pleasure and instruction" (*Hero*, 74). But though he argues on the one hand that it is only "because Ishmael has learned the lessons of Queequeg that he is able to function on the ship as an exponent of restored sexuality" (91), he is forced to confess on the other that Ishmael is not always "faithful to the values expressed in these early chapters" (72). To account for this gap, which is made even more evident by Queequeg's diminished role in the later chapters, he declares that the values of nonaggressive touch "remain there as a foundation to which [Ishmael] can return once he has freed himself from the lure of the Ahabian quest" (72–73). He briefly acknowledges that it is a foundation that is only there if we insist that it is—"one must keep in mind the Ishmael-Queequeg relationship throughout the entire novel, even though it is only alluded to occasionally once the ship has set sail" (90)—before naturalizing it again in his conclusion: the "pastoral vision of a restored harmony" is "first glimpsed in New *Bed*ford, and nothing can finally erase its memory" (94; his emphasis).

18   Crain, "Lovers of Human Flesh," 33. Though Crain suggests that it was Melville's innovation "to associate this cannibalism and voluptuousness with each other" (32), it was in fact a familiar association, as the examples above should indicate.

19   Labillardiere, *Account of a Voyage*, 2:204, 225.

20   Bennet and Tyerman, *Journal*, 2:135–36. Because there is so often a resistance to the suggestion of homoeroticism in encounters between men, colonial or otherwise, it might be useful to record a few more instances. An officer in Marion du Fresne's ill-fated New Zealand expedition of 1772, Lieutenant Roux, observes that the Maoris "are peculiarly fond of kissing each other, and this they do with great intensity. They were never weary of admiring our skins, especially their whiteness, but when we permitted them to place their lips, either upon our hands or our faces, they sucked the flesh with a surprising greediness" (McNab, *Records*, 2:403). The missionary Walter Lawry reports that upon landing on a Fijian island, "a stout cannibal attempted to ascertain whether Philip Johns, one of the seamen, was fit to eat, by laying hold of his leg and turning up some of his clothing, to see how the matter stood" (*Friendly and Feejee Islands*, 204). And Peter Bays writes in 1831 that soon after he and his shipwrecked companions beached their open boat on an island near the Fijis, "three or four of the savages came and laid hold of Mr. Garret, and led him away a few pace from the party, and began to examine him: first they opened his bosom, then pulled off his jacket and waistcoat; and, lastly, stripped him to the skin." Aided by the sight of "the large fire blazing up at this instant," and by their preconceptions of "the bar-

barous character of the Fegee islanders," this slow exposure of their companion's naked body became, in their minds, a decisive sign of an appetite for human flesh: "we really felt as though they were going to butcher him, and that instead of getting among friends, we were among cannibals" (*Wreck of the* Minerva, 47).

21 Some selected passages may help to clarify what Melville means by "gameness." Upon discovering that Queequeg is a Pacific islander, Ishmael confesses that "I was so afraid of him that I was not game enough just then to address him" (22). In a similar usage, Ahab attempts to shame Starbuck into acquiescence by asking him, "art not game for Moby-Dick?" Stung, Starbuck answers, "I am game for his crooked jaw, and for the jaws of Death too, Captain Ahab, if it fairly comes in the way of the business we follow; but I came here to hunt whales, not my commander's vengeance" (163). In part, then, to be game is to be as fearless and tenacious as a gamecock; this is the association that Pip draws on in his rhapsody over Queequeg and that the captain of the *Town-Ho* draws on when he calls Steelkilt "my fine bantam, that wouldn't give up" (253). But it also implies that these qualities are governed by the provisional spirit of play that operates in a game. Although the "gamesome" things that are said about Jonah's furtiveness (43), Nantucket's barrenness (63), the vulgarity of whalers (240), the nervousness of the captain of the *Town-Ho* (245), and a dying whale (369) are all expressive of contempt—unlike the "spirit of godly gamesomeness" expressed in a round of huzzahs (144)—that contempt is at least qualified by the staged quality of the statements. A "game" act is an essentially *performative* enactment of masculinity, in other words; it is a provocation or a response to provocation that occurs in the suspended time of the contest or the joke.

22 J. K. Campbell, "Greek Hero," 132; Ayers, *Vengeance and Justice,* 21.

23 Bourdieu, "Sentiment of Honour," 202.

24 Pitt-Rivers, "Honour and Social Status," 25.

25 J. K. Campbell, "Greek Hero," 134.

26 S. Stewart, *On Longing,* 127. Subsequent page references will be cited parenthetically in the text.

27 In Craik, for instance, we learn that when a Maori named Tupai was being sketched in England, "he was above all solicitous that the marks on his face should be accurately copied," for they constituted "the distinctive mark of the individual; and one part, indeed, of that on his own face, the mark just over the upper part of his nose, Tupai constantly called his name; saying, 'Europee man write with pen his name,—Tupai's name is here,' pointing to his forehead" (*New Zealanders,* 330–31). According to John Bright, such representations of identity were less common among the Maori after New Zealand was annexed. He writes in 1841 that "the circles on the nostrils were formerly described on a deed as the signature of the marker, and termed by them their *amoko;* now they generally sign their names" (*Hand-Book for Emigrants,* 77).

28 Irwin, *American Hieroglyphics,* 323.

29 The chapter from which these quotations have been taken, "Queequeg in his Coffin," may at first appear to belie my assertion that Queequeg essentially disappears from the narrative once the *Pequod* has gone to sea. As these quotations should suggest, however, what returns at this point is nothing more than a "partial presence" (Bhabha, *Location,* 114). Though the tattooing on his body hints at the advent of a mystically symbolic meaning, it is ultimately nothing more than a "devilish tantaliza-

tion." Insofar as it is unreadable, and will molder away with the flesh and the wood, its promise of immaterial truth is betrayed by the materiality of its representation.

30 For the classic statement of this assumption, see Thorstein Veblen's socioevolutionary analysis of "conspicuous consumption" in *The Theory of the Leisure Class*.

31 Beginning in the 1840s, Fiji was increasingly linked to cannibalism; by the end of the nineteenth century, it had replaced New Zealand as the Pacific island group that was most widely associated with the practice. The link between cannibalism and Erromanga, an island in the New Hebrides chain, was more topical. In 1839, the missionary John Williams and a companion were killed by the natives of Erromanga soon after stepping on shore. One of Williams's first biographers, Ebenezer Prout, reported that "the wretched creatures confessed that they had devoured the bodies, of which nothing remained but some of the bones" (*Memoirs*, 394). In the less temperate words of Thomas Jacobs, Williams had been "most barbarously massacred by the savages upon this island; his body was roasted and eaten!" (*Scenes*, 235). Melville was obviously familiar with these events; when he quotes from Williams's *Missionary Voyage* in *Omoo*, he refers to him as "Williams, the martyr of Erromanga" (*O*, 187).

32 For an excellent discussion of this point, see David Simpson, *Fetishism and Imagination*.

33 Pease, "Cold War," 116, 144.

34 As Leland S. Person Jr. has recently observed, "Critics have generally agreed that *Moby-Dick* is a man's book and that Melville's representation of seafaring manhood inscribes a patriarchal, anti-female ideology that reinforces nineteenth-century gender separatism—a manhood based on differentiation from women" ("Melville's Cassock," 1). But once we have acknowledged this point, Person says, we must go on to ask whether Melville essentializes this opposition by stabilizing its masculine pole. I disagree with Person's conclusion that Melville ultimately decenters masculinity by plunging it into "the fluid, unmanageable depths of both world and self" (7); as I have been suggesting, it is not the encounter with plenitude that inspires this reorientation, but the encounter with lack. I think Person is right, however, in attributing to Melville a desire to "destabilize a manhood predicated on difference" (4). For a version of this argument that is somewhat closer to my own, focusing on the impasse that Melville's male narrators discover when they intrude into feminine realms, see Judith Hiltner's "Disquieting Encounters."

35 Palgrave, "Superstition and Knowledge," 449. For a discussion of the relationship between this review essay and Melville's notes in his Shakespeare volume, see Sanborn, "Name of the Devil."

36 As far as I have been able to tell, Robert K. Wallace is the only other critic who has suggested this connection, arguing that Melville encountered Goethe's theory through his reading of Charles Eastlake's "Extracts from the Translation of Goethe's Theory of Colours" (Wallace, *Melville and Turner*, 170). It is not my intention here to resolve the question of where Melville encountered this theory, only to show that the parallels between "The Whiteness of the Whale" and Goethe's text are both direct and extensive.

37 Goethe, *Theory of Colours*, 60. Subsequent page references will be cited parenthetically in the text.

38 Melville was not alone in his interest in this feature of Goethe's theory. In "Self-

Reliance" (1841), Emerson deprecates time and space by calling them "physiological colors which the eye makes," as opposed to the soul, which "is light: where it is, is day; where it was, is night" (*Selected Essays*, 189). And in "Fanny McDermot" (1845), Melville's Berkshire neighbor Catharine Sedgwick describes her seduced heroine as having "no true coloring or proportion to her perception; she was like one, who, having imprudently gazed at the sun, sees every object for a time in false and brilliant coloring. But these illusions fade by degrees to blackness; and so, as Fanny recovered from the bewilderment of passion, the light became shadow—ever deepening, immovable shadow" (130–31).

39   Lacan, *Ecrits*, 296.

40   Crary, *Techniques of the Observer*, 98.

41   In a hologram, Jean Baudrillard observes, "things seem to be made of a more unreal substance; they seem to turn and move in a void as if by a special lighting effect, a fine membrane you pass through without noticing it. . . . The hologram is akin to the world of phantasy. It is a three-dimensional dream and you can enter it as you would a dream." But "[e]verything depends on the existence of the ray of light bearing the objects"; if that light wanes or scatters, you are left in the void you have been seduced into entering (*America*, 29–30).

42   Quoted in Bennett, "Rivals Unravelled," 423. The emphasis on the number fifty continues in later verses, as the remaining fifty wives steal off with fifty chiefs, and the king sends "cannibal slayers" to "put an end to all their lives / The fifty chiefs and the fifty wives." It is probably no accident, then, that when Queequeg is counting pages in the book in the Spouter-Inn, he pauses "at every fiftieth page" to express amazement before beginning again "at the next fifty; seeming to commence at number one each time, as though he could not count more than fifty, and it was only by such a large number of fifties being found together, that his astonishment at the multitude of pages was excited" (*MD*, 49).

43   Bennett, "Rivals Unravelled," 420; Reid, *Odd People*, 169.

44   Melville's own sense of Queequeg's unreality is further suggested by the fact that many of the details that he used in constructing Queequeg's character were not drawn from life but from a book. The book is an at least partially imaginary travel narrative by Thomas Jefferson Jacobs called *Scenes, Incidents, and Adventures in the Pacific Ocean*, published by Harpers in 1844 and purchased by Melville in 1847. Like *Mardi*, the book takes advantage of the fact that the southwestern Pacific is still "an unknown and unexplored region" (*Scenes*, 64), using the novelty of the field as both a source of interest and an opportunity for invention. In his opening paragraph, Jacobs makes it clear that he is attempting to capitalize on the popularity of earlier representations of Melanesians, alluding to the fact that "[a]bout ten years ago, as many of my readers may recollect, two savages, named Sunday and Monday, and advertised as cannibals, were publicly exhibited in New-York and other cities of the American Union" (1). The voyage he is about to describe is a kind of sequel to that exhibition, he says, insofar as it follows one of those cannibals, Sunday, on his trip back to his native island, whose precise position had never been disclosed. This cannibal, whose native name is Telum-by-by Darco, bears an unmistakable resemblance to Queequeg. "His dexterity in throwing the spear was very great," Jacobs tells us, and he "had a most inveterate and praiseworthy habit of minding his own business" (23, 24). Whenever he speaks, moreover, his broken English is rendered

exactly as Queequeg's is; at one point, he shouts from the lookout post, "Me tink-e me see land-e! . . . Him look-e too much-e far off!—plenty high!—me no hab fool-e you dis time!" (24). After dropping Sunday off on his native island, Jacobs's ship picks up a substitute, a cannibal prince named Garry-Garry who has "a great desire to accompany us to [civilization]" (193). Garry-Garry, too, is a proto-Queequeg: soon after his arrival in Sydney, "[a] wheelbarrow took his fancy, as being a very useful thing for his people to become acquainted with" (248). After extended expo-sure to the sight of white men swearing and drinking, however, "he looked as if his moral principles had received a severe shock, and said, "My people no do so bad; me wish'e me in Bidera" (248). On the way back to Bidera, he develops a fever "that made him quite delirious. He imagined that he would surely die, and what troubled him more than all was the thought that his body would be cast into the sea, and thus prevent his people from performing over it the rites of sepulture" (250). He "recovered rapidly" (251), however, and was eventually restored to his island.

45 Žižek, Metastases of Enjoyment, 82.

4 Walking Shadows: "Benito Cereno" and the Colonial Stage

1 Mandel, "Two Mystery Stories," 637.

2 Phillips, "Good Captain," 190; Putzel, "Source and Symbols," 194.

3 Putzel, "Source and Symbols," 199; Green, "Diabolism, Pessimism, and Democ-racy," 288; T. J. Martin, "Idea of Nature," 168.

4 By my count, eight critics have *stated* that Aranda was eaten: in chronological order, they are Gaillard, "Melville's Riddle for Our Time," 481; McElroy, "Canni-balism in Melville's 'Benito Cereno,' " 206–18; Dillingham, *Melville's Short Fiction*, 241; Wright, "New Psychoanalysis and Literary Criticism," 102; Rogin, *Subver-sive Genealogy*, 214; Richardson, "Melville's 'Benito Cereno,' " 67 n. 50; Baines, "Ritualized Cannibalism in 'Benito Cereno,' " 163–69; and Hattenhauer, " 'Follow Your Leader,' " 14–15. Thirteen more have *suggested* that Aranda was eaten: again in chronological order, they are Kaplan, "American National Sin," 22; Putzel, "Source and Symbols," 205; Nicol, "Iconography of Evil and Ideal," 28; Pops, *Mel-ville Archetype*, 155; Thompson, afterword, 127; Johnson, "American Innocence and Guilt," 431; Hilfer, "Philosophy of Clothes," 224; Newman, *Reader's Guide*, 121; Sundquist, "New World Slavery," 99; Levine, *Conspiracy and Romance*, 291 n. 91; Crain, "Lovers of Human Flesh," 44; Kiely, *Reverse Traditions*, 73; and Bartley, "Creature," 457.

5 My argument picks up on certain elements of an earlier challenge to the assump-tion that the slaves on the *San Dominick* cannibalize their master. In a 1992 essay, Sterling Stuckey argues that during the three days in which Aranda's corpse was concealed below decks, Yau "telescoped" the Ashanti custom of allowing the bodies of dead kings to decay for eighty days, scraping the flesh off, and preserving the bones (" 'Follow Your Leader,' " 192). Within the terms of Ashanti culture, Stuckey suggests, the compression of the process to three days could have signified, con-temptuously, that Aranda was "sort of a king without honor" (192). In reminding us that black men plus human bones does not necessarily equal cannibalism, Stuckey offers a useful critique of the standard reading of the story. But in assuming that the locus of the story's meaning is below deck—that the bones are signs proceeding

from and operating within an authentic Ashanti context, rather than signs produced within the context of the colonial encounter—Stuckey reproduces the fundamental assumption of that reading: that a Shekinah of truth may be made to radiate from the interiors of the ship's hull and Babo's skull. When we replace the truth of "savagery" with the truth of "culture," we too often avoid asking questions about the ways in which *each* of these truths is produced.

6 Though the absence of collaborative speculation in "Benito Cereno" may seem to indicate that Melville had given up entirely on the project of meeting his readers on their ground, and though Melville had indeed begun to despair of making any meaningful contact with those readers, there is still an imagined audience here, and a pedagogy appropriate to it. As Sheila Post-Lauria has observed, there is a noticeable difference in strategy between the stories Melville wrote for *Harper's* in the 1850s, like "Bartleby," and the stories he wrote for *Putnam's*, like "Benito Cereno." When writing for *Harper's*, he employed "the sentimental mode both to represent and to change conservative middle-class views in what appears to be an attempt to instruct readers" (*Correspondent Colorings*, 209). When writing for *Putnam's*, whose more liberal readers "expected critical treatments of political, social, and ideological positions" (209), he enacts, in order to move beyond, the blitheness and gloominess that sometimes envelop such critics.

7 Parkinson, *Journal of a Voyage*, 116.

8 Roquefeuil, *Voyage Round the World*, 33, 34. The French admiral D'Entrecasteaux similarly reported that while in Van Dieman's Land, "[o]ne of the naturalists found some bones, which he concluded to belong to the body of a very young girl; they were discovered among the ashes of one of the places apparently used by the natives for cooking their victuals. Some fragments of broiled flesh were attached to these bones." He immediately warns us, however, that "[a] fact, thus isolated without other indications, especially among a people of such simple manners, is not sufficient to authorize conjectures so reproachful to human nature, sinking it below the most ferocious beasts of prey, which at least spare their own species" (quoted in Barrow, "Dentrecasteaux," 30).

9 Sheldon, "Brief Account of the Caribs," 418. Subsequent page references will be cited parenthetically in the text.

10 Humboldt and Bonpland, *Personal Narrative*, 2:414. Subsequent page references will be cited parenthetically in the text.

11 Irving, *Columbus*, 2:14. Subsequent page references will be cited parenthetically in the text.

12 Byron, *Voyage of H.M.S. Blonde*, 12.

13 If the colonial encounter cannot be aligned, in the final analysis, with these other encounters, then there is indeed something contradictory about Bhabha's "employment of the transcendental categories of psychoanalysis for the analysis of the historical phenomenon of colonialism" (Young, *White Mythologies*, 144). At the same time, the specificity of the colonial encounter should not be sunk into the vortex of a universal truth. As Ernesto Laclau has pointed out, "to say that everything is contingent . . . is an assertion that would only make sense for an inhabitant of Mars. It is true that in the *final instance* no objectivity can be referred back to an absolute ground; but no important conclusion can be drawn from this, since the social agents never act in that final instance" (*New Reflections*, 27).

14 Kavanagh, "That Hive of Subtlety," 357.

15 Ibid., 370.

16 Fanon, *Black Skins, White Masks,* 109.

17 Haegert, "Voicing Slavery through Silence," 29.

18 In a similar argument, Charles Martin and James Snead have suggested that although "[s]ome literary critics, like Delano, may consider that once successive veils have been removed, something has been solved or disclosed," it is more reasonable to conclude "that not any particular lesson, but the entire sequence of them, and the illusion of correctness at each stopping point, was perhaps the 'moral'" ("Reading through Blackness," 234, 245).

19 From our perspective, it is relatively obvious that Babo is the subject-who-knows-most; as several recent critics have noticed, he is, in the world of the story, the closest analog to Melville himself. In his resolutely nontransparent activity—plotting, staging, hinting, and falling silent—Babo points us in the direction of a selfhood that accepts the uncertainty of signs and transforms that uncertainty into the source of its power. For modern readers who are more interested in *threatening* "white" consciousness than in reformulating it, Babo is a particularly powerful "leader," though his murderousness, like Cereno's suicidalness, is likely to be an obstacle to the desire to take on his identity as our own.

20 Halttunen, *Confidence-Men and Painted Women,* 125.

21 According to David Stannard, the "familiar death's-head carving" of the late seventeenth and early eighteenth centuries gave way in the mid-eighteenth century to "more optimistic and spiritual representations." As early as the 1740s, "the grim visage of death had metamorphosed into a pleasant cherubic image," and "by the close of the century both styles had been replaced by the familiar and full-blown Romantic 'urn and willow' motif" (*Puritan Way of Death,* 157).

22 Benjamin, *Origin of German Tragic Drama,* 217, 176.

23 Ibid., 214.

24 Sontag, *Illness as Metaphor,* 11–12.

25 Quoted in Dubos and Dubos, *White Plague,* 127.

26 It is hard to say whether Melville was aware of the work of the English epidemiologist William Budd, who published an influential essay on the contagion theory of tuberculosis in 1867, but the connection is at least possible. Knowing that explorers had reported that there were no signs of tuberculosis among Africans in the interior of the continent, Budd was struck by the fact that African sailors in England contracted the disease and died from it at an alarming rate. After reflecting on this phenomenon, he became one of the first Western scientists to convert from the theory that consumption is produced by disappointment to the theory that it is "disseminated through specific germs contained in the tuberculous matter cast off by persons already suffering from the disease" (quoted in ibid., 97). *Billy Budd,* which begins with an image of a radiantly healthy African sailor striding the docks in Liverpool, is similarly concerned with the mechanisms by which disorder enters an individual or social body, though the book rocks back and forth between the theory that it develops from within and the theory that it is "caught" from without. In the passage I quoted in the text, Melville subscribes to the older, moralistic account of the genesis of disease. When describing the Nore mutiny of 1797, however, Melville shifts to the more modern theory, comparing it "to the distempering irruption of contagious fever in a frame constitutionally sound, and which anon throws it off" (*BB,* 55).

27 *Macbeth,* 3.4.20–21, 5.5.24–28.

1 Heffernan, *Stove,* 29. Subsequent page references will be cited parenthetically in the text.

2 For a partial list of borrowings from Bennet and Tyerman in *Mardi,* see Jaffe, "Some Sources of Melville's *Mardi.*" For an account of the use of the Pollard interview in *Moby-Dick,* see Pommer, "Herman Melville and the Wake of the *Essex.*"

3 These quotations and those that follow are from *Clarel* (ed. Harrison Hayford, Alma A. MacDougall, Hershel Parker, and G. Thomas Tanselle [Evanston, IL: Northwestern University Press/Newberry Library, 1991]), part 1, canto 37.

4 One of the clearest signs that he thought of himself as a student of cannibalism is his reference in an 1849 journal to an "Allusion to *Cannibals*" on the "17th page of Sir Thomas Browne." "Also," he added in parentheses, "page 57 of B. Jonson" (*J,* 142). Probably at around the same time, he wrote three words centered at the top of a page in a miscellaneous entry notebook: "Cannibals," "Execution," and "Terrapin." In all likelihood, the entry was inspired by Poe's *Narrative of Arthur Gordon Pym,* in which the survivors of a wreck develop cannibal desires, proceed to the execution and consumption of one sailor, and then discover, below deck, a terrapin that could have served as food. Like the other entry, it is of interest as a sign of Melville's ongoing engagement with tales of cannibalism. In its terse summation of the narrative's cruel irony, moreover, it calls attention to Melville's equally ongoing engagement with the abandonments and mockeries of "humanity." As he suggests in a later journal entry, in which "Cap. Pollard. of *Nant.*" is written after the words "*Noah after the Flood*" and "*Eclipse,*" these tales of shipwreck cannibalism represent, for him, both the testing of humanity and the veiling of the face of the Tester.

WORKS CITED

Ahmad, Aijaz. *In Theory: Classes, Nations, Literatures*. London: Verso, 1992.

Alberti, John. "Cultural Relativism and Melville's *Typee:* Man in the State of Culture." *ESQ* 36 (1990): 329-47.

Anderson, Charles. *Melville in the South Seas*. New York: Columbia University Press, 1939.

Archer, Christon. "Cannibalism in the Early History of the Northwest Coast: Enduring Myths and Neglected Realities." *Canadian Historical Review* 61 (1980): 453-79.

Arens, William. *The Man-Eating Myth: Anthropology and Anthropophagy*. New York: Oxford University Press, 1979.

Armstrong, Richard. "A Sketch of Marquesan Character." *Hawaiian Spectator* 1 (1838): 6-16.

"*Ashantee and the Gold Coast*." *The Athenaeum*, 11 September 1841, 707-8.

Atkins, John. *A Voyage to Guinea, Brasil and the West Indies*. London, 1735.

Ayers, Edward L. *Vengeance and Justice: Crime and Punishment in the 19th-Century American South*. New York: Oxford University Press, 1984.

Baines, Barbara J. "Ritualized Cannibalism in 'Benito Cereno': Melville's 'Black-Letter' Texts." *ESQ* 30 (1984): 163-69.

Baker, Houston A., Jr. *Modernism and the Harlem Renaissance*. Chicago: University of Chicago Press, 1987.

——. "Scene . . . Not Heard." In *Reading Rodney King/Reading Urban Uprising*, ed. Robert Gooding-Williams, 38-48. London: Routledge, 1993.

Bancroft, Edward. *An Essay on the Natural History of Guiana*. London, 1769.

Barber, Ian. "Archaeology, Ethnography, and the Record of Maori Cannibalism before 1815: A Critical Review." *Journal of the Polynesian Society* 101 (1992): 241-92.

Barker, Anthony J. *The African Link: British Attitudes to the Negro in the Era of the Atlantic Slave Trade, 1550-1807*. London: Frank Cass, 1978.

Barratt, Glynn, ed. *Bellingshausen: A Visit to New Zealand: 1820*. Palmerston, New Zealand: Dunmore Press, 1979.

[Barrow, John]. "Anderson's *Mission to Sumatra*." *Quarterly Review* (June 1826): 99-110.

——. "Beechey's *Voyage to the Pacific and Beering's Straits*." *Quarterly Review* (April 1831): 57-97.

——. "Cruise—*New Zealand*." *Quarterly Review* (April 1824): 52-65.

——. "Dentrecasteaux—*Voyage a la Recherché de la Perouse*." *Quarterly Review* (February 1810): 21-43.

———. "*Expeditions on the Amazon.*" *Quarterly Review* (September 1836): 1–29.

———. "Langsdorff's *Voyage round the World.*" *Quarterly Review* (July 1813): 433–43.

———. "Porter's *Cruize in the Pacific Ocean.*" *Quarterly Review* (July 1815): 352–83.

———. "Russian Embassy to Japan." *Quarterly Review* (December 1811): 357–91.

Bartley, William. " 'The Creature of His Own Tasteful Hands': Herman Melville's *Benito Cereno* and the Empire of Might." *Modern Philology* 93 (1996): 445–67.

Baudrillard, Jean. *America.* Trans. Chris Turner. London: Verso, 1988.

———. "The System of Collecting." In *The Cultures of Collecting,* ed. John Elsner and Roger Cardinal, 7–24. London: Reaktion Books, 1994.

Bays, Peter. *A Narrative of the Wreck of the* Minerva *Whaler of Port Jackson.* Cambridge, England, 1831.

Beaglehole, J. C., ed. *The* Endeavour *Journal of Joseph Banks.* London: Angus and Robertson, 1962.

———. *The Journals of Captain James Cook on his Voyages of Discovery.* 4 vols. Cambridge, England: Hakluyt Society, 1955–1974.

Beechey, Frederick. *Narrative of a Voyage to the Pacific and Bering's Straits.* 2 vols. Philadelphia, 1832.

Belcher, Edward. *Narrative of a Voyage Round the World, 1836–1842.* 2 vols. London, 1843.

Benjamin, Walter. *The Origin of German Tragic Drama.* Trans. John Osborne. London: Verso, 1977.

Bennet, George, and Daniel Tyerman. *Journal of Voyages and Travels.* 2 vols. Ed. James Montgomery. London, 1831.

Bennett, Anthony. "Rivals Unravelled: A Broadside Song and Dance." *Folk Music Journal* 6 (1993): 420–45.

Bentley, Nancy. *The Ethnography of Manners: Hawthorne, James, Wharton.* Cambridge: Cambridge University Press, 1995.

Bergman, David. *Gaiety Transfigured: Gay Self-Representation in American Literature.* Madison: University of Wisconsin Press, 1991.

Bhabha, Homi K. *The Location of Culture.* New York: Routledge, 1994.

Bolingbroke, Henry. *A Voyage to Demerary.* London, 1807.

Bourdieu, Pierre. *Outline of a Theory of Practice.* Trans. Richard Nice. Cambridge: Cambridge University Press, 1977.

———. "The Sentiment of Honour in Kabyle Society." In *Honour and Shame: The Values of Mediterranean Society,* ed. J. G. Peristiany, 191–242. Chicago: University of Chicago Press, 1966.

Bousquet, F. Marc. "Mathews's Mosses? Fair Papers and Foul: A Note on the Northwestern-Newberry Edition of Melville's 'Hawthorne and His Mosses.' " *New England Quarterly* 67 (1994): 622–49.

Breitwieser, Mitchell. "False Sympathy in Melville's *Typee.*" *American Quarterly* 34 (1982): 396–417.

Breton, William. *Excursions in New South Wales, Western Australia, and Van Dieman's Land.* 2d ed. London, 1834.

Bright, John. *Hand-Book for Emigrants, and Others, Being A History of New Zealand, Its State and Prospects.* London, 1841.

Brooks, Peter. *The Melodramatic Imagination: Balzac, Henry James, Melodrama, and the Mode of Excess.* New Haven: Yale University Press, 1976.

Bryant, John. *Melville and Repose: The Rhetoric of Humor in the American Renaissance.* New York: Oxford University Press, 1993.

Burns, Barnet. *A Brief Narrative of a New Zealand Chief, Being the Remarkable History of Barnet Burns, an English Sailor.* Belfast, 1844.

Burrow, J. W. *Evolution and Society: A Study in Victorian Social Theory.* London: Cambridge University Press, 1966.

Busby, James. *Authentic Information Relative to New South Wales, and New Zealand.* London, 1832.

Butler, Judith. *Gender Trouble: Feminism and the Subversion of Identity.* New York: Routledge, 1990.

Byron, George Anson. *Voyage of H.M.S.* Blonde. London, 1826.

Byron, George Gordon. *Don Juan.* Boston: Houghton Mifflin, 1958.

Campbell, J. K. "The Greek Hero." In *Honor and Grace in Anthropology,* ed. J. G. Peristiany and Julian Pitt-Rivers, 129–50. Cambridge: Cambridge University Press, 1992.

Campbell, Mary B. *The Witness and the Other World: Exotic European Travel Writing, 400–1600.* Ithaca: Cornell University Press, 1988.

Carlyle, Thomas. *A Carlyle Reader.* Cambridge: Cambridge University Press, 1984.

Carver, Jonathan. *Travels through the Interior Parts of North America.* London, 1778.

Chamerovzow, Louis. *The New Zealand Question.* London, 1848.

Charvat, William. *The Profession of Authorship in America, 1800–1870.* 1968. Reprint, New York: Columbia University Press, 1992.

Clendinnen, Inga. " 'Fierce and Unnatural Cruelty': Cortes and the Conquest of Mexico." In *New World Encounters,* ed. Stephen Greenblatt, 12–47. Berkeley and Los Angeles: University of California Press, 1993.

Cook, James. *A Voyage towards the South Pole and Round the World.* London, 1777.

Cook, James, and James King. *A Voyage to the Pacific Ocean.* London, 1784.

Cooper, James Fenimore. *The Red Rover.* Albany: State University of New York Press, 1991.

Copjec, Joan. *Read My Desire: Lacan against the Historicists.* Cambridge: MIT Press, 1994.

Coulter, John. *Adventures on the Western Coast of South America.* 2 vols. London, 1847.

Craik, George. *The New Zealanders.* London, 1830.

Crain, Caleb. "Lovers of Human Flesh: Homosexuality and Cannibalism in Melville's Novels." *American Literature* 66 (1994): 25–53.

Crary, Jonathan. *Techniques of the Observer: On Vision and Modernity in the Nineteenth Century.* Cambridge: MIT Press, 1990.

Crawfurd, John. *History of the Indian Archipelago.* 3 vols. Edinburgh, 1820.

Cruise, Richard. *Journal of a Ten Months' Residence in New Zealand.* London, 1823.

Dalyell, Sir J. G., ed. *Shipwrecks and Disasters at Sea.* 3 vols. Edinburgh, 1812.

Dana, Richard Henry. *Two Years before the Mast.* Harmondsworth, England: Penguin, 1981.

Darwin, Charles. *Journal of Researches into the Geology and Natural History of the Various Countries visited during the Voyage of HMS Beagle.* 2 vols. New York, 1846.

Defoe, Daniel. *The Life and Adventures of Robinson Crusoe.* Harmondsworth, England: Penguin, 1965.

Delbanco, Andrew. "Melville in the '80s." *American Literary History* 4 (1992): 709–25.

Derrida, Jacques. " 'Eating Well,' or the Calculation of the Subject: An Interview with Jacques Derrida." In *Who Comes after the Subject?,* ed. Eduardo Cadava, Peter Connor, and Jean-Luc Nancy, 96–119. New York: Routledge, 1991.

A Dialogue between Farmer Trueman and His Son George, about the Cannibals in India. London, 1818.

Dickens, Charles. "The Lost Arctic Voyagers." *Household Words,* December 2 and 9, 1854.

Dieffenbach, Ernest. *Travels in New Zealand.* London, 1843.

Dillingham, William B. *Melville's Short Fiction, 1853–1856.* Athens: University of Georgia Press, 1977.

Dimock, Wai-Chee. *Empire for Liberty: Melville and the Poetics of Individualism.* Princeton: Princeton University Press, 1989.

———. "*Typee:* Melville's Critique of Community." *ESQ* 30 (1984): 27–39.

Douglass, Frederick. *Narrative of the Life of Frederick Douglass, An American Slave.* Harmondsworth, England: Penguin, 1982.

DuBois, W. E. B. *The Souls of Black Folk.* Harmondsworth, England: Penguin, 1989.

Dubos, Rene, and Jean Dubos. *The White Plague: Tuberculosis, Man and Society.* Boston: Little, Brown, 1952.

Duncan, Archibald. *The Mariner's Chronicle.* 4 vols. Philadelphia, 1806.

Earle, Augustus. *Narrative of a Residence in New Zealand.* London, 1832.

Elder, John Rawson, ed. *The Letters and Journals of Samuel Marsden.* Dunedin, New Zealand: A. H. Reed, 1932.

Ellis, William. *Polynesian Researches.* 4 vols. New York, 1833.

Emerson, Ralph Waldo. *Selected Essays.* Harmondsworth, England: Penguin, 1982.

Erskine, John Elphinstone. *Journal of a Cruise among the Islands of the Western Pacific.* 1853. Reprint, London: Dawsons, 1967.

Evelev, John. " 'Made in the Marquesas': *Typee,* Tattooing and Melville's Critique of the Literary Marketplace." *Arizona Quarterly* 48, no. 4 (1992): 19–45.

Fanning, Edmund. *Voyages Round the World.* New York, 1833.

Fanon, Frantz. *Black Skin, White Masks.* Trans. Charles Lam Markmann. New York: Grove, 1967.

———. *The Wretched of the Earth.* Trans. Constance Farrington. New York: Grove, 1963.

Fliegelman, Jay. *Declaring Independence: Jefferson, Natural Language, and the Culture of Performance.* Stanford: Stanford University Press, 1993.

Forster, George. *A Voyage Round the World.* London, 1777.

Forster, John Reinhold. *Observations Made during a Voyage Round the World.* London, 1778.

Foucault, Michel. *Discipline and Punish.* Trans. Alan Sheridan. New York: Random, 1978.

———. *The History of Sexuality: An Introduction.* Trans. Robert Hurley. New York: Random, 1978.

———. *Madness and Civilization.* Trans. Richard Howard. New York: Random, 1965.

Fox, William. *Colonization and New Zealand.* London, 1842.

Fried, Michael. *Absorption and Theatricality: Painting and Beholder in the Age of Diderot.* Berkeley and Los Angeles: University of California Press, 1980.

Gaillard, Theodore L., Jr. "Melville's Riddle for Our Time: 'Benito Cereno.' " *English Journal* 61 (1972): 479–87.

Gilmore, Michael T. *American Romanticism and the Marketplace.* Chicago: University of Chicago Press, 1985.

Goethe, Johann Wolfgang. *Theory of Colours.* Trans. Charles Lock Eastlake. London, 1840.

Green, Jesse D. "Diabolism, Pessimism, and Democracy: Notes on Melville and Conrad." *Modern Fiction Studies* 8 (1962): 287–305.

Greenblatt, Stephen. *Marvelous Possessions: The Wonder of the New World.* Chicago: University of Chicago Press, 1991.

Griffiths, Gareth. "The Myth of Authenticity: Representation, Discourse, and Social Practice." In *De-Scribing Empire: Post-Colonialism and Textuality,* ed. Chris Tiffin and Alan Lawson. New York: Routledge, 1994.

Guzman, Gregory G. "Reports of Mongol Cannibalism in the Thirteenth-Century Latin Sources: Oriental Fact or Western Fiction?" In *Discovering New Worlds: Essays on Medieval Exploration and Imagination,* ed. Scott D. Westrem. New York: Garland, 1991.

Haegert, John. "Voicing Slavery through Silence: Narrative Mutiny in Melville's *Benito Cereno.*" *Mosaic* 26:2 (1995): 21–38.

Halttunen, Karen. *Confidence-Men and Painted Women: A Study of Middle-Class Culture in America, 1830–1870.* New Haven: Yale University Press, 1982.

———. "Early American Murder Narratives." In *The Power of Culture: Critical Essays in American History,* ed. Richard Wightman Fox and T. J. Jackson Lears, 67–101. Chicago: University of Chicago Press, 1993.

Harner, Michael. "The Ecological Basis for Aztec Sacrifice." *American Ethnologist* 4 (1977): 117–35.

Harris, Marvin. *Cannibals and Kings: The Origins of Cultures.* New York: Random, 1977.

Harvey, Bruce A. " 'Precepts Graven on Every Breast': Melville's *Typee* and the Forms of the Law." *American Quarterly* 45 (1993): 394–424.

Hattenhauer, Darryl. " 'Follow Your Leader': Knowing One's Place in *Benito Cereno.*" *Rocky Mountain Review of Language and Literature* 45 (1991): 7–17.

Hawkesworth, John. *An Account of the Voyages Undertaken by the Order of His Present Majesty for Making Discoveries in the Southern Hemisphere.* 3 vols. London, 1773.

Hawthorne, Nathaniel. *The Marble Faun.* Harmondsworth, England: Penguin, 1990.

Heffernan, Thomas Farel. *Stove by a Whale: Owen Chase and the Essex.* Middletown, CT: Wesleyan University Press, 1981.

Heflin, Wilson. "Herman Melville's Whaling Years." Ph.D. diss., Vanderbilt University, 1952.

Hegel, G. W. F. *The Philosophy of History.* Trans. J. Sibree. New York: Dover, 1956.

Herbert, Christopher. *Culture and Anomie: Ethnographic Imagination in the Nineteenth Century.* Chicago: University of Chicago Press, 1991.

Herbert, T. Walter. *Marquesan Encounters: Melville and the Meaning of Civilization.* Cambridge, MA: Harvard University Press, 1980.

Higgins, Brian, and Hershel Parker. *Herman Melville: The Contemporary Reviews.* Cambridge: Cambridge University Press, 1995.

Hilfer, Anthony Channell. "The Philosophy of Clothes in Melville's 'Benito Cereno.' " *Philological Quarterly* 61 (1984): 220–29.

Hiltner, Judith. "Disquieting Encounters: Male Intrusions/Female Realms in Melville." *ESQ* 40 (1994): 91–111.

Hulme, Peter. *Colonial Encounters: Europe and the Native Caribbean, 1492-1797.* London: Methuen, 1986.

———. "Making No Bones: A Response to Myra Jehlen." *Critical Inquiry* 20 (1993): 179–86.

Humboldt, Alexander von, and Aime Bonpland. *Personal Narrative of Travels to the Equinoctial Regions of America, during the Years 1799-1804.* Trans. and ed. Thomasina Ross. 3 vols. London, 1852–53.

Huntress, Keith. *A Checklist of Narratives of Shipwrecks and Disasters at Sea to 1860, with Summaries, Notes, and Comments.* Ames: Iowa State University Press, 1979.

Irving, Washington. *A History of the Life and Voyages of Christopher Columbus*. London, 1828.

Irwin, John. *American Hieroglyphics: The Symbol of the Egyptian Hieroglyphics in the American Renaissance*. New Haven: Yale University Press, 1980.

Jacobs, Thomas Jefferson. *Scenes, Incidents, and Adventures in the Pacific Ocean*. New York, 1844.

Jaffe, David. "Some Sources of Melville's *Mardi*." *American Literature* 9 (1937): 56–69.

Jameson, Fredric. *The Political Unconscious: Narrative as a Socially Symbolic Act*. Ithaca: Cornell University Press, 1981.

Jan-Mohammed, Abdul R. "The Economy of Manichean Allegory: The Function of Racial Difference in Colonialist Literature." In *"Race," Writing, and Difference,* ed. Henry Louis Gates Jr., 78–106. Chicago: University of Chicago Press, 1986.

Jehlen, Myra. "History before the Fact; or, Captain John Smith's Unfinished Symphony." *Critical Inquiry* 19 (1993): 667–92.

———. "Response to Peter Hulme." *Critical Inquiry* 20 (1993): 187–91.

Johnson, Paul David. "American Innocence and Guilt: Black-White Destiny in 'Benito Cereno.'" *Phylon* 36 (1975): 426–34.

Journal of the Resolution's *Voyage*. London, 1775.

Kaplan, Sidney. "Herman Melville and the American National Sin: The Meaning of 'Benito Cereno.'" *Journal of Negro History* 41 (1956): 311–38 and 42 (1957): 11–37.

Karcher, Carolyn. *Shadow over the Promised Land: Slavery, Race, and Violence in Melville's America*. Baton Rouge: Louisiana State University Press, 1980.

Kavanagh, James H. "That Hive of Subtlety: 'Benito Cereno' and the Liberal Hero." In *Ideology and Classic American Literature*, ed. Sacvan Bercovitch and Myra Jehlen, 352–83. Cambridge: Cambridge University Press, 1986.

Kiely, Robert. *Reverse Traditions: Postmodern Fictions and the Nineteenth Century Novel*. Cambridge, MA: Harvard University Press, 1993.

Kilgour, Maggie. *From Communion to Cannibalism: An Anatomy of Metaphors of Incorporation*. Princeton: Princeton University Press, 1990.

Kotzebue, Otto von. *A New Voyage Round the World*. London, 1830.

Krusenstern, Adam. *A Voyage Round the World, in the Years 1803, 1804, 1805, and 1806*. 2 vols. London, 1813.

Labillardiere, Jacques de. *An Account of a Voyage in Search of La Perouse*. 2d ed. 2 vols. London, 1802.

Lacan, Jacques. *Ecrits*. Trans. Alan Sheridan. New York: Norton, 1977.

———. *The Four Fundamental Concepts of Psycho-Analysis*. Ed. Jacques-Alain Miller. Trans. Alan Sheridan. New York: Norton, 1981.

Laclau, Ernesto. *New Reflections on the Revolution of Our Time*. London: Verso, 1990.

———. "Power and Representation." In *Politics, Theory, and Contemporary Culture*, ed. Mark Poster, 277–96. New York: Columbia University Press, 1993.

Lang, John Dunmore. *View of the Origin and Migrations of the Polynesian Nation*. London, 1834.

Langsdorff, George von. *Voyages and Travels in Various Parts of the World*. London, 1813.

La Perouse, Jean François Galoup. *A Voyage Round the World*. Ed. L. A. Milet-Mureau. 2 vols. London, 1799.

———. *A Voyage Round the World*. Boston, 1801.

Lawry, Walter. *Friendly and Feejee Islands: A Missionary Visit to Various Stations in the South Seas, in the Year 1847*. Ed. Elijah Hoole. London, 1850.

Lazarus, Neil. "National Consciousness and the Specificity of (Post) Colonial Intellectualism." In *Colonial Discourse/Postcolonial Theory*, ed. Francis Barker, Peter Hulme, and Margaret Iverson. Manchester, England: Manchester University Press, 1994.

Ledyard, John. *A Journal of Captain Cook's Last Voyage.* 1783. Reprint, Corvallis: Oregon State University Press, 1963.

Lery, Jean de. *History of a Voyage to the Land of Brazil, Otherwise Called America.* 1578. Trans. Janet Whately. Berkeley and Los Angeles: University of California Press, 1990.

Levine, Robert S. *Conspiracy and Romance: Studies in Brockden Brown, Cooper, Hawthorne, and Melville.* Cambridge: Cambridge University Press, 1989.

Lewis, R. W. B. *The American Adam.* Chicago: University of Chicago Press, 1955.

Leyda, Jay. *The Melville Log: A Documentary Life of Herman Melville, 1819-1891.* 2 vols. New York: Harcourt, Brace, 1951.

Lisiansky, Urey. *A Voyage Round the World.* London, 1814.

Locke, John. *An Essay Concerning Human Understanding.* Oxford: Clarendon Press, 1975.

Long, Edward. *The History of Jamaica.* 3 vols. London, 1774.

Mandel, Ruth B. "The Two Mystery Stories in 'Benito Cereno.'" *Texas Studies in Literature and Language* 14 (1973): 631-42.

Manuel, Frank. *The Eighteenth Century Confronts the Gods.* Cambridge, MA: Harvard University Press, 1959.

Marsden, William. *The History of Sumatra.* 3d ed. London, 1811.

Martin, Charles, and James Snead. "Reading through Blackness: Colorless Signifiers in *Benito Cereno*." *Yale Journal of Criticism* 4 (1990): 231-51.

Martin, John, ed. *An Account of the Natives of the Tonga Islands.* Boston, 1820.

Martin, Robert K. *Hero, Captain, and Stranger: Male Friendship, Social Critique and Literary Form in the Sea Novels of Herman Melville.* Chapel Hill: University of North Carolina Press, 1986.

Martin, Samuel. *New Zealand in a Series of Letters Containing an Account of the Country.* London, 1845.

Martin, Terry J. "The Idea of Nature in *Benito Cereno*." *Studies in Short Fiction* 30 (1993): 161-68.

Matthew, Patrick. *Emigration Fields.* London, 1839.

McCrae, Alexander. *Journal Kept in New Zealand in 1820.* Ed. Frederick Revans Chapman. Wellington, New Zealand: Skinner, 1928.

McElroy, John Harmon. "Cannibalism in Melville's 'Benito Cereno.'" *Essays in Literature* 1 (1974): 206-18.

McNab, Robert, ed. *Historical Records of New Zealand.* 2 vols. Wellington, New Zealand: John McKay, 1908-14.

Meares, John. *Voyages Made in the Years 1788 and 1789, from China to the North West Coast of America.* London, 1790.

Montaigne, Michel de. *Essays.* Harmondsworth, England: Penguin, 1958.

Morrell, Benjamin. *A Narrative of Four Voyages.* New York, 1832.

Morrison, Toni. *Playing in the Dark: Whiteness and the Literary Imagination.* Cambridge, MA: Harvard University Press, 1992.

"Narrative of a Four Months' Residence in the Marquesas." *The Athenaeum,* 21 February 1846, 189-91, and 28 February 1846, 218-20.

Nelson, Dana D. *The Word in Black and White: Reading "Race" in American Literature, 1638-1867.* New York: Oxford University Press, 1992.

Newman, Lea Bertani Vozar. *A Reader's Guide to the Short Stories of Herman Melville.* Boston: G. K. Hall, 1986.

Nicholas, John Liddiard. *Narrative of a Voyage to New Zealand.* 2 vols. London, 1817.

Nicol, Charles. "The Iconography of Evil and Ideal in 'Benito Cereno.'" *ATQ* 7 (1970): 25-31.

Norris, Robert. *Memoirs of Bossa Ahádee, King of Dahomy.* London, 1789.

Obeyesekere, Gananath. *The Apotheosis of Captain Cook: European Mythmaking in the Pacific.* Princeton: Princeton University Press, 1992.

——. "'British Cannibals': Contemplation of an Event in the Death and Resurrection of James Cook, Explorer." *Critical Inquiry* 18 (1992): 630-54.

Odell, George C. D. *Annals of the New York Stage.* 15 vols. New York: Columbia University Press, 1928.

Oliver, James. *Wreck of the* Glide, *with Recollections of the Fijis, and of Wallis Island.* New York, 1848.

Pagden, Anthony. *The Fall of Natural Man.* Cambridge: Cambridge University Press, 1982.

[Palgrave, Francis.] "Superstition and Knowledge." *Quarterly Review* (July 1823): 440-75.

Parker, Hershel. *Herman Melville: A Biography.* Vol. 1, *1819-1851.* Baltimore: Johns Hopkins University Press, 1997.

Parkinson, Sydney. *A Journal of a Voyage to the South Seas.* London, 1784.

Parley, Peter. *Tales about Shipwrecks, and Disasters at Sea.* London, 1847.

Parry, Benita. "Problems in Current Theories of Colonial Discourse." In *The Post-Colonial Studies Reader,* ed. Bill Ashcroft, Gareth Griffiths, and Helen Tiffin, 36-44. New York: Routledge, 1995.

Patterson, Samuel. *Narrative of the Adventures and Sufferings of Samuel Patterson.* Palmer, RI, 1817.

Pauw, Corneille de. *Selections from M. Pauw.* Bath, England, 1795.

Pearce, Roy Harvey. *Savagism and Civilization: A Study of the Indian and the American Mind.* 1953. Reprint, Berkeley and Los Angeles: University of California Press, 1988.

Pease, Donald E. "*Moby-Dick* and the Cold War." In *The American Renaissance Reconsidered,* ed. Walter Benn Michaels and Donald E. Pease, 113-55. Baltimore: Johns Hopkins University Press, 1985.

Person, Leland S., Jr. "Melville's Cassock: Putting on Masculinity in *Moby-Dick.*" *ESQ* 40 (1994): 1-26.

Phillips, Barry. "'The Good Captain': A Reading of *Benito Cereno.*" *Texas Studies in Literature and Language* 4 (1962): 188-97.

Pitt-Rivers, Julian. "Honour and Social Status." In *Honour and Shame: The Values of Mediterranean Society,* ed. J. G. Peristiany, 19-78. Chicago: University of Chicago Press, 1966.

Poe, Edgar Allan. *The Narrative of Arthur Gordon Pym of Nantucket.* Harmondsworth, England: Penguin, 1975.

Polack, Joel Samuel. *Manners and Customs of the New Zealanders.* 2 vols. London, 1840.

——. *New Zealand.* 2 vols. London, 1838.

"Polack, *Manners and Customs.*" *The Athenaeum,* 11 April 1840, 287-88.

"Polack, *New Zealand.*" *The Athenaeum,* 18 August 1838, 579-82.

Pommer, Henry F. "Herman Melville and the Wake of the *Essex.*" *American Literature* 20 (1948): 290-304.

——. *Milton and Melville.* New York: Cooper Square Publishers, 1970.

Pops, Martin Leonard. *The Melville Archetype.* Kent, OH: Kent State University Press, 1970.

Porter, David. *Journal of a Cruise Made to the Pacific Ocean.* 2 vols. Philadelphia, 1815.

Post-Lauria, Sheila. *Correspondent Colorings: Melville in the Marketplace.* Amherst: University of Massachusetts Press, 1996.

Prescott, William H. *History of the Conquest of Mexico.* 3 vols. New York, 1843.

"Prescott's *History of the Conquest of Mexico.*" *North American Review* (January 1844): 157-210.

"Prescott's *History of the Conquest of Mexico.*" *Quarterly Review* (December 1843): 187-235.

Priest, Josiah. *Slavery, as It Relates to the Negro, or African Race.* Albany, NY, 1844.

Prout, Ebenezer. *Memoirs of the Life of the Late John Williams.* New York, 1843.

Putzel, Max. "The Source and the Symbols of Melville's 'Benito Cereno.'" *American Literature* 34 (1962): 191-206.

Raffles, Sophia. *Memoir of the Life and Public Services of Sir Thomas Stamford Raffles.* 2d ed. 2 vols. London, 1835.

Reid, Mayne. *Odd People.* London, 1860.

Reynolds, Jeremiah. *Voyage of the United States Frigate* Potomac. New York, 1835.

Richardson, William D. "Melville's 'Benito Cereno': Civilization, Barbarism, and Race." *Interpretation* 11 (1983): 43-72.

Robertson, William. *The History of America.* 2d ed. Leipzig, 1786.

Rogin, Michael Paul. *Subversive Genealogy: The Politics and Art of Herman Melville.* New York: Knopf, 1983.

Roquefeuil, Camille de. *A Voyage Round the World.* London, 1823.

Rowe, John Carlos. "Melville's *Typee:* U.S. Imperialism at Home and Abroad." In *National Identities and Post-Americanist Narratives,* ed. Donald E. Pease, 255-78. Durham, NC: Duke University Press, 1994.

Russell, Michael. *Polynesia: or, an Historical Account of the Principal Islands in the South Sea.* New York, 1843.

Sagan, Eli. *Cannibalism: Human Aggression and Cultural Form.* New York: Harper & Row, 1974.

Said, Edward. *Orientalism.* New York: Random, 1978.

Samson, John. *White Lies: Melville's Narratives of Facts.* Ithaca: Cornell University Press, 1989.

Sanborn, Geoffrey. "The Name of the Devil: Melville's Other Extracts for *Moby-Dick.*" *Nineteenth-Century Literature* 47 (1992): 212-35.

Sanday, Peggy Reeves. *Divine Hunger: Cannibalism as a Cultural System.* Cambridge: Cambridge University Press, 1986.

Sandberg, Robert A. " 'The Adjustment of Screens': Putative Narrators, Authors, and Editors in Melville's Unfinished *Burgundy Club* Book." *Texas Studies in Language and Literature* 31 (1989): 426-50.

Saunders, Ann. *Narrative of the Shipwreck and Sufferings of Miss Ann Saunders.* Providence, 1827.

Savage, John. *Some Account of New Zealand.* London, 1807.

Schueller, Malini Johar. "Colonialism and Melville's South Seas Journeys." *Studies in American Fiction* 22 (1994): 3-18.

Sealts, Merton M., Jr. *Melville's Reading: A Check-List of Books Owned and Borrowed.* Madison: University of Wisconsin Press, 1966.

Sedgwick, Catharine Maria. "Fanny McDermot." In *Rediscoveries: American Short Stories by Women, 1832–1916,* ed. Barbara H. Solomon, 113–55. Harmondsworth, England: Penguin, 1994.

Sheldon, William. "Brief Account of the Caribs, Who Inhabited the Antilles." *Transactions and Collections of the American Antiquarian Society* 1 (1820): 366–433.

Shillibeer, John. *A Narrative of the Briton's Voyage, to Pitcairn's Island.* Taunton, England: 1817.

Siebers, Tobin. *The Romantic Fantastic.* Ithaca: Cornell University Press, 1984.

Silverman, Kaja. *The Threshold of the Visible World.* New York: Routledge, 1996.

Simpson, A. W. Brian. *Cannibalism and the Common Law: The Story of the Tragic Last Voyage of the* Mignonette *and the Strange Legal Proceedings to Which It Gave Rise.* Chicago: University of Chicago Press, 1984.

Simpson, David. *Fetishism and Imagination.* Baltimore: Johns Hopkins University Press, 1982.

———. *Romanticism, Nationalism, and the Revolt against Theory.* Chicago: University of Chicago Press, 1993.

Slemon, Stephen. "The Scramble for Post-Colonialism." In *De-Scribing Empire: Post-Colonialism and Textuality,* ed. Chris Tiffin and Alan Lawson, 15–32. New York: Routledge, 1994.

Sontag, Susan. *Illness as Metaphor.* New York: Farrar, Straus and Giroux, 1978.

[Southey, Robert.] *"Life and Public Services of Sir Stamford Raffles."* *Quarterly Review* (March 1830): 405–50.

"Southey's *History of Brazil.*" *Eclectic Review* (September 1810): 788–800.

[Sparks, Jared.] "New Zealand." *North American Review* (April 1824): 329–55.

Spivak, Gayatri Chakravorty. *Outside in the Teaching Machine.* New York: Routledge, 1993.

Stannard, David E. *The Puritan Way of Death: A Study in Religion, Culture, and Social Change.* New York: Oxford University Press, 1977.

Stern, Milton R. *The Fine Hammered Steel of Herman Melville.* Urbana: University of Illinois Press, 1957.

Stewart, Charles. *A Visit to the South Seas, in the U.S. Ship* Vincennes, *during the Years 1829 and 1830.* New York, 1831.

Stewart, Susan. *On Longing: Narratives of the Miniature, the Gigantic, the Souvenir, and the Collection.* Durham, NC: Duke University Press, 1993.

Stuckey, Sterling. "Follow Your Leader': The Theme of Cannibalism in Melville's 'Benito Cereno.'" In *Critical Essays on Herman Melville's "Benito Cereno,"* ed. Robert E. Burkholder, 182–95. New York: G. K. Hall, 1992.

Sundquist, Eric J. "*Benito Cereno* and New World Slavery." In *Reconstructing American Literary History,* ed. Sacvan Bercovitch, 93–122. Cambridge, MA: Harvard University Press, 1986.

Taylor, W. Cooke. *The Natural History of Society in the Barbarous and Civilized State.* 2 vols. London, 1840.

Terry, Charles. *New Zealand, Its Advantages and Prospects as a British Colony.* London, 1842.

Thomas, Nicholas. *Entangled Objects: Exchange, Material Culture, and Colonialism in the Pacific.* Cambridge, MA: Harvard University Press, 1991.

Thomas, R. *Interesting and Authentic Narratives of the Most Remarkable Shipwrecks, Fires,*

Famines, Calamities, Providential Deliverances, and Lamentable Disasters on the Seas. Hartford, CT, 1837.

Thompson, Lawrance. Afterword to *Benito Cereno,* by Herman Melville. Barre, MA: The Imprint Society, 1972.

Thomson, Arthur S. *The Story of New Zealand: Past and Present—Savage and Civilized.* 2 vols. London, 1859.

Thomson, Robert. *The Marquesas Islands: Their Description and Early History.* 2d ed. Ed. Robert D. Craig. Laie, HI: Institute for Polynesian Studies, 1980.

Todorov, Tzvetan. *The Conquest of America.* Trans. Richard Howard. New York: Harper, 1984.

Tolchin, Neal. *Mourning, Gender and Creativity in the Art of Herman Melville.* New Haven: Yale University Press, 1988.

The Travels of Hildebrand Bowman. London, 1778.

Turnbull, John. *A Voyage Round the World.* 2d ed. London, 1813.

Twain, Mark. *The Adventures of Huckleberry Finn.* Harmondsworth, England: Penguin, 1985.

Veblen, Thorstein. *The Theory of the Leisure Class.* Harmondsworth, England: Penguin, 1979.

Viaud, Pierre. *The Shipwreck and Adventures of M. Pierre Viaud.* Trans. Mrs. Griffith. London, 1771.

Voltaire. *Candide.* Harmondsworth, England: Penguin, 1947.

————. *Philosophical Dictionary.* New York: Basic Books, 1962.

Wakefield, Edward Gibbon. *British Colonization of New Zealand.* London, 1837.

Wakefield, Edward Jerningham. *Adventure in New Zealand, from 1839 to 1844.* 2 vols. London, 1845.

Wallace, Robert K. *Melville and Turner: Spheres of Love and Fright.* Athens: University of Georgia Press, 1992.

Ward, R. Gerard, and Ernest S. Dodge. *American Activities in the Central Pacific, 1790-1870.* Ridgewood, NJ: Gregg Press, 1967.

Wilkes, Charles. *Narrative of the United States Exploring Expedition, 1838-1842.* 6 vols. Philadelphia, 1845.

Winterbottom, Thomas. *An Account of the Native Africans in the Neighborhood of Sierra Leone.* London, 1803.

Wright, Elizabeth. "The New Psychoanalysis and Literary Criticism." *Poetics Today* 3 (1982): 89-105.

Yanella, Donald. " 'Seeing the Elephant' in *Mardi.*" In *Artful Thunder: Versions of the Romantic Tradition in American Literature in Honor of Howard P. Vincent,* ed. Robert DeMott et. al., 105-17. Kent, OH: Kent State University Press, 1975.

Yate, William. *An Account of New Zealand.* 2d ed. London, 1835.

Young, Robert. *White Mythologies: Writing History and the West.* New York: Routledge, 1990.

Žižek, Slavoj. *The Metastases of Enjoyment.* London: Verso, 1994.

————. *The Sublime Object of Ideology.* London: Verso, 1989.

INDEX

Addictiveness of human flesh, 27-28, 45-46, 60, 80
Anderson, John, 71, 178
Archer, Christon, 70
Arens, William, 30, 36
Athenaeum, 36-38, 59, 71-72, 86
Atkins, John, 30-36, 61

Baker, Houston, 11-12
Bancroft, Edward, 31
Banks, Joseph, 23, 32, 36, 177-78
Barker, Francis, 28
Barnum, P. T., 130, 230 n. 11
Barrow, John, 6, 33-37, 62, 71-72, 178
Battas. *See* Sumatra
Baudrillard, Jean, 136, 234 n. 41
Beechey, Frederick, 131
Bellingshausen, Faddey, 68-69
Benjamin, Walter, 195
Bennet, George, 138, 181-82, 202-4
Bennett, Anthony, 167
Bhabha, Homi, xiii, 8-11, 13, 16, 116, 122, 175, 185-86, 197, 232 n. 29
Bolingbroke, Henry, 25-26
Bones: as evidence of cannibalism, 111-12, 174-84
Bourdieu, Pierre, 60, 149
Breton, William, 56-57, 60, 64, 223 n. 9
Busby, James, 51-52, 132
Butler, Judith, 60
Byron, George Anson, 181
Byron, George Gordon, 46

Cannibalism, reports of: in Africa, 23, 24, 26-27, 28, 46, 70, 215 n. 9; in Asia, 24, 51, 61; in the Caribbean, 179-82; in North America, 23, 24, 43-44, 47-48, 53, 61-62, 69-70, 178-79, 216 n. 9; in South America, 23, 24, 25-26, 31, 39-40, 61, 179-180, 225 n. 19. *See also* Fiji; Hawaii; Marquesas; Melanesia; New Guinea; New Zealand; Samoa; Sumatra; Tahiti; Tonga
Carver, Jonathan, 61-62
Charvat, William, 75-76, 84, 118
Chase, Owen, 202-5
Colonial encounter, xiii, 7, 9, 17, 72, 186, 194, 236 n. 5
Colonialism, 28-30, 51-52, 59-60, 72, 94, 132; discourse of, 9-13, 16, 77, 101, 103, 116, 122, 174-75
Columbus, Christopher, 28, 179-84
Cook, James, xi, 21-24, 31-32, 38-39, 53-56, 68-69, 83-84, 110, 177-78, 181-82, 221 n. 115, 223 n. 9, 227 n. 33, 229 n. 9
Cooper, James Fenimore, 46
Copjec, Joan, 17, 60
Craik, George, 28, 51, 56, 64, 230 n. 11, 232 n. 27
Crary, Jonathan, 164
Crawfurd, John, 51
Cruise, Richard, 34, 223 n. 7
Culture, xii, xiv, 17, 57-58, 77, 100, 134, 140-41, 236 n. 5
Curiosities, xv, 121-24, 126, 130-32, 168, 186

Dalyell, J. G., 41

Darwin, Charles, 39–40
Dean, John, 43
Defoe, Daniel, 27
Denial of existence of cannibalism, xiv,
    23, 30–38, 85–90
Dickens, Charles, 44
Dickinson, Emily, 199, 200
Dieffenbach, Ernest, 91, 223 n. 7
Douglass, Frederick, 11–14
DuBois, W. E. B., 12–14
Duncan, Archibald, 42

Earle, Augustus, 4–8, 17
Emerson, Ralph Waldo, 9, 234 n. 38
Enlightenment, 24, 31, 35, 47, 58, 61, 84,
    160, 177, 211 n. 10
Erromanga. See Melanesia

Famine: as explanation of cannibalism,
    xiv, 22–23, 38–46, 100, 203–7
Fanning, Edmund, 15–16, 216 n. 9, 226
    n. 23
Fanon, Frantz, 93–94, 116, 187
Fetishism, 8, 9, 79, 108, 110, 121, 134
Fiji, 23, 26–28, 54, 93, 95, 130, 150, 152–
    53, 167, 209 n. 3, 224 n. 16, 225 n. 18,
    227 n. 33, 231 n. 20
Forster, George, 21, 31, 39, 47
Forster, John, 47, 49–54, 63
Foucault, Michel, 48–49, 60–61, 64–65
Fox, William, 29

Geertz, Clifford, xii, 58
Goethe, Johann Wolfgang, 158–60, 163–64
Greenblatt, Stephen, 7
Griffiths, Gareth, xiii

Haegert, John, 191
Harner, Michael, 39
Harris, Marvin, 39
Hawaii, 23, 68, 83–84, 110, 151, 181–82,
    218 n. 44, 221 n. 115, 225 n. 18, 227
    n. 33, 229 n. 9
Hawkesworth, John, 38–39, 53
Hawthorne, Nathaniel, 17, 18, 119, 161,
    164, 171, 202, 205
Heads: embalmed, 108, 127–33, 140, 178.
    See also Skulls

Hegel, G. W. F., 26
Herbert, Christopher, 58
"Homosexual panic," 138
Honor, 149–51
Hulme, Peter, 16–17
Humanism, 17, 18, 36, 59, 126, 134, 140–
    41, 155, 185
Humanity: coexisting with savagery, 53,
    91; dependent on savagery, xv, 80–81;
    displaced by savagery, 43–46, 100, 174;
    expressed in horror, 4, 5, 6, 24–26, 29,
    42, 58, 104, 146, 186; femininity of, 89–
    90, 114–15, 155; as racial or universal
    instinct, 30, 32, 33, 40, 70–71, 101;
    radical critique of, 19, 42–43, 46, 68;
    reduced, 41–42, 58
Humboldt, Alexander von, 179–81
Huntress, Keith, 40

Irving, Washington, 180–81
Irwin, John, 150

Jameson, Fredric, 44
Jan-Mohammed, Abdul, 11
Journal of the Resolution's *Voyage,* 3–4,
    215 n. 4
Justice, 48, 143–44

Kavanagh, James, 187
"King of the Cannibal Islands," 166–67
Kotzebue, Otto von, 69
Krusenstern, Adam, 81–82, 178, 226 n. 23

Labillardiere, Jacques de, 138
Lacan, Jacques, xii, 8, 65, 68, 158, 162, 185
Laclau, Ernesto, xiii, 236 n. 13
Lang, John Dunmore, 55, 78
Langsdorff, George von, 27, 45, 65–68,
    223 n. 7
La Perouse, Jean François Galoup, 53, 218
    n. 44
Ledyard, John, 68
Lery, Jean de, 61
Lisiansky, Urey, 111–12, 182
Locke, John, 33
"Looseness," 154–56, 166, 168–69
Lust, as explanation of cannibalism, xiv,
    21–30, 39, 52, 60, 78–85

Maori. *See* New Zealand

Marquesas, xiv, 15–16, 23, 27, 65–68, 72, 75–118, 178, 182, 216 n. 9

Marsden, Samuel, 29, 55–56, 58, 223 n. 7

Marsden, William, 31–33, 63–64

Martin, John, 48, 51, 182

Masculinity: as ideal, 50–51, 54, 92, 94, 96, 101, 140; as phantasm, xii–xiii, xiv, xv, 18, 109, 126, 155–56, 169

McCrae, Alexander, 131

Meares, John, 69–70, 179

Melanesia, 23, 27, 138, 150, 223 n. 9, 234 n. 44

Melodrama, 117–18, 211 n. 10

Melville, Herman: "Authentic Anecdotes of 'Old Zack,'" 230 n. 13; "Benito Cereno," xi, xii, xv–xvi, 80, 118, 171–201, 205; *Billy Budd*, 143, 156, 199, 206, 237 n. 26; *Clarel*, 205–7; *The Confidence-Man*, 166, 174, 185, 187; "The Encantadas," 196; "Hawthorne and His Mosses," 17, 161, 214 n. 30; "House of the Tragic Poet," 227 n. 33; *Israel Potter*, 120, 151–53, 227 n. 33; *Mardi*, 75, 119, 122–25, 166, 171, 174–75, 204, 227 n. 33, 228 n. 5, 229 n. 9; *Moby-Dick*, xv, 14–15, 75–76, 103, 118, 119–69, 171–72, 185, 186, 191, 201, 204–5, 228 n. 33; *Omoo*, 119–22, 129, 145, 149, 150, 167, 229 n. 9, 233 n. 31; *Pierre*, 143, 171–74, 191–96, 199, 227 n. 33; *Redburn*, 75, 124, 135, 228 n. 33; "Rich Man's Crumbs," 227 n. 33; *Typee*, xii, xiv, xv, 25, 75–126, 134, 141, 145, 162, 167, 171, 174, 185, 186, 229 n. 9; *White-Jacket*, 75, 227 n. 33

Metonymy, 7–8, 107, 112, 116, 130, 145, 149, 151, 152

Milton, John, 119, 215 n. 37

Morrell, Benjamin, 56, 182

Morrison, Toni, 18

New Guinea, 27, 229 n. 8

New Zealand, xi, 3–8, 21–25, 28–29, 31–38, 48–60, 62–64, 68, 71–72, 91, 127, 130–33, 138, 149, 151, 177–78, 182, 209 n. 3, 223 nn. 7, 9, 227 n. 33, 229 n. 8, 230 n. 9, 231 n. 20

"Newness," 9–12, 14, 16, 18

Nicholas, John Liddiard, 25, 53–56

Norris, Robert, 70, 215 n. 9

Obeyesekere, Gananath, 16–17, 210 n. 8

"Ocular proof," 6, 8, 31, 174–75, 178

Oliver, James, 25, 58–59

Orientalism, 79, 81, 84, 101

Ornamentation, 65, 105–8, 112, 116, 149–52, 182

Parkinson, Sydney, 177

Parley, Peter, 42

Patterson, Samuel, 27

Pauw, Corneille de, 38, 39

Pearce, Roy Harvey, 18

Pease, Donald, 155

Pedagogy, xv, 75–77, 103, 175

Polack, Joel, 28, 36–38, 71

Pollard, George, 202–7

Pommer, Henry, 204, 215 n. 37

Porter, David, 25, 93, 95, 102, 112, 182

Postcoloniality, 8–10, 12, 14, 72, 78, 122, 185, 198; of Melville's work, xiii, 16, 18, 77, 174

Priest, Josiah, 27

Quarterly Review, 33–36, 86, 155

Racism, xi, xv, 24, 26, 28, 33, 39, 46, 62, 81–82, 122, 129–30, 140–41, 153, 155, 185

Raffles, Stamford, 64

Reid, Mayne, 167

Reynolds, Jeremiah, 64

Robertson, William, 47–48

Roquefeuil, Camille de, 178–79

Russell, Michael, 26, 219 n. 84

Said, Edward, 79, 81, 101, 115, 116

Samoa, 69

Sanday, Peggy Reeves, 57–58

Saunders, Ann, 43

Savage, John, 62–63

Savagery: as "cause" of humanity, 4–6, 19, 24–25, 39–40, 58, 80–81; characterized by gameness, 148–154; characterized by inconsistency, 141–44; characterized

Savagery (*continued*)
by irreverence, 144–48; as commodity, 122, 130–31; discourse on, xii, 14, 36; as homeostatic condition, 50; as masculinist ideal, 52, 54, 100–101, 103, 126, 140; as masculinist phantasm, 135, 166–69; as masquerade, 8, 65, 105, 109, 114–18, 185–86; as product of colonial encounter, xv, 71; as product of "error," 59–60; as racial or universal instinct, xi, xiv, 17, 43–46, 173–74, 183, 187
Shakespeare, William, 3, 6, 155, 161, 199–200
Sheldon, William, 179–82
Shillibeer, John, 85
Shipwreck narratives, 40–46, 202–7
Silverman, Kaja, xv, 211 n. 10
Simpson, A. W. Brian, 40
Simpson, David, 33, 87, 226 n. 26
Skulls, 65–67, 111–12, 174, 176–78, 182. *See also* Heads: embalmed
Snelgrave, William, 70
Souvenirs, 112, 195–96
Sparks, Jared, 24, 25, 209 n. 3
Spectacles, 136–39, 147, 190; of postcolonial melancholy, 198; of punishment, 64; of savagery, xv, 4, 5, 6, 8, 24, 25, 127–30, 133–34, 145, 175
Spivak, Gayatri, 122
Stewart, Charles, 99–101, 183
Stewart, Susan, 149, 196
Sumatra, 23, 31, 63–64, 71–72, 178, 209 n. 3, 217 n. 43, 228 n. 33
Superstition: as explanation of cannibalism, xiv, 23, 53–61, 97–103

Tableaux, 5, 25, 172, 200, 211 n. 10
Tattoos, 65, 104–13, 116, 127, 130, 133, 134, 136, 141, 149–52, 168
Tahiti, 24, 203, 223 n. 9

Taylor, W. Cooke, 45, 57
Terror: as explanation of cannibalism, xiv, 8, 23, 38, 61–72, 103–15, 227 n. 33
Terry, Charles, 60
Theory: resistance to, 33–35, 87–88, 101
Thomson, Arthur, 63
Thomson, Robert, 103
Tonga, 48
Todorov, Tzvetan, 7–8
Touch: as basis of subjectivity, 136–39, 168
The Travels of Hildebrand Bowman, 33
Trophies, 108–13, 131, 150–51, 179, 182–83
"Truth," 161–62, 165–66, 168, 186
Tuberculosis, 198–99
Tyerman, Daniel, 138, 181–82, 204

Vancouver, George, 23, 182
Vengeance: as explanation of cannibalism, xiv, 22, 23, 47–56, 62, 90–97, 227 n. 33
Viaud, Pierre, 43–45
Voltaire, 38, 39

Wakefield, Edward Jerningham, 29
Wales, William, 22, 23, 39, 47, 53, 70
Whiteness: as color in spectrum, 77, 157–65, 185; as subject position, xvi, 12, 14, 16, 18, 26, 29, 104, 175, 198
Whites: as cannibals, 40–46; as contributors to postcoloniality, xiii, 14, 18; as makers of trophies, 151; as merchants of heads, 130–33; as objects of spectacle, 130; as postcolonial readers, 175, 194; as spectators of savagery, 67, 130
Wilkes, Charles, 28, 131, 132, 224 n. 16
Winterbottom, Timothy, 70

Yate, William, 48, 131–32
Young, Robert, 186, 212 n. 16, 236 n. 13

Žižek, Slavoj, xiv, 61, 133–34, 169